The Dialectic
of Ideology
and Technology

The Dialectic
of Ideology
and Technology

The Origins, Grammar,
and Future of Ideology

Alvin W. Gouldner

A Continuum Book   THE SEABURY PRESS • NEW YORK

The Seabury Press, Inc.
815 Second Avenue
New York, N.Y. 10017

Printed in the United States of America

LIBRARY OF CONGRESS CATALOGING IN PUBLICATION DATA

Gouldner, Alvin Ward, 1920–
  The dialectic of ideology and technology.

  (A Continuum book)
  Bibliographical Notes
  Includes index.
  1. Communism and society. I. Title.
HX542.G68   335.43'8'301   75-29393
ISBN 0-8164-9275-1

Dedicated to the memory of an historical non-person:
Frederick Lewis (Henry) Demuth
(23 June 1851–28 January 1929),
son of Helene Demuth
Who knew something of the dark side of the dialectic

Ideas like that, thought Skelton, could set a man to barking. Even a brief soulful howl beside the garbage would help . . .

There was a knocking on the door of the fuselage. Skelton opened it. It was the wino drill sergeant from next door. "Come in."

"Thank you, sir. Do you have a dog?"

"No, I don't."

"I thought I heard barking."

"I was clearing my throat."

THOMAS MCGUANE,
Ninety-Two in the Shade

o o o

Where there is a kinship of languages, it cannot fail, due to the common philosophy of grammar—I mean, due to the unconscious domination by similar grammatical functions—that everything is prepared from the outset for a similar development and sequence of philosophical systems . . .

NIETZSCHE

o o o

Not ideas, but material and ideal interests, directly govern men's conduct.

MAX WEBER

o o o

. . . our conclusions agree with the general point of view expressed by Chomsky that dialects of a language are apt to differ from each other in low-level rules, and that superficial differences are greater than those differences found (if any) in their deep structures.

WILLIAM LABOV

Contents

Preface

This study is about ideologies as a form of discourse; i.e., as a culture of critical speech; i.e., as an elaborated sociolinguistic speech variant. It is part of a larger work, including two other volumes: *On Marxism*, and *Revolutionary Intellectuals*.

Being about such topics, inevitably this present study has implications for the ongoing world convulsions, although these are exhibited only in a set of side-steps. For who longs to address *these* head-on? In such a situation one must lay one's cards on the table, but there is no obligation to read them out loud. In a serious game, the convention is always the same: it is the cards, not the player, who speaks. But one should never forget, this is a convention.

Like anyone else, I write out of the interaction between where I have been and where I now find myself, inevitably tacking between what I did previously and the work remaining to be done. Some will remember the last serious effort as being *The Coming Crisis of Western Sociology*. Unless, however, their memory is a bit longer, and can go back to my *Enter Plato*, they will not altogether understand the present offering.

Since "ideology" is now a topic of inquiry historically continuous with the problematic formulated by Marx and Engels (rather than with the earlier French "ideologues"), I have naturally asked myself: What is the relationship of this work to Marxism, and is it Marxist at all?

To answer this in the flat negative seems both ungrateful and, in my case, just plain wrong; for I am well aware of how much I have learned from the work of Marx and from Georg Lukács, whom I think the greatest Marxist theorist of the twentieth century.

At the same time, simply to *affirm* the connection also seems presumptuous in the manner of a "name dropper," who seeks to borrow luster by intimating a closeness with the great. This view of the matter may seem strange to "normal," academic sociologists who commonly know little, and think less, of Marxism. My judgment, however, differs. I think of *certain* Marxists as having made Promethean achievements; as having risked and accomplished much in the world; of *some*, as brave men who have torn their lives out on behalf of their convictions; and of some few as men of intellectual genius and heroic action with whom I, as a rather unworldly scholar, have no urge to connect myself.

What, then, is my relationship to Marxism? A British reviewer (of my last book, *For Sociology*) has seen fit to characterize my position as a "critical Maoism." The reader will be better able to judge whether this designation is apt after he reads my chapter on Maoism, in my as yet unpublished book on Marxism. For my part, I am all too keenly aware that, if I am Marxist at all, I belong to no Marxist *community*, and certainly to no Marxist establishment. If my own view is solicited, I would have to label myself as a—Marxist *outlaw*.

For essentially what I am engaged in here, in the larger project, is a demystification of Marxism, which often proceeds by grounding itself in certain Marxist assumptions. It is an exploration of the limits of Marxist consciousness. It is therefore necessarily a study of the linkages between Marxism as an articulate, self-conscious technical theory, as an extraordinary and elaborated linguistic code, with the less reflexive reaches and (hence less articulate or more silent) paleosymbolic levels in Marxism.

A concern with the demystification of Marxism is grounded in and justified by the assumption that Marxism today—as a real historical movement—has not produced the human liberation it had promised. Certainly there are great parts of the world, such as China, in which Marxism has successfully overthrown archaic systems of exploitation and colonial domination. When one remembers the unbelievable misery to which such societies had been subjected, there seems little doubt that the new societies by which Marxists have replaced them are much to be preferred, allowing as they do both more human dignity and more adequate subsistence.

At the same time, however, Marxism has also helped to produce, in other parts of the world, grotesque political monstrosities such as Stalinism. The need to conceal Marxism's own partial implication in the political and human catastrophe of Stalinism is one central source of Marxism's contribution to social *mystification*. Paralyzed by defensive impulses, many Marxists have either refused to speak at all about the implications of Stalinism for Marxism, while others who confront the issue sometimes act as if Marxism had absolutely nothing to do with it, and allege that Stalinism is to be explained solely in terms of certain peculiar historical or Russian characteristics, "Asiatic backwardness."

The concealment of Marxism's implication in (which is *not* equal to saying its *causation* of) Stalinism, has been one major reason for the blunting of Marxism's own demystifying edge and for the corresponding growth in its own role as a social mystifier. One way of documenting this would be to study the reactions of even non-Soviet Marxists to Alexander Solzhenitsyn's *Gulag Archipelago*; this detailed exposure of Soviet prison camps has often caused Marxists great anguish and generated a kind of repressive impulse toward the book, either by not talking about it at all or else by softening the impact of its correct exposures by emphasizing Solzhenitsyn's own religious, nationalistic, and (truly) often right-wing ideologies, as if the truth of the former was somehow made less by the falsity of the latter.

The growing *détente* between the government of the United States under the Nixon, Kissinger, Ford, Rockefeller leadership, with the governments of both the USSR and of China, very largely means the curtailment of the *de*mystifying role that Marxism once played in the modern world. For while the Marxisms of these two countries do *not* exhaust the variety of Marxisms in the world, together they now largely dominate it and control the foci of discussion among Marxists. Extract the influence of both Peking and Moscow from the world community of Marxists today—"factor" it out—and what is left are small groups whose intellectual interest has little corresponding political influence. Even where successful, as in Cuba, the latter are under great pressure to accommodate either to Peking or Moscow.

The new *détente*, then, means that a powerful sector of the Marxist community throughout the world is disposed to repress or modify definitions of social reality at variance with the maintenance of that alliance. For example, this was plainly evident in the Soviet Union when, until shortly before President Nixon was forced from office, the Soviet media largely concealed the weakness of Nixon's political position, and the imminence of his impeachment, from the Soviet people; Soviet authorities feared that this would make it seem that they had associated themselves politically with the most reactionary and corrupt section of American political life—exactly what they had done!—and that could not, in any event, keep the promises for which the Soviet leadership had "compromised" themselves.

Marxism, then, has become increasingly implicated in a world process of social mystification. Such native inclinations toward mystification as it always had are now intensified by the requirements generated by the *détente* between the leading capitalist and leading Marxist powers. In this new context, then, efforts to demystify the social theories held by both sides become increasingly necessary. In my book, *The Coming Crisis of Western Sociology* (Basic Books, New York, 1970), I sought to contribute to the demystification of certain conventional *academic* social theories in capitalist society; and, particularly, in the United States. Here in the larger project, of which this is one volume, the aim is the demystification of the other, Marxist, side of the modern world's sources of mystification. Justification for this last project, however, is not alien but intrinsic to Marxism itself. For the first commandment of the dialectic is contradiction, negation, critique. Which is why Mao has said repeatedly: "To rebel is justified."

"If one apprentices himself to a master," writes E. P. Thompson in a similar vein, "one does not do so to become a copyist . . ." Marx, of course, who was the product of his own transcending assimilation of Hegel (among others), knew this in his bones, and, therefore, issued the paradoxical disclaimer in which he held: "I am not a Marxist." This was not, as some vulgar Marxists might like to believe, a trivial act of empty playfulness, but manifested Marx's profound rejection of the reification of his own social theory. It is in that spirit that I confront the question of the demystification of Marxism. As those who have actually read *The Coming Crisis of Western Sociology* will know, my intention in examining Marxism critically is not to pay my dues to the corrupt and imperialist polity that dominates so much of the world today. At its most fundamental levels, my standpoint remains very much that of the C. Wright Mills whose own radicalism and reflexivity was never expressed as a commitment to Marxism.

My own standpoint is essentially that of the ridge rider: half sociologist and half Marxist, and rebel against them both. In a general way, I also sense that my own position is more "European" and less "wholesomely" American than Mills', being the standpoint of a kind of intellectual mulatto, a kind of theoretical Gênet, but certainly not that of a "Saint" Gênet. My own position rather reminds me of the prisoner-soldier, Cruz, in Jorge Luis Borge's stunning story who, at last, came to understand that the other cavalry men and his own calvary uniform had become a burden to him, and who saw that the man he had hunted was much like himself; Cruz finally discarded his uniform, threw down his kepi, and began to fight the other soldiers alongside the man he had been hunting, Martin Fierro. One does not discard one uniform to don another.

Paradoxically, a Marxist outlaw is a man of the law. He insists on using one law for all and believes that such consistency is essential to the justice he seeks. Specifically, he wishes to use the dialectic to study Marxism itself. It is precisely because of this that he comes to be defined as an outlaw, for most Marxists (like most academic sociologists) reject the idea that they and their theory are the bearers of contradiction, false consciousness, and mystification. The Marxist outlaw is characterized by the fact that he also speaks about Marxism; that he is reflexive about Marxism and that he does not simply view Marxism as a resource but also takes it as a topic. The Marxist outlaw is attempting to speak the rules by which Marxism lives; to discover and articulate the grammar to which it submits. The Marxist outlaw, then, holds that even Marxism must be subject to critique.

To the extent that a Marxist insists on following the law of Marxism *universalistically* he is certain to be treated as an outlaw. This, for several reasons: "normal" Marxists seek to transcend, unmask, and critique the world around them and seek to set themselves apart from it. Normal Marxists regard the social world as their "topic" and view themselves as the "resources" that will clarify, transform, and set it right. Normal Marxists distinguish tacitly, but sharply, between themselves and the world they critique. Normal Marxists focalize differences between themselves and the world, but they defocalize the continuities.

In some part, this derives from the pressure to secure our speech, to make it seem certain, which in turn invites the speaker to obscure his own presence in his speech. For if his presence is visible, if it is clear that what he calls the "world" and its contradictions are *statements* that he makes and speeches *he* utters, it then becomes evident that the world's structures are *attributes*, not "properties," and have all the chancy contingency and problematicity of any "subjective" pronouncement. "Objectivism," which conceals the presence of the speaker in the speech, thereby conceals the contingent nature of that speech and of the world to which it alludes. Reflexivity, however, makes that contingency obvious. It inhibits the feeling of conviction so necessary for the high and sacred moments of practice. For practice is politics; and politics is, in the end, killing. For practice, therefore, one seeks surety and purity.

We seek to be sure of what we want and to be sure of the world in which we pursue it. From the standpoint of normal politics, however, reflexivity is the "pale cast of thought" that slackens the finger on the trigger. Thus those who wish to make Marxism (or, for that matter, normal academic sociology) a *topic*, are inevitably inhibiting it as a practice and as a way of life. They are, therefore, outlawed.

Moreover, many Marxists mistakenly understand "contradiction" as a deplorable or stigmatic condition. Hence to speak of the contradictions of Marxism is, in their view, to attribute a defect to it; it seems to say that Marxism shares the defective existence of the way of life it wishes to abrogate. Normal Marxism wishes to raise itself above what it critiques; but a reflexive, nonnormal Marxism also acknowledges important continuities between the critic and the criticized, between the subject and the object, itself and the other. The reflexive Marxist knows there are subterranean links between the revolutionary "subject" and the reactionary "object." The reflexive Marxist, like the reflexive sociologist, must therefore be outlawed. For he subverts the conventional hierarchy and the elite claims to privilege of normal theory, Marxist or sociological.

The normal Marxist says this of the reflexive Marxist: "He takes sides with the *status quo* against which Marxism struggles." If you critique me, warns the normal Marxist, you are "objectively" giving aid and comfort to the dominant bourgeois establishment. The defensive rhetoric of normal academic sociology is to tell us how "young" it is. The defensive rhetoric of normal Marxism is to tell us how oppressed and put upon it is, concealing the fact that it now controls half the world.

Normal Marxism fundamentally premises that the world is divided into two and only two conflicting parts. But this view freezes the world into an immobility behind the mask of a speciously radical dialectic. This view is based on a dialectic that only knows thesis and antithesis, but forgets that the antithesis itself is the child of the very thing it opposes and therefore has certain of its parents' limits built into it. The very victory of an antithesis overthrows part, but ensures the *continuance* of at least another part, of what it had struggled against. Antitheses must also be subject to critique and the antithesis' own limits must be overcome. It, too, must dance to its own music. "Negation of the negation" *consolidates* escape from and victory over the present. This is the bridge-burning essence of Maoism and its Cultural Revolutions.

The Marxist outlaw's insistence on the absoluteness and inescapability of contradiction, his insistence on a critique grounded in such a universalism, means that the Marxist outlaw is a Socratic, or a Marxist Socratic.

The Socratic does not believe he must pay a ransom—by offering a positive doctrine—for his right to criticize. Not preaching any positive doctrine, the Socratic will not exchange one unexamined life for another, and he therefore subverts both the present and the antipresent. Being the critic of all positive doctrines, searching out their limits, the Socratic is necessarily suspect in the eyes of all who offer (and all who *ache* for) a positive doctrine. In the end, then, the establishment *and* those who aspire to succeed it—in other words, both the old and the young—will accuse him of "poisoning the mind of the youth." Thus Socratics are, and are made, outlaws. Clearly, however, Marxist outlaws have not surrendered the dialectic, but continue to probe and wander its dark side. Only those who can move without joining packaged tours of the world can afford such a journey.

I thank Marion de Groot-Schmitz for typing this manuscript and organizing our sprawling notes. My relationship to Derek Phillips, as American sociologists living in Amsterdam, has been a uniquely gratifying one, and was nourished by his encouraging generosity and his unflinching intellectual integrity.

I can think of no words properly to thank my wife, Janet Walker Gouldner, nor our daughter, Alessandra, for the burdens that this work has inflicted upon them.

Washington University
St. Louis
November, 1975

PART ONE

Ideology and the Communications Revolution

chapter I

The Splitting

In the ordinary language of everyday life, as in the extraordinary language of sociology (be it academic sociology or Marxist), "ideology" is commonly stigmatized as a pathological object. It is seen as irrational cognition; as defective discourse; as false consciousness; as bad sociology. That low opinion was one (not the most important, but *one*) reason why some scholars prematurely celebrated "The End of Ideology." As the subsequent history of the 1960s demonstrated, the rumors of the death of ideology were much exaggerated.° The truth, of course, is that ever since Auguste Comte's critique of "metaphysics," sociologists have been cheerfully celebrating such a death.

1

Sociology's perspective on ideology, holds S. N. Eisenstadt,† was shaped by "the strongly a-religious or anti-religious thrust of much of the Enlightenment, of rationalism . . . which tended to belittle the significance of non-rational or non-scientific ideas." But this, of course, is not so much a confession by sociology as an accusation against ideology, equating ideology as it does with the "non-rational." Eisenstadt's point, however, tacitly expresses one paradox of the sociological tradition: it acknowledges (and sometimes even insists on) cognitive distortions derivative of *religious* convictions, even for sociologists. Since Comte, sociology has felt free to express distaste for religion, as E. A. Shils has correctly observed. Nonetheless, sociology does not seriously acknowledge those different cognitive *distortions* that may result from other, "extrascientific," involvements such as, say, class membership and privilege. The everyday life of normal sociology is contradictory, for there is no good reason why one should guard sociology against religious bias but not from distorting economic interests.

° One problem was that the "party" had been called two years earlier. By the time that it was held it was becoming clear, even to the celebrants, that the celebration might be ill-advised. But what could one do: the hall had been hired, the guests invited, the budget appropriated.

† S. N. Eisenstadt, "Ideology and Social Change," in T. Parsons (ed.), *American Sociology*, Basic Books, New York, 1968.

It is as if sociologists can admit to being biased only by "higher" spiritual commitments, but feel constrained to deny the biasing effects of economic interests because these are morally "base." But the low moral position of an "interest" does not make it any the less distorting than high moral passions. An excess of religious zeal or of atheistic piety can surely cripple a thinker, but this is sometimes viewed as at least manifesting his high moral character.

In the view of social science, as well as of respectable common sense, ideology's social "dysfunctions" are commonly held to be those that might just as well be realized by numerous other "adaptive" responses to cultural "strain": alcoholism, psychosomatic symptoms, and nail-chewing. It is in the judgment of ideology's *cognitive* functions, however, that one discerns a certain Manichean dualism. As cognition, ideology is cast in the role of the force of darkness, the nonrational.

When speaking of ideology, sociology loses its hushed voice and opaque language; its technical language suddenly joins forces with blunt and lively common parlance. It characterizes ideology as the mind-inflaming realm of the doctrinaire, the dogmatic, the impassioned, the dehumanizing, the false, the irrational and, of course, the "extremist" consciousness. Without doubt, there are ideologies that fully deserve these characterizations. But would one really want to characterize *vegetarianism* with such violent adjectives? Prohibitionism? Liberalism? The nonviolent movement for Black rights? All versions of Women's Liberation? Gomperism? The Movement for Universal Manhood Suffrage? Anti-Monarchical beliefs in England or Holland? Psycho-analysis? Even if all are "ideological," surely some of these views are better reckoned eccentric than demonic. The readiness with which social science declares ideology *non compos mentis,* seems to manifest a self-serving one-sidedness. That, at any rate, is the view I propose to explore.

1.1

The conventional social-science view of ideology fails on three counts: first, it manifests one-sidedness. If, as Hegel said, the truth is the whole, then the normal social-science view of ideology is untrue. Secondly, the conventional view also fails because it is lacking in historical seriousness. The historical perspective on ideology commonly used by sociologists is largely a prudent nod of conformity to the formal requirements of historical analysis. In other words: the historicism of sociologists commonly verges on the ritualistic. Third, I will suggest that the conventional social-science view of ideology fails because it is not reflexive. It glimpses, but never really grasps, the way it *itself* is ideologized because of its own structural situation.

Discussions of ideology by social science often take place with the prosecutory haranguing of an adversary proceeding. Social-science views of ideology are vulnerable to distortion by reason of the contestful relation between the two. The claims of social science thus deserve to be scrutinized closely, for their own "disinterestedness" is scarcely above suspicion.

2

Academic sociology and Marxism each begin in a similar manner. Each starts in part by affirming that it wishes to extend the method of the exact sciences into a new area that requires it, the study of human relations. Positivistic sociology certainly does that overtly.

Marxism, too, occasionally defines itself as a science of society, searching for laws as other sciences do. There were occasions when Marx enjoyed being taken for a scientist. But the self-defining acts of both Marxism and positivism are not confined to indicating the paradigm they wish to emulate; each also defines itself negatively by specifying what it *rejects*, by stigmatizing certain cognitive enterprises as *negative* paradigms.

Marxism constitutes itself by developing a critique of "ideologies"; by setting itself over and apart from what it calls "ideology." Early Comteian positivism proceeds in a manner that is structurally similar. It begins not simply by affirming Newtonian mechanics as a paradigm, but by drawing a *line* between itself and other modes of cognition that it holds to be defective: religion, metaphysics, and the work of "publicists" (who perhaps correspond most closely to the "ideologues" denounced by Marx).

Saint-Simon, Auguste Comte's protean mentor and the creative genius whose work he selectively systematized, had argued in his 1813 "Essay on the Science of Man" that psychology must "rid itself of the religious assumptions on which it had hitherto been based." (22) He stressed (elsewhere) that all the sciences had been able to advance by reason of "the weakening of belief in God . . . and that the idea of God should not be used in the physical sciences." (19, 20) (On this matter, Heidegger and Saint-Simon complement one another.) Saint-Simon's followers, "Saint-Simonians" such as Père Bazard, while having a more sophisticated epistemology than Comte, agreed that they must set themselves apart from philosophers who juggle a "few historical events" with some "old metaphysical notions," as well as from publicists with their "contradictory theories."

Comteianism and positivistic sociology began by separating themselves from traditional religion and metaphysics. This is a paradoxical beginning, to say the least, for this beginning could *not* have been grounded in the very method of "observation" that positivism's program proclaimed as the basis of its own authority. The separation of positivistic sociology from metaphysics then was a *philosophical* act, not a scientific one. It was, in Gaston Bachelard's (and Louis Althusser's) terms, a *coupure épistémologique*, an epistemological break. Yet, as Jürgen Habermas has noted, positivism really had no epistemological argument against the beliefs it stigmatized, and none was given. They are taken as having a *prima facie* weakness that needed no demonstration.

Why was this so? In some part, this happened because the old metaphysics had been an *other*-grounded belief system; it was grounded hierarchically, from above, by traditional authorities, clerical and aristocratic, whose authority had deteriorated. In France, at any rate, the rejected "metaphysical" standpoints were grounded in institutions and social classes that had been defeated historically; their views, therefore, did not command the *credit* commonly given to powerful establishments.

To have "credit" is to be believed in *advance* of demonstration; without demonstration; or with only loose demonstration. Intellectuals and intellectual products have "credit" when they are associated with prestigious and powerful social forces, or are media-sponsored. For example, professors from great universities are taken more seriously (and take themselves more seriously) than those who are not. Theorists associated with *successful* revolutions—for example, Lenin and Mao—are read more widely and more carefully than those whose revolutions failed. Who now reads Sukharno, Nkrumah or, alas, Allende?

I am not saying that "might makes right." I am saying that viewpoints grounded in powerful social forces are taken more seriously than they might otherwise. In short, they are *credited.* Metaphysics and religion in France were associated, after 1789, with the past and with the defeated. They had entailed a reliance upon authorities whose authority had been undermined. Science was associated with the forces that had defeated them; with industry, with the new professions, with the future. That is why Comte never had to *justify* his rejection of metaphysics and epistemology, for they had already been *defeated* historically.

2.1

Marx's critique of "ideology" emerges sharply in his critique of the leading social science of his time, political economy, and which he by no means rejects *in toto.* But Marxism does not constitute itself by drawing a line only between itself and ideology; it also places on the other side of the dividing line it draws, in a manner akin to Comteian positivism (I say akin, not identical), both religion and philosophy or metaphysics, whose cognitive failures it specifies and condemns as "mystifications" and ideological "inversions." In both positivism and Marxism, philosophy has come upon hard times. In the former, it is banished from the provinces of "modern" social theory; in the latter, it has become suspect.

One might add parenthetically that Marx's critiques of "inversion" and "mystification" focus on knowledge and knowing. His critique of ideology, however, focalizes the failure of the *knower*, the ideologue, grounding his cognitive failure in the social situation of the knowing subject, in his relation to the larger society. The concept of ideology in Marx thus manifests the fuller surfacing of his materialism, in which the knower is seen not as the self-grounding actor autonomously producing truth, but as an *object* itself shaped by class forces and social interests, as the spoken as well as the speaker.

2.2

The split between the new social sciences and ideology was a one-sided break, emerging largely from the initiatives of would-be social science rather than from the new ideologies. At any rate, after Napoleon made "ideology" a disparaged symbol, few wished to define themselves as ideologists, preferring the garb of the new sciences. To that extent, the development of science conditioned the development of modern ideology.

The rise and development of modern ideologies was shaped by the rise of modern science, by the growing prestige of technology and new modes of production, and by the development of publics whose favorable judgment of modern science was rooted in the decline of older authority-referencing discourse. Science became the prestigious and focally visible paradigm of the new mode of discourse; it was this mode of discourse, which diffuses the seen-but-unnoticed set of background assumptions, on which science itself was tacitly grounded.

The connection between science and ideology was well, but often tacitly, understood by Marx. This is implicit in the fact that his sharpest attacks against "ideology" are mounted against belief systems that present themselves in a specific way, as *science*—witness, for example, his critique of classical political economy and most especially of "vulgar" political economy. It is belief systems about society that present themselves as sciences that are most *problematic* to him and most forcibly criticized as ideology.

Marx, we might say, "inherits" (from Ludwig Feuerbach and David Strauss) the essential parts of his critique of religion, especially Christianity: an understanding of it as a projective belief system grounded unconsciously in man's alienated social condition. For Marx, this is one of the essential *givens* of his analytic strategy. For Marx, this inherited critique of religion is then creatively generalized into a critique of philosophy, a critique that sees philosophy as the continuation of religion "by other means." In this, however, philosophy is not seen as essentially religious in character but, rather, as rooted ultimately in certain social and class conditions, as religion itself was held to be. From this extension of the critique of religion to a critique of philosophy, which he shares with other Left Hegelians, Marx then moved to a critique of political economy as an *ideology* and, particularly, to a critique of the "vulgar" economists.

2.3

There is one way in which Marx's critique of political economy as ideology is particularly justified. For political economy took its own intellectual autonomy for granted. As belief systems "evolved" from religion to philosophy to science, the claim to *self*-grounding autonomy was increasingly built into them. Christianity had traditionally seen itself as a revealed religion, and philosophy and theology were long interlinked; they were institutionally separated only during the eighteenth century; only modern, post-Cartesian philosophy begins to conceive itself as self-grounded. It is with Newton's mechanics that science's characteristic claim to intellectual autonomy is made in a nondefiant, unpolemical way.

Marx's critique of the "ideological," meaning specifically that the thinker falsely thinks himself *autonomous,* was, in a way, *least* applicable to classical Christianity, for that of course defined itself as created by, rather than autonomous from, God. The charge of "ideology" is *most* applicable to would-be social science which paradoxically, held (and holds) itself not only autonomous from God, but even more emphatically from society as well. Sociology paradoxically affirms, at one and the same time, the vast penetrating power of society and its own escape from that power.

The new social science's claim to intellectual autonomy, then, was astonishingly self-contradictory; it embodied a pretentiousness that fully justified the critique of ideology that Marx levelled against it so forcibly. For the charge of "ideology," in Marx's lexicon, aimed centrally to refute nineteenth century social science's claim to be a science, itself free of the influence of the very object that it had discovered and whose importance it affirmed. In this sense, to speak against "ideology" was a critique of intellectual pride. These latent implications of Marx's notion are plainly indicated in his position on romanticism. Romanticism was, of all nineteenth century outlooks, most *anti*scientific and was, indeed, most *anti*-Enlightenment, at least in its extreme versions. Nonetheless, it was *not* the most romantic views that Marx characteristically labels as "ideological" but, rather, the beliefs that romantic views had themselves most *opposed.* In a way, Marx would not have been altogether consistent, in speaking of a "*Romantic* ideology."

The entire notion of ideology then, *as Marx used it,* was most crucially *a critique of the scientific pretensions of the new social science.* That Marx extended "ideology" to embrace metaphysics and religion alike, derived from the fact that his analytic attention was focused elsewhere, on the economic *infra*structure. In comparison with this infrastructure, differences among different belief systems were merely residual issues. But if one attends to the structure of Marx's argument on "ideology," and the specific *uses* to which he puts this concept, it may be seen that he directs it most forcibly against beliefs about society that make scientific claims, claims he holds to be unjustified.

The Hegelian tradition from which Marx had emerged had attacked romanticism as soft-headed, sentimental, and intellectually befuddled; Hegelianism had sought to counterpose itself to romanticism as more rigorous, hard-edged, and intellectual. It was exactly because romanticism never paraded as science that it was not the main target of Marx's critique of "ideology." The modern interest in "ideology" thus emerges as a Marxist category whose underlying, latent paradigm is: *a belief system that makes pretentious and unjustified claims to scientificity.* This solves a problem. It explains why Marx does not condemn Newtonian mechanics any more than Romantic poetry, in that theoretically special way, namely as *ideology*.

There is thus implicit in the Marxist concept of ideology an understanding of a very special way *in which ideology and science were mutually implicated; specifically, for Marx, ideology was failed science, not authentic science.* Implicit in his critical rejection of ideology was an image of *true* science that was to be a standard. Those failing to measure up were "ideologies" and "ideologues."

Even for Marx, then, ideology was a residual category; for it implies that ideology is, in part, that which is *not* science. It is precisely this *residual* character of ideology, its negative definition, that allows Marx to call other belief systems—such as religion and metaphysics—"ideologies," for clearly they are *not* sciences, even though they are not for Marx the truly paradigmatic case of an ideology; to wit, a belief system with *pretensions* to *science*.

It is clear, then, that any historical view of social science and ideology must stress their historical connections—the reality and strength of their historical connectedness.

Sociology begins by stigmatizing certain modes of cognition, by asserting or developing a critique of them, and by proclaiming a *coupure épistémologique* from them, rather than simply by affirming its alliance with the exact sciences. It constitutes itself as a preferred method and authorizes its program by positing ideology and metaphysics as negative paradigms. It defines itself by identifying its enemies as well as its allies.

In raising the problem of "ideology" one is not simply raising a question about one of many possible *objects* that sociology might study. Unlike phenomena such as social classes, political parties, or property institutions, which are indeed objects, objects of knowledge for sociology, "ideology" is not just a cognitive object of sociology but is also its claimed *boundary*. Ideology is not therefore an out-there thing, to be clarified simply by careful observation, by researches, by empirical studies. Its ultimate significance brings us to the problem of the self-understanding, to the mandate, to the mission and the character of sociology. When the problem of ideology is placed on the agenda of sociology it has not simply set itself the task of researching another object but of defining and affirming its own purposes.

This boundary between ideology and sociology, then, is not some long-forgotten outpost that the march of intellectual empire has left behind unwatched. Ideology is not some acned condition that sociology outgrows in its maturity. It remains, rather, a boundary wall that is manned, watched, and recurrently repaired. When Talcott Parsons tells us that the "essential criteria of ideology" are to be found by contrasting it with science, and that ideology manifests itself as a "discrepancy between what is believed and what can be established as scientifically correct," it is clear that, in Parsons' view (as in positivism and in Marxism), ideology is boundary-defining for sociology. Clifford Geertz is, therefore, quite right in indicating that Parsons' view of this is essentially Comtean.*

Ideology, then, is as important as it ever was for understanding sociology. Indeed, one reason for exploring ideology is that it provides an occasion to deepen and extend an understanding of sociology itself and of what it might require for the development of its own rationality.

3

It has perhaps become clearer why it is dubious to define "ideology" simply as an out-there thing, a thing totally apart from sociology, that could, presumably become a topic of sociology. What sociologists are studying in studying ideology inevitably embodies their interests and commitments and is an object they themselves have participated in making.

In pursuing an understanding of ideology, then, we necessarily face a *two*fold task: to see it as an object in a theoretical region, and to see the region within which it is constituted as an object. It is thus inescapably a study of both a social object (or world) and, also, a social theory. To conduct a study of social objects or worlds without simultaneous reflection on some social theory is to generate a false consciousness that believes that all that it is doing is mirroring passively an out-there world, and which fails to understand

* See Talcott Parsons, "An Approach to the Sociology of Knowledge," *Transactions of the Fourth World Congress of Sociology*, Milan, 1959. See also, Clifford Geertz, "Ideology as a Cultural System," in David E. Apter (ed.), *Ideology and Discontent*, Free Press, New York, 1964, p. 50.

how it itself has participated in constructing the very object it takes to be problematic.

Reflexive study, then, proceeds simultaneously with an interconnected study of social objects and of the enregioning social theory that defines their symbolic identity. If we need to understand how social theory and theorists are always implicated in the objects they study, we also need to comprehend how these objects are something apart from our speech, how they are a not-us, but an-Other. To ignore the first, our implication in things, is mindless empiricism. To ignore the second, the not-us character of the object, is an egoistic subjectivism whose ultimate fantasy is that *we* are all there is, or all that matters.

4

So far as we know, the term "ideology" was first used by Destutt de Tracy (Antoine Louis Claude Destutt de Tracy) in 1797. De Tracy used "ideology" in a eulogistic way, to name and recommend a new science—the science of ideas. This was to be a positive science that would not imply any "first causes"; that would eschew metaphysics; that had a sense of certainty (or of the positive) since "it does not hint of anything doubtful or unknown . . ."

As such, "ideology" would provide the intellectual grounding of a new society. Stripped of old, erroneous modes of thinking, and confidently rooted in the sure knowledge of a science, rather than in ancient and discredited metaphysics, ideology was also to be the grounding of the other sciences, accounting for the manner in which they too did and should develop their ideas.

In both cases, the new science was to sort out and separate false from true ideas primarily in terms of *empirical* considerations. Thus de Tracy rejected any doctrine of innate ideas, doing so as part of a secularizing critique of religious assumptions concerning soul or mind, rejecting them as invisibles that could not be justified by observation. The *idéologues,* as de Tracy's group came to be known, essentially continued the Enlightenment tradition that had premised changed ideas as the key to a reformed society, especially if changed in conformity with the indications of their new science, and if embodied in a reformed system of public education liberated from the errors of churchly superstitions.

One connection between sociology and ideology, then, is evident immediately even from this brief sketch: the *idéologues* are the grounding of both sociology and positivism, as these emerged in interconnection in post-Revolutionary France. There is scarcely an epistemological doctrine of the new positivistic sociology (formulated by Henri Saint-Simon and his one-time secretary, Isidore Auguste Marie François Comte) that is not clearly stated or plainly implied in de Tracy. Comte's sociology and de Tracy's ideology also share a doctrine of social reconstruction, centering on the role of a scientifically transformed system of ideas, diffused by a reformed system of public education.

4.1

For Comte, then, the intellectual vice against which he pits his own new science of sociology will be "metaphysics"; "ideology" will not be the central negative symbol for him that it became for Karl Marx (who, like Comte, also wished to transcend and "abolish" philosophy). Thus positivistic sociology and Marxism each begin with a *common* concern to overcome certain cognitive defects of social theory; but each has a somewhat different diagnosis of the nature of the cognitive deficiency it wishes to surmount. Comte's sociology sees the paradigm of cognitive vice as "metaphysics." It aims to overcome this by grounding itself in an *empirical* account of the world. It thus reduced cognitive deficiency to that which was not properly grounded *empirically*. Marx's, however, sees the paradigm of cognitive deficiency as "ideology"—i.e. thinking that was grounded in the *economic interests* of the bourgeoisie and was distorted because of these interests.

The matter is also somewhat more complicated for Marx, because he views ideology itself as entailing a certain kind of metaphysics, thereby converging with Comte. For Marx, however, metaphysics is rejected as, and in part because it is, a *specific* metaphysics, an *idealistic* metaphysics. There is, then, a certain ambiguity in the Marxian rejection of metaphysics. What is rejected, focally and polemically, is one specific type of metaphysics, idealism. At the same time, however, Marx also rejects metaphysics in *general*, partly as a secular disguise for (and sublimation of) religion; and partly as an ideology grounded in and sustaining an exploitive class system.

Although this generalized rejection of metaphysics is *de*focalized in Marx, it is nonetheless there: particularly when Marx and Engels characterize it as having come to an end in Hegel's work; as needing to be "abolished"; and when they invidiously contrast this presumably outmoded form of thinking with the new, modern, and powerful *sciences* that are emerging. Comte and Marx thus converge on a critique of metaphysics that commonly identifies it with obsolescent and outmoded forms of thought.

Comte and Marx both invidiously counterpose metaphysics with the new, modern, mode of thought: science. But the epistemological problematic for each differs: for Comte and the sociologists following him, the epistemological problematic becomes the *empirical* grounding of cognition. For Marx and Marxists, the epistemological problematic becomes the *class* grounding of cognition, being concerned with how social thinking is distorted by the class system and by the interests of the privileged in maintaining that system.

For the sociologists, then, the solution to the epistemological problem becomes proper "method"; for the Marxists, the solution is to change the world. For sociology, then, the cognitive problematic is not *ideology*, as it is to Marxism. Correspondingly, for Marxism the empirical *per se* is not the cognitively problematic.

4.2

For the *idéologues*, ideology was clearly a *positive* symbol. It was only after Napoleon's attack on their group as impractical, unworldly, and unrealistic theorists, that "ideology" came to be viewed negatively, as it was by Marxism and in subsequent usage. Our own juxtaposition of "ideology" on the one side, and of Marxism on the other, may be interpreted as, first, implying that Marxism is here viewed as an ideology—which it *is*—and, secondly, as seeking to attach to Marxism the public discredit commonly connected with ideology. However, speaking of Marxism as an ideology is not intended here as a discrediting dyslogism. Indeed, to term Marxism as ideology is scarcely my invention. Marxism, or "Marxism-Leninism," has been called an ideology by Marxists as different as Louis Althusser, Georg Lukács, and Nicolai Lenin.

It is true, however, that this is paradoxical, for Marx and Engels themselves had used "ideology" negatively. In *The German Ideology*, for example, they firmly broke with de Tracy's positive evaluation, and, instead, characterized ideology negatively. Marx and Engels emphatically condemned "ideology" as a system of ideas made with a false consciousness that inverted social reality and that was subservient to the interests of the bourgeoisie, helping them dominate society. To some extent, then, Marx and Engels' judgment on ideology was continuous with Napoleon's condemnation of it. It is, therefore, ironic that certain subsequent Marxists should have reversed Marx's usage, reverting to a view of ideology as positive, and, indeed, as almost synonymous with rational social theory or science.

Marx and Engels' break with de Tracy's positive evaluation of ideology was a great and profoundly important theoretical contribution, on the one side, and, on the other, it was the source of an ambiguous theoretical legacy. In either case, however, their transvaluation of ideology exhibits *the* central symbolic commitment of Marxism, its essential character-defining act, its movement from "idealism" to "materialism."

4.3

Insofar as Marx's view of ideology entailed a critique resonating the Napoleonic contempt for theory's impracticality, it is vulnerable to philistine views deprecating the role of consciousness in practice and of reason in life. On the level of practice, this creates possible moorings within Marxism for an irrational politics. On the intellectual level, it creates an opening toward positivism. Suspecting philosophy as archaic, it provides no ground onto which one can step back to appraise the new science it proclaims. It therefore provides no basis in whose terms one can critically examine the assumptions of science itself; science—and social science—now become isolated from a larger, more encompassing view of reason.

One should bear in mind that this is no condemnation of "Marxism" *tout court,* if for no other reason than that Marxism itself (like all other social objects) contains internal contradictions, ambivalences, and ambiguities. We are speaking here only of *one* tendency in Marxism and have, for that reason, spoken of its vulnerabilities, not its "vices;" of the space it opens rather than of its thrust and drive. We have tried to intimate complexities requiring a careful exploration that will have to await later discussion.

If Marx's break with de Tracy's use of ideology held such dangers, it was also a major step forward for social theory. For by this break, Marx resisted the powerful momentum of the Enlightenment consensus which seemed to advance a naively optimistic view of reason, ideas, and consciousness, which premised that reasonable argument and discussion alone sufficed to change the world, or were the decisive agents for doing so. Clearly there was a tacit theory of social change built into this view of reason. In breaking with the *idéologues,* Marx broke with a view that had obscured the *limits* on reason.

In affirming that ideologies and social consciousness were not autonomous but, instead, were grounded in "social being," Marx affirms that there are *limits* on reason and rational discourse; he insists that these limits are not a matter of an eternal human nature, but are grounded in the historical nature of the society, its class conflicts, and in the speakers' relationship to these. This is a momentous and historically consequential advance in social theory (even though it builds on the prior work of Henri Saint-Simon, and of Saint-Simonians such as *les pères* Enfantin and Bazard).

4.4

From this point, there were several different ways forward for Marxist theory. In one of these, Marx could have taken (and largely did) the optimistic stance that, since social consciousness is determined by social being, the defects of the old (bourgeois) consciousness and social theory would be removed as the bourgeois conditions determining them were themselves overthrown. From this standpoint, there was no need for a special analysis of ideologies and consciousness; attention had, instead, to be focused on the social conditions producing them and on revolutionizing these conditions. Never for a moment does Marx simply regard himself as the merely curious, Olympian ethnographer of capitalism. In this respect Marxism adopts a critical position toward society. Here, the critical focus is on a specific and limited aspect of life—on the infrastructure, the economic institutions, and class system.

That, at any rate, was *one* way forward for Marxism after it had made its character-defining commitment to break with Enlightenment optimism, to affirm the limits of consciousness, and to make a *critique* of ideology rather than to propose a science of ideology.

Marxism's critique of ideology as such, however, focused primarily on sounding the alarm about the limits of ideology, dwelling on the negation of ideology's claims to autonomy and summoning the contrary, the imprisonment of consciousness in social structure: "social being determines social consciousness." Now *that* form of ideology critique had a curious, tacit, but consequential strain of positivism buried in it. Underneath the critique of ideology, underneath the exposure of its false claims, underneath the impulse to reject and transform it, the operating assumption was that one could take as given the transformation and the overcoming of ideology's limits.

The critical focus was on the distortions of a bourgeois consciousness derived from a society doomed by its own inescapable inner contradictions. As these unfold, capitalism will be replaced by socialism—either that or barbarism, said Marx—and, with this, there will be a new socialist consciousness.

Marxism's focus, then, was on the defective consciousness of *bourgeois* society, ideology; it problematicized the historical *limits* of bourgeois consciousness. The factors limiting it are essentially taken to be known. Hence the question of *what* kind of social structure would strengthen and extend the role of consciousness and reason in life is never fully confronted with analytic clarity. The Marxist focus comes to be placed on transforming the capitalist infrastructure that determines consciousness.

Whether the newly emerging socialist society coincides with the specifiable requisites of a rational consciousness or discourse, whether the new social structure also imposes certain (even if different) *limits* on consciousness, and whether and how far these might be modified to protect and strengthen reason, is not made problematic.

The role of consciousness in the new society will, presumably, be what the new social structure allows; and *this*, seen only as an overcoming of the old bourgeois limits, rather than as the imposition of new limits, is fundamentally accepted and accommodated to, rather than itself being appraised critically.

There is a positivistic acceptance of the future consciousness. Assuming that what must be must also be *better*, this Enlightenment vein of optimism could allow certain Marxists to feel that "history was on our side" and they could thus submit to its inevitability without qualms. Indeed, this inevitability was the guarantee of fulfillment.

The "scientific Marxism" that developed, then, took subterranean strength from the optimistic structure of sentiments that was its legacy from the Enlightenment. In the modern period, however, that legacy has been expended. Optimism wanes as the promise of technological expansion is seen to have approaching ecological limits and when scientific achievements threaten a military peril of planetary proportions. Now, once-rosy optimism has greyed and gives way to a growing sense of being lost in history. There is no longer a sense of riding an upward drift and the dimming prospect reopens once-closed Malthusian issues.

This is true of the bourgeoisie and middle classes, many of whom begin to sense "an end to civilization as we know it." Pessimism spreads also, however, among certain Marxists, particularly those of "humanistic" bent. Looking at the first socialist societies, they begin to suggest that they are only the "dinosaurs" of socialism and that they are not really "Socialist." They see themselves as caught in a double historical failure: in the emergence of Stalinism *and* in the failure of the Soviet effort to overcome it—the abortive "thaw." They begin to reconstruct the socialist timetable, putting off to a more distant future the hope for a true socialist fulfillment. A new whisper of millennianism is heard.

Marxist disorientation and pessimism began to be visible with the paradoxical success of the October revolution in the backward economy of Czarist Russia, and with the revolution's failure in the advanced industrial societies in Central Europe. It is in some part in response to the failure of Scientific Marxism's promise that it comes to be challenged increasingly within the Marxist community by another Marxism, a "Critical Marxism," that places a greater emphasis on the role of consciousness, will, and struggle and which is, in different ways, exemplified by Fidel Castro's Cuba and by Mao's revolution in permanence.

5

Modern social theory—sociological or Marxist—begins, we might say, with epistemological anxiety. Marxism and normal, academic sociology come into conflict with and become structurally differentiated from one another, in some part, because of the different ways they seek to resolve their epistemological anxieties.

In speaking of an "anxiety," I intend no mere literary conceit, but to call attention to the way epistemological concerns characterize the modern era. They are not simply the technical interests of a few academicians, but are grounded in a massive social transformation, in that great historical watershed that marks the decline of the "old regimes," of their once established system of authority, and consequently of the traditional culture of discourse by which they had been characterized and sustained.

This was a transitional period in which the old clerical and aristocratic authorities had lost their public credit and in which the new bourgeoisie was still far from established. In a transitional era, the problem arises as to how, or on what, public discourse will ground itself, if the old authorities—on whom the old discourse had formerly relied to ground its assertions—were being discredited, and if new ones were not yet accepted. In effect, public discourse could no longer ground or justify itself on *authority* per se, as it once had done.

The epistemological anxiety of the era tokened the decline of an old culture of discourse and hastened the rise of new forms of discourse, the new ideologies and the new social "sciences." The transitional era then was an era of nothing less than profound linguistic change.

In this context, it is clear that both ideology and social science alike are post-traditional, modern symbol systems. Each seeks to solve the problem that the crisis in the authority system had generated for the old culture of discourse. Now discourse could less readily justify assertions by authority-supported references to tradition, or to the authoritative interpreters of tradition.

In contrast to the old mode of discourse, both the new ideologies and social sciences were part of the modern, rational culture. The new ideologies and social sciences shared modes of discourse in which the correctness of world-referencing assertions had become *problematic*, and in which these could not be justified by invoking the public authority of the speaker. This further undermined the old-regime authorities and it also fostered a situation in which even the new *bourgeois* authorities were now open to question.

Vis-à-vis the old traditionalism and the emerging bourgeoisie, the new positivistic sociology at first had a liberative and rational function. It brought into question the self-understanding of all elites, so far as these could not be given an "empirical" grounding. Definitions of social reality advanced by any of the elites, old or new, could now be subject to systematic questioning, to examination, to a demand for justification. *En principe,* pronouncements were now no longer credited by virtue of being affirmed by persons of authority. The new sociology's empiricism might then question the most ancient traditionalism or the newest ideology's claims. A man's social position or political allegiance no longer sufficed to credit his discourse. And now all formerly authoritative definitions of social reality—the conventional, the sacred, or the privileged—came into tension with the new modes of discourse, with its new mode of justification.

5.1

The ideologies then proliferating were, historically speaking, relatively rational modes of discourse. As modes of discourse, ideologies were akin to the new social "sciences" rather than simply being their contrasting foils. And as kin, the new ideologies and the new social sciences were, from the beginning, therefore, also competitors. From the standpoint of new positivistic sociology, the new ideologies were condemned as defective in their *empirical* grounding. Sociology proposed to resolve the babel of their competing tongues by examining their empirical credentials. In this, however, the new sociology gave its competitors short shrift, *under*estimating the ways in which ideologies themselves embodied new rational modes of discourse, and *over*estimating its own emancipation both from metaphysics and from the society in which it existed.

The inescapable paradox of the new social science was this: sociology had set itself up as the study of society, stressing the profound power and influence of the objects it studied—society, groups, social structures—and then it proceeded to claim that its own researches were free of biases derived from these same powerful influences. One need not accept the Marxist counterclaim to see the logical contradiction in which positivistic sociology had placed itself. The more one believed the claims of sociology, the more one had to concede that it, too, must necessarily embody social limits on its cognition, which gave it no clear cognitive superiority to ideologies.

At the same time, however, simply to transform "social being," as the Marxists sought, simply to overthrow the old bourgeois limits on knowledge and consciousness, could surely not be taken to imply that any new belief about society that subsequently emerged was true. There still had to be some express set of criteria that one had to follow, including "empirical" standards, by which the validity of belief might be tested. Correspondingly, insofar as one held that theory and consciousness were grounded in and limited by social being, then the problem arose as to *which* social arrangements led to the acceptance of these criteria and encouraged their consistent application.

5.2

It is this last question that constitutes the farthest point toward which our study probes, establishing the vector of its ultimate interests. Clearly, however, from all that has been said before, we do not mean to allow our exploration to be confined to the usual polemic between ideology and sociology. We do not suppose that sociology as we know it can surmount the limits of ideology as we know it, or that ideology is the sickness for which sociology is the remedy.

We had best remember that sociology and ideology are competitors— which means adversaries, and the arguments they invoke against one another will be limited by that. It is a central intention of our study of ideology to inhibit the conventional stereotypes that each has of the other; to inhibit sociology's view of ideology as primarily "dogmatic"; to inhibit ideology's critique of sociology as merely "academic," or as just a "bourgeois ideology."

We shall have to understand, however reluctantly, that sociology is substantially more ideological and far less scientific than it claims, and that ideology is often more rational and even scientific, than sociology conventionally grants. It will also be acknowledged that there are rational grounds for a *negative* critique of ideology.

If sociology is not all that it claims, neither is ideology. In short, there will be occasions to probe ideology's irrational side, seeking to clarify what it is and on what it rests. From this perspective, however, such irrationalities as ideology will be seen to have will no longer be a glib cliché grounded in a competitor's animus. If we see that ideology and social science both exhibit the new modes of rational discourse of the post-traditional era, then there is indeed a common basis for appraising the claims to which both must submit. We are thus not necessarily faced with the relativism of incommensurable paradigms.

The study here is part of an effort to lay a basis for developing a third form of discourse that eludes the pretentiousness, false consciousness, and limits of both social science and ideology, as we have lived them historically. It is a probe toward a more transcending form of discourse that we might call reflexive rational social inquiry, toward a critical theory that wonders about itself and about the world.

Bibliographical Note

Bibliographies essentially have to do with "proof," and I had therefore better attempt to speak briefly about my epistemological "position" before presenting bibliographical notes.

Like many Americans, I have been much influenced by Thomas Kuhn's *The Structure of Scientific Revolutions*, which is congenial to sociologists in its stress on the role (and mechanisms) of consensual validation as the grounding of knowledge in science. Through Louis Althusser's work, I was also led to Gaston Bachelard's complementary interest in scientific and intellectual *dis*continuities—"revolutions" in science. I have also been influenced, or at least much attentive to, the debate that Kuhn's work launched among philosophers of science: P. K. Feyerabend, I. Lakatos, and K. Popper. Apart from them, my epistemological concerns have been sharpened most by Jürgen Habermas, Michel Foucault, Gerard Radnitzky, and Alan Blum.

In the end, I remain most persuaded of the *fruitfulness* of Kuhn's insistence that the validity of some truth-claim is grounded in the consensus of some scholarly community. What science means by "truth" is the consensus of those it defines as competent and full members of its community. My own preference, however, is to think of this group consensus as a *mediation* and a continuing dialogue, rather than in the nature of a jury verdict.

At any rate, the consensus of the knowledgeable must be a *necessary* condition for believing some truth-claim to be valid. Since it is possible, however, that this consensus may be achieved in an "unreasonable" way, e.g., by political coercion, such consensus is not *sufficient*. More than anyone else, Habermas has seen the problem here clearly. Obviously, then, the general *standards* employed in coming to consensus must be judged separately before a specific consensus it reaches can be accepted as reasonable. But how are the *standards* established if not, also, by some consensus of the same group?

There seems an infinite regress here, yet not entirely. For in the last analysis, the group must win acceptance of its procedures and conclusions by some *larger* group. The scientists' actions must be deemed reasonable by the larger community of *non*specialist scholars, because it conforms to some grammar of rationality or culture of critical discourse which it accepts and which cuts across the diverse paradigms within each science. There is, then, a place to "step back" onto and away from the each individual scholarly speciality, and in terms of which *certain* of its procedures may be judged.

There are language variants *shared* by scholars enabling a reasonable judgment to be made by outsiders of *parts* of technical work. There is a *culture of discourse* shared by scholars, scientists, and educated persons of no scholarly occupation, enabling them to make a reasonable judgment about *aspects* of specialized work. To that extent, then, scholars operating in some technical speciality are not a law unto themselves, even though, in the end, we have not escaped attending to the judgment of some group, albeit now a larger group.

What I am saying, then, is that all the "artificial" or technical languages of science and scholarship are language variants—sociolects—of some shared language, some shared "elaborated" linguistic code, some shared grammar of rationality, some shared culture of critical discourse, so that, in the end, outsiders can speak about and judge, in *part*, the activity and intellectual work of even highly specialized physicists. Certain historians and philosophers of science do that quite competently without being physicists. (At this linguistic level, we come close to Feyerabend's position in his "Against Method," in vol. 4 of *Minnesota Studies in Philosophy of Science*, edited by Radner and Winokur, 1970.)

Discourse conducted across specialities and across technical languages is made possible by a commonly held culture of discourse which made it *reasonable*, for example, for *non*specialists to suspect Lysenko's genetic work. Science is distinguishable from, say, theology, which also produces consensus in churchly quarters, insofar as science's world-referencing claims are accepted as having conformed with distinct standards deemed reasonable (to science's distinct objectives) by the larger community of nonspecialists sharing a common culture of discourse. Thus the mere consensus of certain *limited* groups of specialists need not be definable as validating *certain* kinds of truth-claims.

But in the end, there is no escaping the judgment of *some* (albeit larger) group and there is no "truth" seen, spoken, and validated except in *some* language variant. Given this concern with the consensual groundings of truth-claims, it must also be acknowledged that, like any consensus of persons, those processes held to produce "truths" also have an inescapable political dimension. There is an unavoidable "politics of science," not only in the trivial sense of who gets to become a government's science advisor, but, in the more profound sense of how diverging views in the scientific community are brought to a consensus, when or if they are. This means that structures of domination will be found at the boundaries and *limits* even of a culture of rational discourse. The more this is denied or repressed, the more difficult it is to diminish their influence on, and prevent their subversion of, the grammar of rationality. The "friends of rationality," therefore, do not deny but must *insist* upon (and remain alert to) the political requisites of consensus, and especially domination, in the life of the mind. (At this point, the divergence from Feyerabend appears.)

Such validity as truth-claims possess, then, are to be understood as proposals and counterproposals in a dialogue in a community of the interested who share a culture of critical discourse. They are moments in an ongoing process of talk; responses to what has been said before, as well as remarks about a world outside the speakers; addresses to others expected to be interested, understanding, and ultimately responsive, and from whose collective work and talk a certain selection and rejection, agreement and disagreement, will in time emerge.

I do not then think of myself as having here done more than establish a reasonable case, that those interested in "ideology" should attend to and critically sift my discourse, accepting and using part of it, and changing or discarding other proposals. My concern is not to demonstrate that I have produced "truths" about ideology but to make a responsible contribution to the conversation of interested others, as well as making responsible reactions to their prior work.

The footnotes and bibliographical notes that follow are shaped by this sense of shared intellectual enterprise and are designed to indicate something about the dialogue, its present "state of play," its old or new concerns and foci, and where it has been and is going. The problem of producing a bibliography for a "topic" such as "ideology," is oppressive considering that, aside from works specifically making mention of "ideology," there are all manner of closely connected, overlapping areas of discussion of considerable relevance: the sociology of knowledge, the history of ideas, epistemology, the philosophy of science, the phenomenology of knowledge, the anthropology of belief-systems, the new semiotics, and the older sociolinguistics, not to speak of communications studies and theory, and the philosophy of symbolism and communication. A systematic bibliography would require a book of its own, and I do not intend to provide it. I will instead use my footnotes and bibliographical remarks to indicate those contributions that I was, sometimes to my own surprise, influenced by, interested in, and responsive to, even though I may not at all agree with them.

A useful small bibliography will be found at the end of Edward Shils' article on ideology in the appropriate volume of the *Encyclopedia of Social Science* published by the Free Press. Useful, although overlapping bibliographies, will also be found in H. M. Drucker's, *The Political Uses of Ideology*, Macmillan, London, 1974. This slim book's modesty of style hides its usefulness for certain historical problems in the development of ideology. David E. Apter's, *Ideology and Discontent*, Free Press, New York, 1964, also has a supplementary bibliography of value because of its sensitivity to some of the periodical literature; it also does some international scanning. Nigel Harris, *Beliefs in Society*, Pelican, 1971, also has an interesting bibliography which helpfully explores the literature in the recent Marxist tradition. Needless to say there are other things of considerable value in all these works in addition to their bibliographies.

Books that have actually influenced my thinking about ideology and which might be mentioned at this juncture are: the marvellously incisive book by Albrecht Wellmer, *Critical Theory of Society*, Herder and Herder, New York, 1971; the dark Heideggerian brilliance of Alan Blum's *Theorizing*, Heinemann, London, 1974; one would also want to read France's Talcott Parsons, Louis Althusser, *Lenin and Philosophy and Other Essays*, New Left Books, London, 1971; the elegant and erudite Rodney Needham's, *Belief, Language and Experience*, Basil Blackwell, London, 1972; *Aspects of Sociology*, Heinemann, 1973, which is a collective enterprise "by the Frankfurt Institute for Social Research"; the excellent selections in Chaim Waxman's (ed.) *End of Ideology Debate*, Simon and Schuster, New York, 1968; and the lively *Knowledge and Belief in Politics*, edited by R. Benewick, R. N. Berki, and Bhikhu Parekh for Geo. Allen & Unwin, London, 1973. The "father of us all," fallen upon especially hard times since Theodor Adorno's biting but one-sided critique is, of course, Karl Mannheim's, *Ideology and Utopia*, Harcourt, Brace, and Co., New York, 1946, which reared the generation of post-World War II sociologists in the United States and which may be read with great profit with the critical commentaries of Robert K. Merton, *Social Theory and Social Structure*, Free Press, Glencoe, Ill., 1957. And the "grandfathers" of the problem of ideology, as conceived in a contemporary vein, are of course Karl Marx and Friedrich Engels, *The German Ideology*, International Press, New York, n.d. (with a foreword by R. Pascal). To reiterate, these are mentioned without any pretense of comprehensiveness or completeness. Recently published items were often of more influence on my thinking than their newness might seem to allow because, in some cases, they were published previously in articles; sometimes I had the great fortune of being quartered back-to-back with the authors as they were writing their work; or to work for them as a junior colleague long before their work appeared or became known. My relation to the first generation of the Frankfurt School, for and with whom I worked while they were in exile in the United States, has been a lasting, if hybridized influence.

chapter 2

Ideological Discourse as Rationality and False Consciousness

Ideology premises the existence of "normal" participants or normal speakers; of normal situations in which they conduct their discourse; of the rules admitting them to the discourse, and governing their conduct during it. This is as true of ideological discourse as of others. In ordinary language it is significant that we do not usually speak of *children* as having an ideology. Commonly, ideology is taken to imply a normal speaker beyond a certain minimum age, of a certain imputed maturity and linguistic competence. In short, reference is made to a responsible and potent subject.

But it is not just because children are defined as immature intellectually that they are *not* commonly seen as having ideologies. For the normal expression of ideological adherence is an act in the public sphere, to which children have only limited access. Ideologies entail discourse among members of different families, not just within them; discourse among strangers, not just among friends.

Ideologies may organize social action and social solidarities in ways irrelevant to, or cutting across, the traditional structures of society—family, neighborhood, or church. Ideologies can bind men who may have little in common except a shared idea. Ideologies thus premise the possibility of powerful affinities, of claims and obligations among persons bound only by common belief. In some part, it is possible for them to do so because of the deterioration of traditional social structures in the transition from old regime society to modern bourgeois societies.

1

The ideological mobilization of masses (like the use of ideology as a basis of social solidarities), premises a detraditionalization of society and of communication, of what is allowed to be brought into open discussion, to be sought and claimed. In traditional societies only relatively fixed and limited claims might be made; and these were already known and established, for the legitimate in traditional societies is the What Has Been, the Old; only fairly fixed, limited, and stereotyped claims may be made under traditionalism. The manner in which claims could be justified was correspondingly limited. Speech was, more typically, authorized by the authority or social position of the speaker.

The emergence of ideology, however, premises that new kinds of claims and new kinds of legitimations (for them) are now possible and, at the same time, that the old stereotyped limits on what is claimable have been removed. Now, almost anything might be claimed. In this limitlessness of possibility some begin to experience themselves as potent Prometheans or, from another standpoint, as anomically insatiable. As Lucien Goldmann puts it, ". . . once the possibility of supernatural interference was destroyed, everything became both natural and possible." (26) Everything: including both man's terror and his reification.

An intact traditional society, then, leaves little room for the play and appeal of ideologies. But, at the same time, ideologies have their own reciprocally deteriorating impact upon traditional structures and on people's involvement in them.

1.1

Ideologies weaken traditional structures by refocusing the vision of everyday life and, specifically, by calling to mind things that are not in normal evidence, not directly viewable by the senses, not in the circumference of the immediate—they make reference to things not "at hand." One cannot, for example, *see* a "class," or a "nation," or a "free market," but the ideologies of socialism, nationalism, and liberalism bring these structures to *mind*. In doing so, they provide a language that enables interpretations to be made of some things that *may* be seen or heard within the immediate. Ideologies permit some of the seen-but-unnoticed aspects of everyday life to be seen *and* newly noticed. Ideologies permit interpretations of the everyday life that are not possible within the terms of everyday life's *ordinary* language: an argument between workers and foreman may now, for example, be interpreted as an intensifying "class struggle." Ideologies become the self-consciousness of ordinary language; they are a metalanguage.

The tradition-dissolving consequences of ideology arise, in part, because they enable actors to acquire distance from the at-hand immediacies of everyday life, to begin to see the world in ways that go beyond the limits of ordinary language; and they may create new solidarities that distance persons from traditional involvements, from family and neighbors. Ideologies, then, enable people more effectively to pursue interests without being restricted by particularistic ties and by the conventional bonds of sentiment or loyalty that kinsmen and neighbors owe one another. Ideology serves to uproot people; to further uproot the already uprooted, to extricate them from immediate and traditional social structures; to elude the limits of the "common sense" and the limiting perspective of ordinary language, thus enabling persons to pursue projects they have *chosen*. Ideologies thus clearly contribute, at least in these ways, both to rational discourse and rational politics, but to a rationality that is both activated and limited by anxieties exacerbated by an uprooting from at-hand, everyday life. Ideologies capture and refocus energies involved in free-floating anxieties. Anxiety liquidates old symbolic commitments, allowing men to seek new ones and to judge them in new ways; but anxiety also means that this must be done urgently.

1.2

Eric Hobsbawm's discussion of the transition from the older traditionalism to the newer age of ideologies quite properly stresses that it is a passage from the dominance of religious thought systems to more secular ones: "For most of history and over most of the world . . . the terms in which all but a handful of educated and emancipated men thought about the world were those of traditional religion. . . . At some stage before 1848, this ceased to be so in part of Europe. . . . Religion stopped being something like the sky . . . became something like a bank of clouds. . . . Of all the ideological changes this is by far the most profound. . . . At all events, it is the most unprecedented. What was unprecedented was the secularization of the masses. . . . In the ideologies of the American and French . . . Christianity is irrelevant. . . . The general trend of the period from 1789 to 1848 was therefore one of emphatic secularization." °

If men like de Maistre, de Bonald, or Burke spoke well of religion and tradition, they spoke with a rationality and awareness that manifested that these were no longer the things they had once been, but something quite new. Most great and articulate defenses of traditionalism are, and can only be, made from a standpoint outside of it. Outside of the time when it was a viable and uncontested force, as de Maistre and de Bonald wrote *following* the French Revolution; or outside of the membership boundaries that the tradition had marked out, as Edmund Burke was. An Irishman seeking his fortune in England, Burke embraced its cracking traditions with the fervor of

° Eric J. Hobsbawm, *The Age of Revolution*, Weidenfeld and Nicolson, London, 1962, pp. 217, 222.

the new convert and with the ability to see it as a boundaried whole possible only to someone not born to it. In like manner, it was only the sharp crisis of established religion that could then enable Madame de Stäel to speak of the need to believe *something*, and which led Georg Brandes to speak of men looking at eighteenth-century religion "pathetically, gazing at it from the outside, as one looks at an object in a museum." As Karl Mannheim observed, tradition was being transformed into *conservatism* via this self-awareness and via the justification of rational discussion. Tradition was, in short, being modernized into an "ideology."

1.3

Like conventional religion, ideology too seeks to shape men's behavior. Religion, however, focuses on the *everyday life* and on its proper conduct. Ideology, by contrast, is concerned not so much with the routine immediacies of the everyday, but with achieving especially mobilized projects. Ideology seeks to gather, assemble, husband, defer, and control the *discharge* of political energies. Religion, however, is ultimately concerned with the round of daily existence and the recurrent crises of the life cycle. Ideologies assemble scarce *energies* for focused concentrated discharge in the public sphere. Religion constantly monitors, disciplines, and inhibits discharges of energy into the everyday life. Birth, puberty, marriage, death, and grief are its central concerns. Ideology functions to change institutions by mobilizing energies and concerting public projects freely undertaken, which are justified by world-referencing rational discourse. Ideology seeks earthly reaction, reform, or revolution, not transcendental reconciliation. Religions are concerned with the sacred and thus those powers within whose limits, or under whose governance, men act. Religions thus see men as limited, created, or other-grounded beings and foster a sense of men's limitedness; ideologies, by contrast, focus on men as sources of authority and as sites of energy and power. If religions and ideologies are thus disposed to a different ontology of man, they are also, correspondingly, disposed to different epistemologies, religion making knowledge (or *part* of it) a phenomenon that is *bestowed* on men and vouchsafed by higher powers and authorities, while ideologies give greater emphasis to the self-groundedness of men's knowledge, involving his reason and his experience: *cogito ergo sum*.

Yet if ideologies (conceived in their modern historical uniqueness) are secularized and rational belief-systems, they embody and rest upon a unique secularization that is linked in the West to the last great revival of religious zeal, the emergence of Protestantism. Auguste Comte's instinct here was correct, especially in his tacit linking of Protestantism to the proliferation of ideologies, which he offered to transcend via his positivism. When Comte deplored the "anarchy" brought by the modern "liberty of conscience" he tacitly contended that this ideological diversity had a *religious* root. Certainly, modern ideological diversity was partly grounded in Protestantism's insist-ence on liberty of conscience. More than that, this liberty of conscience goes to the core of modern ideology's tacit but characteristic insistence on the individual's right to make his own judgment about the truth of claims and, correspondingly, on the importance of persuading him of that truth in its own, new ways. Modern ideology is grounded in Protestantism's conception of the rights and, as I shall stress later, of the *powers*, of individuals.

The age of ideology premised the prior experience of the band of emerging protest-ants; it is grounded in the diffusion of this concrete historical experience into a *tacit*, secularized paradigm for a broader politics of protest. Modern ideology premised Protestantism's this-worldly ascetic activism and, on a different level, modern ideology premised the activistic inclinations with which this religious transformation—among other forces—had sedimented the modern character.

1.4

Ideology also premises the deritualization of public communication so characteristic of the Puritan revolution. In this, the sermon exhorting men to abide by the Word was substituted for the ritualized Mass.° Through the sermon, men were called to a unity of theory and practice and to a conforming enactment with the Word in *everyday* life and in all their deeds, rather than in the occasional Sunday ritual set apart from men's everyday life. Unlike the Mass, which tranquilized anxieties, the sermon probed and proded them. In the sermon, the age of ideology could find a paradigm of righteous and energetic persuasion, the paradigm of a rhetoric that could mobilize men to deeds. Ideologists assume that words matter, that they have a power that can change men and their worlds, sometimes dropping the scales from their eyes or the shackles from their hands. Ideologists, in brief, believe in the power of the idea as vested in the word.

Protestantism commonly encourages a pattern of coping with anxiety by work, rather than by ritual or magic. Resting on a sublimated Protestantism that survives the "death of God" at the level of character structure, grounded in activistic and ascetic this-worldly impulses, modern ideological politics comes to be defined as a kind of *work*.† From this standpoint, both work and worklike politics are expected to be performed diligently and methodically,

---

° Cf., P. Miller, *The New England Mind.* Beacon Press, Boston, 1961.

† Cf. Michael Walzer, *The Revolution of the Saints*, Harvard University Press, Cambridge, Mass., 1965.

with a scrupulous surmounting of self, precisely because it is defined as pursuing a higher moral obligation that is all the more binding because it is freely chosen. Sedimented with Protestantism on the level of character structure, ideology was the Gospel of Labor in Politics.

In much the same way, Protestantism had undermined Renaissance magic and alchemy by linking control of the environment to the conduct of disciplined, routine work, thereby laying the cultural infrastructure for modern technology and science. Science and technology arise when the will to know is grounded in an impulse to *control, and* when this control is felt to be possible through routine *work*. Both modern ideology, on the one side, and modern science and technology, on the other, have a certain affinity because both in part rest on Protestantism's assumption that work is anxiety relieving.

Michael Walzer tells us of Calvin: as he "firmly believed that the terrors of contemporary life could be politically controlled, he became an activist and ecclesiastical politician. . . . In his political as in his religious thought, Calvin sought a cure for anxiety not in reconciliation but in obedience . . . he promptly engaged in sharp polemic against the Anabaptists, whose goal was not so much reconstruction as the dissolution of the political world. . . . Calvinism was thus anchored in this worldly endeavor; it appropriated worldly means and usages . . ." °

1.5

It was in this manner that Protestant-grounded modern ideology premised the doctrine of the unity of theory and (worldly) practice and thereby unleashed a vast political force in the modern world, a force still powerful and far from spent. This great political power also premises that great importance is attributed to ideas. It supposes that people can have an obligation by reason of having an idea or a theory. It premises the capacity and duty of men to commit themselves to the logic of an idea, to endure its implications, despite its costs to other interests: family, friends, or neighbors.

Obedience to the word is here defined as a supreme value and as a decisive test of character. Ideologies premise that the word can lay binding obligations on persons. This is one important basis enabling ideology, as *address*, to counter the effect of conventional duties and institutions. It is thus that ideologies can serve as a counterweight to the "heaviness" of interests. Ideology thus implies a view of rational discourse as a potent source of world change, on the one hand, and, on the other, as a source of tension with conduct grounded in interest. Ideologies foster the suppression and repression of some interests, even as they give expression to others.

° Michael Walzer, ibid., p. 28.

In fighting for his ideas (or "principles"), the ideologue now experiences himself as engaged in a new, purified kind of politics. He understands and presents himself as not just engaged in politics for the old, selfish reason—to further his own interests or to advance himself "materially." Ideological politics now claims to be a historically new and higher form of politics; a kind of selfless work. It thereby authorizes itself to make the highest claims upon its adherents. It obliges them to pursue their goals with zealous determination, while authorizing them to inflict the severest penalties on those opposing such goals.

Moreover, as politics is transformed into a sacred labor, there is greater pressure for practitioners to conceal, from themselves as well as others, any "base" motives they may have for their political activity; they thus become dulled by that distinct kind of false consciousness called "piety." They may come to believe that, unlike others, they are disinterested in personal perquisites. One specific way this is done is to define the power they seek (or exercise) solely from the standpoint of the functions it has for the group interests, rather than as an enjoyable privilege that its possessors may consume privately. More generally, their claim is that when *they* seek office, power, livings, tenures, or income, they do not seek them as private enjoyments but only because they advance collective interests. Ideology thus serves, on the one hand, to permit ruthlessness to others in the name of high values, and, on the other, to present oneself as having a selfless ambition, that nonpartisanship which legitimates any claim to power. Ideology thereby permits the mobilization of power and, at the same time, allows its full and unrestrained discharge.

Ideology fosters a politic that may be set off, radically and profoundly, from prosaic bourgeois society with its moral flabbiness, its humdrum acceptance of venality, and its egoism. The conservative ideologist, no less than the radical, is in tension with a bourgeois society that is unashamedly self-seeking and egoistic. The ideologue, by contrast with the bourgeois, claims to be altruistic, never seeking his private interest but speaking only in behalf of "the Word." In this tension between the normal corruptness of bourgeois society and the abnormal altruism of the ideologist, political conflict emerges as a higher dramaturgy in which one side presents itself as acting out the impersonal pursuit of an idea. The vulgar venality of the bourgeois thus finds its match in the unembarrassed righteousness of the ideologist.

2

Ideologies entail projects of public reconstruction and require that believers support actively the accomplishment of the project and oppose whoever rejects it. This call for support is now justified by formulating a conception of the social world, or a part or process in it. In short, each ideology presents a map of "what is" in society; a "report" of how it is working, how it is failing, and also of how it could be changed. Ideology is thus a call to action—a "command" grounded in a social theory—in a world-referencing discourse that presumably justifies that call. Granted that it does not pursue "knowledge for its own sake"; nonetheless, ideology offers reports or imputes knowledge of the social world; its claims and its calls-to-action are grounded in that imputed knowledge.

Note: I am not saying that a specific view of the social world offered by ideology is necessarily "correct;" I am saying merely that ideology is a rational mode of discourse. (Thus a Socrates might use rational discourse to argue for the immortality of the soul.)

2.1

Ideology thus entailed the emergence of a new mode of political discourse; discourse that sought action but did not merely seek it by invoking authority or tradition, or by emotive rhetoric alone. It was discourse predicated on the idea of grounding political action in secular and rational theory. A fundamental rule of the grammar of all modern ideology, tacit or explicitly affirmed, was the principle of the *unity of theory and practice* mediated by rational discourse. Ideology separated itself from the mythical and religious consciousness; it justified the course of action it proposed, by the logic and evidence it summoned on behalf of its views of the social world, rather than by invoking faith, tradition, revelation or the authority of the speaker. Ideology, then, premised policies shaped by rational discourse in the public sphere, and premised that support can be mobilized for them by the rhetoric of rationality.

This is no new view, but is offered by a surprising variety of modern theories and ideologists. Thus Irving Kristol remarks: "Ideologies are religions of a sort, but they differ from the older kinds in that they argue from information instead of ultimately from ignorance. . . . Ideology presupposes an antecedent 'enlightenment'; before it can do its special job of work, facts must be widely available, and curiosity about the facts quickened. Men must be more interested in the news from this world than in the tidings from another. The most obdurate enemy of ideology is illiteracy . . ." °

Much the same view is affirmed by Stephen Rousseas and James Farganis, although from an ideological position opposed to Kristol's: ideology's "major function," they affirm, "is to apply intelligence—the fusion of passion and critical reason—to the problem of the modern world." † Erik Erikson also

° Chaim Waxman, ibid., p. 108.
† Ibid., p. 216.

makes the same point from the standpoint of his psychohistory: ideology, he holds, is an unconscious tendency underlying religious and scientific as well as political thought; the tendency to "make the facts amenable to ideas, and ideas to facts, in order," he adds, "to create a world image convincing enough to support the collective and individual sense of identity." ° The unspoken point here, however, is that what makes a "world image" *credible* differs under different historical conditions. Erikson, however, is essentially correct about the construction of world views in the *modern* epoch.

Ideology makes a diagnosis of the social world and claims that it is true. It alleges an accurate picture of society and claims (or implies) that its political policies are grounded in that picture. To that extent, ideology is a very special sort of rational discourse by reason of its world-referring claims. It defends its policies neither by traditionalistic legitimation nor by invoking faith or revelation. As a historical object, then, ideology differs from both religion and metaphysics in that it is concerned to make "what is" in society a basis of action.

In Jürgen Habermas' terms: ". . . what Weber termed 'secularization' has two aspects. First, traditional world views and objectivations lose their power and validity as myth, as public religion, as customary ritual, as justifying metaphysics, as unquestionable tradition. Instead, they are reshaped into subjective belief systems and ethics which ensure the private cogency of modern value-orientations (the 'Protestant Ethic'). Second, they are trans-formed into constructions to do both at once: criticize tradition and reorganize the released material of tradition . . . existing legitimations are replaced by new ones. The latter emerge from the critique of dogmatism of traditional interpretations of the world and claim a scientific character. Yet they retain legitimating functions, thereby keeping actual power relations inaccessible to analysis and to public consciousness. It is in this way that ideologies in the restricted sense first came into being. They replace traditional legitimations of power by appearing in the mantle of modern science and by deriving their justification from the critique of ideology. Ideologies are coeval with the critique of ideology. In this sense there can be no prebourgeois 'ideologies.' " †

2.2

Ideologies are reports about the world, or social theories, that are both rationally and empirically supported. Almost all the major "scientific"

° David Apter, ibid., cited by Apter, p. 20.

† Jürgen Habermas, *Toward a Rational Society*, Beacon Press, Boston, 1970 (German volume, 1968), pp. 98–99.

theories of society had the plainest ideological linkages. When Adam Smith sought to reform the relationship between government and business in England he wrote *The Wealth of Nations* (1776). This rational effort to persuade "established government to abandon the errors of mercantilism and to adopt the policy of internal free trade" became one of the foundations of classical political economy. And it is obvious that Karl Marx's argument for socialism produced one of the great and comprehensive social theories, as consequential for the nineteenth century in which it was written, as for our own. Correspondingly, when men like Edmund Burke, de Maistre, and de Bonald, spoke vauntingly of tradition as a foundation of social order, as the bulwark against men's susceptibility to passion, and as the repository of the group's experience so critical to its survival, they were (as Robert Nisbet rightly says) contributing to the conceptual foundations of an entirely new intellectual discipline, sociology itself.

In ideologies, the question of the cognitive validity or "truth" of the beliefs set forth may be raised. This is inherent in the fact that the ideology, on the one hand, serves to consolidate the unity of those who already believe, the community of believers; and, on the other, it shapes their communication with nonbelievers whom they seek to recruit (or neutralize). Especially in its communication with nonbelievers, ideology is open to challenge and must stand ready to justify its claims about the world, to counter disagreement with rational rebuttal.

It is of course inherent in language that any affirmation implies the logical possibility of a negation. As Roger Trigg says, "the fact that these claims may be true also means that they could be false. . . . When I say something to you . . . you are free to disagree." ° At any rate, it is always logically possible, but not always sociologically feasible, to disagree with any assertion. The logical possibility can be actualized only under certain historically limited circumstances, essentially when there is a relative equality between speakers and listeners; when one cannot readily frighten or starve the other into agreement; and when the other is defined as a full person to whom a rational appeal may and should be made. It is then that there develops a distinctive mode of justifying assertions that does not ground itself in the societal position of the speaker.

Ideologies justify problematic or challenged truths without invoking the authority of the speaker because, in addressing nonbelievers, ideologues cannot rely on "outsiders'" acceptance of those whom the ideologues view as authorities. Insiders and outsiders do not share authorities in common. Characteristically, ideologies justify assertions without relying on tradition, revelation, faith, or the speaker's authority, but place distinctive emphasis on the importance of recourse to "evidence" and reason.

° Roger Trigg, *Reason and Commitment*, Cambridge University Press, 1973, p. 153.

2.3

The purveyor of an ideology, thus, in effect, says to those whose adherence he seeks, "You may believe that this is true 'objectively', true in its own right and *not because I*—who may be an interest-limited person—say so." Thus while ideologies are rooted in interests, their impersonal or "objective" rhetorics function to conceal the presence of persons who might be suspected of "reality"-distorting interests.

Thus intimating emancipation from a distorting partisanship, ideology may now claim that its beliefs warrant acceptance by others. This, then, is the more or less tacit objectivistic grounding of all ideological affirmations about the social world. Correspondingly, it is the explicit claim of "social science" in general and positivism in particular.

It is when, as in the passage from the old regime to the new bourgeois societies, that the culture, the roles, and social structures of traditionalism are waning, that the validity of the expectations of everyday life becomes (or may be made) problematic. Ordinarily, in a traditionalistic setting, the established consensual validation of the group's beliefs suppresses questions of their validity, and questions that do arise may be settled by the decision of a commonly accepted authority. Failing consensual validation, as the new industrialism succeeds and replaces the old traditionalistic arrangements, beliefs do indeed become problematic and must be given some justification— a new kind of justification, in reason and evidence, precisely because the older authorities (and, consequently, modes of justification grounded in them) have lost credit.

Ideologies, then, are belief-systems distinguished by the centrality of their concern for What Is and by their world-referencing "reports." Ideologies are essentially public doctrines offering publicly scrutable evidence and reasoning on their behalf; they are never offered as *secret* doctrines.

The secret doctrine is that which is made available to followers, or to those already committed to a group, and who by oath or membership promise to keep secret the doctrine revealed to them. Here commitment is made to a group *prior* to knowledge of the doctrine it upholds. In ideology, the process is reversed; commitment to the group is made because of prior belief in the doctrine it affirms and because of that belief. In the framework of ideological discourse, it is premised that membership follows from belief, rather than belief from membership. The premises are clearly "sectarian" rather than "churchly."

Again, ideologies differ also from "propaganda" which is not believed in—at least at first—by those spreading it. Ideologies are intended to be believed in by those affirming them publicly and by all men, because they are "true," and they thus have a universal character.

With the waning of traditionalism, there is now an increased struggle over "ideas." This means a greater struggle over which definitions of social reality (or reports) and which moral rules (or commands) are to be dominant. Social struggle in part takes the form of contention over What Is and what should be done about it. Since the latter comes to be defined as grounded in the former, political struggle increasingly takes the form of a contention among competing versions of social reality, through the mutual undermining of adversary versions of reality, and by the development of articulate "methods" or epistemologies as rhetorical recommendations for the version of reality offered.

The social definition of What Is becomes a political question, for it affects the question of which groups are subordinate and which dominant, and hence affects who gets what. "Reports" about What Is are shaped by the structures of social dominance—especially by the credit commonly given elite definitions of social reality—and these "command" actions that, in turn, affect that system of stratification. Classes and parties are thus concerned about and struggle over definitions of social reality, all the more so as no one group's definition is established authoritatively. Both ideologies and social science contain reports about social worlds and both are thus inevitably *competitors* rather than simply being alternatives to one another. We might say that a social science is that distinctive form of discourse which makes focal its reports about What Is and, like both academic sociology and Marxism, holds that it does not "moralize" about what should be, but simply describes what is happening and what will happen. In other words, a "social science" does not make focal its *command* implications, allowing the latter to be placed in only an auxiliary awareness.

But all speech contains a command, even if only tacitly and by implication. There is always something that the speaker wants the listener to *do;* at the least, he wants him to listen in a certain way, with friendly care, which means that he wants the listener to adopt a certain social relationship to himself. He commonly wants the listener to *change* himself and his beliefs by becoming more similar to the speaker. He wants the listener to adopt the same or a similar relationship to the world, to persons and social objects in it, as he himself does. He wants the listener to see the world as he does.

The speech of both ideologies and social sciences are thus alike, both commonly contain commands and reports, statements about What Is that have implications for the listener's actions. It is not that the command is a conclusion that follows with *logical necessity* from the report. A command is nonetheless supported by some reports and is dissonant with others. Thus, for instance, a military order (or command) is held to be grounded in reports ("intelligence") about the enemy's disposition and strength. For example, a command to mobilize one's forces is grounded in reports that the enemy is mobilizing or has begun an attack. Yet that command for a countermobilization does *not* follow with *logical* necessity from that report, since the group attacked always has the option of surrendering. At the same time, once a government grounds its order to mobilize in reports about the enemy's approach, then a claim that such reports are inaccurate will be dissonant with the mobilization command and will reflect discreditably on the government.

Ideologies and social science alike, then, contain both commands and reports. Reports always have implications about what may be done or might be done—to us or by us—and are thus always relevant to our values and, in that sense, are never "value free." To be value free, then, is not to be devoid of command implications but only to be silent about them. It is in part by such silence that the social sciences attempt to assert their superiority over other symbol systems, ideologies.

Conventional ideologies, for their part, however, tacitly claim a *moral* superiority by holding that they do not simply limit themselves to diagnosing reality, but also seek to remedy it in the light of their knowledge. In short, ideologies tacitly claim *moral* superiority in the name of the "unity of theory and practice" that they advocate. The social sciences, however, explicitly claim *cognitive* superiority precisely because their *rejection* of that unity presumably allows them a dispassion and disinterest that better enables them to say What Is. It is very doubtful, however, that social science's claim to a *general cognitive* superiority, or ideology's claim to moral superiority, has ever really been established.

2.4

Ideology and social science are both responses to the newly problematic nature of social reality in post-traditional society. It deserves remembering that social science, like outright ideology, also sought in its beginnings to live by the doctrine of the unity of theory and practice and to impose certain obligations for public action on its adherents. For both Auguste Comte and Henri Saint-Simon, the new "religion of humanity" that they propounded was to be their applied science, the site for the unity of theory and practice.

At first, the new social science also sought to reconstruct society, no less than to know it. But as social science accommodated to societies, and to the growing universities in which it slowly won a place for itself, it renounced the doctrine of the unity of theory and practice. In its beginnings, however, social science's ambitions were not much different from those of other outright ideologies. It, too, believed—and believed openly—in the unity of theory and practice. In time, however, its ambition to reconstruct society was suppressed; some of social science's adherents were—as those of some other ideologies—persecuted and harried. Both the carrot and the club were used against the new social science, finally inducing it to withdraw from the public arena into the isolation of the university.

But the early sociology was, from its very beginning, essentially inimical to the idea of a politics that would be open to *all* and conducted in the *public* arena. Positivism's essential posture was that public issues were now to be studied as scientific and technological problems, to be resolved by the exclusive discussion of qualified *social scientists*. Ideology, however, had kept the public arena open to all on the basis of men's interests and their common possession of reason; the emerging social sciences denied that mere interest and reason sufficed to admit men to discussion concerning public matters; they claimed that now such admission should be open only to those with *technical* credentials.

At the same time, however, the conception of a Vanguard Party of "professional" revolutionaries, later emerging out of Karl Kautsky's and V. I. Lenin's reading of Marxism, seems essentially similar. Academic technicians and vanguard revolutionaries both define themselves as the repository of a superior knowledge that can and should be the basis of a social reconstruction. Both are elite conceptions that place other segments of society in a tutelary role, although one commonly serves to reform and integrate the *status quo* while the other seeks to revolutionize it.

The common view that sees ideology as a halfway house between tradition and science, and the corresponding assumption that the defects of ideology may be overcome by an ideology-free social science, lose their force the closer one looks at them. For the historical task of ideology is not simply a critique of tradition which, once completed, may allow ideology to abdicate in favor of true social science.

If social science embarrasses ideology with questions about its empirical justification, ideology embarrasses social science with a critique of both its social grounding and of its philosophical position. In particular, ideology develops a critique of *science* and of the scientific *Lebenswelt*, no less than of *tradition* and its *Lebenswelt*. It is one of ideology's essential social functions— of considerable cognitive relevance—to stand outside of science itself, and to reject the idea of science as *self*-sufficient or *self*-grounded. In other terms, ideology's critique of science, its refusal to let science be the only judge of itself, its public exposure of science's selfishness, of its irrelevance to everyday life, of its implication in the war machine, and of the egoism, the barbarism, and the *limits* of science, mean in effect that: ideology functions as an epistemology of everyday life. The task of ideology, then, could not end with its victory over the old regimes and their traditionalism. Ideology's face was turned forward, as well as backward; for it was in effect the only standpoint which, in a secularizing society, could provide a grounding for a critique of science and technology and thus resist their domination of the public arena.

2.5

It was (and is) of the essence of sociological positivism that something new was believed necessary to persuade modern men—the "facts." That is, facts were needed as a "rational" *rhetoric*, precisely to persuade. Positivism expressly assumed that in the modern era only science could persuade reasonable men, yield consent, and thereby mobilize *consensus*. It was *not* "knowledge for its own sake" that was sought by classical French sociological positivism, but knowledge for the sake of social consensus, social order, and social reconstruction. This sociological positivism, then, was characteristically ideological in its insistence, at least at first, on such a *unity* of theory and praxis.

In effect, positivism, most especially Comteian sociological positivism, is the generalized self-awareness of the new, postrevolutionary consciousness of ideology-in-general. It was in the midst of the welter of contesting ideologies, following the French Revolution, that sociological positivism first put itself forth as the *arbiter* of ideologies, as providing a *method* that could resolve the contention of ideologies in a new consensus grounded in science. It was this rhetoric of consensus that exhibits that sociological positivism is an ideology about ideologies. Observation-grounded "facts" would presumably resolve the anarchy born of a "liberty of conscience." Thus the sparseness of positivism, the Puritanism of its cognition (in Theodor Adorno's terms), was at first placed in the service of a consensual Catholicism. Against the divisive ferment of new ideologies, positivism asserted itself as the new, *non*ideology, as the *supra*ideology, when it was also the new *super*ideology of societal unity and "organization."

Positivism saw the religious infrastructure of the emerging new ideological politics, but not its own religious infrastructure. When Comte decried the prevailing "liberty of conscience," he was complaining not so much about Christianity, as Bazard had claimed, but about the new Protestantism that had fragmented the old Catholic European order. Convinced that Protestantism provided no way forward to a new consensus, and Catholicism no way back, positivism opted for a new, engineered religion of its own devising; for a "religion of humanity" founded on science. It also sought a model of verification consonant with the Protestant insistence on individual choice but which, also, required that this choice be subjected to the rigorous disciplining of a method superintended by a new priesthood. Positivism, then, premised a new emphasis on the facts, resting on the infrastructure of a *sectarian* consciousness: "the Puritanism of cognition," in which what had been placed in question was the ordinary individual's *right* and his capacity to *think*.

Essentially, then, positivism itself was grounded in a specific ideology and politics: the politics of "what is." It is the tacit affirmation that "what is," the *status quo*, is basically sound; that it only needs to be fine tuned through the use of the new social science and by a "positive" *appreciation* of "what is," scientifically formulated by the new sociological priesthood. It is not simply that the early sociological positivism of Saint-Simon and Comte functioned as a substitute for a waning traditional religion; it also put itself forth *expressly* as a new religion appropriate for modern men. But if one sees elements of continuity between the old religion and positivism's new ideology of humanity, it is also important to see the differences and the *dis*continuities. Even the efforts to protect and revive the old religions were then being made in newly secular ways; one can no more revive an old religion than an old love and one must not expect to restore either faith or passion.

Comte believed that the new age was to be the age of science. His genius was to foresee the future social importance of science, as his mentor Saint-Simon had foreseen it before him. Their weakness was to foresee that dim future as a vivid immediacy; they mistook what was only dawning for what had fully arrived, thereby offending the "common sense." In the meanwhile, the dominant reality was that the new age was also an age of *ideology*, in which positivism took its place as an equal among equals but could not accept such equality. What positivism failed to acknowledge was that ideology was an improvement over the intellectual methods and vision of traditionalism. Positivism one-sidedly stressed the prescientific inadequacy, rather than the *post*tradition accomplishment, of ideology.

3

Ideologies are not the one-sided thing that their enemies and friends both commonly suppose; they are not merely the false consciousness condemned by their critics nor the emancipated rationality that their adherents like to believe. Rather, ideology is both: false consciousness *and* rational discourse. Indeed, the same historical factors that help foster modern rationality also establish a limit on it. As a nonauthority-referencing discourse, ideology submits to the grammar of modern rationality. No ideology holds that *sheer* reference to any authority *suffices as a reply to those challenging* its reports and commands about the world. It is *what* an authority has said and its intrinsic merit on which ideologues claim to rely; the propriety of citing an authority, it is held, derives from what he knows.

It may be said that this is only a "claim," but that the reality is otherwise. It may be said that, in reality, the ideologue is "dogmatic" and actually does rely on authority *per se* to resolve issues and justify his assertions. But in this there is, I would suggest, a misunderstanding. The rationality of ideologists or of ideology does not reside in its practice but in the rules, in the grammar of rationality, which is acknowledged as binding. In other words, "dogmatism" may be a speech mistake, a departure from a grammar of rationality acknowledged to be the standard even by speakers departing from it. Dogmatism, we would say, is "deviant" behavior from the standpoint of the grammar of proper usage to which the normal believer of the ideology submits, even though it is systematically patterned by the speech variant of which ideology is one sociolect—as I shall later argue.

There are, however, difficulties here. For example, how do we know that the erring speaker really believes in the grammar he violates? If he violates it frequently, we might well wonder whether he really does believe it or is simply giving "lip service" to it out of expedience. But this would imply that the ideologist knows that a rational grammar is expected of him, and that he is subjected to pressures or temptations to accept it. This, of course, is the typical socialization situation, much like that in which young children find themselves *vis-à-vis* parental belief, and which, in the end, they commonly internalize and "genuinely" believe even though they begin with only "lip service." So we are back then, to a situation in which ideologists are oriented—either by inner conviction or outward circumstance—to a grammar of rationality.

To speak of rational discourse, then, is to speak of a culture of critical discourse which accepts certain rules and commonly makes an effort to conform with them, acknowledging as wrong lapses or departures from them. Rational discourse is an historically specific culture. That is, the rationality referred to here is not some theoretically perfect mode of cognition of timeless validity. It is, rather, an historically developed set of rules for discourse which (1) is concerned to justify its assertions, but (2) whose mode of justifying claims and assertions does not proceed by invoking authorities, and (3) prefers to evoke the voluntary consent of those addressed solely on the basis of the arguments adduced.

This is a culture of discourse that rests on the sociological premise that the coercive power and the public credit of societal authorities has been undermined, restricted, or declared irrelevant, and that the use of manipulative rhetoric is limited either by institutional and moral restraints or by the prevailing technology of mass communication.

3.1

The culture of discourse that produces ideology was historically grounded in the technology of a specific kind of mass (or public) media, printing, and its specific mode of production: privately owned, small-scale, widely diffused, competitive and decentralized units. The technology of printing and its mode of organization were both independently important in the construction of modern rational discourse. Printing helped make it possible and necessary to mobilize political support among the masses. Printing could reach the great numbers concentrated in the growing urban centers.

With the spread of literacy, it became possible and necessary for elites to ensure that these new publics would support their policies, or, at least, remain neutral to them. The decentralized structure of the printing industry also made public support (or neutrality) a necessity since the public might be reading the opposition press and be mobilized by opposing forces. Even as early as the French Revolution, the power of the Jacobin leaders was dependent on their ability to mobilize the Parisian masses which, in turn, depended in part on the support of various newsletters, newspapers, and journalists.

The age of ideology presumed literacy, the literacy of substantial publics that might be mobilized, as well as the literacy of dominant classes and political elites. A ruling class such as that of feudalism which was often illiterate, and might think of reading as an effeminate thing best left to the clergy, could not have established the sociological requisites of the age of ideology. The development, spread, and organization of printing produced the growing supply of pamphlets, newsletters, newspapers, books, and journals that were partly a response to and partly a source of the growing literacy.

In one part, what printing does is establish the increased influence of written culture—it spreads writing and reading, and the forms of rationality to which the written, as distinct from an oral tradition, is disposed.

In Western cultures, rational thought pressed forward to the exclusion of the ephemeral and contingent with a corresponding selective focus on the imputedly enduring—that is, on austere abstraction. The abstract is the reduction of complexity to the "essential" via selection and simplification. Abstraction is thus a mode of decontextualization, removing or constructing a thing apart from the complexity which is its normal context in ordinary language and everyday life. Simplification, decontextualization, and abstraction permit greater concentration and control, symbolic or otherwise.

As Ernest Gellner has suggested, writing confers and is thought to confer permanency. To that extent, writing may evoke more careful thought in writer and reader. It establishes that the topic is to be taken with a certain seriousness, not having the fleeting quality of speech. And this is strengthened to the extent that writing is the scarce skill of a limited elite of scribes or literati. That something has been written, then, is often taken to impute importance to it, to claim it ought to be taken seriously, to be considered with *reflection*.

What the revolution in printing technology did was to democratize the culture of writing. It was consequential, though scarcely alone in this, for a quantitative increase in public discourse and, also, for qualitative changes in its character. Like writing, printing and printed objects *de*contextualized speech and tended to reduce the modalities of communication.

Face-to-face talk is *multi*modal, allowing persons to see and to hear speakers. Force, tone, pronunciation, dress, manner, gesture, and movement, all convey information providing a context for interpreting talk. Sometimes such multimodality facilitates interpretation, providing necessary information not conveyed linguistically. Sometimes, however, it might distract the listener from the speech itself or overload him with irrelevant or useless information, thereby impairing interpretations of talk. Printing separates the talk from the talker, allowing and requiring it to be appraised without the seen-but-unnoticed, without the given-but-unintended, supports of the nonlinguistic modalities of communication.

This *de*contextualization can make appraisal of the validity of an argument more rigorous. It may allow it to be appraised somewhat more deliberatively and impersonally, without pressure for the rapid rebuttal of contest-like conversation. Such distancing and depersonalization may, also, permit a greater control of affectivity thus, again, reinforcing a certain kind and measure of rationality.

Printing strengthened rational discourse both by its effect upon responses to arguments and, also, by its effects upon those offering the argument. The printed exposition of writing requires an author to finalize his argument. It disposes him to think of himself as having to prepare the "final draft" that will be printed and which, once printed, cannot easily be changed or improved, and which may be stored and read long after publication.

An author of a printed work is thus under considerable pressure to perfect his argument, prior to its publications. In conversation, however, a speaker may not think of any one statement as definitive. He does not have to try to anticipate the various objections to his argument in advance but may simply answer them *ad hoc*, as they are made. Involvement in face-to-face dialogue means that a speaker is concentrating upon the specific viewpoint of the other who is present. But the writer has no such limiting confinement; he may range imaginatively over a variety of possible audiences anticipating their various responses and seeking to formulate his argument so as to deal with them. A writer prepares his argument to be read by different audiences and, often, by people in later historical periods. Printing decontextualizes argument. The argument is thus less susceptible to the idiosyncratic characteristics of an immediate or local environment, and less under its influence or control; the writer is thus more likely to attend to the grammar by which he feels he should be bound.

Given the (relative) decontextualization of printing, a writer cannot rely on the seen-but-unnoticed premises, or seen and noticed reactions, of a face-to-face audience. The printed exposition of arguments requires (and allows) a writer to make *explicit* the chain of his assumptions and to articulate the grounds of his argument. He can allow himself to develop and present a long-linked complex argument; for he knows his reader can read it over as frequently as necessary, without having to rely only on his memory of the argument, as would a listener. It was in part for that reason that Socrates had insisted that the dialogue required short questions and short answers. But printed argument is not constrained by the same limitation.

It is not only that printed form *allows* a longer, more complex argument; it also *requires* this because readers and writers cannot rely on their sharing a common context to interpret the other's casual, compact or cryptic speech. Given the greater diversity of his audience, the writer often cannot know what assumptions or interests his readers will bring to his work, and whether these will coincide with those he himself uses. The writer, therefore, must spell out his assumptions in greater detail if he wishes to be convincing. Oral discourse is more tolerant of *casual* styles of discourse, but writing fosters *careful* styles of discourse. With the spread of printing, then, the structure of what is regarded as a convincing argument begins to assume a specific character. This involves the ideal of a full explication of all the assumptions necessary to support the conclusions. This, too, becomes an important rule in the emerging grammar of modern rational discourse. The fullest exemplifications of this ideal, with its structure of axioms and theorems, is the geometric proof which becomes the concrete paradigm of that ideal of rational discourse.

It is in that sense that Martin Heidegger was correct in speaking of the "mathematical project" as characterizing modern science.* For my part, I would prefer to say that the mathematical project with its ideal of self-sufficiency, is *one* of the grounds of modern science, most particularly of its rational (rather than its empirical) structure. Both science and ideology are grounded in a culture of careful discourse, one of whose main rules calls for *self-groundedness*, requiring as it does—as a regulative ideal—that the speaker be able to state articulately all the premises required by his argument, and to show that his conclusions do not require premises other than those he has articulated.

This aspect of the grammar of rational discourse is, to repeat, an ideal; an ideal not of the ordinary languages of everyday life but of the various extraordinary, technical, or specialized languages characteristic of the intelligentsia. It is an ideal partly grounded in and reproduced by the special exigencies of a printed communication that increasingly decontextualizes communication, creating a situation where writers and readers may not share one another's assumptions—or if they do, may not know it—and where these must therefore be defined.

* Martin Heidegger, *What Is a Thing?* Henry Regnery, Chicago, 1967.

Certainly, however, this element in the grammar of modern rationality is not only rooted in the technology of printing. The ideal of a self-grounded rationality was also furthered by the Enlightenment impact on religion. With the decline of conventional religious conviction and of the givenness of God, persons—and particularly the intelligentsia—were less likely to define man as God's creature and, instead, inclined more and more to believe that "man makes himself." Similarly, the political revolutions following the Enlightenment also heightened the sense of potency of ordinary persons. Enlightenment assumptions and revolutionary experience coalesced with printing technology to foster *self-groundedness* as a critical rule of rational discourse. This rule also spread because it corresponded to the specific status experience and the vested interests of the emerging intelligentsia. This was an intelligentsia that often freed itself of conventional churchly loyalties that moved through different social and political organizations, from the old regime salons to the revolutionary assemblies, and that travelled widely and was interested in different countries, developing a cosmopolitan self-image as "Citizens of the World."

With the decline of the traditional clerical and aristocratic authorities of the old regime societies, the older grammars of discourse that had entailed or allowed justification by invoking authority were losing force. Discourse was now unable to justify its claims by referring to the supporting authority of another, and it was constrained increasingly to become *self*-authorized. The ideal of rational discourse as self-grounded discourse thus became increasingly both more possible and more necessary in that transitional era, when the old regimes were waning and when the new bourgeoisie was far from fully established. (It was precisely because this assumption of self-groundedness had been so entrenched in the grammar of modern rational discourse that Kurt Gödel's 1931 paper was of epochal importance, showing as it did that formal systems are unavoidably lacking in self-sufficiency and must rest on assumptions *outside* their own stipulations.)

If the coalesced forces of printing technology, the decline of old-regime traditionalism and the emergence of new Enlightenment assumptions contributed to the development of modern rationality, they also built *limits* into it, fostering a certain false consciousness. Specifically, as they increased the *de*contextualization of discourse—strengthening the speaker's orientation to his grammar and focusing attention on discourse as embodied in printed objects, there was a corresponding defocalization of those *persons* to whom it was addressed and of the *speaker* making the address.

The *dialogue* character of discourse thus tends to become occluded, as focal attention is given over to the printed object or to its words or ideas. The latter come to be increasingly separated from those producing them as a speech, and from the patterns of social interaction that are its meaning-bestowing context. Dialogue is thus hidden behind monologue. Talking and listening give way to a reading and writing that may take place alone and apart from others. With the increased decontextualization of communication, and with the spread of depersonalizing print, communication becomes a kind of ghostly, disembodied voice separated from its speaker. Communication as speech produced by a speaker (and hence dependent on and varying in character with the *language* spoken) becomes less visible. It is therefore now easier to assume that the *meaning* of a communication (as distinct from its *validity*) may be understood apart from the intent and occasion of the speech and the speaker.

3.2

The critique of ideology developed by Marx out of the Left Hegelian critique of religion, which had affirmed that man made god (and religion) rather than that god had made man, centered on denying the decontextualization and autonomy of ideas. Indeed, Marx defines this decontextualization as a fallacious philosophy—idealism. Marx's critique of ideology is an effort to resist the decontextualization of communication and aims to *re*contextualize it—to *recover* the context of communication as speaker-implicated. The specific goal of a Marxist recontextualization of communication is the recovery of the *class character* of the speaker. Ideology is thus defined by Marx as the false consciousness of speech that mistakenly believes itself to be autonomous and which serves the bourgeoisie's interests in social domination.

At the same time, however, this Marxist recontextualization of speech is itself limited and faces certain problems. Specifically, a Marxist recontextualization of speech, recovering the occluded class character of the speaker, inevitably invites universalization. This was essentially the tack that Karl Mannheim took, in developing his own sociology of knowledge. Mannheim regarded the self-imposed limits of Marxism's recontextualization of speech as irrational because it was not universalized to include and to make reflexive reference to the Marxist-*self*. Whatever one may think on Mannheim's sociology of knowledge, he was right in seeing that Marxism resisted efforts to see *itself* as a speech produced by speakers, who may also be limited by their own social context.

To view its own theories as a speech like other speeches, and its own theorists as speakers like other speakers, undermines Marxism's (and any ideology's) capacity to mobilize the action it seeks and to persuade men to pay the costs of their commitments. Relativism may foster a worldly tolerance of different gods and discourage costly sacrifices on behalf of one's own beliefs, since these are taken to be far from certain. Its attitude may promote neutrality rather than struggle against the "error" of opposing outlooks.

Marxism, therefore, could not allow its recontextualization of speech to be extended to include itself.

In this respect, Marxism like other ideologies is a rational mode of discourse that embodies a specific communication pathology—"objectivism." *Objectivism* is discourse lacking in reflexivity; it one-sidedly focuses on the "object" but occludes the speaking "subject" to whom it is an object; objectivism thus ignores the way in which the spoken object is contingent in part on the language in which it is spoken, and varies in character with the language—or theory—used.

The analytic essence of ideology, common to all concrete "isms," is precisely that it is speech that does not recognize or make problematic its own grounds, and rejects such reflexivity as unworldly "navel-gazing." It is thus exemplified by Napoleon's contempt for the *idéologues*; but it was he rather than they who, from our point of view, was the ideal ideologue.

3.3

There are *two* forms of objectivism and thus, in this respect, *two* types of ideology. One of these is "idealistic objectivism," where the focus is given over to the logical, intellectual, or linguistic grounds of speech, while simultaneously taking as given the "material" or sociological grounding of the speaker. The second is "materialistic objectivism" where attention is focused on the socioeconomic grounding of the speaker but where the nature of speech as speech grounded in and contingent on language or theory is occluded. For all its critique of ideology, then, Marxism does not itself transcend all ideology. Marxism's ideology critique powerfully illuminated the limits of one form of ideology, that based on *idealistic* objectivism; but Marxism itself also generated a materialistic objectivism and remains bound by the specific, linguistic, nonreflexivity of a materialist ideology.

Correspondingly, "normal" academic social science, including sociology, remains limited by its own essentially idealistic objectivism, particularly evident in its paradoxical vision that it itself is able to elude the very social forces to which it attributes such power. The idealistic objectivism of academic sociology sometimes makes *theory* problematic, but commonly takes the *theorist* and his social situation as givens.

3.4

If ideologies are grounded in a culture of rational discourse they are also, and indeed, for that very reason, a mode of discourse that is limited by objectivism, speaking of the world in an omniscient voice, as if the world itself rather than men were speaking. Ideology thus lacks reflexivity. As we will later elaborate, the reason for ideology's objectivism is that it is grounded in an interest that does not wish to make itself problematic and refuses to put itself in question, and hence it generates silence about itself and about the limits on its rationality.

But interests are the interests of persons or groups which also need furtherance and protection by the cooperative action of others. The problem is how to secure the support of others for an interest that one does not wish to discuss, or at least to make problematic. Depersonalized objectivistic speech does this by defocalizing the presence of such interests in part by occluding the presence of speaking persons whose visibility would underwrite the contingency of what was said, being all too evidently speech spoken by men with inherent limitations and distorting interests.

A second limitation on ideology's rationality has to do with its relation to the empirical. We might say that ideology has a certain "overconfidence" concerning its own empirical grounding. It takes this grounding as given rather than treating it as problematic and as susceptible to critical reexamination. In effect, ideology acts as if all relevant empirical issues have been resolved satisfactorily. For ideology, then, there no longer seems to be any question of fact or, more exactly, questions of fact that have policy relevance. In some part this is an expression of the frequently remarked-upon "dogmatism" of ideology, but the problem is a broader one to which we will later have to return in a more systematic way. For the moment, a few phenomenological observations about this may be in order.

Consider the Other's phenomenology of the ideologue, how the ideologue is seen and experienced by another. The ideologue is experienced as one who does not want to "bend"—as "rigid"—while he wants the Other to "bend." There is an *eristic* element of struggle for sheer dominance; discourse itself has here become contest. There is a fundamental lack of reciprocity of perspectives, for the ideologue is experienced as wanting the Other to change, to see the world through the ideologue's perspective, but himself cannot or will not reciprocate by seeing the world through the Other's perspective. The ideologue is accused of violating a fundamental if tacit rule of discourse, the mutality or reciprocity of perspectives. He is seen as being one-sided, "his"-sided. Discourse is thus experienced not as an "exchange" but as an agency of control by one party over another. Ideology is seen as being uncontrollably and compulsively one-sided. As out of touch with the "Other." This is an aspect of a critical phenomenology of the ideological.

The ideologue, however, experiences himself differently. Most preeminently, he experiences himself as possessing a significant truth, a truth he does not experience as dubitable, although he does view it as embattled, subverted, precarious. For him, however, his truth is not just one other truth in a world of truths and half-truths, but something special which he must put forth special efforts to safeguard. The ideologue is on guard against those who, he feels, are trying to talk his theory to death. He experiences discourse as fraught with great danger, thus speaking frequently of its "traps."

The ideologue's truth is not just a knowledge about some part of the world but simultaneously transforms the ideologue's relation to it, and does so in a way that is liberating in relation to some other, older conception of the world. It has become a center around which the ideologue's identity becomes rearranged. It is thus more than empirical bits of information that are decisive in their effects on the ideologue; there has been a larger and more subtle conceptual shift that rearranges the total architecture of his perspective on the world, and hence of his place in it. With this new truth, the whole world has a different feel. Part of what is experienced is in the nature of a rebirth of self; for with the adoption of the ideology, a boundary line has been drawn in the periodization of the self into a before-and-after the coming of the ideology, into a division between the early, "archaic" self and the new, "reborn" self. The ideology is thus in some measure *self*-transforming.

But now that the whole self has been reorganized in terms that hinge on the ideology, the latter cannot be lightly opened up for examination; it cannot be kept perpetually open to continual, critical reexamination or challenge. Known with an inward conviction, there seems nothing more, or at least nothing more of comparable importance, for the ideologue to know. It is not that he feels he knows all. But he feels that what he knows is decisive. To the extent that ideology becomes the grounding of identity, a person's being becomes contingent on the maintenance of that ideology and thus sets limits on the capacity to change that ideology rationally. In other words, insofar as it is self-constituting, ideological discourse generates an identity that, like an *interest*, is taken or takes itself *as* given, and thereby also constitutes a limit on rationality.

The ideologue's task, then, is not an empirical one but something else. First he has the task of spreading the word; to tell and convince others, to help them see something of the extraordinary thing he sees. Secondly, he has the task of doing what is needed, of adopting a practice appropriate to his own new knowledge. What is needed, then, is an effective rhetoric, organization, or practice and also vigilant countermeasures to defend this knowledge from those who mean to discredit it. But what is *not* needed is more "research" or more "critical thinking."

3.5

It would be erroneous, however, to conclude that this demonstrates the general inferiority of ideology's rationality in comparison with science's. It is likely, rather, that this simply demonstrates that the points at which their rationality is limited differs, rather than implying that ideology has limits while science has none. The limits of scientific rationality are located precisely in what Thomas Kuhn defines as the hallmark of its maturity, in the very "paradigm" which is shared by members of the scientific community. "Normal science," in Kuhn's terms, is science that operates within the limits of a paradigm, "testing" and working on "puzzles" via bits of research that are implied by the paradigm.

It is just this readiness to focus on "puzzles" and tests within the paradigm that indicates that, for the most part, it remains a given for the scientific community, being that about which questions are not raised, until it produces an accumulation of anomalous findings. The limited rationality of the process is suggested, further, by the fact that the production of even anomalous findings within the framework of a paradigm does not readily generate a critical review of the paradigm. Before this commitment is surrendered or brought into question the anomalies must grow and/or there must be available alternative or competing paradigms. But Kuhn himself comes rather close to saying much the same, about the limited rationality of normal science, when he says that it *begins with the end of critical reason*. Kuhn thus remarks that "when I describe the scientist as a puzzle solver . . . I use the term 'puzzle' in order to emphasize that the difficulties which *ordinarily* confront even the very best scientists are, like crossword puzzles, challenges only to his ingenuity. *He* is in difficulty, not current theory." ° And again: ". . . it is precisely the abandonment of critical discourse that marks the transition to a science. Once a field has made that transition, critical discourse recurs only at moments of crisis . . ." † This strongly suggests that what Kuhn calls "normal science" can be conceived of, from the standpoint of the grammar of rationality, as a cognitive pathology.

4

If the analytic essence of ideology is its stunted reflexivity, concerning its own ideal or material groundings, this is in effect a critique of ideology as a limited rationality. To judge ideology in this way views it from a tacit standpoint, in terms of a certain ideal of rationality, and reproaches it for falling short of that ideal. Essential to this ideal of rationality, as already adumbrated, is the standard of self-awareness. This prizes the speaker's capacity to speak the assumptions of his perspective, to know the rules to which he submits.

° In I. Lakatos and A. Musgrave (eds.), *Criticism and the Growth of Knowledge*, Cambridge University Press, 1970, p. 5.
† Ibid., p. 6.

Rationality is here construed as the capacity to make problematic what had hitherto been treated as given; to bring into reflection what before had only been used; to transform resource into topic; to examine critically the life we lead. This view of rationality situates it in the capacity to think *about* our thinking. Rationality as reflexivity about our own groundings premises an ability to speak about our speech and the factors that ground it. Rationality is thus located in metacommunication. But the critique of a set of assumptions depends, in its turn, on using a set of assumptions; and these, in turn, must also be susceptible to critique, *ad infinitum*. There are probably very definite limits on any individual's capacity to reflect upon the assumptions he uses to examine the assumptions he uses, etc. Perhaps a third- or a fourth-order reflexivity is the very most that can be sustained by any one person.

4.1

The grounding of such a rationality can therefore be secured only in the right of the listener to question and critique the speaker's assumptions. Such rationality, then, depends not only on the speaker but, no less, on the listener and on their *inter*relationship. Rational discourse entails a kind of *rotating* division of labor, the speaker of the moment having a vested interest in *his* assumptions, while the listener challenges, and, indeed, has a vested interest in his capacity to challenge, the assumptions made, and so on. Such rationality, then, is in the *dialogue* and in rules that permit assumptions to be examined regressively. But one should note that under these rules the particular set of assumptions at any given moment—the cultural *status quo*—is always subject to challenge. Inherent in this structure of rationality, then, is potential revolution in permanence, the "permanent revolution." It is the drive toward unending perfection, that unceasing restlessness and lawlessness, that was first called *anomos* and later, *anomie*.

Ideology, then, is indeed a mode of discourse with a limited reflexivity. But it is a mode of *rational* discourse, too, in part because it is grounded in another norm emphasizing its self-groundedness. In other words the norm of rationality that requires *meta*communication—the transformation of assumptions into problematized topics—is a form of critique limited by that other norm of rationality which seeks to make discourse autonomous, either from the language in which it takes place or from the social conditions on which it rests. This criterion of self-groundedness is a norm of modern rationality which allows its premises to be criticized, rather than to be placed above criticism. At the same time, however, the claim that it is a *self*-grounded discourse generates systematic silences about those substantial conditions, in language and society, on which the conduct of that discourse depends. It thus produces, as noted above, that pathology of cognition called "objectivism":

communication that conceals the presence of the speaker; a sociology that conceals the presence of the sociologist; thinking that ignores the language or theory in which thought is taking place. Objectivism is that pathology of cognition that entails silence about the speaker, about his interests and his desires, and how these are socially situated and structurally maintained.

Such a rationality does not understand itself as an historically produced discourse but as suprahistorical and supracultural, as the sacred, disembodied word: *Logos*. Imagining itself valuable only to the extent it escapes history and society, this historical form of rationality maintains a heavy silence about its own grounding. The objectivism that characterizes ideology, then, is not peculiar to ideology. It is a cognitive flaw it shares with all discourses grounding themselves in the culture of modern rationality. The objectivism that is a limitation of reflexivity, then, is in part grounded in modern, historically contingent rationality itself. Objectivism is a cognitive "deviance" produced and reproduced by an effort to *conform* with that rationality's requirement of self-groundedness. For conformity with that norm fosters deviance from modern rationality's other norm, that demanding self-aware-ness and self-examination. Objectivism and the critique of objectivism, then, are *both* produced by the grammar of modern rationality, and are sympto-matic of its internal contradictions.

4.2

Our view of ideology, then, sees it as grounded in a mode of discourse that is an internally limited form of rationality. Neither the emancipation of this discourse from traditional authority, nor the false consciousness built into its grammar, emerges under any and all historical conditions. Our view of that rationality—as reflexivity about our groundings—premises an ability to speak about our speech. It is thus profoundly rooted in the decline of traditionalistic cultures and in the corresponding demystification of speech—or forms of it—as god-inspired or as revelation, or as fused with the sacred as in *Logos*. In Western societies this at first most visibly emerges in the Greek city-state; its fullest development is reached, however, only after the termination of feudalism and its political system.

The specific sociocultural conditions under which the modern grammar of rationality matures is: the waning of once traditional cultures; the decline in the sheer givenness of its values; the corresponding increased visibility of the rules that had hitherto remained largely unnoticed; the rise of cities and of urbanism; the rise of new social classes, the decline of older established elites, and the intensifying struggles among them; increasing travel, commerce, improved modes of transportation and communication, bringing increased *confrontation* among different cultures and within their bearers. All this makes more visible, and more problematic, the older, once unnoticed rules by which persons had customarily lived.

The model of rationality tacitly employed in the critique of ideology as flawed rationality sees men as *properly* bound only by rules they can articulately justify. It premises men who have *not* spent their lives in viable tribal, rural, or traditional communities; who, rather, have been uprooted and anomically detached; who are now bound together less by an unnoticed, hence unexaminable culture, and more by common interests; by commitments to which they may in part attend deliberately, and whose protection or pursuit is no longer limited by traditional structures; and who have to "negotiate" with one another, to come to terms and arrive at settlements, understandings, and alliances and who arrange exchanges through persuasion, rather than direct domination. It premises an ecology of speakers who cannot give one another orders, because they have a relative equality; who have some means enabling them to resist compulsion and who must therefore be persuaded, "rationally."

4.3

The Marxist critique of ideology had focused on certain very important specific sources of the lack of reflexivity, particularly class "interests." The Marxist critique was thus a major step in demystifying rational discourse, pointing as it did to certain of the social conditions by which rationality might be subverted and on which it depended.

At the same time, however, "class interest" was a special case that ignored *other* limits on rationality; for example, the cultural limits of language. This became belatedly clear, at least to certain in the Marxist community, when Joseph Stalin launched his critique of the Soviet linguist N.Y. Marr, and plainly affirmed the ambiguous place of language in Marxist theory. Marxism had, also, occluded the cognitive consequences of desire. The "passions," in short, are also important in limiting rationality: e.g., "when you're in love, smoke gets in your eyes."

Ideology, then, is *one* concrete, sociologically grounded limit on rationality and thus by no means exhausts such limits. To have raised the question of the effects of class interests was a profound but limited step toward understanding the hazards to rational discourse. What I am saying is that ideology is only one set of forces that limit, or may be used to strengthen and extend, rationality. The study of ideology has its value because it is part of that larger family of problems but it has a limited role in that family, for it is only a part. While my analysis here will largely focus on ideology and interests, rather than, say, desire, I shall try to remain alert to the limits of my own inquiry.

An ideology critique has a certain ambiguity, for it both accepts and challenges the validity of the very standard of self-groundedness or autonomy implied by modern rationality. On the one hand, ideology critique condemns speakers for failing to abide by the standard of self-groundedness they affirm, and the "critique" itself proceeds by exhibiting (or "unmasking") those hitherto unspoken grounds. To that extent, critique *accepts* the grammar of rationality calling for self-grounded, autonomous speech. On the other hand, in calling attention to the force of external influences, critique denies the very possibility of fully autonomous speech and thus calls into question the norm requiring such autonomy.

If the naive, unreflexive affirmation of autonomy fosters a false conscious-ness, the corresponding denial of such autonomy is, on the one side, a liberative critique of that false consciousness, while on the other side, it is an opening to a positivistic accommodation to the sheer fact of limits on rationality. In short, it does not yet pose systematically the question of what may be done to *overcome*, to pierce, stretch, struggle against, and at least limit these limits themselves, if not remove them.

4.4

To speak of ideology critically is to condemn rational discourse when it fails by its *own* standards. This implies that these standards are workable and that rational reflection can transcend the interests, desires, and languages that commonly limit it. But how is it possible to transcend these limits? This seems almost like jumping over one's own shadow; for these interests, desires, and language *are* the very speaking subject himself. In what sense, and how, can thinking transcend the interests and desires and languages for which and with which persons think? In some part, this depends on what happens to us as we pursue our interests, or submit to our passions in our living experience and practice. Interests and desires that fail to be achieved in practice generate a very different sort of experience than those that succeed. Failures of practice subvert intentions; they liquidate commitments even to great interests and passions and they ready us for new ones, from wherever they might come.

But how can our thinking transcend the "prisonhouse of language" with which it thinks? In some part, (to repeat, *some*, not *all* of) our thinking and the language in which we think is in the service of our interests and desires; when it fails in practice to embody, to express, and to achieve them, our ways of thinking are undermined and we become ready for new ways, which is to say, new languages. Certain forms of practice can activate passions, desires, anxieties, panics, lusts, powerful sentiments, and ambitions that overwhelm grammars and liquidate, at least partially, old linguistic investments and habits, leading us to "speak in tongues," in new ways that we may not at first recognize as different and as our own. This means that we think and reason within the perimeters of our interests, desires, and language, and not—indeed, never—outside of them, or without them.

Sentences that are true, while not necessarily dictated by grammar, are always sentences within some language, which we utter in part because of some motivating interest, desire, or intention. A language allows for the possibility that certain correct things *may* be said, but does not by itself ensure the truth of what is correct or require any particular true sentence to be spoken. Desire, interest, and experience are needed to actualize the possibilities of speech and of speaking truly. But whatever is spoken truly always depends on, varies with, and is limited by language.

The problem, then, comes down to whether thinking with language makes it impossible to think *about* language, to develop reflexivity about it. Obviously, however, metacommunication *is* possible. But what we say or think about a language is limited by the language we use to do so. Yet, several things need adding: First, as Bertrand Russell long ago said, in his introduction to Ludwig Wittgenstein's *Tractatus Logico-Philosophicus*, ". . . every language has . . . a structure concerning which, *in the language,* nothing can be said, but . . . there may be another language dealing with the structure of the first language and having itself a new structure, and that to this hierarchy of languages there may be no limit." In short, we need not limit our thinking about language$_1$ to language$_1$-thinking; we may use another, or several other languages$_{2-n}$, to think about language.

Again, this does not mean that our thinking has become language-*free*. We are still limited by the language we use, our subject language, even if not by the language we think about, our object language. Still the specific limits on our thinking may have changed and differ from those imposed by language$_1$. Multilinguality, then, constitutes a structurally different situation than monolinguality. It enhances our reflexivity about and ability to elude the limits of any one of our languages, even if not of language in general. Multilinguality is qualitatively different from monolinguality because it changes our awareness of language, increasing our reflexivity and distance toward *all* languages, including the one we happen to be using, as well as the one we are talking about. When one only knows and speaks one language, social reality and communication are experienced as intuitively *given* and it is more difficult to see that communication and social reality is language constructed and language mediated.

Persons may thus have different *relations* to languages, as well as having different languages. Some use a language without ever noticing that they are using it, others may make their language and its grammar objects of critical awareness. Such variations in critical awareness establish differences in the limits imposed, or the slippage allowed, by a particular language. As Ragnar Rommetveit has trenchantly remarked: ". . . the issue of imprisonment of thought in a bodily-perceptual-motivational perspective represents very different issues, depending on whether we study the inferences that Piaget made when he was four years old about another child's preference ordering of toys, or whether we consider his reflections, fifty years later, on the protocols derivable from such observations of egocentrism under carefully controlled conditions." *

But it is not only multilinguality or reflexive distance toward language that may allow a certain escape, but, also what is *done*, on the basis of or with languages. Men are, but are not only, speaking subjects. They are also sensuous actors engaged in a *practice* which may be spoken but is not identical with that speech. Words mediate between deeds and experiences; but there are deeds that overwhelm the capacity for speech, thus imposing silences and dissatisfaction with our ability to communicate or understand our experience. If language imprisons, it is also true that our experiences and feelings may also be imprisoned for *lack* of a language adequate to them; and this imprisonment fosters a readiness to accept or to fashion new languages. What we call the "imprisonment of language" was likely, at some point, to have been a liberation from imprisonment in an individually unique, and hence noncommunicable, prelinguistic experience. As a practice, experience, and sentiment change, a once emancipatory language may become wooden and no longer express (but newly imprison) the changed men.

The meaning of our imprisonment in language depends fundamentally on the fact that we are *not* just speakers, but that our languages are part of a larger life of practice, and vary with the nature of that practice. Those who largely live a passive contemplative existence, or others who relate to the world with sensuous aesthetic appreciation, and still others who view the world as an object to be acted upon, changed and used, all engage in fundamentally different forms of practice. If their language limits what they may say and know about the world, their different practices also affect the manner in which their languages are used, the purposes they seek, the meanings they acquire, and the limits imposed by the language. The limits of a language will be more readily tolerated in some forms of practice, while in others they will chafe and foster a transcending resistance.

5

We began by stressing our most elemental notion of ideology as a system of symbols and of rules for using them. Ideologies, in short, are languages and our approach to them was largely that of an historical sociology of language. More narrowly, ideologies were seen as symbol systems that serve to justify

* In J. Israel and H. Tajfel (eds.), *The Context of Social Psychology*, Academic Press, London, 1972, p. 221.

and to mobilize public projects of social reconstruction; projects which, of course, can have different magnitudes, ranging from minor civic reforms to permanent world revolutions.

We emphasized that ideology accomplishes its project-mobilizing function in an historically distinctive manner—"rationally." We also suggested that this very rationality is an historically emergent mode of discourse, having an historically grounded grammar. The rationality of specifically ideological symbol systems is, in part, expressed in the way it connects its "reports" and "commands"—to use W.S. McCulloch's and Gregory Bateson's terms.

Ideologies require that the command, or the "what is to be done?" side of language should be grounded in the "report" side, the side that makes reference to "What Is" in the world. Ideologies are thus "rational" symbol systems in that they have a "deep structure" (an analytic or a set of more or less tacit rules) requiring "the unity of theory and practice." To that extent, Marxism is only one instance of such a symbol system, albeit a relatively aware and reflexive one. (For the moment, we need simply suggest that "reflexivity" means self-awareness concerning the rules to which one submits and by which one is bound, thereby referring to a kind of "theoreticity.")

In ideological symbol systems, then, the report side is taken, under certain conditions, to institute a secured justification for the command, practical, or policy implications of the symbol system. The practical or policy implications, correspondingly, are taken to be securely grounded in the report side of the ideology which speaks What Is or What Is Becoming.

5.1

Ideologies, then, are emergent, historically distinct symbol systems, posttraditional systems that emerge along with bourgeois social and cultural structures. Ideologies thus differ from traditionalistic value systems, religions, or myths, and have certain convergences with those symbol systems called "science." Both scientific and ideological symbol systems entail the negation of traditional value systems and share a certain rationality. Both formulate their reports about the world, or social world, in relatively *focalized* ways; both treat the correctness of such reports as grounded in facts and logic; and both place high value on the importance of cognitive correctness.

"Social Sciences," we may say, *defocalize the command implications of their reports*; contrariwise, they focalize the report side of their contents. In contrast to self-styled social sciences, what are commonly called "ideologies" focalize *both* their command *and* their report sides, grounding the former in the latter. Ideologies thus produce a new mode of public discourse in which there is a mobilizing appeal to "publics." Publics, we suggest, are persons to whom there may be access via discourse; "persons" are those persuadable through discourse; but more on this, shortly.

Ideologies thus premise certain historical, sociological, and socio-psychological conditions. For one, they premise the emergence of certain nontraditional social structures—the "public" sphere—characterized in part by a certain residuality; for publics are nontraditional structures, arrangements in part negatively defined by their *release* from the control of traditional social arrangements. By reason of this release, publics are those persons available for political mobilization, on the basis of a rational appeal to interests they are imputed to share. Again, I shall discuss this in greater detail later.

5.2

It is implied that the *normal* routines of such persons, their *everyday* lives and ordinary languages, do not suffice to produce a shared consciousness, a common policy, or solidary social action on behalf of it. Ideologies seem, then, at some level, to premise that the community reconstitutions they seek require a "consciousness"; and that this must come from an "outside," because the requisite consciousness will not be produced "spontaneously" by these persons' everyday lives and ordinary languages; and that therefore the ideology itself is necessary, if not sufficient, to produce a shared consciousness of the desirability of some policy and a solidary effort to enact it. This, too, is another aspect of the deep structure (or the analytic) of all ideologies.

In this respect again, Marxism (particularly in its Kautskian-Leninist variant with its stress on a "vanguard"), is simply a special case of the importance of "outsiders" as the site from which a consciousness-changing ideology will be *brought to* some enacting historical agent. "Vanguards," hold onto or seek to conserve and to "bring" an ideology to some public-historical agent, tensively protecting the ideology from distortion by the public to which it is brought, while simultaneously modifying it to make it intelligible and attractive to that public.

The discourse through which ideologies mobilize publics thus premises the dissolution of traditionalistic, "old regime" social structures, constituting the initial social grounding for the emergence of the Age of Ideologies. These "old regime" social structures entail this overlap: the end of traditionalistic regimes with the beginning of the new bourgeois structures, but before the latter have yet entrenched themselves.

5.3

Beyond this *sociological* premise of ideology, the latter is also grounded in the emergence of new kinds of social *selves* or identities; these are commonly characterized by their possession of a newly heightened sense of potency. That is, the persons constituting the new publics are defined (or define themselves) as foci of power who have a moral responsibility, who both can and should change their community in ways defined as rational.

The Age of Ideologies, then, implies the development of both new social structures and new selves. The self is viewed increasingly, as a rational "subject," a locus of rational social transformation.

Posttraditional ideological discourse is rational in the follosing sense: it does not justify its reports or commands by claiming them to be sanctioned by authorities external to its own discourse. Its culture of discourse affirms relatively context-independent criteria of argument and persuasion. Modern ideologies thus distance themselves from prior epistemological positions which had commonly allowed reliance upon authority to justify policy recommendations. Now, in the newer modes of ideological discourse, policy can no longer be justified by making reference to the social position of those recommending it. Indeed, persons' social position may be defined, as in Marxism, as a source of their cognitive *un*reliability.

5.4

In ideological discourse, then, the societal status of the speaker is not seen as authorizing his speech. Rather, conformity to a given "method"—seen as separate from the speaker's social position—is put forth as the grounding of the reports on which proposed policies are held to rest. To that extent, then, both ideologies and social sciences are inherently *non*dogmatic, in terms of their *grammars*, or of the rules to which they claim to submit.

That concrete ideologies (and social sciences) do become dogmatic is not necessarily *intrinsic* to their deep structure; it may be due to certain special social conditions under which they enact their grammar. For example, "dogmatism" may be due to anxieties that become exacerbated under conditions of conflict and struggle, with all their dangers and risks.

It need not follow, however, that both social science and ideology are equally dogmatic. The point is simply that both are prone to a similar dogmatism when enacted under similar anxiety-inducing conditions.

Ideology, then, constitutes a language variant with a distinct mode of justifying assertions, whether commands or reports. This distinctive aspect of ideologies makes them similar to what Basil Bernstein has called *relatively* context-independent, "elaborated linguistic codes." Such codes are in contrast with those linguistic codes usually dominant in everyday life and which are (again, in Bernstein's terms) "restricted linguistic codes" that allow the justification of assertions in terms of the speaker's societal status.

5.5

In these terms, then, the Age of Ideologies refers to the development of new, elaborated linguistic variants; to their increasing infringement on older, authority-referring restricted linguistic variants; and to the increasing importance of elaborated speech in public-political discourse. In effect, what Marxism spoke of negatively as "ideologies" were precisely cognitive systems which, it held, had claimed but *failed* to be context-independent. Ideologies were submissive to the interests of the bourgeoisie, all the while presenting themselves as if they were the products of autonomous thought processes. This Marxist critique of ideologies, then, correctly noticed the emergence of that very standard of careful speech, a (relative) context-independence to which ideological discourse claimed to submit and which exposed it to critique when it failed to live up to its own standards.

But all ideologies imply that their policies are no longer justified by the societal position of their adherents. Ideologies commonly imply that such justification can no longer be grounded in traditional ways. They thus cast doubt on the epistemologies of everyday life. In particular, they are dissonant with the everyday epistemologies of restricted linguistic variants. They make problematic the cognitive justification of ordinary reports—i.e., the "common sense"—about the social world. The question of what constitutes a sufficient grounding for reports and commands becomes a matter of increasing concern and there is a spread of epistemological anxiety.

6

Central to the analysis in this chapter has been the work of Basil Bernstein, or at least my reading of that seminal work, the core of which began with his distinction between "elaborated codes" and "restricted codes." Originally focused on studies of the education and socialization of children, Bernstein saw the difficulties of lower-class children in school as largely derivative of the disjunction between the speech patterns they commonly learned at home and those dominant in the public school. The educational problems consequent upon these language differences, however, as well as their imputed class connections, are of secondary concern here. What most concerns us now is Bernstein's analysis of the differences in the two speech modalities—the two syndromes of elements by which he sees each language variant typified.

In Bernstein's most recent formulations—see the volume edited by Sebeok, mentioned below—what he once spoke of as the elaborated and restricted linguistic "codes" are now, rather more precisely it seems, characterized as sociolinguistic speech variants. The *elaborated* variant, or my reading of it, converges with what I have here called the "culture of critical speech," or "discourse." The tacit comparison is with (what William Labov has termed) "casual speech" in which minimum attention is being paid by the speaker to his speech and which is, for *that* reason, convergent with Bernstein's "restricted" variant, both being relatively nonreflexive speech modalities.

Having said this, it is then immediately apparent that the distinction, when held coordinate with class differences, seems to have invidious implications discreditable to the lower or working class. Bernstein's views then drew a withering critique, some of which he seems never to have deserved. Clearly, Bernstein never intended to imply more than differences in the statistical frequence of these "codes" among classes, or in their realization among classes. Variance then exists among classes as well as—the work of Labov and others shows—among different kinds of speech situations confronted by any one class. But the existence of the latter does not make the existence of the former variance less important.

The Marxist response to Bernstein has sought to affirm the importance of class differences without, also, implying the *inferiority* of working-class speech. This has, in turn, led some Marxists to a paradoxical situation in which they find themselves denying that the deprived social situation of the lower classes has had any depriving consequences for their *speech*. In some cases, it has also led some Marxists to a paradoxical linguistic *liberalism* in which there is a dogmatic affirmation of the equal utility of all speech variants. This would seem to be internally contradictory, for if this were actually so, of what use then is Marxism itself?

To summarize: in his most recent formulations, Bernstein describes the "elaborated" sociolinguistic variants as discourse situations in which "principles and operations are made linguistically explicit," while in the case of the "restricted" variant they are relatively implicit. Self-conscious reflexivity° and theoreticity are thus, in effect, the central value dimensions in terms of which the distinction between elaborated and restricted variants is made. But whether or not Bernstein grounds *himself* in this value distinction is irrelevant, so long as the speech modalities of some consequential speech community also accept the same value grounding, thus orienting their speech to it, for this would in part make them a distinguishable speech community.

Given only tacit or implicit discourse principles, says Bernstein, meanings will more likely be context dependent; in the elaborated variant, where they are more explicit, meanings will more likely be (relatively) context independ-

---

° The important convergence between Bernstein and Labov, despite other differences, can be seen from Labov's comment: "There are a great many styles and stylistic dimensions that can be isolated by an analyst. But we find that styles can be ranged along a single dimension measured by the amount of attention paid to speech. The most important way in which the attention is exerted is in audio-monitoring one's own speech . . ." which Bernstein calls "editing." (See Labov, below, p. 208.)

ent, less closely linked to local social structures, relationships, or situations. The elaborated variants with their greater explicitness of guiding principles, notes Bernstein, allow persons fuller access to their own culture grounding. I take it that this is a way of speaking of the "examined life" and, in referring to it as entailing "rationality," Bernstein clearly places himself in the "classical" tradition—in the fullest possible sense.

In this classical vein, the elaborated variant is also seen as entailing articulated symbols, while the restricted variant is more fully grounded in condensed symbols and metaphors. At the same time, however, Bernstein also emphasizes that ". . . a restricted code gives access to a vast potential of meanings, of delicacy, subtlety, and diversity of cultural forms . . . to a unique aesthetic . . ." Correspondingly, the elaborated speech variant is characterized by more careful "editing" of lexical and grammatical components. There are two value modalities from which this same observation might be judged, and it seems likely that both are correct. One views such "editing" as implying a desirable carefulness, self-inspection and watchfulness, self-discipline and seriousness. The other, negative modality, no less persuasive, implies that the elaborated variant would manifest a certain loss of spontaneity, pathological self-consciousness, stilted convuluted speech, inhibition of the imagination, of play, and of feeling.

Bernstein manifests increasing sensitivity to these negative value implications—potential "dysfunctions" or costs?—of the elaborated speech variant. He notes that they give access to *alternative* realities, and hence have a relation to the status quo which is *critical* and transcendent; it thereby makes them of decisive relevance for *ideologies,* and thus far from merely expressive of the status quo in a conservative way. At the same time, Bernstein also insists that elaborated variants "carry the potential of alienation, of feeling from thought, of self from other, of private belief from role obligation," and, I would add, of theory from practice.

The elaborated variant's critical discourse entails a self-watchful discipline bent on making speech conform with a set of known rules that specify the proprieties of speech. Thus the elaborated variant is a two-sided process; on the one, productive of reflexivity and, on the other, of a certain *loss* in spontaneity and warmth. A culture of critical and serious speech is committed to the value of speech about speech, of metacommunication, in which particular heed is taken of the certainty (or uncertainty) of assertions made, whether reports or commands. One is expected to be alert to the possibility that *any* affirmation may be negated, is inherently negatable, open to challenge and criticism and, therefore, must have justification ready to hand.

Although Bernstein does not put it this way, we may say that one critical speech act, that serves as a boundary beweeen elaborated and restricted variants, is the act of "justification," when arguments are offered in support of challenged reports and commands. Restricted variants will accept references to the speaker's role in society as a legitimate rhetoric. Elaborated variants, however, tend toward the rule that a good reason is not a reference to the speaker's position in the group and, it seems, references to ascribed positions are particularly proscribed as modes of justification. Correspondingly, we might add that if the elaborated speech variant inhibits references to societal position as a mode of justifying assertions so, also, does it reject the purely "personal."

In David Silverman's terms, "bad speech is speech which arises from personal biases and commitments of the author ('halo effect,' personal sympathies, personal political views, personal value judgment)." Correspondingly, good speech in the elaborated variant means speech that "is in-accord-with-a-community-rule, both by attending to the order of things which the community sanctions . . . and by purportedly basing its analysis in communally-sanctioned methods." It is thus not the person alone that judges the speech; "the community is to be the final arbiter of the goodness (validity, accuracy, insightfulness) of any account. It must judge whether the account is properly rule-governed . . ." *

From the standpoint of this chapter, then, an ideology is to be understood as a case—or a "sociolect"—of an elaborated speech variant. Correspondingly, this constitutes the shared culture of critical speech to which concrete ideologies—and social sciences, as well—commonly claim and seek to conform. To revert to our earlier observation that children are not ordinarily said to have an ideology, we may now see an auxiliary reason for this: the obligation to abide by the culture of careful discourse is imposed on persons in some correlation with age, the younger being less under the obligation.

The conjunction here of the notion of ideology, on the one side, and of an elaborated speech variant, on the other, has a certain incongruity of promising fruitfulness. This, because when we see ideology as an elaborated variant we are sensitized to its possession of a rationality that, in the common view, it is usually denied; and when we see the elaborated variant "set" from the standpoint of ideology, as one case in it, we are alerted to the possibility that elaborated (no less than restricted) codes may have blocked access to their own grounding. That is, seeing the elaborated variant from the perspective of ideology focalizes the *limits* of the reflexivity of this most reflexive speech variant. Let us develop the latter implication briefly from the standpoint of an ancient distinction in literary criticism, that between "classical" and "romantic" cultures.†

With their common emphasis on the editing of speech performances in conformity with explicated principles and reflexively held rules, elaborated

---

* David Silverman, "Speaking Seriously," *Theory and Society*, Vol. 1, No. 1, 1974, pp. 1–16.

† See my extended discussion of romantic and classical, in A. W. Gouldner, *For Sociology*, Basic Books, New York, 1975, pp. 323–366.

speech variants including ideology, are essentially in the nature of a cultural *classicism*. (This again resonates a certain dissonance between ideology and the *romantic*, which I have alluded to in Marx's work.) The elaborated variant is "classical" in the sense conventional to that terms' usage in literary criticism, in being rule oriented, grammar and pattern oriented. Correspondingly, the restricted variant's openness to metaphor and condensed symbolism is characteristically "romantic," as that term has been responsibly used in literary criticism. The restricted variant, like the romantic, is open to the ramifying *sense* of words, while the elaborated variant seeks to repress "sense" and focus on and admit only legislated, explicated *meanings*, the literalness of relatively decontextualized conceptualizations. (I intend here the distinction between sense and meaning used by Lev Semenovich Vygotsky, in his *Thought and Language*.)

To characterize the elaborated speech variant as "classical," then, is to signal that the conventional critique of ideology, namely, that it is "dogmatic," does not identify a fault peculiar to it but, rather, refers to a fault generated by the rule-oriented theoreticity that ideology *shares* with other elaborated speech variants, including "methodologically" committed social science. On the one side, the very reflexivity that is the prized virtue of the elaborated speech variant is a reflexivity about the grounding of speech in a relatively context-free set of rules—rules which are seen as *governing* contexts. From this, however, derives the other, "dark" side of that same reflexivity, in which there is an inflexibility in the face of differences in concrete contexts, a compulsive insistence on "one word, one meaning," and on hewing to the legislated rule; and where, further, the force and consequence of the context for the speech and speaker is denied, being dissonant with his image of himself as a consistency-bound conformer with articulate rules. It is this inflexibility about, and insensitivity to, the force of differing contexts that is precisely the common implication of the "dogmatism" of ideology. The limits of ideology, then, are not limits peculiar to *it* but are shared by other sociolects of the elaborated speech variant, and they are not divorced from but grounded in the very historically specific *rationality* of that variant.

7

Elaborated speech variants, including their ideological sociolects, are manifested most fully in the speech of intellectuals and intelligentsia; they are the deep structure of the common ideology shared by these groups. That is to say, the *shared* ideology characteristic of intellectuals and intelligentsia is an ideology about *discourse*: the culture of critical discourse, the historically specific mode of rationality implicated in the elaborated speech variant. Apart from the specific ideological sociolect spoken by different intellectuals and intelligentsia, they are *commonly* committed to a culture of critical discourse. A theory of ideology thus implies a theory of intellectuals and intelligentsia, even if only implicitly. Which, in turn, implies that whatever else a concrete, specific ideology is about, whatever specific project of community reconstruction it proposes, there is also and always tacit within it some place assigned to intellectuals and intelligentsia, in the movement from the old order and in the new, reconstructed order.

Since the elaborated speech variant that is the unifying culture of intellectuals and intelligentsia inhibits reference to the *speaker,* to his personal character or his societal status, then the implication of the speaker in his speech is commonly repressed, and thus the implication of intellectuals in ideologies and ideological projects of social reconstruction is commonly occluded, even as it is invariably inserted. One latent function of elaborated speech variants, then, is to *de*authorize all traditional speech, all speech grounded in traditional societal *authority,* and to authorize only the speech of those speaking impersonal and deauthored speech which is, characteristically, the speech of the "well"-educated.

Intellectuals are "mass produced" only with the end of traditional society and the corresponding rise and reform of modern systems of public education, education away from the home, and firmly differentiated from the kinship system. This develops in the course of that process of secularization in which some of the intelligentsia and intellectuals cease being "organic" intellectuals, trained by, living within, and subject to the close supervision of a churchly organization and thereby separated from the everyday life of their society. Such secularization is important because it desacralizes authority-claims and allows the emergence of a culture of critical discourse that insists that the reasons given may be negated and criticized, and are not to be grounded in the imputedly privileged and sacred status of the speaker. Secularization helps constitute a culture of critical discourse in which *self*-groundedness, in Heidegger's sense of the "mathematical project," is central.

Along with this, there is the rise of vernacular languages and the corresponding decline of Latin as the language of intellectuals. This further thins out the membrane between everyday life and intellectuals, readying them to propound projects of this-worldly social reconstruction, ideologies. At the same time there is, also, the attenuation of the old regime system of personalized patronage relationships between specific members of the old hegemonic elites and individual members of the intelligentsia or intellectual stratum. The other side of this development is one in which there is a growing anonymous market for the products and services of intellectuals, thus allowing them to make their livings apart from close supervision and personalized controls by patrons. Their residence and their work, both, are now less closely supervised by others, and they are now capable of more personal initiatives in the public sphere, while also having a "private" life. Thus the claims and force of established authority, and of modes of discourse grounded in it, are diminished.

This is further reinforced by the development of a relatively insulated and more highly differentiated system of public education whose teachers define themselves, not as having an obligation to reproduce the class values of their students' parents, but as responsible for and representative of "society as a whole." In some part, an elaborated speech variant is required and fostered by the new public system because the school claims to be above the conflict of different sections of the society with their differing regional dialects and class sociolects; and the elaborated speech code thus has universalistic implication. The public school emerges in coordination with the "public," and is a microcosm of that larger communal public—being a setting in which communication is addressed to linguistically diverse groups. An elaborated speech variant thus serves in some part as a *unifying* culture of discourse, permitting the collaboration of different social sectors and speakers of different language variants, of various restricted variants, without manifestly siding with or speaking the speech of any one of them. As later chapters will develop, this is precisely one of the functions of "ideology."

At the same time, the elaborated speech variant is the language of bureaucratic rationality, which is the *organizational* instrument of societal unification on the level of the modern state apparatus or the private rational economy. The public schools' commitment to the elaborated speech variant, then, constitutes the socialization of bureaucratic personnel, at the level of the state or the enterprise, no less than of intellectuals and intelligentsia. There is thus a characteristic interchangeability and social mobility between intelligentsia and bureaucracy. The modern public school system educates those intellectuals who, for the most part, produce ideologies, as well as providing them with a mass-produced audience of readers and purveyors.

Bibliographical Note

It is perhaps now altogether evident that our analysis of ideology is a compound of historical perspective and the sociology of language; a straightforward sociology of language, rather than the technical fascinations of linguistics and sociolinguistics. As a biographical aside, I confess that I found social psychology theoretically sterile for the project at hand. With the exception of Milton Rokeach's work, to which I will later make reference, I found the usual discussions of "attitudes," "beliefs," and "values" to situate me in a theoretical tradition that lacked specific, substantive "middle-range" theories that could help unpack the package of "ideology." In contrast, the sociology of language has built-in comparative concerns and an openness to historical evolution that was precisely right for the problem of ideology. More than that, it had a set of middle-range theories of sociological and historical specificity that had an almost pinpointed relevance. Once I could see the sterility of the tradition of social psychology for the *ideology* problem, and had made the shift to a semiotic symbolic conceptualization of the problem, the utility of the sociology of language became immediately apparent.

One of the most straight-forward *sociologies* of language of which I am aware is presently being written, in my view, by Joshua A. Fishman who has an encyclopedic sense of the field, an awareness of its crucial theoretical dialogues, and a total command of its relevant empirical research. See, for example, his edited volumes *Readings in the Sociology of Language*, Mouton, The Hague, 1968; *Advances in the Sociology of Language*, Mouton, The Hague, 1971; see also his important contribution, "The Sociology of Language," in Thomas A. Sebeok ed., *Current Trends in Linguistics*, Mouton, The Hague, 1974. I have also found the work of the sociologist Allen D. Grimshaw sensitively open to the crucial theoretical issues of relevance here. See, for instance, his articles in *Contemporary Sociology* in Volumes 2 and 3, 1973, 1974. An important collection for the sociologist is that of John J. Gumperz and Dell Hymes, editors, *Directions in Sociolinguistics*, Holt, Rinehart, and Winston, New York, 1972. See also J.G. Gumperz, *Language in Social Groups*, Stanford, 1971. The best introductory statement of the ethnomethodological contribution to, and perspective on, language is Aaron V. Cicourel, *Cognitive Sociology*, although the microlevel on which the ethnomethodologists' focus is difficult to align with historical interests such as those here. The rediscovered volume by V.N. Volosinov, *Marxism and the Philosophy of Language*, Seminar Press, New York, 1973, provides a valuable indication of the potential utility of Marxism for a sociology of language.

The sociologist of language that has influenced and excited me most is Basil Bernstein, precisely because his central interests are so classically sociological, centered as they are on the question of the interaction of the symbolic order and social structures, which he pursues from a standpoint that is fundamentally Durkheimian, with a comparative and anthropological sensitivity that is worked through in a quasi-Marxist idiom and where the central comparisons are *class* comparisons. Bernstein's papers begin to appear in the early 1960's, and his by-now controversial classic on "Elaborated and Restricted Codes," appears in Gumperz and Hymes, editors, The Ethnography of Communication, *American Anthropologist*, 66, 6, 2, pp. 55–69. Since then, Bernstein has edited three major volumes reporting his work and that of his research group: *Class, Codes, and Control*, Volume 1, Theoretical Studies Towards a Sociology of Language; Volume 2, Applied Studies towards a Sociology of Language; Volume 3, Towards a Theory of Educational Transmissions; Routledge and Kegan Paul, London, 1972, 1973, 1975. For myself, I have found the perspectives and criticisms of Bernstein's work—said and implied—in the work of Dell Hymes and William Labov to be congenial and important in developing my own appreciation of Bernstein as a sociologist. Hymes' work seems to be a unique blend of the anthropological tradition with its relativistic sensitivities, and a sustained capacity for theoretical analysis. The most important example of this, from a sociologist's view, is perhaps his *Towards Communicative Competence*, University of Pennsylvania Press,

Philadelphia, 1972, and his prior work, On Communicative Competence, Ferkauf Graduate School, Yeshiva University, 1966, which Bernstein characterizes as the explicit source of Chomsky's view of "the potentiality of competence and the degeneration of performance"; B. Bernstein, "Social Class, Language and Socialisation," in T.A. Sebeok, ed., 1974, Ibid. The other critique of Bernstein that I have found most informative is that of William Labov, whose important summary volume, *Sociolinguistic Patterns,* University of Pennsylvania Press, 1972, applies techniques of systematic survey research within the framework of a theory of class structure and with a concern for systematic cumulation and continuity. The dialectic between the Englishman Bernstein, and the Americans Hymes and Labov, not always dramatically visible in their writings, has produced one of the richest discussions in the sociology of language, if not from the standpoint of technical linguistics then certainly from that of the sociologist. Let me repeat that these comments are made from the perspective of a working sociologist who is not a linguist, and who is primarily concerned about the work cited here for its sociological relevance in general, and its usefulness in analysing the ideology problem in particular. With that qualification in mind, I would also mention that I have found the work of Umberto Eco and Ferrucio Rossi-Landi most suggestive, even though I know only the relatively limited part of it that has been translated into English from the Italian, in addition to having heard Eco lecture in Barcelona and Amsterdam.

chapter 3

Surmounting the Tragic Vision: Generic Ideology as Idealism

Like any part of culture, an ideology structures the roles people can play and, thereby, influences the very kind of persons they become; more than that, ideologies (like any language) are person-constituting. They produce speaking subjects. The very existence of "persons" of any sort may be affected by ideologies. For ideologies both premise and contribute to very special kinds of human qualities, particularly to a sense of potency, which is in turn essential to person-being.

1

"Our modern ideologies are all based, in one way or another," says Frederick Watkins, "on a belief that life here on earth is capable of being perfected by human knowledge and effort." * The premised unity of theory and practice, combined with the doctrine of human perfectibility, is grounded in a very specific—if tacit—conception of the normal actor as an adult person possessed of power. In calling men to transform their convictions into institutions, ideologies tacitly convey a conception of the normal person to whom their discourse is directed as a center of power and decision. Ideologies thereby foster in the actor the sense of his own *subjecthood*. They imply, and thus ask him to think, that he has power.

* F.M. Watkins, *The Age of Ideology—Political Thought, 1750 to the Present*: Prentice Hall & Co., Englewood Cliffs, N.J., 1964, p. 2.

On the one side, this enables him to resist traditional claims and bonds; and, on the other, it endows him with self-confidence and the hope that he shall "overcome," that he can change the world. Ideologies reinforce conceptions of persons as potent actors; in other words, as mature subjects able to commit themselves without permission of patrons, family, friends, neighbors, and even *against* their wishes.

In learning specific ideologies, individuals learn certain tacit premises of an ideology, they learn that part of the grammar of generic ideology which holds that individuals have an obligation to enact their beliefs, which implies that they have the power to do so, if only they persevere. An ideology's doctrine about the *social world* is the focalized belief learned by the believer; but, at the same time, he also learns the defocalized, auxiliary belief it implies about *himself*. Ideologies thus serve to define and interpret social situations explicitly, and thereby serve to redefine *persons tacitly*.

In mobilizing the self, ideology transforms it. We might say ideology enables the modern self to overcome "terror," the anxiety of isolation from traditional supports and from ascribed positionings of the self. It thus enables the self to feel strong enough to act, either without or against the traditional, the authoritative. It is thus that ideologies help create speaking subjects.

I am *not* saying that ideologies *premise* the existence of persons (which they do), but I am saying that ideologies themselves actually help produce them as persons. What are "persons?" Persons are human beings socially defined as having certain attributes. A person is a human being believed (1) to be a locus of potency or power, and *hence* (2) to be morally responsible for his actions. A person is someone subject to reproach in moral terms when he is believed *able*, but unwilling, to conform to a moral norm. In implying that the human beings who endorse ideologies are strong enough to enact them, and are obliged to do so, ideologies reinforce the personhood of human beings. As ideologies reinforce personhood, they help create the human conditions requisite for vast public projects and, indeed, of great revolutionary undertakings.

In linking person to ideology I have not, however, meant to suggest that ideologies were the *only* symbol systems supportive of personhood. Certainly, many religions have done much the same.° But ideologies began to assume this function after traditional religion waned and as secularization ensued. As ideologies were associated with secularization, personhood was no longer linked to the sacred. A new ambivalence was thereby installed in the new subject-person.

° But only by allowing some scope for human *potency*. For example, "freewill"; or by identification or communion with the power of a personal Deity; by premising that there is something above even the gods—Moira; by premising that men's ritual initiatives may call them to the favorable notice of the god; by premising a hierarchy of gods, so that men may seek the help of a higher god against a lesser, etc.

On the one hand, his potency is not acted out under the imputed supervision of a Super Being who *limits* it. Thus the new potency of the person can be near-Promethean. Any task becomes possible for him. On the other hand, just as the limits are lifted on his potency, so, too, is there removed any sacred limit on what can be *done* to him. No longer under a supernatural protection, he becomes a thing like any other; usable like any other. His unlimited potency is now matched by his unlimited vulnerability. What he conceives himself able to do, and what he can have *done* to him, are both no longer limited. His craving for power and his sense of terror may now feed upon one another.

1.1

Ideology is grounded in (and further contributes to) an historically evolving, new sense of the potency of *ordinary* men and not just of great kings, generals, or the rich. This historically evolving sense of potency has one root in Greek antiquity, especially perhaps in the *demos'* assimilation of the heroic ideal and in the democratization of the aristocracy's values and self-concepts. It has another root in medieval and feudal societies where it is also especially sustained by the nobility's notion of honorific bellicosity. A good part of the sense of men's potency rests on *conflictual* validation: the conduct of *successful* conflict, struggle, contest, and also war.[*]

In some part, the modern sense of power is rooted in a similar kind of warfare; this time, however, in the sublimated contest to dominate nature, on the one hand, and, on the other, in the sublimation of the quasi-sacred ideal of warrior heroism into the modern form of secularized contest, *politics*. To reverse Clausewitz's dictum, politics is the conduct of war by other means. The culminating reinforcement of the modern and specifically Western sense of potency was the French Revolution which made politics a game not only for an elite but one that all could play, *en principe*.

With the French Revolution, the "people" were no longer what they had been. They were no longer mere *sans culottes*, no longer disease-ridden starvelings to be mud-spattered with impunity by the hurtling carriages of the high and the mighty. No longer merely the wretched, the lowly were now the "people," a word that brought a new pride. If this new People had a single voice, they might have spoken in the following way:

"We have shown conclusively that Kings and Cardinals can be brought to justice. We no longer need to wait for the gods to resent their *hybris* and to bring them toppling down. We do it. By ourselves and for ourselves. The

[*] This general thesis is developed more fully in A.W. Gouldner and R.A. Peterson, *Notes on Technology and the Moral Order*, Bobbs-Merrill and Co., Indianapolis, 1962, Ch. 3.

revolution, our revolution, is real and powerful and we are that revolution. We the new People are no longer what we were, no longer subjugated objects. In fact, our rooting goes beyond all political systems and regimes; we People are the deepest of enduring things, the very stuff of which nations are made. We are audacious. We exist without permission. Self-grounded, we now exist for ourselves. We can master the streets and we can master politics. We can achieve. We have one unified being. We have a new name, and, in some quarters, that name brings bad dreams. We are no longer parcelled-out beings that are given—like lands and castles—into the keeping of kings or clergy. We are no longer isolated and restricted to a tiny, backward locality. We have friends and comrades everywhere. We expand out into and fill great nations and we citizens of the world now live in a larger universe. It is no longer our leaders who connect us to this world; we are part of it without mediation. No longer the small link in a large chain, we are the very center of it."

2

In this we may see how modern ideological thought differed from the tragic thought of classical antiquity or even of Christianity. In the classical worldview the vulnerability of even the *powerful* was evident in the most sudden and drastic overturns in fortune; classical thought took as a truism that even the powerful might be trapped in the net of slavery. The Christians believed in the limits imposed on all (and even great) men by original sin and by their common corruption; and both classical and Christian thought believed in the *vulnerability* of reason to the confusions of the passions.

Ideology differs, however, in believing in the great power of *ordinary* men, in the mass if not individually, as well as in the great power of the extraordinary person. Part of the age of ideology coincides with the reign of Napoleon, who was viewed as a towering colossus even by Europe's most sensitive thinkers, artistic geniuses, and profound philosophers. The age of ideology also coincides with the vision of the romantic "genius," and his exceptional, almost supernaturally bestowed, powers.

If power is taken to count for so much, then those who have more of it will count for more, even in the cultivated judgment. It is consistent then that, after the revolutions of 1848, the age of *Realpolitik* begins to flourish. Ideology, then, entails a redefinition of the sites of power, on the one hand, and of the sheer amounts of power deemed to be present in the social world, on the other. It correspondingly implied a transition in how others are judged, morality waning in importance as a standard while power becomes an increasingly salient concern. There is a growing tension between the growth of power and the waning of conventional morality. With this, there is an attenuation of transcendental morality, or Christianity, and, correspondingly of the tragic vision.

2.1

What we must consider here is the dialectic between the tragic vision and the ideologic vision. By the ideologic vision, I do not refer to this or that concrete ideology but rather to their communality, to their shared character as ideologies. The "ideologic vision" is generic ideology, one of the common dimensions underlying concrete and specific ideologies.

Paradoxically, there is no way adequately to understand the specific *historicity* of ideology except by first clarifying the most generalized analytic nature of the ideological vision. In the seventeenth and eighteenth centuries, this ideologic vision succeeds the tragic vision as the salient form of consciousness. It does not, however, replace or destroy, but, rather, primarily *represses* the tragic. The ideologic vision is grounded in an optimistic estimate of man's power and, as such, reinforces man's confidence in himself and his ability to reconstruct society, as well as increases his sense of moral responsibility to do so. The weak man's excuse for his refusal to try to remedy conditions is manifest in his condition. But no such weakness rationalizes the passivity of the man who feels himself powerful, and is seen that way by others. For him, the Kantian slogan is reversed, and "can implies ought," at least on the level of everyday life.

The crux of the matter is that both the tragic and ideologic visions entail doctrines governing man's relation to the world and worldliness. The ideologic vision pronounced men strong, and imposed an obligation to change the world. The tragic vision, however, fostered an endurance of suffering by cathartic sacred dramas, by rituals, and by the everyday solidarities of family existence. While the tragic vision is not at all incompatible with the existence of a public sphere and of political struggle, as in ancient Greece, still the tragic vision places firm limits on what politics can do. In ancient Greece, politics might have put one in the way of making (or replenishing) a private fortune and foster a "fame undying," but, in any event, it was seen that even the politically high might be overturned drastically at a stroke. The Greeks saw a fickleness in fame and fortune and thus knew the *limits* to politics.

Moreover, in classical antiquity, politics were not yet so fully individualistic and separated from the family system. Finally, there was a continual see-saw struggle between the popular faction or *demos* on the one side, and the oligarchical or aristocratic faction on the other. In effect, this meant that a small but powerful segment of society, the oligarchs, were bent on continually narrowing down the public sphere as an arena for politics. The Christian societies that succeeded these largely did eliminate that public sphere and made politics a matter of family or of a limited ruling stratum. In contrast, however, a "public sphere" is in its modern sense a sphere open to all, or to all "men with an *interest*," and who have a measure of competence in the ordinary language spoken.

Insofar as the quest for repute in antiquity was concerned, this might be achieved by poetry, honorific expenditure, athletics and, preeminently, military success, all situated within the competitive zeal of a contest system. Politics was an uncertain instrument of clearly limited use, as indeed were all the others. And so far as certain goals are concerned—the fantasy of immortality—politics was a hopeless business. Philosophy's importance grew, in part, as a mode of discourse that might justify *rationally* a belief in immortality, the immortality of the soul—"such immortality as men might have."

A society with a pervading sense of the tragic, then, cannot have the same relationship to politics as one with an ideological vision. The ideological vision has slipped free from the limits of which tragedy was so acutely aware. The reconstruction of society through a differentiated political system, operated by ideological men having a sense of their new potency, broke with the serenity that tragedy sought to cultivate. The tragic vision sought to prepare men to survive, and to carry on bravely, despite the threatened failure of their highest aspirations. It sought to preserve the self. The ideologic vision's historical mission, however, was to overcome the inertia and inhibiting sense of limits fostered by the historically prior, traditional, tragic vision of life. (Much the same can be said about the sonata form which entered Europe about the same time as the Age of Ideology.)

2.2

The best statement of the tragic vision of which I am aware was that formulated by Lucien Goldmann in *The Hidden God.*° Rather than distilling Goldmann's conceptions in my own words, I propose to use a selection (with all the dangers this implies) of Goldmann's own words, chosen from many different parts of his acute study of Jansenism:

". . . natural philosophy did not replace Thomism by a similarly precise and stable system. It abolished the miraculous intervention of the divinity by integrating it into the natural world, but once the possibility of supernatural interference has been destroyed everything becomes both natural and possible (26). . . . the Calvinist groups studied by Max Weber practised

° Lucien Goldmann, *The Hidden God*, Routledge and Kegan Paul, London, 1964. The page of the citation is indicated in the text.

self-denial but remained active in society. . . . The extreme Jansenist groups, on the other hand, refused to take part in any worldly activity of any kind, whether social, economic, political or even religious. (8) . . . the central problem of tragedy is that of discovering whether a man can still live when the eye of God has lighted on him. . . .

"[The] view the tragic mind takes of the world . . . is that the world is at one and the same time both nothing and everything. It is nothing because tragic man lives forever with God's eye upon him, because he can demand and select only completely clear, absolute and unequivocal values, because for him 'miracles are real,' and because, measured by these standards, the world is essentially confused, ambiguous and therefore non-existent. (48) . . . It is, in short, because tragic man is aware neither of degrees nor of a transitional plane between nothing and everything, because for him anything which is not perfect does not exist. . . .

"This means that tragic man finds the world as it normally is both non-existent and inauthentic, and that he lives solely for God, finding nothing in common between Him and the world. (49) . . . tragedy believes neither that the world can be changed, and authentic values realized within the framework it provides, nor that it can be simply left behind while man seeks refuge in the city of God. (50) . . . It is however precisely this 'Yes' and 'No,' both equally complete and equally absolute . . . which allows the tragic mind to achieve on the plane of knowledge, a degree of accuracy and objectivity of a type never before attained. The man who lives solely in the world, but remains constantly detached from it, finds that his mind is freed from all the current illusions and limitations which beset his fellows. (56)

". . . Tragic man never gives up hope, but he does not put his hope in his world; that is why there is no truth either about the structure of this world or about his place in it which can cause him to be afraid. (57) . . . What, however, is the concrete meaning of the expression: to refuse this world? . . . it means setting up against a world composed of fragmentary and mutually exclusive elements a demand for totality that inevitably becomes a demand for the reconciliation of opposites . . . his real task lies in trying to create the whole and complete man who will bring the two together. (57) . . . It is from this that spring the two paradoxical elements of the tragic mind . . . its extreme realism and its demand for absolute values . . . what the tragic mind accepts as its first absolute value is that of truth, and this demand is inevitably accompanied by the realization that all the possibilities offered by this world are limited and inadequate . . . the tragic mind becomes aware of the limits prescribing both it and the external world. (58) . . . 'Death,' [remarks] Lukács, 'which is an absolute limit, is for tragedy a constantly immanent reality indissolubly linked with everything the tragic soul experiences! (59) . . .

". . . it is precisely the fact that it does not accept ambiguity and, instead,

keeps alive the demand for reason and clarity, that makes tragedy what it is.
(61) . . . [of] the two essential characteristics of tragic man . . . the first is
that he makes this absolute and exclusive demand for impossible values . . .
the second is that, as a result of this, his demand is for 'all or nothing' . . . he
is totally indifferent to degrees and approximations, and to any concept
containing the idea of relativity. (63) . . . everything temporal or psychological forms part of this world, and has therefore no existence for the tragic
mind, which has moved out of time and into eternity and life in the eternal
instant. (64)

". . . The fundamental characteristic of tragic man is his demand for
absolute truth. (66) . . . The consequences which spring from this attitude
are the absolute primacy accorded to morality over abstract effectiveness, the
abandonment of any hope of material victory or even of future life in this
world, and, at the same time, the absolute certainty of the final moral and
spiritual victory. (70) . . . In the perspective of tragedy, clarity means first
and foremost awareness of the unchangeable nature of the limits placed on
man, and of the inevitability of death. . . . Tragic greatness transforms the
suffering which man is forced to endure because it is imposed on him . . .
into a freely chosen and creative suffering . . . going beyond human
wretchedness by a significant action which rejects compromise and relative
values in the name of a demand for absolute justice and truth. (81) . . . 'The
wisdom of the tragic miracle,' wrote Lukács, 'is a wisdom of limits.' (75)"

2.3

In the West, the concrete historical grounding of the tragic includes, on one
side, the radical disorder of fragmented cities and societies, the Greek and
Medieval fragmentations. In these, men could be exposed to even the grossest
changes in fate, to the most radical disruption of everyday life—to brute
violence, death, and to total slavery. A second concrete historical rooting of
the tragic in the West was, of course, Christianity itself. Periodically
vulnerable to pessimism about this world, Christianity affirmed a sense of
man's ineradicable finiteness along with a simultaneous commitment to
absolute values.

After the waning of the first wave of ideologic consciousness, after the
Enlightenment critique of the tragic vision had exalted the hope for
happiness, the tragic vision crept back again in the form of cultural pessimism
and in romanticism—in, for example, the "fated hero." The tragic and
ideological visions do not simply succeed one another in the public sphere or
within individual persons. So long as persons hold high and absolute values,

the tragic potential is not destroyed but forms a repressed infrastructure of ideology. Each vision then lives on in tension with the other.

The resultant consciousness has a profound internal rift; it is susceptible to abrupt restructurings in which one vision may suddenly supplant another. The structure of the *modern* consciousness, then, is divided; there is continual tension in it between tendencies toward cultural pessimism, on the one side, and technological optimism, on the other. An essential characteristic of the modern consciousness, then, is precisely that it is *not* just ideological, but that it is precariously divided internally so that one decade may be passive and profoundly gloomy while the very next is activistic and optimistic.

The tragic and the ideological visions each makes salient what the other represses. Each speaks the other's silences. Each speaks the bad news the other hides; each dreams the hope the other represses. The ideological vision remains stubbornly silent about what it does not hope to attain, those regions to which its optimism does not extend. It conceals that, within itself, there is another level, encompassing those things about which it is not optimistic and which have been hidden. The ideological vision entails the tacit, hence unexamined, belief that politics and social action can solve *all* problems.

Ideology, then, dulls the tragic vision's alertness to limits. Ideology, however, does not suppose that what it offers is "the best of all possible worlds." Ideology is countertragic because it seeks to better, not to perfect, the world, offering what is "only" a substantial *improvement.* It dismisses the idea that man can have or make the best possible city; it rejects passivity and depression when it sees that it can only have the "second best" city; it holds that this is quite enough to fight, and if need be, to die for. The ideological rejects the idea of an eternal and absolute limit, and thus of biological or theological limits. It assumes men to be limited *ultimately* only by conditions they themselves create or, at least, not by any beyond their influence. It carries the suspicion that thwarting "conditions" are only the phenomenal disguise of human enterprise. Men are seen as making and unmaking themselves. Under the grammar of ideology there is the social ontology of human self-groundedness.

Thinking historically, the ideological seeks such improvement in men's lives as seems possible *under given circumstances.* It expects that historical conditions will not always be limiting in the same way, and that present limits will, in future, give way. The "historical," then, was the specific nineteenth-century therapy for the tragic. This "therapy" defocalized the issue of permanent limits by diverting attention from things men might never achieve and by focusing it, instead, on what men might achieve under certain limiting, but changing, historical circumstance. The tragic vision had said the imperfect was not worth struggling for. The ideological vision accepts universal imperfection and settles for the better. The tragic view summoned men to transcend tragedy by the courageous endurance of the unchangeable. It thus saw such transcendence as an essentially individual heroism. The ideological vision, however, saw men facing circumstances that their courage might collectively surmount.

The ideologic view, then, stresses that some limits are more amenable to change and that, even if all men must finally die, it makes some difference (to them) whether they die at age 29 or age 65. The tragic view, however, denies that this matters. It is an "all or nothing" consciousness that rejects a world in which it cannot fulfill its highest values.

It was one of the more remarkable accomplishments of Marxism to harness the ideological vision to the repressed hopes of absolute fulfillment on the paleosymbolic level of the tragic vision. It pursued those improvements in men's conditions that each socioeconomic arrangement allowed, and, once these were achieved, Marxism sought to overthrow the society which then unnecessarily limited further advances. More than that, it also linked these historically progressive and cumulative changes to a vision of an ultimate achievement, in the Hegelian manner. "It is the *final* battle," sang the *Internationale*. While this surmounting of all limits was not the focus of Marxism, it was a fugitive fantasy to which it was open and from which it drew a hidden, extra strength.

The tragic vision represses awareness of what is possible; the ideologic vision represses awareness of what is *impossible*. Each, then, has its false consciousness. The first leads to existence sustained by some relation to the god; the second leads to a politics of precarious humanistic complexity— which is such politics as people may have. Tragedy's false consciousness is the pretense that it *chooses* to go to its defeat; by a proud act of his own free will, man asserts himself as something more than a pawn of reality. (Tragedy thereby preserved, for later historical development, a sense of man's power.) Ideology's own false consciousness is that defeats are only temporary and that things will sooner or later turn out pretty much as decent, courageous, and enlightened men strive to have them.

2.4

One specific mechanism by means of which the nineteenth-century ideologic vision fosters the sense of its own reality and rationality, while undermining that of the tragic, is the development of *historismus*. In this, the social changes occurring in different periods are seen as profound, rather than as superficial changes in those costumes and props that conceal the similarity of essence between different epochs. *Historismus* stresses the continuity and reality of social change, the reality of even "small" social changes and their importance by reason of their cumulativeness, either slowly or in sudden revolutionary spurts of "quality into quantity." *Historismus*, then, premising that change is real, serves to legitimate social reconstruction through public projects.

Conservative *historismus* opposed *revolutionary* ideologies by stressing the gradualness of change; but by endorsing even that gradualness it was consistent with the deeper antitragic impulse of the essentially ideologic. Revolutionary ideologies, of course, do not reject but *radicalize historismus*. Seeking a guarantee that the *status quo* is improvable and can be transcended, all ideologies must resort to history, but all do not find it equally congenial. It is history that becomes the bestower and repository of immortality, and of the ultimate meaning of politics,° after the surfacing of secularization. But such a "history," a history that can be "on our side," is vulnerable to recurrent reification.

It is important to make certain qualifications here between conservative or reactionary ideologies, on the one side, and liberal or radical ideologies, on the other. All ideologies commonly imply the possibility of rational public projects to change society, even if only to restore it to the *status quo ante* or to prevent further revolutionary change. There is thus a tendency for conservative or reactionary ideologies to ground their projects in an *extra*historical agency, such as "human nature" seen as an absolute constant, or in racism, or in a biologically supported evolutionism. These in effect converge, but they are scarcely *identical*, with the tragic vision in their emphasis, implicit or otherwise, on the limits within which rational social change is deemed possible. To that extent, reactionary ideologies that ground limits in the earthy rather than the sacred, are clearly different from, yet adjacent to, the tragic vision. Reactionary ideologies that are secularized have a notion of man as bound by his animality, and thus as higher than but still linked to the ape; tragedy saw man as lower than, but still linked to, god.

Reactionary ideologies, then, are ideologies that stress the limits on change. They seek to reorganize the present to forestall revolutionary change by stressing the power of certain limits, which they ground in a secular legitimation. There is thus a strange ambivalence in "right-wing" ideologies. On the one hand, they have an affinity toward old *religions* that stress the finiteness of men, and, on the other, toward those new *social sciences* which, being synchronically oriented toward ongoing systems, do not easily point toward significant social change. Right-wing, like other ideologies, thus also ground themselves in "science" or in certain new social sciences. Right-wing ideologies conceive the object of such science as a synchronic system, while left ideologies lean toward more historical and diachronic paradigms. It is thus that certain social sciences are lacking (not in an affinity toward ideology in general but) in an affinity toward *certain* ideologies, those of the right or

° Cf. Hannah Arendt, *Between Past and Future*, Viking Press, New York, 1968, pp. 62 *et seq.*

those of the left. Commonly normal academic sociologists assume that their rejection of right- or left-wing ideologies justifies their claim to be ideology-free and *value*-free. They forget, of course, that their *liberalism* is also an ideology.

To speak, as I have earlier, of ideologies as entailing public projects of social reconstruction does not, then, imply that the *status quo* needs and has no ideologies. Far from it. For even conservatives, not to speak of reactionaries, do not accept the *status quo* as it *is,* believing as they do that the present is in danger from various quarters, where it has not already succumbed to these dangers. The conservative and reactionary, then, also have a vision of an ideal society from which the present is seen to depart and toward which they, like the liberal and revolutionary, wish to move and for which they require ideologies.

2.5

Historicity is one aspect of the more general problem of the temporality associated with ideology—the kinds of time perspectives and (in Julius Roth's sense) the kinds of "time tables" involved in ideology. There is in ideology a kind of openness to sheer temporality that seems quite different from either the tragic or the utopian. Seeking some sort of change, ideology takes time to be real and treats it seriously. For ideology, time is the dimension in which the project shows progress, has a start and a culmination, and produces returns on energies invested.

Yet the historicity with which ideology is associated has tacitly internalized writing as a time index, and the paradigm of "historical peoples" are those who read and write and thereby, fortunately for historians, leave records to be studied. For the historical, literacy tends to constitute an invisible boundary of historical time, and what went before, the preliterate, has less interest, tends to be chunked together, mythologized, or tacitly assimilated with the more recent, better known time: "all history is a history of class struggles," to which Engels was subsequently enjoined to add a demurring footnote.

Put another way, the historical sense of time is more nearly like the sociological than the anthropological which sees the distinctiveness of culture but also sees culture as species grounded and the human species as one evolving from others. The anthropologist's time is a much "longer" time than historians' or sociologists', and the latter are much closer to ideology's time. Thus as the new *historismus* sensitized moderns to the reality of time, in linking it to literacy it also truncated the modern sense of time.

There is a certain ambivalence in the modern sense of time: it is the dimension in which we *can* achieve something and in which we *must;* for with secularization the realm of a timeless beyond evaporates, and we must achieve what we can *urgently*. Secularization thus begins to make time a scarce good to be husbanded or used efficiently. The organization of the bourgeois economy, which is based upon the purchase and sale of labor power, hinges on an exchange: one group promises a wage in return for the other group's promise to obey the first, *for a certain period of time*. The workday and the contract require performances within a limited time period.

Finally, there is a complementary consideration of a Durkheimian kind to which Mary Douglas sensitizes us. Certain corporate groups, she has remarked, and those identifying with them, will last beyond the lifetime of their present members who take a longer view of things. But those without such corporate membership, living in a world where the extended kinship system is shrinking down to the nuclear family, where urbanization, social mobility and travel surround one with strangers, and where other entities such as the estate and neighborhood are declining, do not have groups on whom they can rely for future performances, cannot easily think across generations, and therefore come to limit their hopes to what can be accomplished within their own life cycle.

Modern ideologies embody such limited time tables. They must produce results within a single life span or risk disillusioning their adherents and they are thus constantly under pressure to generate the false consciousness of progress and successful achievement. In turn, this suggests that there is a way in which ideologies are essentially projects for—or commitments made by—young men. Or at any rate we must suspect that an ideology's meaning varies profoundly with the age of its adherents, the young seeing it as a project they will harvest in their own lifetime and the older, seeing how long things take, beginning to view it as their own or someone else's dream, and each accusing the other of being limited by his age.

3

I have said that it is characteristic of the grammar of ideology that it calls for the unity of theory and practice; that it seeks to change the world; that it is discourse on behalf of public projects of social reconstruction. It is in this that the ideological rejects the limits of the tragic. The next question, of course, is *how?* How does ideology expect to surmount What Is? What are the assumptions that any ideology necessarily makes in proposing these public projects?

Ideology proposes, whatever else it also does, to surmount the world by way of a rethinking. Change is expected to require a new and allegedly correct rethinking, and it is this that is assumed necessary. We may say, then, that the concept of ideas-as-potent constitutes a generic, underlying communality, being one of the basic dimensions of concrete ideologies or specific "isms." "Generic ideology," then, is a belief in the potency of "ideas." Ideologies suppose that if the world is to be changed (for the better, rationally) there must be a prior change in persons' thinking.

3.1

This assumption is not always evidenced by what ideologues say expressly about the relations between thinking and world-changing. It is, however, commonly exhibited by the potency attributed to ideas by the very act of communicating them emphatically through writing, by the importance they attribute to writing, by the sheer amount of time and energy they devote to writing. Not to speak of reading. Whatever their politics or their public project—whether reactionary or revolutionary—ideologies are regarded by their speakers as having their authoritative expression in writing.

A Socratic preference for the *spoken word,* and a corresponding rejection of writing, is inherently nonideological. It is, however, profoundly symptomatic of ideological discourse that, at some point during discussion, meetings, or conferences, there will commonly be the buying, borrowing, and circulating of books, articles, or pamphlets. There will also usually be much talk about this writing and reading. (That this makes it difficult to distinguish between ideology and, say, academic social science, that it focalizes a rational dimension in ideology, is true. It *is* difficult to distinguish the two.)

To bring the potential adherent to a reading is to bring him into a sympathetic and open relation to the authoritative expression of the ideology and with a highly valued, if not quasi-sacred, embodiment of the idea. This reading is something that can occur apart from face-to-face dialogue and apart from the potentially distracting presence of a troupe of believers. As we have said, there is an ambiguity here. On the one side, this conceals the man-implicated character of the writing, focusing attention on the printed object. (The printed object may also be a way that an ideological group penetrates the person's private life, reinforcing their public pressure on him.) On the other side, however, the printed object does allow for a more patient rational appraisal, a more reflective judgment than is sometimes possible in conversation.

There are many forces molding persons' consciousness other than ideologies, hence many ways consciousness can be "remolded." Whether men live in feudal society, or live where commodities—including labor power—can be bought and sold for money, has a profound and perhaps decisive effect on men's consciousness. This may indeed be more influential than what they read or hear about the state of the social world. The relative impact of various forces on consciousness is, however, not the issue here. The point is simply to acknowledge that ideology is, and effects, only a *part* of consciousness, certainly not the whole.

3.2

Ideology, however, remains a very special part of consciousness; it has a very special relationship to the consciousness (and *unconsciousness*) of persons and to the social relations of their collectivity. The ideological is a part of consciousness that can be given words: it can be *said*. Though this is not to equate ideology with all verbalizable consciousness, it shares certain characteristics unique to all verbalizable forms of consciousness: it is an intersubjective part of consciousness that can be debated, disconfirmed, or validated in the course of deliberate communication with others. Ideology is that special part of consciousness which has a public objectivity and thus allows the public projects to which it makes special reference to be discussed among strangers.

Ideology, then, is that part of consciousness which is focused linguistically on public projects. With it, it is now possible (not necessary) to have rational political discussion with others who commonly possess the shared language it provides. Somewhat more precisely: ideology is grounded in the utilization of an ordinary language, but it is the restructuring of an ordinary language in special ways: partly by selectively focusing the ordinary language on certain public projects; partly by changing certain of the meanings of the ordinary language, giving it a somewhat new or extraordinary meaning, extended redefinition, or focusing; partly by taking certain parts of ordinary language and making them newly problematical, thus assigning a new significance to them; partly, by the invention of new signs. Consider, for example, what Marx did with such concepts as social "classes" or "labor power." In other words: ideology constructs itself as a sociolect of an "elaborated" sociolinguistic variant by using parts of ordinary languages and restricted variants as a raw material.

Ideology, then, separates its adherents from nonbelievers, allowing the former to cooperate with one another for the achievement of their special public projects, while at the same time allowing discourse with nonbelievers; allowing continued efforts to win them over to the ideology. Ideology is thus both a bridge and a moat; it both separates believers from nonbelievers and, also, connects them.

A boundary between believers and nonbelievers, ideology is a dividing line that has a special osmotic character. When optimally constructed according to its own inner logic (or fantasy), ideology allows the believer to influence, *but not to be influenced reciprocally* by the nonbeliever. It thus constructs a boundary with a special, one-way permeability. The ideologues can speak the ordinary language from which their own has emerged and in which it continues to be grounded. But now they elaborate what is a special (not an "artificial," but nonetheless an) extraordinary language, from the standpoint of ordinary language-speakers. Ideology thereby permits a solid linguistic community-within-a-community.

The extraordinary sociolect that is an ideology rests on and transcends, remains grounded in and yet refiexively aware of, the ordinary language; elaborated code speakers are grounded in and control restricted codes, but not necessarily the reverse. They provide distance from but allow access to the speakers of the ordinary language. Specifically, ideology provides a symbolic structuring mechanism, a sifting and sorting, an admitting and rejecting structure. Ideology selects some and rejects other aspects of consciousness; it mobilizes some and it demobilizes others; and thereby it reorganizes consciousness as a whole. Ideology resonates (links up with) and activates certain affects; that is, certain selected contents of consciousness. It permits these to be communicated via reflexive, articulate, and shared ideas. In that very selective symbolic articulation, old aspects of consciousness are transformed. In their new public availability they are no longer exactly what they had once been.

Ideologies provide for both the selective resonance of personal affect, and also, for the selective verbal intercommunication of consciousness, spoken and written; they allow for both personal experience or feelings and for interpersonal speech. The symbolic articulation and resonance of affect permitted by ideology consequently does not merely transmit but *transforms* the contents of consciousness. Ideology does *not* simply "express" consciousness unchanged; it does not simply provide a new costume for an old actor. Ideology does not simply lift previously formed aspects of consciousness unchanged, from some an existing reservoir; it transforms them into something new.

Ideology permits the selective "publication" of consciousness. That is, ideology permits new modalities of *communication*. It is thus that ideology performs its "consciousness-raising" social function. It is just such publication that objectifies selected aspects of consciousness by making them available for public presentations, without which rational appraisal could not be complete.

So, ideology, then, premises it can transform society and surmount the tragic vision by the symbolic articulation and resonance of consciousness; by making it publicly accessible and visible through symbolic articulation. It links individual to society, person to group, by allowing certain selected components of individual consciousness to be shared with other persons with whom they may now be debated, disconfirmed or confirmed, in public discourse. Ideology thereby grounds itself in the infrastructure of individual persons, in their individual consciousness and *un*consciousness, on the one side, and, on the other, as a dimension of a social collectivity, a dimension of communality, a language.

Ideology, of course, thereby allows only certain (limited) things to be communicated, objectified, and discussed. If, on the one side, ideology functions "expressively," it also functions—as expression always must—selectively; which is to say, it functions *re*pressively in relation to certain other matters. Ideology both focuses attention and diverts it. It allows the expression of some and *dis*allows the expression of other contents of consciousness. It thus generates a public discussion and communication which both includes and excludes; it is the latter that creates a public "unconsciousness."

The public "unconsciousness" consists of those shared concerns of persons from which ideology systematically diverts attention, systematically rejects and will not express, and hence represses, suppresses, distorts. Expression and repression via ideological structuring are not mutually isolated but are, rather, both mutually *constructive*. The suppressed, we may say, is that which is expressed only *inadvertently*. By focalizing certain and defocalizing other matters, ideologically structured communication creates audible silences— seen-but-unnoticed omissions, or in Michael Polanyi's terms, an "auxiliary awareness."

If we ask, how do ideologies propose to change the world, we may now say that they aim to do so through "ideas" and through the rational appeal these may have to "consciousness." Seen from their communicative standpoint, an "idea" is no longer a pellet in the mind of an individual, but a meaning formulable only in a shared language. To say, then, that ideologies and ideologues expect to change the world through "ideas" is now, from this standpoint, to refer to the constitution and operation of a system of communication that is objective relative to individuals.

3.3

How the world is to be changed finally comes down to the linguistic relation between the ideological believer and nonbeliever. This is the nuclear problem. Their relationship is nothing less than the core paradigm of modern world transformation. In it, the ideological believer is at first constrained to use the nonbeliever's language, to use it in the latter's own way if he is to be understood. In time, however, the ideologue turns the ordinary language against itself. The nonbeliever is taught to speak in ways somewhat different from his former, ordinary language, so that this language becomes an object distanced from him. Restricted variant speakers are taught a new elaborated variant.

Thus the ideological believer teaches the nonbeliever *a new language* and, through this, he develops (in the latter) *a new self—emancipated from the old language:* a self poised more instrumentally toward the old and distanced from the old social world it had embodied, constituted, and protected. *Ideological change is a linguistic conversion that carries with it a reorganization of the self,* on the one hand, and an alienation from old social conventions, on the other; that permits the *new* self to act *against* the old world. It is this conversion from an older, unreflexive and restricted linguistic variant to a more elaborate and reflexive variant, or from an old to a new elaborated variant, which is always involved in learning an ideology, and that unifies social and personal change.

3.4

The perspective on ideology formulated here, then, is one which moves the focus from a concern with "consciousness" to a concern with communication and language. Still, my own emphasis is not at all to supplant a concern with consciousness or thinking with a focus on communication. In focusing on ideology *qua* communication, my intent is to *add* a perspective on ideology rather than to replace consciousness with communication. Indeed, I would stress that, far from simply being two ways of conceptualizing one underlying structure, communication and consciousness are mutually interdependent forces on different levels of existence; communication being the dimension of a sociocultural group structure while consciousness is an attribute of a skinbounded individual person, even though it is commonly shared with others and thus has aggregate characteristics.

To speak of ideology as premising the power of ideas, or of thinking and consciousness, is to make reference to a latent continuum underlying all concrete "isms" and is to suggest that this is a dimension common to all concrete ideologies. Reference to or assumptions about the potency of ideas is, then, *generic* ideology. To stress the potency of ideas and consciousness means that human consciousness is a center from which power radiates out into the world and which it can, at least to some degree, change. That is the premise of generic ideology. Stated in this way, it is obvious that, viewed as a philosophy, this generic dimension underlying all concrete ideologies is in effect: "idealism."

4

The question arises as to why ideologies are idealistic. Essentially, this is related to their character as projects of public reconstruction. As such they are a *politics*, and the grammar of all politics must, at some point, assume that some have the initiative and ability to win the allegiance of others, by some form of persuasion and rhetoric.

The idealism of ideology is grounded in the fact that all ideologies reject the world as it is; they find the world as it is, defective. This implies that, at some level, they must distinguish between what is and what should be, between the real and the ideal, contrasting the former invidiously with the latter. Ideologies as an idealism suppose that what is real can and should be brought under the control or influence of the ideal, even if not guaranteeing the triumph of the ideal. This is one aspect of the idealism of ideology.

A second aspect of ideology's "idealism" is its supposition that men are open to persuasion by an appeal to their reason and to their ideals. Ideology claims, tacitly or overtly, that the public project for which it calls is a deserving cause, and that its call will be heeded in part for that reason, and not simply because adherents expect to gain spoils from joining the cause. Ideology premises that some persons, at least, will do what is right and good, when and if they can be made aware of that. In effect, ideology *per se* is an effort at persuasion; it is a rhetoric designed to exhibit an imputed good, to authorize it as a good, and to mobilize for it the power and support it deserves, because it is good. Ideology, then, is grounded in a part of the universal grammar of all social action: the effort to "normalize" relations between the two most fundamental dimensions of semantic space, power and goodness, making that which is good, powerful, and that which is powerful, good.

Ideology, then, is a politics. It is a special kind of politics, concerned to mobilize power not simply to procure partisan advantage; to advance what is held to be a good and to do so through rational persuasion. To be engaged in a *politics* is, inherently, to premise that some things are contingent and not totally determined in advance of persons' efforts. To be in politics is not simply to have the kind of control that a scientist-engineer has over certain objects, or that a slave master or prison guard has over prisoners. "Politics" transcends sheer domination. For to be in politics means that one is pursuing goals whose achievement is, on the one hand, recognized as *uncertain* and, on the other, is seen as in part dependent upon the *willing* conformity, the *motivation* of others which can, in turn, be mobilized by initiatives undertaken by certain of the actors.

Whatever means are ultimately used in politics, all politics presumes some role for rhetoric as a starting mechanism; it presumes that men can be persuaded through speech, implying that power may be generated by words and the ideas they convey. At an everyday, ordinary language level, then, *all politics is inherently idealistic.* Ideology, in its more distinctive form, is a symbol system that is rationally articulated and pursues power by persuading men through rational discourse, among other means. Ideology thus seeks to mobilize power by uniting men in new solidarities, by their common allegiance to ideas, where they might otherwise be divided by their different interests.

4.1

It seems evident from this that although modern ideology emerges and identifies itself with the age of emerging science that, nonetheless, it is a distinctively Western symbol system ultimately grounded in the Judaic-Christian tradition that makes a sharp distinction between the ordinary *way* of the everyday world, and the extraordinary world of a god that stands above the world's way, seeking to command and impose himself upon it. This Judaic-Christian tradition also has important continuities with Platonism, whose metaphysics firmly distinguished between the Eternal Ideal Forms, on the one side, and the natural matter of the world, on the other. Platonism also distinguished both the Ideal form and the world from a third thing, the power to imprint the form on the world of matter. In Plato's theology, god's power over the world was mediated through the hyperspatial Eternal Forms, so that if the Platonic godhead was a fusion of power and the good, the making of that very distinction also introduces a certain contingency into their relationship: the problematicity of the relationship between power and the good becomes *systematically* discernible. The Platonic theology, then, intimates a possible *divergence* between power and the ideal, while simultaneously denying that that possibility is actualized. Indeed, the Platonic theology was a response to a common view of the Greek gods that saw them as not bound morally. It is clear, then, that in certain essential (although not all) respects, the Judaic-Christian tradition was continuous with Platonism.

Modern ideology, then, is a branch of *that* massive historical continuity in the West. Modern ideology seeks the unity of the real and the ideal by transforming the world into some conformity with the good. The tragic vision accommodates to this distinction in everyday life; it accepts the failure of the world to be what it should be, and provides a compensatory gratification in the promise of a better world after life, or has rituals that provide symbolic resolutions of the tension between real and ideal. In contrast, the ideological vision seeks *practically* to unite the ideal and the real, through everyday *practice in the world*. Between the tragic vision, grounded in classical Greek-Judaic-Christian idealism, on the one side, and a this-worldly rational and political ideology, there was the historical mediation of that last great revival of religious zeal in the West, the various Protestant reformations, which, as noted earlier, accented the use of work as a mode of anxiety reduction; these helped to transform magic into methodical "normal" science and, also, helped to form a new politics, politics as a disciplined work governed by the conscientious enactment of the ideal, which is the unity of theory and practice.

The Ideological vision, then, is grounded in the same idealism as the Tragic vision. Both premise a split between the real and the ideal, and both premise a certain power in ideas that can help overcome that split. In the tragic vision, however, the word and the ideal have the power to help by reconciling men to What Is, to an essentially unchangeable fate, by giving men the capacity to *endure* the world's failures and disappointments. In the ideological vision, the word and the ideal are seen as having the power practically to change What Is, here in this world, and it intimates that this world is all there is, thus making the outcome in it a matter of some urgency, if not of desperation. Although grounded ultimately in the Judaic-Christian tradition, ideology always secularizes transcendence.

5

Finally, we need to link the notion of the ideological back to something related to the tragic, namely, the utopian. The linkage between the ideological and the utopian is, of course, owed to Karl Mannheim. I hasten to add, however, that his is not the responsible source of my own usage. I do not at all think of the ideological as did Mannheim, i.e., as connected only with the defense of the *status quo*, and contrasted with the utopian as, presumably, future oriented. My own special vantage point sees the utopian as linked to the tragic. In short, I would stress how both the tragic and utopian share a latent structure.

The historical character of ideology as a mode of rational discourse is made more visible by contrasting it with the tragic. This rationality of the ideological is linked to its character as an alternative-generating elaborated speech variant, and can, as such, escape merely traditional definitions of social reality. This historical rationality of ideology faces in two directions, one toward the *world* itself and one toward the *self*, as it faces the world. In the first case, the rationality of the ideological implies a declining hold in traditional and in sacred definitions of social reality, thus allowing them to be made *problematic* and to be examined from the standpoint of whether they are true or logical and whether they might be otherwise. In the second case, the rationality of the ideological predicates a self that feels self-confident and potent enough to pit itself against familiar versions of reality and to question, prod, and probe them.

From this standpoint, then, the ideological is not merely more activistic than the tragic but, also, more rational, at least by its own standards. For it does not take "what is" as given, but insists on making it problematic. In treating the world, or parts of it, as deliberately transformable, the ideological assumes that the world is susceptible to rational diagnosis. The fuller rationality of the ideological, however, becomes visible only by extending the background against which it is viewed to include the "utopian," as well as the tragic and, above all, to see the subterranean links between the utopian and the tragic. Both *share* certain structures, assumptions, rules. If the tragic and the utopian are involved in a tensionful dialectic they are, also, brothers-under-the-dialectic; if the utopian is *dis*continuous with the tragic it is, also, profoundly *continuous* with it. The utopian is, we may say, the tragic inverted.

Like the tragic, the utopian is grounded in the split between an imputedly transcendent ideal and an imputedly separate definition of social reality. The tragic response to this chasm between real and ideal is a radical avoidance of an imputedly corrupt world; avoidance saves risking pollution of the ideal or of the self committed to it. The tragic vision entails a refusal, a "great refusal" to "compromise" with the world. The utopian response, like the tragic, seeks also to avoid compromising the ideal and refuses to accept something less than the ideal world. But rather than refusing the defective world, the utopian plunges into headlong confrontation with it in an effort to change it at once and bring it into full conformity with the ideal. The utopian is thus "utopian" in that he acts as if he fully expects to get *all* that he defines as right and ideal. The utopian, then, treats value commitments as a set of "nonnegotiable" demands on reality, exactly as does the tragic; but the utopian seeks to *enact them in the world* rather than to protect the ideal by world-avoidance. The utopian view, then, is that definition of the relation between the ideal and real in which the latter is seen primarily from the standpoint of the former and where the moral ideal alone constitutes the instructions in terms of which reality is to be acted upon.

In the utopian view, the difference between the real and ideal, then, is defined as a surmountable, continuously reducible *distance*. Any difference between real and ideal is regarded as a "blurred" vision which can (and should) be corrected fully so that the two become one, and that in a particular way, namely, by moving the (vision of the) real until it is completely isomorphic with that of the ideal. It is one of the paradoxes of the specifically utopian view that, in seeking to eliminate all distinction between real and ideal, it is incapable of being satisfied even by its own successes. Insofar as the utopian embodies nonnegotiable demands on reality, however great its previous achievement in closing the gap between the real and ideal, the remaining gap is experienced as profoundly unsatisfactory even if smaller than ever. Thus, the utopian view is nonhistorical. It does not see the present from the standpoint of the previous situation but, rather, from the standpoint of the differences between present and ideal. The utopian standpoint, then, is in profound tension with *whatever* is, however much this is an improvement over the past. The utopian standpoint therefore can find little that is gratifying to itself, whether in the world or in its own action upon the world.

The utopian entails moments of seemingly boundless optimism about what may be achieved in the world. But precisely because its focus is not on what has been accomplished, it is continuously poised on the brink of a new despair and pessimism, to which it is vulnerable, so that one unintended outcome of the striving to enact the utopian vision is to regenerate the tragic vision. The pursuit of utopia prepares for a regression to the tragic view.

In the utopian vision, each achievement toward the ideal is immediately the basis for a recalibration, the new focus being immediately fastened on the remaining difference between the real and ideal; this distance is viewed precisely as a *non*temporal event and as an *a*temporal *distance;* as an apartness rather than as a *new* closeness or even as a "remaining" distance; for "new" and "remaining" are both temporal qualifiers and *any* temporalization of the perspective will include a view of what has already been accomplished, encompassing the "improvement," as well as what yet needs to be done. The utopian, like the tragic, thus accents the distance between "what is" and what should be. The tragic separates and removes itself from the real, while the utopian ceaselessly moves toward, against and aims to overcome and transform the real.

The utopian, then, is a high-minded, morally-grounded form of *anomie*. It is that insatiability deriving not from the *absence* of norms but from an existing absolutism of norms. Utopianism is that insatiability that derives from detemporalization, such that one is always oriented toward a future seen only in relation to a what-might-be but never in relation to what-has-been. The utopian entails an ahistorical commitment to moral perfectibility, which is to say, to an absolutistic moralism. It is thus a commitment to progress with*out* history, and is thus the anomie of progress. Utopianism, then, is "permanent revolution," or continual cultural revolution, grounded in an uncompromising moral revulsion from what is.

The ideological and the utopian are not at all identical. Rather, the utopian is a pathology of the ideological, not its normal condition. Neither tragic nor utopian, the ideological vision premises a temporal sensitivity, of the "what is" seen as a point (or space) in a lineal extension of time, defined both by what lies ahead and what has been before, and in which the latter is seen as the implicit grounding of the former. Neither utopian nor tragic, the ideological experiences itself as imbued with a sense of "practical realism." It does not acquiesce in what is, but neither does it affirm ceaseless struggle against it. It believes that some projects are, indeed, accomplishable in the world. It believes that they are indeed worthwhile, even if limited, even if less than perfect, even if leaving a residual distance between what is and should be. To that extent, the ideological is "compromising" and possesses an inherent potential for "opportunism."

The tragic and the utopian, then, are siblings, Siamese twins united and joined at the back. If the first is all resignation, the second is a readiness for rage against the world; both, however, are grounded in a focus on the *distance* between "what is" and what should be, and on a refusal to compromise with it. Both the utopian and the tragic, seen from another standpoint, are directions in which the ideological can break down.

The ideological presumes that the world is not simply and not entirely an object of *moral judgment*. The ideological thus *rejects* the view that the world is a "moral gymnasium," a place in which all that men need do is flex their moral impulse and make moral judgments. The ideological presumes that the world has a *being* of its own. What the world *is*, or is taken to be, makes a difference and affects our effort to bring it into conformity with our moral standards, and may limit our ability to achieve our values and affect the *extent* to which we achieve them. The ideological implies that what should be done is in part a function of what *can* be done and not only of our moral ideals. It implies a limit on the claims of morality. It says that what we are morally bound to do does not depend solely on a judgment of what is right and good but, also, on what is *possible*. It says that commands should be grounded in reports. The ideological embodies the Kantian view that "ought implies can." The ideological premises a *politics* that embodies but transcends morality.

The ideological, then, exhibits the rationality of the elaborated speech variant by refusing to take the world as a given, and by insisting on seeing it from the standpoint of what might be, counterposing project to tradition, and, secondly, by fostering *encounters* with the world such that, in seeking to enact the project, we also experience a resistance that fosters a sense of the independent reality and weight of the other; the world can now become an object of attention, as something real apart from us, and not as viewable simply from our moral standpoint. By limiting the scope of our moral response to the world, the ideological allows more scope for the autonomy of the cognitive even while linking it to moral givens and publicly committed projects that must, at some point, *limit* that autonomy.

chapter 4

The Communications Revolution: News, Public, and Ideology

There is a profound interconnection, as I have observed earlier, between the new Age of Ideology—the eighteenth and nineteenth centuries proliferation of ideologies—and the "communications revolution" grounded in the development of printing, printing technologies, and the growing production of printed products. The fuller ramifications of these developments, of their reach both forward and backward in time, and across social subsystems, are exhibited with exceptional clarity by Morse Peckham, whom I quote at length below.

1

"One of the most striking facts about the nineteenth century, perhaps time will show it to be the most important, is the population expansion in the area of western European culture. . . . To clothe this new population would have been impossible—that is, the population increase itself would have been impossible—had it not been for the perfection, in the county of Lancaster in England, of cotton spinning and weaving machinery, shortly followed in the 1790s by the invention in America of the cotton gin. For the first time the perennial textile shortage of Europe was relieved. . . .

"Another consequence of cotton production was. . . . A by-product of cotton . . . an immense increase in worn-out clothes, or rags. Rags were the raw-material of the paper-making industry which, so long as linen was the only source for rags, perennially suffered a shortage of raw materials. There had been a consequent shortage of paper itself in Europe ever since its innovation in the late Middle Ages, which prevented the expansion of the printing and publishing industries. Books, which for economic reasons could command only part of the available paper supply, were luxury goods, printed in editions of about a few hundred. The coming of cotton meant that the shortage of raw material for paper disappeared.

"It is no surprise to learn, therefore, that in the first decade of the nineteenth century, England perfected a paper-making machine, named after the men whose fortunes went to develop it, the Fourdrinier brothers. . . . It was as important as the invention of the printing press. . . . This invention involved a whole chain of reactions.

"First, paper making could move from a hand process to a machine process, run by the newly exploited energies of water and steam. Paper became cheap and plentiful. The next step was to apply water and steam to printing, for there had been no point in improving the original fifteenth-century model of the printing press so long as there was not enough paper to keep the presses from standing idle. Now there was enough, and printing also became part of the industrial revolution. Bookbinding also could now profitably be taken out of the stage of handwork and made a machine process. The huge quantities of books manufactured could be profitably distributed because of the new energies available for transportation.

"By 1830, publishing had been revolutionized. Printed matter was now cheap—for the first time in human history literacy could be massively extended through all levels of the population. In England the population grew by a ratio of one to four; but the literate population grew by a ratio of one to thirty-two. Not merely book manufacture was affected, but every type of communications and record keeping involving paper—magazines, newspapers, letters; business, government and military correspondence and orders. . . . The nineteenth century experienced a communications revolution which, though a part of the industrial revolution, may very well have been the most important of its results." °

1.1

Peckham notes one exceedingly important consequence for the writing of history, the hitherto dominant, intellectually serious, and secular effort to account for and describe the social world:

"The historian's technique was developed centuries before the communications revolution. It was a product of the fact that documents were limited in number. A single human mind could master them. All the surviving

° Morse Peckham, *Beyond the Tragic Vision*, George Braziller, New York, 1962, pp. 25–27.

documents of ancient Greece can be intimately studied within a few years.
. . . Consequently, we have a clear picture of the history of ancient Greece.
That clarity is a consequence, not of our understanding, but solely of the fact
that there is so little to understand. When the historian attempts to grapple
with any period after the communications revolution had begun, he is lost in a
chaos of documents. His technique no longer serves him. . . . He is forced to
recognize that history is a construct; he can no longer delude himself into
thinking that what happened was identical with what was recorded in a very
small number of surviving documents; he cannot escape the conclusions that
his construct is an instrument which he uses to organize the documents." °

There was, then, a tremendous increase in information due to the
accelerating availability of printed materials, newspapers, or official documents. This sheer increase in the information intensified the problem of
information *processing* and, above all, of clarifying the meaning of the
information. Acquiring *meaning*, not information, became increasingly problematic.

It became clearer that meaning did not simply spring forth from
information itself, that meaning was not dictated by the number of
documents, by the facts or bits of information, but depended, at least in *part*,
on prior commitments to conceptual schemes, theories, and perspectives.
Differences in intra- or inter*national* news accounts, for example, became
evident to travelling readers who could compare diverse accounts, of the
"same" event. Meaning could thus be seen to depend on the *interests*—national, political, religious, and emphatically, economic—of both publishers
and readers. The sheer increase in information, and in the diversity of the
reports concerning "one" event, generated a new public problematic: the
need for publicly shareable *meaning*. The proliferation of ideologies, the Age
of Ideology, was one fundamental response to the new communications
revolution; it was, in part, an effort to supply meaning where the overall
supply of public information was greater than ever.

1.2

The Age of Ideology, then, may be looked upon as that proliferating
production of symbol systems that responded to the increased market for
meaning; and, in particular, for *secularized* meanings, due partly to the
attenuation of older value systems and religions that were tied to the dying
old regime; due partly to the new social structures and revolutionary events
that needed to be synthesized; and due greatly (as I have stressed above) to
the sheer increase in *bits* of information that the communications revolution
spread in every direction.

° Ibid., pp. 27–28.

More than that, there was also the fragmented image of the world that was inherent in "news" itself. As Robert Park commented: News deals ". . . with isolated events and does not seek to relate them to one another in the form of causal or teleological sequences. . . . News comes to us . . . not in the form of a continued story but as a series of independent incidents . . . small, independent communications." Focused on the *newness* of news, each news story tends to constrict attention to the present, and thus generates a loss of those connections with the past that is "history." It decontextualizes "events."

It is thus consistent that the Age of Ideology is not only to be seen as responsive to the fragmentation of news, but also corresponds with the modern development of history, with the development of *modern* history, that connects distant with recent events over time, and, what is newer, soon presses on to interconnect the seemingly isolated subsystems of society—for example, to write about the relationship between economics and politics. The interconnectedness of economics and politics can now be told as a kind of revelation, and history is no longer an isolated chronicle of crowns and courts. The new history is *re*contextualizing as are the new ideologies; they both seek new meaning-bestowing *contexts*.

2

With the diffusion of literacy, the technology of printing, and the development of the modern newspaper, there was, then, the development of the modern notion of "news" itself. Indeed, between, say, about 1780 and 1830, the growth of journals, newsletters, and newspapers was so great in Europe that a fundamentally new social phenomenon comes into being—the "news"-reading public.

In Germany, newspapers began to be issued with some regularity, in the very early seventeenth century. The first French paper, *Gazette de France* appeared in 1631. Between 1700 and 1789, some 85 journals were started in France. The *London Gazette* appeared in 1665, containing articles by Jonathan Swift and Daniel Defoe, among others, and by 1774 there were seven London dailies. As early as the mid-eighteenth century, about 7½ million newspaper stamps were sold in Britain and by about 1830 these had almost reached 25,000,000. Robert E. Park notes that "the first newspaper in America, at least, the first newspaper that lasted beyond its first issue, was *The Boston News Letter* . . . published by the postmaster."

At first, such publications were more likely to combine commentary on literature with "news." But by 1830 the news predominated, as parliaments and political centers became of wider interest, and as the spread of markets into national and international systems meant that distant events could affect local prices and supplies. The new media, then, appealed to a variety of audiences, including one in Leipzig (1725–26) written for women, while about 1830 working-class newspapers began appearing in London and Paris (e.g. *Le Populaire* and *L'Atelier*). Even in 1620, Ben Jonson had described subscribers to his newsletter as "of all ranks and religion." Subsequently, and with the development of different departments and features within one newspaper, the paper spreads itself across different "publics" who become amalgamated and connected with one another through the newspaper's "layout." Typography and layout become visual ways of organizing meanings and audiences.

2.1

The emergence of the mass media and of the "public" are mutually constructive developments. A "public" emerges when there is an attenuation between culture, on the one side, and patterns of social interaction, on the other. Traditional "groups" are characterized by the association and mutual support of both elements; by the fact that their members have patterned social interactions with one another which, in turn, fosters among them common understandings and shared interests which, again in turn, facilitates their mutual interaction, and so on. A "public," "refers to a number of people exposed to the same social stimuli," and having something in common even without being in persisting interaction with one another. (John Bennett and Melvin Tumin.) "Publics" are persons who need not be "co-present," in the "sight and hearing of one another." (E. B. Reuter and C. W. Hart.)

In most traditional societies, however, markets and holidays constituted the basic specialized structures periodically spreading information to the larger community, among strangers or members of different families; and this, of course, was transmitted by word of mouth, in a context-sustained face-to-face conversation that allowed clarifying feedback and questioning. With the growth of the mass media, exemplified at first by printing, numerous persons were now exposed to a continuous flow of information, at more or less the same time. Information becomes *de*contextualized, for it must be made intelligible, interesting and convincing even to persons of diverse backgrounds and interests, persons who do not know one another and do not meet and interact.

With the growth of the mass media, social interaction was less requisite for cultural communality. People might now share information and orientations, facts and values, without mutual access and interaction. The problem now arises as to how persons can evaluate information. The shared beliefs people defined as true and worthy, could now be controlled from a remote distance, apart from and outside of the persons sharing the beliefs. Insofar as the control of media comes to be centralized and its reach becomes extended, competing values and definitions of reality no longer check one another; rational persuasion is then less necessary, and manipulation from a central source can substitute for voluntary persuasion.

Historically speaking, then, a "public" consists of persons who habitually acquire their news and orientations from impersonal mass media where they have available to them diverse information and orientations diffused by competing individual entrepreneurs or corporate organizations, and where this diversity increases *talk* among those sharing news but seeking consensus concerning its meaning. That is a *bourgeois* public.

A *"socialist"* public differs in that talk is generated by the commonly understood lacunae of the news, by the distrust of the univocality of the news, and by the immensely greater difficulty in voicing interpretations divergent from those sanctioned officially, because of the lack of *open* support for (deviant or) dissenting views. A bourgeois public clearly has its limits in property interests, class-shaped cultural assumptions and educational backgrounds; but it also supports diversity, eccentricity and dissent among persons by allowing deviants the supportive consensual validation of a public organ, however small and poorly supported.

2.2

Newspapers strengthen enhanced public rationality in certain obvious ways. First, they provide a larger supply of information. This transcends local conditions, going beyond it to bring information concerning distant events. News thus has a cosmopolitanizing influence, allowing persons to escape provincializing assumptions, and thereby enabling them to *compare* their own conditions with others. News allows alternatives to be defined as "realistic" by showing different conditions to exist already, thereby fostering more ready transcendence of the immediate and the local. News also enables men to see what might be coming, partly as a "weather report" permits adjustments based on crude extrapolation, thus limiting possible costs or reaping greater gains. News itself, then, enhances rationality in these several ways.

Increasing news and information was also rationality-enhancing in the early bourgeois period by the way news came to be structured, by the separation of news and editorials, as well as because competing papers might present different reports of the same event. Both of these circumstances were fostered by bourgeois profit-seeking and competitive enterprise.

News was separated from editorial policy in part because an "imprudent" pursuit of the paper's policy might offend and limit its market. This became enormously more important as advertising spread, intensifying concern with the size of the readership, and clearly linking income from advertising to sheer size of readership. This, then, controls the editor's single-minded pursuit of policy, splitting the presentation of news from the editorial. Indeed, it may make both news and editorial opinion subordinate to entertainment: to feature writers, "human interest" stories, romance stories for the "ladies," sports for the "gentlemen." As entertainment develops, the newspaper as a source of rationality is profoundly undermined. But, until then, and so long as newspapers present information that requires interpretation, it fosters discussion and rational dialogue.

2.3

It was central to the pioneering analysis of the public, and of the news made by the "Chicago School," that news *constructed* a public by stimulating face-to-face conversation. Talk was intensified to resolve uncertainties about the *meaning* of the news, whether uncertainty was fostered by lacunae or by conflicting accounts.

But such talk premises motives for clarification. These, in turn, premise an *interest* in integrating the often fragmented bits of information that character-ize news; the varied, ambiguous, or conflicting reports of news. The system at bottom premised: the publisher's dependency on the successful marketing of his product, which meant *interesting* his audience and generating a larger market; it implied a socioeconomic-political system that allowed for a multiplicity of semiautonomous producers of printing, publishers, outlets, and distributors, free to purchase writing and writers, whose work they thought would sell for a profit. It also premises writers who could sell their writing on a labor market, and who might therefore by-pass the censorship of one publisher by using another, competing publisher; or who might even be published by a publisher who disliked their views simply because they sold newspapers.

Bourgeois rationality transcended the rationality of classical antiquity primarily because it was grounded in the new technology. The class systems of classical slave society, and of capitalist society, both premised the exclusion of great parts of the society from participation in rational public dialogue. The limits of rationality in both class systems were, in part, the class and property interests of the dominant classes—slave owners and bourgeoisie.

The Greeks, however, give little or no *evidence* of ever having made slavery a problematic institution open to public discussion, except insofar as it was implicated in the politics of Greek solidarity against the Persians. While some resisted the Greek enslavement of Greeks, their own enslavement of "barbarians," however, seems never to have been questioned publicly in classical antiquity, nor was the institution of slavery as such. Bourgeois society, however, very swiftly generated a public critique of its most fundamental property assumptions. Quite unlike classical antiquity, it moved with breathtaking speed to plant "the seeds of its own destruction." Scarcely had the French Revolution been completed when the liberating mission of the proletariat was announced. Indeed, this had been partly anticipated and heralded by the Babeuvian "conspiracy of the equals," in the very midst of the Revolution itself.

Publics imply a development of rational discourse because they imply the existence of a cleared and safe space in the community available for *face-to-face* discourse, concerning a commonly shared body of news-disbursed information, that is motivated by a quest for the interpretation of that shared news. Such discourse is "rational" precisely in the sense that it is *critical;* meaning that what has been said may be questioned, *negated* and *contradicted.* This, in turn, is possible if and only if people may speak "openly" without fear of sanctions, other than those imposed by the deficient logic and factuality of their speech, and only insofar as such sanctions are inflicted by co-speakers in their *private* capacity. The rationality of "public" discourse thus depends on the prior possibility of separating speakers from their normal powers and privileges in the larger society, especially in the class system, and on successfully defining these powers and privileges as irrelevant to the quality of their discourse. Publics thus require men to be treated as "private" persons.

2.4

News-grounded conversation, as a vehicle of public rationality, thus depends importantly on the *absence* of state-sponsored spies, informants, censors, and a secret police governmentally mandated to search out heresy, dissidence, or immorality.

The class system and the state, then, must *both* be excluded from the dialogue, if the public is to actualize its potential for critical rationality. Any social transformation of the class system alone will, therefore, *fail* to enhance public rationality if it does not, at the same time, prevent the *state* from the surveillance and punishment of dissident talk, or at least forbid surveillance as a routine activity that does not require extraordinary justification. It is in that sense that it is not only class power but *any* source of societal domination that inhibits dialogue and undermines rationality.

The development of a public in bourgeois society clearly entailed the interaction of growing news, printing media and technologies, and a cleared, safe space within which *face-to-face talk* about news and its meaning could occur. This development begins within the confines of liberal aristocratic society, well before the bourgeois revolution. It begins in the aristocratic salons and is only later "democratized" by the development of public cafés in bourgeois society—places where a limited group could gather and talk, without fear of either class snobbery or police spies. In the case of the salon, of course, conversation concerning public matters is within the space of a *private* home, and is a form of common entertainment. One had to be invited, otherwise one could not participate. This meant that conversation was limited by the tacit requirement that it not impair conviviality and "good taste," as defined by a presiding hostess. This, in turn, meant that rationality was tacitly limited by a *class*-shared cultivation and tact. (On these matters, Lewis Coser's *Men of Ideas* is superlative.)

With the development of the public café open to all with the price of admission, there remained only one fundamental limit on participation, and that was the limit on rationality that had persisted since antiquity: leisure. To spend time in a café talking with others implied, if it was during the *day*time, that one was not accountable to others for his time. It implied that "he" was his own "master" because "he" was a reputable independent professional or entrepreneur, or a dubiously reputable "bohemian" who had rejected a routine occupation, and/or a student supported by others. It is important to add that even a wealthy entrepreneur who employed others might be excluded from such participation by reason of his need (or wish) actively to superintend those whom he employed.

2.5

To spend time in a café talking with others also implied, especially if it was a *night*time activity, that it was a male-dominated group. Presence at the café premised a family system having men-dominated households from which they could depart or return at their own pleasure, without time-consuming participation in child care or housekeeping. The bourgeois public then was not just class-grounded; it was also grounded in a *patriarchical family system*. It was open primarily to those who were economically *and* sexually privileged.

In both bourgeois society and in classical antiquity, public rationality was grounded in class privilege and in unchallenged male domination of the family. Both provided that indispensable requisite for rational discourse: leisure, free from time-consuming work in the household and in the work-place, and the freedom to allocate one's own "free time" without the control or permission of another. Patriarchical subjugation of women and private property, then, were the unmistakable conditions and limits of the post-Enlightenment development of public rationality in bourgeois society.

The existence of owning-publishers also generated a set of limits within which the distinction between editorials and news could not be altogether real; for the publisher, after all, hired both the editorialist and the head of the news department. But the sheer problem of profitability imposed its own constraints. It meant that the publisher could neither hire nor publish only in terms of his own ideological preferences. Precisely because the publisher was a capitalist and subject to the imperatives of profitability and of competition, he had to *limit* his own impulse to infuse the news with his own ideological views. For there was the compelling consideration of printing what would not offend others and could sell and turn a profit.

2.6

Ideologies serve to mobilize "social movements" within publics through the mediation of newspapers and other media. Movements are sectors of the public committed to a common public project and to a common social identity. Movements are those sectors of the public responsive to the mobilizing efforts of ideologies; they share an ideology that, on the one side, interprets the news and, on the other, provides an awareness of their own social identity from reports in the news media. News generates ideology-centered social identities which, in turn, are now media-constructed and defined. Thus social movements in the modern world are both ideology- and news-constructed.

Indeed, between the later spread of a social movement, and an earlier formulation of an ideology, there is often the intervening organization and production of a newspaper. In the period of the consolidation of the bourgeoisie, newspapers were often instruments of parties; and parties were often mobilized and organized through the newspapers. The modern political party, which is the enduring cadre *organization* and elite of a movement, is fostered by the newspaper and its commitments and interests; in many cases, newspapers are essentially "in-house," party organs.

Newspaper editors sometimes doubled as editors and party chiefs. One way that the party cadre could secure livings, leaving them time for party involvement, was as party journalists or editors. No one understood this better than V. I. Lenin who deliberately undertook to mobilize a Marxist cadre in Russia by the specific tactic of launching a newspaper that was appropriately called *Iskra, The Spark*, highlighting its mediating significance. Correspondingly, one of the reasons that Marx and Engels never became the active *leaders* (but only remained the "senior consultants") of mass socialist parties was that they *refused* to be the editors of party newspapers, even of socialist papers.°

° Thus Engels remarks in a letter of November 18, 1892, written to August Bebel: "Marx and I always agreed that we would never accept such a position [as editor of a party journal] and could only work for a journal financially independent even of the Party itself." They regarded this as a

2.7

The meaning of a "public" develops along with the socially emergent idea of the "private." The relations between the two, however, are not always the same in all countries. In typical form, in eighteenth- and nineteenth-century France, the relation is one in which the "private" constituted the complement and grounding of a "public." In Germany, the private was often a *substitute* for the public, a place of the "mind" where one could be free, even if not openly free in public discourse. Here, the private is compensatory; a consolation prize for the stunting of a public. And even that is more complicated than it might seem, for the private here is not simply the *absence* of all dialogue but is *intense dialogue* limited to close friends and intimates. The German dwelling on *innerlichkeit* (inwardness) in the nineteenth century, in effect, made the mind (consciousness) and the close friendship a site of sanctified retreat from the repressions and dangers of a truly public discourse. In the French case, the effort was to insulate private life from the stresses of the public; above all, to prevent one's public involvements from intruding on the nuclear family.

In England, of course, the "public" school is not one open freely to all, but a school that is conducted away from the family home and hence away from direct parental supervision. Here "public" is that which is outside the family and is thus congruent with the French understanding. Indeed, it is not so much that the German situation differs in its *understanding* of the public as in its ability to *enact* it. There is the sociological stunting of the public in much of nineteenth-century German life. In one part, the present focus of the Critical School on the "communicative competence" of ego-and-alter seems continuous with that tradition and, overemphasizing the early bourgeois public, depresses the value of the present public and strives to conceive of "freedom" *apart* from the *public*. The freedom of the "ideal speech situation" with its "communicative competence" is not a consciousness *in* the mind, but is in the intimate communion of some abstract, timeless, and technologically innocent dyad.

Public and private thus develop together. To make matters "public" means to open them even to those who are not known personally, to those who do not ordinarily come into one's sight and hearing. On the paradigmatic level, to make things public is to take them (or allow them to go) beyond the *family*, where all is in the sight and hearing of others, and which constructs a context for communication that may, in consequence, be cryptic, allusive, seemingly vague. The simultaneous growth of the public and private meant the

---

"barren position" inhibitive of their freedom of discussion. Cf. A. Bebel, *Briefe an Bebel*, Berlin, DDR, 1958.

development of a limit on the power of the public, the drawing of a firm boundary beyond which the public could not intrude. One could be a public being, with all the exhaustion and tension that generates, only because there was a place—the private sphere—to which one could retreat for repairs; a place in which one could find support for efforts that had failed to find public support. The private was a place where one could speak the silences of the public to a sympathetic and validating hearer.

Structurally speaking, this meant either (1) a patriarchical family system within which (sometimes) loved but commonly subjugated women and children helped the husband-father redefine his defeats, producing favorable private reassessment of unfavorable public verdicts; or, (2) it might also imply a system of well-informed and cultivated *heterae*, such as the ancient Greeks had perfected—the *heterae* were a force that helped maintain rational public discourse in ancient Greece°—but which a puritanical bourgeoisie could not countenance; and (3) the development of close male friendships, as a framework of intimate intellectual expressivity, but which, also, premises (as it did both in ancient Greece and modern bourgeois society) a male-dominated family system. Thus the very strengthening of the sphere of the private is, in these conditions, necessary (not antithetical) to the strengthening of the public.

2.8

The public is a sphere in which one is accountable; but it rests on a private, family system in which dominant males are accountable to other family members only to a very limited extent. To be "accountable" means that one can be *constrained* to reveal *what* one has done and *why* one has done it; thus, the action and the reason for it are open to a critique by strangers who have fewer inhibitions about demanding justification and reasonable grounds. Given the mutual dependency, affection, and tact in family groups, and given the power of males in them, there are severe limits on the questions that males will be asked there. Conversely, given a *lack* of affection, emotional dependency, tact, and of direct power over one another, there will be far fewer constraints in what may be questioned in public.

Publics are, in that sense, unhindered in asking questions and in demanding justification concerning courses of conduct; these will therefore be protected from the demand for rational justification by the use of one major tactic: concealment and secrecy. This, in turn, generates inevitable pressures for censorship, particularly in a world of semiautonomous media.

° Cf., the discussion on "interpersonal strains and homosexuality" in A. W. Gouldner, *Enter Plato*, Basic Books, New York, 1965, pp. 60 *et seq.*

But why, one might wonder, should the realm of the private (and thus of the familial) restrict the flow of information and limit the demand for accountability? Primarily because the *interests* of private persons, and their families, may conflict with the interests of other private persons, and their families; because (or when) they are, to some extent, all playing a zero-sum game against one another; and, also, because they are behaving at variance with the interests of the group as a whole or of the state. Underneath the growth of privacy, then, was a possessive, self-protective individualism rooted in a system of competitive private property. This integration of the patriarchical family system with a system of private property was the fundamental grounding of the private; a sphere that did not routinely have to give an accounting of itself, either by providing information about its conduct or justification for it. Private property and patriarchy were thus indirectly the grounding of the *public*. For if the private sphere limited the public, it by that fact also supported and protected the public sphere, in which, at least, some things were accountable and subject to open rational discourse.

The bourgeois public constituted one of the great historical advances in rationality. It firmly excluded treating the community and the state as the private business of some single grouping of notables. Since two major interests are encompassed in this enclave of the private (property and patriarchy), the critique of the bourgeois order often began with an attack on both of these.

The most notable instance of this was the Saint-Simonians, who became the incubators of the twin socialist critique of property and family, and who launched a "dizzying" internal discussion of "free love" and monogamy. Despite their aristocratic encoding, the Romantics, German or French, are indeed a fundamentally progressive force precisely because they inherit that side of the dual movement—the critiquè of patriarchy and patriarchical repression in the name of the spontaneity and freedom of the sexes. "Romanticism" thus emphatically subverts and rejects the right of the family system to control the relations between the sexes and, most particularly, the subordinate role of the woman. Romanticism clearly destroys the male, patriarchical right to allocate women. Modern "counterculture," as a "drop out" and *a*politicized force, has one of its centers in that continuing critique of patriarchicality, long grounded in romanticism.

The (ambivalent) fantasy of the nineteenth-century bourgeois, namely that communism implied the communization of women, no less than of property (or as another form of property), was not totally mindless. It was the bourgeois counterpart of the Saint-Simonian thrust. It was becoming clearer to all that the property system was protected within a sphere of privacy nucleated by the patriarchical family. But correspondingly, the effort to make modern socialism respectable to a *male* public led to the repressive tabling of the issue of emancipation from patriarchy.

Despite occasional nods at the "woman question," Socialism moved forward primarily as a system of public politics from which women were, for the most part, excluded except as auxiliaries or as tokens of emancipation. (This is all too painfully visible in Marx's own household, in which he sired a son with Helene Demuth, the servant sent as a "present" by his mother-in-law, and then forced Helene Demuth to remove the child from the household.°)

The private sphere, then, is at one and the same time the grounding and the limit of the public. The private sphere is, on the one hand, an arena from which public rationality is excluded and where certain reasons need *not* be given; and, on the other hand, the private is a basis for resistance to a public sphere which can become powerful enough to intrude on and control the private person. The fate of both the private and public spheres is thus inextricable. There can be no transformaton of the public sphere that is not, at the same time, a transformation of the private.

In one part, modern socialism is an effort to take production, productive property, and work, away from the control of the private sphere and to reconstruct it as a public matter. With this, however, the property basis of the bourgeois family collapses. The family now becomes open to direct manipulation and intervention of the state. As a private sphere for the repair and maintenance of social identities, especially male egos, the family is undermined. The monopolization and the execution of the public interest is now appropriated by the state. The "public," as something linking but also buffering the family system and the state, is thereby crippled. With the destruction of the public as a quasi-autonomous network of discussion, the family system becomes increasingly a direct medium of the state apparatus, and is less and less able to serve as an ego repair station and identity-forming group. The family has less and less of a social function; is now less able to serve as an enclave silently supporting the resistance of individuals and helping them to say "no" to the demands of the state and the media. The crippling of the family-grounded sphere of the private, together with the decline of the property-based sphere of the public, means that the surviving force in control of that pulverized social field becomes the state; becomes its mobilizing instrument in the community, the "vanguard" party; and the institutional fusion of the two, the party-state, the "integral state" in Max Horkheimer's terms.

3

The men and women who wrote and read ideologies differed from earlier,

° For the full and quite tragic story see Yvonne Kapp, *Eleanor Marx Vol. I, 1855–1883*, Lawrence & Wishart, London, 1972.

literate persons in that they were a *news-reading public*. Their symbolic environment was profoundly and uniquely altered by the mounting communications revolution based on proliferation of the printed word. Ideologies, then, may be further defined as symbol systems generated by, and intelligible to, persons whose relationship to everyday life is mediated by their reading—of newspapers, journals, or books—and by the developing general concept of "news," as well as by the specific and concrete "bits" of news now increasingly transmitted by the growing media, and is grounded in the experiencing of life as decontextualized events. The emerging ideologies are characterized by their world-referencing discourse, on the one side, and on the other, by their tacit reliance upon news reports about the social world. Ideologies were not grounded in the experience of an unmediated everyday life with its ordinary languages. They were not grounded in what we might call an unmediated and taken-for-granted "localism." Between everyday life and the newly propounded ideologies there were now the newspapers and other mass *media* that selectively defined issues, fragmented experience as "events," focused "public" attention, and brought distant events to notice, thereby defining them as of local relevance, overcoming provincialism and enhancing "cosmopolitanism."

As the mass media spreads, there is a growing disjunction between information (or knowledge), on the one side, and on the other, the attitudes and sentiments—the affect structure—to which that information is related. This implies, from one perspective, that information systems become *relatively* context-free, or at least, freer of the limits imposed by operation of the *affect* structure in face-to-face communication.

In word-of-mouth talk, it is not only information but interpretations, orientation, and appropriate notions of what is to be done, that are communicated. Commands are transmitted with clarity and force, along with reports. Face-to-face talk allows direct feedback with which considerable pressure may be generated to modify feelings in some manner defined as proper to the reports. In face-to-face talk, command and report are mutually contextualizing and are more readily brought into an integration, in which each supports the other. With the mass media, however, the possibilities of a disjunction between the two grow. Given the absence of feedback, or low feedback, there is no way the media can judge whether their reports have elicited proper feelings. And even if they know, there is little they can do to feed back approving or disapproving responses, for proper or improper feelings. Without doubt, the media *intend* to command appropriate actions and to elicit feelings consistent with their news; but the transmission of information has now been isolated from a multimodal pattern of social interaction and feedback that might enforce that intention. Thus, "research findings indicated that the *mass media* can effectively change cognitions (that is, increase knowledge), but *inter*personal communication is more likely to be effective when attitude change is the goal . . ." °

Certainly, there is a continual tendency to respond selectively to information, admitting information consistent with and filtering out information dissonant with the existing affect structure. This *would* maintain an integration of cognition and sentiment, if that were all that was involved. But news is a public (and a public-generating) social phenomenon. It generates public attention and it stimulates talk. Sheer knowledge of news, regardless of its implications for affect structure, thus influences persons' chances of public participation, of group membership and evaluation, and ultimately it influences persons' social identities. People are thus *constrained* to know news, even when it is *not* in keeping with their prior affect structure, and even when they might prefer to forget it. Indeed, persons may be constrained to know such news so that they can counter interpretations adverse to their own feelings and beliefs.

News thus fosters a *de*contextualization of affectivity and information. These are now made relatively context free, and there is a growing possibility of a dissonance between affect structure and cognition. It is in this news-generated disjunction that there is grounded a modern sense of the disparity between the "is" and the "ought," between theory and practice, and between facts and values.

Ideologies, then, are never grounded in an uninterpreted everyday life. Nor are they simply grounded in the oral interpretations of everyday life spoken in ordinary languages. Ideologies always premise tacitly those printed interpretations of everyday life called "news." They are thus not simply commentaries on what is *happening*, but also on what the news *said* is happening. Ideologies are always palimpsestic texts on texts, no less than world-referencing commentaries on "life."

Marx thus subtitled *Das Kapital* as a "Critique of Political Economy"— that is, of the *books* and *articles* published by the liberal economists. Much of Marx's understanding of the concrete working of capitalism was based on his *reading* of books, journals, newspapers, and on the parliamentary investigations published in the "blue books." It was Frederick Engels, now commonly scapegoated for Marxism's "sins against philosophy," who knew capitalism from the inside as a participant observer; from his own experience in managing his father's cotton business, and from his own firsthand study of the conditions of the working class in Manchester—which was itself a remarkable piece of reportage. (Nor, of course, was it only ideologies that grounded themselves in the news but so, too, did many novelists, of whom the most typical are probably Emile Zola and Theodore Dreiser.)

° E. M. Rogers, "Mass Media and Interpersonal Communications," E. de Sola Pool et al., eds., *Handbook of Communication*, Rand McNally, Chicago, 1973, p. 291.

3.1

An interesting dialectic develops between news and everyday life. The "news" is that which is *not* routine and is information not *already* known. It is not the fundamental routines and rhythms of everyday life, of family and work, but the accenting punctuation, the more or less modest departures from them. News, then, tacitly divides the social world into (1) the seen-but-unnoticed regularities of everyday life and (2) the "news" which *is* the seen, noticed, and publicly commented-on accentings of or *departures* from these regularities. As news focuses notice, so it also *de*focalizes notice. As news reports, it therefore also censors and occludes aspects of life; its silences generate a kind of "underprivileged" social reality, a social reality implicitly said (by the silence) to be unworthy of attention.

News is a report about the imputedly unknown which is necessarily selective, partial, and perspectival. "In trying to explain what news is," Harvey Molotch and Marilyn Lester cogently suggest, "we must meet the challenge of explaining how it is that certain phenomena are included as news while an infinite array of other phenomena are ignored. The traditional view . . . inevitably falls back on the notion that some things are just more important than others." ° News is ambiguous; it says and does *not* say What Is. It dramatically accentuates and it keeps silence, it expresses and it suppresses, it exposes and it *censors*. But on what basis does the work of news constructing proceed? First, the news producers—reporters, editors, rewriters, headline writers, layout men, typographers, photographers, publishers— must take notice of something, be able to give it focalized attention and treat it as a spoken, fragmented "figure" against an unspoken "ground." In part, but only in part, this is a function of accenting departures from everyday life, from what is routine in some social sphere. It is the everyday that in time generates a frame of reference within which perception takes place, constituting the basis in terms of which some events will be noticed more or less. To some extent sheer difference from the modalities of the expected are defined as potentially newsworthy, being expected to capture the attention of readers, as they have of the news producers. Things distant will be noticed more readily than events that do not depart from them. Nonetheless, it also happens that when things differ *too* much they may be doubted or become "unbelievable." They may thus be ignored or "seen" as normal, that is, normalized, otherwise the entire pictured order is threatened. There are times, then, when "we could not believe our eyes," because things depart *too greatly* from the norm.

° H. Molotch and M. Lester, "Accidents, Scandals and Routines," *Insurgent Sociologist,* Summer, 1973, p. 2.

Nonetheless, the old saw remains largely true: "Dog bites man," is not news, but "Man bites dog," *is* news. In that sense, the "news" has a time tag attached that in itself assigns value—"news" is that which is relatively "new" and not the long and widely known. News emerges in a world in which, with the breakdown of traditional old regimes, with the emergence of bourgeois society, and with the French and the Industrial Revolutions, there is much that is truly *new*. Yet there is also a great deal that is new, much of which fails to make "news."

3.2

What one "sees," of course, is not simply a function of having eyes or expectations but, also, of having *interests* and these interact with and affect visibility. We are more likely to see what interests us. But whether we take *notice* of and report it as news depends on a further consideration. It depends partly on whether or not the viewed event is consonant with the picture of the social order that is defined as good; and with the identity assigned to the groups, roles, or persons featured in the events to be reported. Events *consonant* with imputedly "desirable" social orders or desirable identities will be more unambiguously "newsworthy" than those felt to be dissonant with them, those that discredit their imputed goodness. Perhaps it is in that sense that one distinguished paper pledges to publish "all the news that is fit to print." The question, of course, is in whose view is it fit or desirable. The answer, of course, must be in the view of the *news-producing system.*

One can only expect that the system will more likely report events that credit persons, social identities, political parties, and institutions that the system believes good. Again, one must expect that the system will more likely report those events that *dis*credit those opposing its "idols." Correspondingly, the system will more likely censor, withhold, or delay reports that discredit persons and groups the system values and credits, than those it *dis*values. The news-producing system is thus also a news *withholding* and *censoring* system.

One may next ask what it is that shapes these judgments of values or disvalues. Here the crux of the matter is the relation of such value judgments to *interest* and especially to "economic" or property interests, and particularly to the interests of those in control of the news-producing system. Since I intend to analyze "interests," at a later point, I will only say here that there is considerable pressure to adjust interests and values to one another, to make our values consistent with our interests and, conversely, to make our interests consistent with our values. *Or*, to see them as such. This implies that interests and values are not always consistent, although we would expect *tendencies* for them to be or, in time, to become consistent.

For the news-producing system, this clearly implies that, in one of its sides, there will be a powerful tendency for the economic and property interests of its owning publishers to shape the news it reports or censors, to influence whether (and how) something is reported. Publishers will, for the most part, not quickly question (or open themselves to disputes that bring into question and discredit) the property system under which those managing the news system are advantaged, by which they are privileged, and on which their very management of that news system rests. In this respect, Molotch and Lester's functional account is correct: "An individual or group promotes one or more of its activities as newsworthy because it is useful for them to do so. If that news is subsequently adopted by the media, we must assume then that they, also, have a use for publishing it." It is important to add, however, that while the two groups' uses may often be similar, they may also be contradictory. For what is scandalous and embarrassing to a "source," and which it would therefore rather suppress, may be useful to the media reporting it, because it attracts an audience and sells newspapers. This would seem to be an inescapable implication of the competitiveness characteristic of capitalist production, in which each economic unit is quite ready to profit from disaster to another. Thus news *dis*creditable to powerful and reputable elements in a society is, therefore, *not* always censored. There undoubtedly do occur events that only "accidentally" bring the hegemonic classes to public attention in a manner discreditable and injurious to themselves; but the fact that these are *published* as news is not itself an accident; it is an outcome structured by the deepest logic of the system.

3.3

I have spoken of the property system's impact on construction of the news; but I have not mentioned *which kind* of property system, whether "private" property or "socialist." As far as one can see, it does not matter. For in either case, the property system will, in part, construct news that helps reproduce the property system, sustaining the power and privileges of those already controlling the media. Any critique of the "mind managers" of capitalist media that fails to affirm this clearly is not emancipatory. It is only giving us a hackneyed bit of demystification in exchange for a new mystification.

The second thing needing emphasis at this point is that a *capitalist* news-producing system, like the capitalist system more generally, has its own internal *contradictions*. In news production, the central contradiction focuses on the difference between what news producers impute to be supportive of their own larger property interests and social values, on the one side, and, on the other, what they impute to be "interesting" to their readers and subscribers. What sells newspapers or wins viewers is not always identical or even consistent with the *publisher's* property interests.

In the decade of the 1960s it became clear that the commercial media were fostering certain values and attitudes, simply because they sold, and that were incompatible with the very property system on which these media were themselves grounded. This, it would seem, is part of the meaning of the "counterculture" or the cultural "revolution" of that decade.

3.4

Irwin Silber's Marxist commentary on this—which tacks back and forth nervously between rejecting the counterculture as a cooptive mechanism, ultimately supportive of capitalism, and affirming it as the harbinger of a socialist consciousness—correctly notes: "The 'revolution' business has become extremely profitable in those sundry cultural outposts of ideas and style which comprise a significant portion of the gross income for book publishers, record producers, clothing manufacturers and the entertainment industry in general." °

After first accusing the counterculture of subverting the working-class's will to oppose capitalism, by telling it to "drop out" rather than to fight back, Silber finally concludes that: the counterculture had fostered ". . . such goals as the destruction of the family, the disintegration of religion, the legalization of psychedelic drugs, the abolition of marriage, a greater sense of eroticism in daily experience, a rational view towards the problems of ecology, a greater looseness in individual and social behavior . . ." He goes on to ask: ". . . is it conceivable that capitalist society can absorb such goals . . . ?" † While it appears so to Silber, it does not seem conceivable to this writer. Indeed, one wonders how it can seem so to Silber who holds that the media-activated counterculture implies that "capitalist society has suffered a massive deterioration in its ability to motivate a sizable portion of its young to pursue individual life goals which coincide with the best interests of the ruling class." ‡

A judgment concerning the "revolutionary" import of a media-fostered counterculture depends greatly on what is used as the paradigm of revolution. If the paradigm of "revolution" is the October Revolution that brought the Bolsheviks to power in Czarist Russia in 1917, then the counterculture will be judged an essentially apolitical, hence nonrevolutionary force, encouraging persons to "dropout" rather than to organize active political struggle. If, however, one is not fixated on that revolution as the paradigm of all revolutions, if one also sees that capitalism's emergence out of feudal society

---

° I. Silber, *The Cultural Revolution: A Marxist Analysis*, Times Change Press, New York, 1970, p. 12.

† Ibid., p. 41.

‡ Ibid., p. 38.

required a long gestation within the "dropout" space of "free" urban enclaves in a surround of feudalism, then one arrives at a different judgment on the ultimate political meaning of the counterculture.

Moreover, whatever one's final verdict on the Weberian thesis about the relation between the emergence of Protestantism and the rise of capitalism, it is clear that the spread of the Protestant reformation and its proliferation of dissenting sects that enforced a this-worldly asceticism cumulatively eroded the cultural foundations of feudalism, lending *unintended* support to the emerging bourgeois society, and to its need for an intensified accumulation of capital. This slow and uneven spread of Protestant culture occurred within the midst of a feudal economic structure, with which it was ultimately incompatible. It spread sometimes by fostering "dropouts" into private existence, i.e., apart from Catholic society, and sometimes by openly and militantly opposing that society. Seen as an element in the long transition to bourgeois society, it would surely be wrong to deride Protestantism and the development of liberated urban space in feudal society as, at bottom, mechanisms by which feudalism bound dissenters back into its own system.

3.5

News is defined against the tacit background of the unspoken premises of everyday life, and by the bench marks these provide. But with the very spread of news these seen-but-unnoticed bench marks in time become *devalued, precisely because they are not given notice in the value-constructing news reports.* All news, then, devalues, censors, and represses certain aspects of everyday life, making these difficult to see and to accept even by the people living them, and thereby further occluding some of the very standards that ground its own selective reports of the newsworthy.

News, then, in time comes to be experienced as lacking in any grounding. It generates the seeds of dissatisfaction that its own public feels toward it. In effect, this means that the question of what is important for people to know about their own lives has become problematic, and can certainly no longer be taken as given. In some part, ideologies are efforts to search out and construct new groundings for the very "news" to which they make tacit or explicit reference.

Thus *ideologies* speak at two different levels: on the one, they speak to the "events" focalized by the news; and, on the other, they may refer to certain news-censored aspects of everyday life, "recovering" certain underprivileged elements in it. Ideologies are thus a "background" to the news—e.g., "the news behind the news," or the "big" news—that premises the reading of certain news-reported events. The tacit, everyday "test" of the intellectual validity of an ideology takes two directions; first, its ability to construct an integrated background *accounting* for the news, and secondly, by bringing to attention what hitherto was seen-but-unnoticed. It does this by "recovering" hitherto censored, defocalized aspects of the everyday experience of the readers which, of course, vary systematically with their social class or other social involvements.

In some part, the "facts" confirming ideologies, and in some part the "relevance" of things spoken of in ideologies, are taken to be commonly available in news. Ideologies can interest readers—and convince them—in part because they refer to news which some already share and, in part, by providing interpretations that go beyond news accounts, by referring to hitherto *publicly* unspoken aspects of people's personal interests, experiences, and everyday lives. Ideologies premise a public which presumes that much of the "facts" are already available in the news, but which now makes problematic the *meaning* of these facts. Ideologies presume a public engaged in face-to-face talk, which does not simply serve to transmit the media's message but to generate interpretations of its meaning by resolving contradictory accounts. It is in part this new *talk* that generates a market for meaning-bestowing and information-integrating ideologies. And it is the ideologies that seek to clarify the cryptic command implications of news reports and to overcome the disjunction between information and affect fostered by news—and so ultimately repairing the rift between theory and practice.

4

In this sense, ideologies are a special form of information-integrating social theory, grounded in news reportage and tested in terms of public knowledge of that news. To state it differently, ideologies are based on (what Robert Merton and Paul Lazarsfeld once called) "secondary research"—i.e., information originally assembled for purposes by agencies other than those of the ideologue. The gap, then, between ideology and social science cannot be a radical one because both are based on research, even if, on the average, on somewhat different types of research. In that sense, Irving Louis Horowitz is correct in asserting that "one of the pleasant fictions of orthodox sociologists is that science is advanced, in contrast to journalism, which is backward." °

Both social science and ideology are grounded in *tensions* generated by news, particularly those involving the dissonance between information and affect structure. Ideologies seek to reduce this dissonance by reaffirming the unity of theory and practice and amplifying the command implications of their reports about the social world. Social science, faced with the same

° I. L. Horowitz, "Sociology and Futurology," *Berkeley Journal of Sociology*, 1974, p. 37.

news-grounded dissonance, seeks to reduce it by *repressing* the command implications of its own reportage about the social world, and by affirming the rationality and propriety of the split between information and affect structure, i.e. of "value-free" sociology.

4.1

Since ideologies are efforts to mobilize publics on behalf of projects, then the issues they address and the ways they address them must have a public character. They must be known to or, at least, be of concern once made known to, relatively large numbers of ordinary-language speaking persons. A very distinctive kind of social theory and sociology is thus fostered by concern with such public issues. It must be able to assimilate, work on, and make sense of distinctive kinds of information sources and supplies. It must be able to interpret *non*technical information, news, concerning what is popularly deemed to be of current relevance. Ideologies must be able to work with information already known and available to a mass public. The use of public media or public documents, for data or communication outlets, thus means that there will be a slower development of a specialized social science vocabulary, since these would impede communication to a diverse lay public. At its extremes, the ideologies rely on and foster a specific type of social theory or sociology: "newspaper sociology."

For ideologues using public documents and news media, the problem is never the mere reliability of the news, or of this or that bit of information, but whether or not the *source* as a whole is inimical or congenial to their own political outlook. The immediate query is, what is their politics? A "newspaper sociology" thus systematically fosters a sense of the *connection* between facts and values, data and policies, information and ideologies. This doubts the very possibility of "value-free" thought—i.e., of "normal" academic sociology—and searches out the ideological and policy implications in social theory and research.

An awareness of how value standpoints are embedded in information is heightened by conflicts among classes and parties *within* a nation, and also, by seeing the same news reported differently in different nations. This, of course, presumes a reading ability in more than one language. Unlike American intellectuals, many Europeans have a comfortable reading familiarity with at least two, sometimes three, occasionally more, languages. They commonly read newspapers in other languages, if only in the course of their travels.

Social scientists' language skills are thus of more general importance for the kinds of social science they produce than is commonly recognized. Such skills not only affect social scientists' information and idea supply, but also their attitudes toward both. It heightens their awareness of the radical diversity of *perspectives* from which the facts can be viewed; it engenders the feeling that facts are inescapably viewed from *some* perspective. It thus makes Europeans less prone to a "methodological empiricism" in which the salient question is the sheer reliability of the facts reported. Indeed, some Europeans are occasionally too ready to gloss over the entire question of the factuality of some statement—and to give greater emphasis to the conceptual construction of facts, to the "meaning" or to the logical analysis of the statements made.

There are still other ways in which an ideologically relevant "newspaper sociology," a sociology oriented to newspaper reports, is of considerable consequence. One is that newspaper sociologists are given daily *consensual validation* of the importance of the problems with which they are dealing and, hence, of themselves and their work. They need not wait for long-delayed professional reviews of their work, or complimentary citations in the work of colleagues, to feel that what they are doing is meritorious. Each morning's newspaper may bring confirmation of the worth of their interests, as may any evening's discussion. Because of their special familiarity with "current events," there are many to whom they can display their competence and from whom they can, in turn, receive prompt recognition of their knowledgeability.

4.2

To put the matter in other terms, a newspaper sociology allows the sociologist to participate in the *public* sphere, to receive recognition in the public sphere, and thus to play a role as a *public* person. He is not confined to a limited professional sphere which, while it may bring him to the attention of colleagues, is, nonetheless, a small sphere, separating him from the life and concerns of ordinary people in his society. There is a way, then, that newspaper sociology prevents the sociologist's sense of lonely alienation and can help him overcome doubts, secret or overt, that all men may experience concerning the value of their lives.

As suggested above, participation in a public sphere has important consequences concerning the conceptual apparatus with which the newspaper sociologist works. He must write in jargon-free terms intelligible to nonprofessionals, and a good part of his conceptual apparatus must focus on problems already visible *without special instrumentation* or techniques. He must, in a way, deal with matters that, being publicly visible, are already part of the "common sense."

He is, however, then vulnerable to criticisms that his "sociology is common sense," having little to add to ordinary public discussion: what need, then, of sociologists? The newspaper sociologist has relatively little motivation to develop the technical apparatus or research instruments with which he works. The newspaper sociologist thus comes to resemble a certain species of anthropologist, who derives his satisfactions by his awesome command of ethnographic detail. He becomes, that is, a subject-matter "specialist" (sometimes a high-class "inside dopester" in some institutional sector) or an "area specialist" focusing on some geographical region of the world. To this extent, then, the newspaper sociologist makes little contribution to the theories he applies, or to the basic disciplines he uses. He trades societal relevance for professional creativity, public appreciation for peer appreciation, intellectual originality for control of the facts. Nonetheless, he is doing something to make the world, as ordinary men experience it, intelligible.

The "normal," academic social sciences commonly affirm the cognitive inferiority of the news, partly because news is clearly responsive to interests apart from knowing What Is, implying, of course, that their own work is free from interests (other than their technical interests). Academic social science sees news as "partial," thereby defining its *own* character as a corresponding effort to overcome the limit of partiality and of world interestedness. Academic social science was thus to be impartial and disinterested, unlike the news. The social sciences were meant to be *news* transcending. Comte's sociology begins with a sneer at, if not a "critique" of, *journalists*. Journalism fostered contention; social science was to generate consensus.

The new social sciences did not, however, differ from the ideologies by their concern for the truth-as-facts, and they did not differentiate themselves from the news primarily by reason of the superior reliability of their information. The social sciences premised new kinds of studies of the social world, they premised "research" and, in particular, "primary" research (as against ideology's secondary research) in which information was assembled by the social scientist himself for his own special purposes, for his "technical" interests as distinct from the *societal* interests of the reading public and publishers. These are premises that they had not, until about the 1940s, been able to satisfy consistently.

Ideology and social science entail qualitatively different structures of investigation shaped by different interests, rather than being information systems, one of which (science) is producing better information than the other (ideology). Given their different interests, there may be no way to rank the cognitive worth of their different findings, for their value is always relative to these different interests.

Social science information will always be evaluated in the larger society, not only from the standpoint of its correctness but, also, from that of its *relevance*. Social science may easily seem lacking in relevance and frequently is, since it is in truth untimely, at least compared with the production of news: and since it is news that constructs the public conception of relevance. Since social science implies primary rather than secondary research, systematic and comprehensive information rather than partial and fragmentary, it is both time consuming and expensive and inevitably requires subventions from "outsiders." But the interests of outsiders, however, are *not* limited to *technical* matters. Ironically, then, the technical interests justifying the social sciences always exist by the sufferance or support of powerful groups whose practical interests constitute limits within which social science's technical interests will be supported or censored. These practical interests are defined in part by the news, and by ideologues relating themselves to the news. The technical interests of social science, while quite real and autonomous, are, however, necessarily pursued within ideologically mediated, news-interpreted interests in domination, precisely to the extent that the social sciences are true to their societal mission and seek to base themselves on *primary* research.

4.3

Countercurrents, in the direction of "critical" theory or "radical" social science have thus far failed to resolve these dilemmas in their relation to the empirical. Largely united by their awareness of the limits of primary research, expressed partly in their critique of "positivism," they are often thrust back to a tacit newspaper sociology. Paradoxically, however, this does not emancipate critical theorists from the perspectives of the *status quo*, since these, of course, are built into the news (or other secondary research) on which they must now rely when they surrender primary researches of their own.

Given a commitment to protect understanding of the social world from the biasing interests of dominant societal groups, there is a tendency to surrender and sneer at primary research. But this means to reduce the sociological enterprise to a *dialectical* exploration of the "implications" of what is *said* about the social world, either by newsmen or by technical social scientists. Efforts to escape the pressures of dominant groups—and their self-serving definitions of social reality—thereby generate that distinct style of investigation known (in its *left*-wing expression) as "critique," and as "the" dialectic in some recent heresies of ethnomethodology, whose ultimate political rendez-vous is surely with the right.

For all its conscientious opposition to the *status quo*, and its sincere striving to elude the limits of a positivistic social science accommodated to What Is—and indeed, *because* of them—critique conforms to *news*-grounded conceptions of the relevant and the factual. If, to condense, critique aims at demystification, then that means to speak the silences of the ordinary language, saying what the news censors and mystifies. While seeking to transcend the news and its ordinary languages, a critical demystification that avoids primary research premises that this can be done by a "right" analysis of the news itself. Critique premises that demystification is possible by the rational rearrangement of bits of news already available. Critique assumes that we already have all the information needed, and that now the problem is to "recover" what is already known but hidden, rather than to "discover" what is unknown.

Critique thereby limits—and obscures the limits—on its own capacity to demystify the present. Critique dramatically focalizes its opposition to What Is, presenting itself as the negation of the news and of merely ideological versions of news. But critique is silent about its own abiding connections with the present, and of the areas in which it shares its assumptions. In presenting itself as a negation, critique conceals that its relation to the present is not just that of opposition, but is a love-hate relation of disunity *and unity* with it. Critique is thus commonly unable to speak the seen-but-unnoticed assumptions that it shares with, and that bind it subterraneously to, the present.

Critique thus vacillates between a rejection of the pseudodisinterestedness of positivistic social science, and a rejection of ideological mediations of the news, manifestly grounded in some partisan interest. And it is precisely because critique cannot "burn its bridges," and must share certain tacit understandings with the world it aims to transcend, that there is (1) a dissonance between critique's call for demystification and its own literary labyrinthianisms and elephantine opacity, as well as (2) a dissonance between critique's epic rhetoric of world "emancipation," on the one side, and, on the other, its essentially Fabian political practice—when it has any politics at all.

chapter 5

From the Chicago School to the Frankfurt School

This analysis of ideologies in the modern world has launched us into a larger universe of discourse: we cannot understand ideology apart from "elaborated" and "restricted" sociolinguistic speech variants, or the culture of critical speech, of the educated, of "intellectuals" and "intelligentsia." Nor can we understand ideology apart from "publics" and public educational systems, both of which are in turn linked to the "communications revolution," to newspaper and "news"; together these constitute part of the grounding for political "parties" and "movements" mobilizing "masses," and generating concern for "opinion."

1

No tradition of sociological analysis better understood the systemic character of these historically new structures than the "Chicago School" which explored them under the stimulus of such men as Robert E. Park, Charles Horton Cooley, Ernest W. Burgess, and E. W. Bogardus, between World Wars I and II. Their pioneering work, however, was limited by two weaknesses characteristic of American sociology of that period; first, a lack of historicity, and secondly, an insensitivity to class stratification, domination, and to the property ramifications of their problem.

The Chicago School saw news, newspapers and publics as an *urban* phenomenon of social psychology, and viewed "the" city as essentially similar even when encompassing greatly different class systems. Cities were viewed as a moment in the transition from "primary" to "secondary" social organization, or from *gemeinschaft* to *gesellschaft*. This abstractly formulated transition was the *de*focalized backdrop for a concern with the public and news that centered on taxonomic issues; it was a classificatory impulse that escaped empty formalism, however, because of its ingrained ethnographic interests.

Because the Chicago School's work developed through a comparative social psychology of structures such as crowds and publics, and indeed, precisely because the Chicagoans saw publics in a contrast with "the irrational" crowd, they stressed the relatively *rational* character of the public. In an essentially liberal vein, they understood the public and news media as having enhanced rationality, as a reflective and critical mode of societal discourse: "The public is any group, aggregate or non-aggregate, that achieves corporate unity through *critical* interaction. . . . The discussion of the members is on the basis of relevant facts, free from sentiment and passion, and it eventuates in a consensus that controls and guides the subsequent activity of the group. . . . In the *crowd* there is an absence of discussion, hence of *reflection* . . . in the *public,* discussion is free and unimpassioned; all relevant facts are received for consideration, divergent and conflicting opinions are expressed and evaluated, all impulses to and proposals for action are criticized in terms of past experience and probable future consequences . . . the public deliberates in regard to issues on the basis of fact and evidence . . . arrives at a consensus through the clash and modification of opinion. The crowd is ecstatic, the public, a rational group." °

1.1

For the most part, the Chicago standpoint saw the *limits* on rationality as due to largely group-activated (or condoned) "passions" grounded in individual persons, rather than in institutional or structural "interests." There was, for instance, no focus on the limits imposed on public rationality by the class and property involvements of publishers, advertisers, and readers. In noting this, however, my point is not carpingly to deny validity to what the Chicago school achieved but to note its serious limits.

It was not always as clear as it might have been, moreover (in the Chicago School's perspective on the "public,") that the very conjunction of the public with urbanism's high ecological and social mobility, individualism, family dissolution, the breakdown of neighborhoods, and personal anonymity, were themselves powerful threats to public rationality, even in the limited *sociopsychological* terms to which they attended. If a "public" implied rational discourse, these proliferating pathologies of urbanism also fostered great insecurities, anxieties, and consequent irrationalities. The Chicago sociologists, then, pioneered the systematic analysis and concrete empirical study of the public, expressly seeing it as constituting the conditions of reflective, critical discourse in modern society. It did so, however, within a

---

° E. B. Reuter and C. W. Hart, *Introduction to Sociology,* McGraw-Hill, New York, 1933, pp. 502–503. Italics added.

framework that tended to separate this rationality from simultaneous potentialities toward irrationality, often missing that a "public" implied contradictory tendencies, and rationality was, therefore, a precarious and perhaps transient phenomenon.

1.2

The Chicago School's analysis of the "news" itself was also immensely rich in opening up a sociology of rationality, even if it did not pursue its structural implications in a historical way. Robert E. Park had clearly brought his analysis of "news" to the point where he saw that news implied a concept of *objectivity* akin to that which academic sociology then accepted. Indeed, Park's sophistication concerning the construction of social reality by the news in many ways transcended that common among sociologists. Park clearly saw that "news" was a constructed account, not a mirror image of what was happening. News, in his view, was not merely "mediated" but produced by journalists. As reporters cannot be at the scene of most of the events they write about, Park saw that many news reports are "second hand," being based on what the reporter was told by someone who had been there, or on what he might glean from hearsay.

Thus Park relates the story of Samuel Johnson acknowledging that it was he who had written a famous parliamentary speech of 1741, long attributed to the elder Pitt. That speech, said Johnson, had not been heard by him but was written from notes, sent by those who had attended the House of Commons on that occasion, which he then rewrote as if it were a verbatim account. When praised for dealing out eloquence and wit with such impartiality, in the many parliamentary speeches he subsequently wrote, Johnson demurred, admitting that, while he "saved appearances tolerably well," he had also taken "care that the Whig dogs should not have the best of it." From Park's standpoint the gap between a "scientific" sociology and the everyday news was not a radical one, sociology simply being the "big" (and, presumably, more enduring) news.* Above all, Park clearly understood that the news had now become the major source for defining social reality in the modern world. Moreover, he also saw some of the specific mechanisms through which news generated a public and consensual validation of itself as a true account. The sheer "publication" of news, in and to the public, with accounts containing real names, specific dates and places, generated the impression that "it was possible for anyone concerned to check them . . ." hence, creating an

---

* R. E. Park, *Society, Collective Behavior, News and Opinion, Sociology and Modern Society*, Free Press, Glencoe, Ill., 1955, pp. 95, 81, reprinted from the *American Journal of Sociology*, March 1940.

*un*checked presumption in favor of its truth. Park addressed himself expressly to the processes by which journalism constructed a *convincing account* of social reality: "News is more or less authenticated by the fact that it has been exposed to the critical examination of the public to which it is addressed and with whose interests it is concerned. . . . The public . . . by common consent, or failure to protest, puts the stamp of approval on a published report.

Had Park any philosophical inclination, and had he not had such strong distaste for a "dialectical" sociology, he could have made an interesting contribution to a sociologically informed epistemology of contemporary relevance. Park's tacit epistemology, of course, premised in a liberal manner the availability to (alert because) interested readers—interests Park took as given—of diverse sources of potentially variable accounts of the imputedly same event. Park had correctly focalized a decisive and necessary condition of public rationality: the manner in which these very interests foster critical reflection by mobilizing attention and openness to relevant information. But he did not explore the manner in which these same interests may also *limit* rationality, by blocking efforts to bring them into question, by censoring and repressing accounts of social reality dissonant with these interests, and by dramatizing accounts consonant with them. Park also failed to weigh adequately that this was not only a matter of the interests of the *readers* but, also, of the advertisers and the owning publishers of the media.

1.3

Park thus pierced but failed to penetrate deeply the dialectic of news. He correctly saw that news came to have its own special standards, which were in a tense relationship to "editorials" and to the practical policy implications of publishers' commitments to economic, political, religious and other groups. Journalists had a special interest in news that would "interest" readers, in the specific sense of *attracting their attention* and hence holding them as buyers, and this differed from other kinds of objective interests that editorials, advertisers, and publishers sought to promote. Park saw that "news" had come to be any account of social reality that claims and holds attention, however briefly and for whatever reason.

News, then, may be interesting but, in some sense, may also be trivial. Interest and importance are thus disjoined in modern news. Even though newspapers contain information, and more information than ever, it is not necessarily such information that contributes to public rationality. To the extent that newspapers are concerned with merely being "interesting" (in the subjective sense of capturing attention), this might be done by *diminishing* the information and by increasing the "entertainment" content. To that extent, news and newspapers might then inhibit critical reflection, and constitute narcotising diversions from rationality or foster escapist, irrational fantasies.

At the same time, however, the submission of reportage to the standard of the *individually* interesting heightens the tension between societal morality and individual gratification, and so undermines conventional morality. "Yellow journalism," we might say, is a journalism that outraged middle-class sensibilities by pandering to what the *middle class* defined as the "base instincts" of the masses, of the poor, of the immigrants and the uneducated, and which failed to provide the "lower orders" with a moral indoctrination acceptable to respectable society. News, as that which seeks and holds attention, implies a *democratization of interests*, holding that all the interests of news buyers have some right to be served. The established value structure's hierarchy is thereby subverted, and news then fosters a measure of *anomie* in the world by publicly sanctioning *de*valued and, indeed, *a*moral (if not *im*moral) interests. In time, then, news comes to service and satisfy its readers' interest in violence, sex, and scandal.

It is, however, precisely because of such a democratization of interests that news develops its own special concept of objectivity. To be an "objective" reporter means to report *anything* one believes true, so long as it is expected to command readers' *attention*, even though it may oppose the editorial policies of the paper's publisher. The mechanism of such "objective" reporting is the tensionful structural separation between the paper's news and editorial departments. The news department knows when it is about to publish reports dissonant with editorial commitments, and expects it must defend itself from possible challenge. It attempts to do this, first, by seeking to establish the sheer *interest* (hence saleability) of the account, and secondly, by exerting pressure on the reporter to make his story defensible by careful investigation.

This standard of objectivity is, of course, applied *selectively*. It is more likely to be enforced when a forthcoming news account is expected (1) to command attention, and (2) to be challenged, either from within or by outsiders. Moreover, it needs adding that—whatever the separation of news and editorial departments—the publisher selects both the news and editorial staffs. Yet Park was correct: the sheer visibility of an account increases the possibility of its being challenged, especially by those whose interests it offends, or by those who have access to alternative accounts. Visibility does strengthen public rationality.

2

Nonetheless, it always remains easier to publish accounts consonant with those offered by the managers of social institutions—accounts which thereby reinforce conventional definitions of social reality and the existent system of stratification. All these contradictory tendencies make it clear that news can contribute both to the irrationality as well as to the rationality of public discourse. Seen in historical perspective, however, the important emergent is that there is any check at all. For there is now a difference in the accounts publicly given by managers of the society's institutions and organizations, and by those offered in the media, and *this* difference is an historically unique development.

News—and the development of boundaried systems of media—means that convincing accounts of social reality may now issue from different quarters. Definitions of social reality now become pluralized, but not simply in the conventionally liberal sense of their being competing newspapers, but in a far more profound way. Those who had traditionally issued authoritative accounts of social reality had been the official managers of social institutions. Those controlling social institutions had largely monopolized the presentation of authoritative accounts of their own management and had thus controlled information bearing on their own success or failure. The cardinal spoke for the church; the baron for the manor; the merchant for the enterprise; the captain for the ship; the masters for the craft. They inevitably proffered self-serving accounts that justified their own management of affairs and relieved others' concerns and anxieties about outcomes.

"News," however, as precisely the *mediation* of official accounts (and regardless of the ideology of newspapers or media) is always a selective *re*presentation. It is *not* that officials cease presenting their own accounts of their management, nor even that they have no special credit in the media. Nonetheless, the media *mediates*. Which means they select and edit, dramatizing some and repressing other events, according to their own standards and rules. They stand *between* the public, on the one side, and, on the other, the official managers of institutions, organizations, movements, or the society's hegemonic elites. Media develop their own machinery and rules for generating convincing accounts of social reality, and of what is worth featuring or reporting at all. To that extent, and quite apart from their "objectivity," media must generate accounts that differ in *some* measure (even if they do not "expose" or criticize), from the accounts rendered by social managers.

2.1

But even this does not quite fully indicate the magnitude and importance of what happens to the position of hegemonic elites and institution managers with the advent of the media, at least within a liberal democracy. The essential point is that, the media and media technicians are often prone to *negate* social reality, to present negative accounts of it, inevitably discreditable to some of the institutions and social strata discussed and to their managers, leaders, or elites. This impulse of the media to negate the society is powerfully limited by a variety of considerations, among the most important being the property and political institutions within which the media operate.

But the *tendency* to negate the society is substantially documented, despite all of Herbert Marcuse's depiction of the society as unidimensional. It has, for example, been documented repeatedly that the (American) press commonly prefers stories featuring violence and, with "reason," for readers' interest is substantially greater for stories depicting violence, and is positively correlated with the amount of violence portrayed.°

The press, in short, dramatizes violence and, more generally, features *conflict*. Indeed, this tends to be greater, the more competition there is among newspapers. It is also generally assumed by editors that a story *praising* institutional managers is less likely to be noticed, read, and remembered than a story entailing accounts of their misdeeds. Of similar import, concerning the society-negating tendencies of media, is a study of the fantasies newsmen have as they write. One of the two main types of fantasies found was that the reporter, if he wrote all he knew, felt himself to have the power to destroy his subject. Newswriters, then, often have feelings toward social institutions that are negative and critical.† It is unconvincing to believe that these negative tendencies will not, in some manner and in some degree, find their way into the published reports.

With the development of the mass media, then, modern society develops a *dual* system of generating accounts of social reality. Inevitably, these reflect on, compete with, and therefore limit one another. The development of the media means the development of a special subsystem, *not* an *independent* system, but, nonetheless, *not* a mere appendage of society's official management. With this, there is inevitably some weakening in the credibility of institutional management and of official accounts that may now be disparaged as "handouts." Authoritative accounts from official sources must now compete with media accountings and, even where they do not compete, official accounts must be transmitted *via* these media, thereby developing a measure of dependence upon them and some vulnerability to their standards.

This new vulnerability of the official managers of society grows, even though the media are only very partially and only relatively independent of them. A new historical situation has now been created for societal managers; their dealing with the public and with one another is now greatly affected by reports carried by the media. The problem of dealing with the media now becomes a central and special problem for all social institutions.

° H. P. Haskins, *Editor and Publisher*, Oct. 19, 1968, p. 38.

† I. de Sola Pool and I. Shulman, "Newsmen's Fantasies, Audiences, and Newswriting," *Public Opinion Quarterly*, vol. 23, pp. 145–158.

2.2

The managers of society are now disposed, to *some* degree, to establish control over the media. At the extreme, they impose some official system of *censorship* on it, or employ such legal instruments as the threat of libel. The emergence of the news-stimulated public intensifies the primitive threat of official censorship to public rationality. It is thus that during the Enlightenment, censorship became a major and distinct source of the alienation of the French intelligentsia. Lewis Coser puts it well: ". . . ever since the printing press made possible a wide diffusion of ideas, censorship has come fully into its own . . . an edict of April 1757 announced the death penalty for authors and printers of unauthorized books; in 1767, the parliament passed a decree forbidding anyone to write on religious questions . . . printers, booksellers, and readers of banned books were often handled with the utmost severity. . . . The forbidden books of the eighteenth century had a wider circulation than the authorized books of the preceding century. Most of the *philosophes* were by no means revolutionaries. Most were, in fact, only too willing to support an enlightened monarchy, but . . . censorship became an unintentional but powerful agency of [their] alienation. . . . Censorship contributed its share to that divorce of the intellectual from the reigning assumptions of the dominant strata that has marked modern history . . . the conflict with the censors gave authors a collective cause . . . a collective consciousness . . . [and] also motivated them to find allies in wider strata of the population . . ." [*]

This rejection of censorship was, in part, based on the grammar of modern rationality that stressed the prime rule of self-groundedness: Only the self may legitimately say what may, or may not, be spoken. It is a central premise of that rule that it is the self that best knows its own interests; that these are at one with the interests of others; and that they motivate an interest in truth. The post-Marxian and post-Freudian critique has questioned each and all of these assumptions.

That critique questions whether the self is one unified "subject" having one harmonious set of interests and, instead, sees men as self-confounded by internally antagonistic strivings. It sees limits on rationality that are built directly into the self, and correspondingly, that these limits vary with the social position occupied. "Id," "ego," and "superego" may thwart one another. If the "superego" is the individual's introjection of the group's grammar of rationality, it may be barred or bent by the lusts of the "id" or by "ego's" narcissism. Correspondingly, the fusion of ego and social privilege may transform a grammar of rationality into an instrumental strategy of

[*] Lewis Coser, *Men of Ideas*, Free Press, Glencoe, Ill., 1970, Ch. 8.

gratification. The ego takes its own survival as a given and not as a problematic object of critical reflection. It is no more prone to regard the continuation of its privileges than the continuation of its sheer existence—if it can separate the two—as an admissible question for open-minded public examination.

2.3

The critique of censorship, then, was at first an eighteenth-century rejection of the limits of rationality that saw them as external and as an offense to the sovereignty of the self. The nineteenth century, however, began exploring the possibility that the self was not unambivalently committed to a grammar of rationality. It began to be seen as a "natural" self, or as a social self constituted by class position (Marx and Engels), by collective memberships, and by the naturally or culturally given categories mediating experience (Kant or Durkheim). These, it began to believe, did not merely *limit* the achievement of rationality, but actually defined rationality. Rationality, then, was not something arrived at after one escaped from these limits, but was itself constituted by them. It was not, then, only a question of political or property interests, external censorship of the self, nor even of "self" censorship. The self and its rationality was seen as constituted, and not merely limited, by censorship, just as a country's boundary does not merely indicate the limits beyond which its power ceases, but also the borders within which it *is* operative and up to which it has already spread itself.

The possibility then emerges that censorship—as that which limits what may be spoken—is not simply a violation of rationality but one grounding for it. If there is not something one could *not say*, rationality is impossible. The grammar of rationality, like any grammar, is itself both a censor and a grounding of speech. Censorship now turned out to be a necessity of rationality. The Enlightenment had come a long way. For *some* things, the traditionalist could now claim, should not and cannot be open to question and should be taken as "given," without any need for justification. But the new grammar of rationality also meant that, in *due time*, all things, including hallowed tradition, could be subjected to critical questioning and would, sooner or later, have to justify themselves. On one side, modern rationality found itself necessarily grounded in nonrational tradition; on the other side, modern rationality was committed to the permanent revolution against tradition. It was one thing to say with Wittgenstein that, in any given argument some things could not be made problematic and had to "stand fast" but quite another to assume that what stood fast was eternal and unchanging no matter the concrete argument.

Yet if the nineteenth century transcended the limited eighteenth-century notion of censorship-as-government-suppression, by adding the notion of *psychic repression* and *social oppression,* it had nonetheless failed to transcend the first. Censorship as state suppression still existed, and grew even stronger in the twentieth century. Movements aiming to overthrow repression and oppression somehow seemed naively to assume that persons could be free in their *minds,* or in their "social" lives, even though suppressed and censored by the state. That revolutionary concept of freedom had, of course, long been congenial to Frederick the Great.

To this time, there is no struggle against censorship that does not buy one form at the expense of the other. Any critical theory of society that conflates state censorship, psychic repression, social oppression, and fails to speak of each openly and directly, serves to accommodate us to the sacrifice of one or more of them. Operating within the opportunities provided by a liberal democracy without a powerful state censorship, critical theorists all too often take the struggle against state censorship as if it was an historically secured victory, when in point of fact it is a danger that rapidly grows greater and more powerful.

Thus in an otherwise cogent analysis of various forms of "distorted communication"—directed, arrested, and constrained communication— Claus Mueller treats censorship in an unintendedly cavalier way in his cryptic, casual, and marginal discussion: "We know of censorship through history . . . in Greece, Spain, Latin America and most of the socialist countries. The nature of censorship has been covered adequately in the literature and will not be discussed here." * But the existence of censorship in (unlisted and unnamed) socialist countries must surely constitute one of the central theoretical puzzles for a generalized theory of distorted communication. It implies, at best, the substitution of one form of censorship, or distorted communication, for another. It implies that the removal of distortions grounded in private property do not at all reduce the level of distorted communication, but may indeed increase it. A critical theory focused on the problem of distorted communication sometimes appears to be drawn, against its own impulses, into a systematic neglect of the single most important and most rapidly developing form of communication distortion in the modern world: state censorship, precisely within socialist societies.

Critical theory thus appears to maintain an opening to a regressive ideology of state censorship. The further development of critical theory requires that that opening be closed. All other struggles for emancipation hinge on this point. The struggle against poverty (or for equality) is a struggle based on the accounts of social reality made by official managers or by movement leaders. Given their censorship of the media, there is no way to know what needs doing and what indeed has been accomplished. The new or old managers of

* *The Politics of Communication,* Oxford University Press, New York and London, 1973, p. 18.

society, it may be relied upon, will invariably tell us that they have done well, or at least the best that could be done, for the poor and underprivileged (considering the circumstances) and that they have, in any event, done better than their competitors would.

2.4

The problem of censorship in its "vulgar" form, as state censorship, during the Enlightenment illuminates greatly two important things: first, the nature of the modern intelligentsia and its special form of vested interest in culture and hence in advanced education, and, secondly, the bases of the intelligentsia's solidarity with that other main sector of the middle class whose interests are based on property rather than education. Much of the early solidarity between these two sectors of the middle class prior to the bourgeois revolution, and much of their subsequent conflict after it, hinges on the problem of censorship. We will be helped in understanding this if we do not confine ourselves to the offense that censorship gave to high ideals, but also (not in place of, but in addition) cast a cold eye on the injury it did to the vested interests and strivings for autonomy of the intelligentsia.

To be specific, censorship erected a barrier between writers and readers at the very moment that the opening of the literary market place began transforming writing and printed products into commodities. The opening of the literary market led writers to produce work that would interest an anonymous public; but the censors intruded on the efficient exploitation of that opportunity. The development of censorship, then, was not just *analogous* to, but was identical with, the mercantilistic intrusion by the state on the emerging businessman's access to a market. Censorship was state restriction of the production and distribution of literary commodities. (Or, to turn the matter around, protectionism was the censorship of commodity production.)

The alliance between the new intelligentsia and the emerging middle classes was cemented by their common suppression and control by the old regime. They had a clearly common enemy and could make a common cause. Censorship meant that some writers led an outlaw existence; the writer was repressed on the level of his workaday existence. Censorship also meant a limitation on the topics writers could write about. It meant pirated editions from which authors would receive no royalties at all. It meant, therefore, raising the price the public would have to pay for their commodity, without a corresponding increase in what the author received. As Lewis Coser puts it succinctly, "censorship robbed them [writers] of their audience and a major portion of their literary property."

This "grubby" side of the process, however, was not something that the new intelligentsia—wily investors and speculators that they sometimes were—commonly made the public point of their grievance. Rather, it was the liberty of all, the needs of the collectivity and of rationality itself, and the manner in which censorship crippled the "market place of *ideas*" that the writers decried. And that, indeed, was what censorship did, even though it also did more than that, badly crimping the private interests of writers. Whatever also it was, and however much it was otherwise justified, the writers' struggle against censorship was not *only* a struggle for universal freedom; it was a struggle for universal freedom that happily coincided with the writers' vested interests.

It was not only the interests of the *bourgeoisie*, then, that were rationalized and universalized by the Enlightenment but, also, the specific status and property interests of the *intelligentsia*. Censorship was a powerful grievance activating the intelligentsia to become the universalizing agency of bourgeois property. Between the political *needs* of the middle class to mobilize a public following in support of their class interests, and the successful achievement of that political aim, *there was the mediating agency of a similarly aggrieved intelligentsia.* The unique symbolic and linguistic skills of this intelligentsia were the media of that universalization; they were placed in the service of the middle class by an essentially similar threat to the intelligentsia's own special vested interests. Here, then, the two main sections of the middle class that will later split—the propertied and the educated—are as yet united.

The universalization of the struggle against the old regime was grounded in part in the old regime's *linguistic* oppression; and in its restrictions controlling the writer's work and inhibiting the sale of his labor power and literary products as commodities. The bourgeois revolution was made by an alliance between the middle class and the intelligentsia, a stratum emerging under the sponsorship of the liberal *aristocracy* and first lionized in their courtly salons. (In that sense, Nietzsche was correct in speaking of Voltaire as the last of the courtiers.) The intelligentsia gave the middle class' aspirations systematic symbolic organization and, more than that, direct access to the new media. The "bourgeois" revolution was thus uniquely grounded in an historical situation that was highly transient—where literary property and other forms of bourgeois property were commonly oppressed and therefore united. This historic alliance was soon severed when the propertied part of the middle class took hold of the political system, after winning control of the economic system. It is precisely the breakup of this alliance that made tenuous the political claims and *legitimacy* of the bourgeoisie, and always made it difficult for them to assert their hegemony openly.

The new media could and did affect political reputations and the mobilization of popular support. With the growth of the media, public repute, political credibility and legitimacy were now mediated by the media which were staffed by an intelligentsia whose vested interests were in the symbolic, cultural, and educational, rather than in older forms of property. Between the *bourgeoisie* and political legitimacy, then, there now stood the working intelligentsia (high and low), the media they worked on, and the media products they assembled and produced. In turn, two very tangible considerations of power were ultimately affected: the "morale" of police and fighting forces no longer depended on their being adequately paid; the media made "morale" a separate contingency. Through the media, there was now also the possibility of mobilizing the masses to support parliamentary factions, for voting, and indeed, for street-fighting.

2.5

What I have been suggesting, then, is that modern rationality itself came into existence along with bourgeois venality and property; the two have been both mutually interdependent and mutually contradictory. It is impossible to imagine a change in one without a change in the other; it is also impossible to imagine the *continuance* of one without a change in the other. The two have been a single whole, but a whole held together precariously and under great tension.

Whatever level of development it attains—whether entrepreneurial or corporate capitalism—the bourgeoisie and neocapitalism cannot survive without the support or tolerance of the media. The entire political system, the modern fusion of state and corporation, cannot, therefore, long survive without the intelligentsia and without its loyalty to or tolerance of that system. The political security of the bourgeoisie is now contingent on either the periodic plebiscitarian mobilization, or the neutralizing immobilization, of the public. A system of "indirect rule" is a characterizing feature of such bourgeois society, and this is inconceivable without the cooperation of sectors of the intelligentsia, once there develops a mass media intervening between the public and elites.

Their cooperation, however, becomes problematic, contingent, and precarious, after the bourgeoisie comes to power. To reiterate: cooperation between the bourgeoisie and intelligentsia grows more (not less) precarious, *after* the bourgeoisie becomes the hegemonic class. Here irony outruns the paradox. For with the political success of the bourgeoisie, the heavy-handed censorship of the old regimes, is amputated, especially in parliamentary democracies. In other words: when the bourgeoisie overthrew the old regimes and eliminated their gross, visible censorship, they also removed one of the major forces that had bound the intelligentsia to the bourgeoisie.

Moreover, as the bourgeoisie came into increasing control of the state apparatus, or allied with it, they were then held accountable for whatever continuing form of state censorship existed, and they would then become the target of an alienated intelligentsia. The bourgeoisie, as partner of the state apparatus with whatever censorship apparatus it had, soon became the butt of an increasingly alienated intelligentsia.

Moreover, with the decline in centralized state censorship, each *bourgeois* was now his own censor as a publisher and a buyer. Each was effectively able to reject literary commodities offered them on the open market by the intelligentsia. All the alienation of the intelligentsia once aroused by the state censor was now transferred to the bourgeoisie, and there arose that special form of contempt against "philistinism," directed toward those exerting censorship through their *economic* power, and who rejected what they did not believe would sell. State censors are *tyrants;* bourgeois censors are "philistines." The permeating contempt of the philistine among many sections of the intelligentsia is, in important part, a hostility towards this historically new form of censorship grounded in private property.

2.6

It is perhaps not amiss here to mention a long-familiar aspect of the life of Karl Marx. Two episodes need brief redrawing—Marx as editor *manqué* and Marx as rejected academician—because both entail forms of censorship.

The *sociological* roots of Marxism are, in important part, to be found in the radicalizing experience of the Left Hegelians with the Prussian censorship of Frederick Wilhelm IV. Philosophy, theology, and politics were here inextricably interwoven. The state censor intervened repeatedly in ways damaging to the practical interests and intellectual pursuits of the young Hegelians. Under the King's pressure, Marx's friend, Bruno Bauer, was forced from the University of Bonn in May of 1842, and with this went Marx's hopes of a normal university career. Marx was thereby forced into a career as a writer and editor where, once again, there was a confrontation with censorship.

Nicolaievsky and Maenchen-Helfen touch upon the frustrations that censorship imposed upon Marx not simply as a thinker, but also as a writer: "Only one of his literary plans was realized. The ever-increasing severity of the censorship made it impossible even to think of founding an aesthetic journal. . . . Marx's essay, "Remarks on the New Prussian Censorship of January and February 1842 . . ." was a devastating and passionate critique. It was written some eight months before Marx took over the editorship of the Cologne, *Rheinische Zeitung* that was soon closed down by the censor. Prussian censorship thus destroyed all of the young Marx's chances of a conventional career within the system. It quite literally forced him out, destroying any "material" basis that might have inhibited his further radicalization.

2.7

With the elimination of a threat common and external to them both, the different parts of the middle class increasingly grow apart; the propertied and educated segments of the middle class become mutually hostile or suspicious. While there is considerable emphasis in bourgeois society on the utilitarian significance (or relevance) of education and knowledge, there are also important factors that attenuate the utilitarianism of that sector of the middle class whose position depended on their education.

Whether "liberally" educated or educated in the civic profession, the educated sectors of the middle class are exposed to pressures transforming the individualistic and venal utilitarianism of the propertied middle classes into a *social* utilitarianism, where the standard is the usefulness of things for the collectivity. The professions also have a long and continuous history in which some *non*utilitarian orientations have been protected by collegial and professional organizations, and these "higher values" are transmitted during training in schools, polytechnic institutes, colleges and universities. To some extent, "knowledge for its own sake" is endorsed; professionals are taught that there are right ways of doing things—the technical proprieties that manifest one's professional competence; they are also taught to provide "service" to clients. The civic professions, then, whether scientific or humanistic, are somewhat uneasy about an individualistic utilitarianism, or by living absorbed in the technical problem-solving efforts—knowledge for its own sake—of their specialty.

Some of the most significant tensions of modern society derive from these differences between the educated or professional sectors of the middle class, the intelligentsia, on the one side and the propertied part, on the other. One contemporary expression of that tension arises when education comes to be administered by the educated sectors of the middle class, and when even the children of the propertied middle class come under such tutelage, thereby being exposed to values diverging from their parents'. Another important modern expression of this split in the middle class arises with the later development of the so-called Welfare State, which is more congenial to the social utilitarianism of the educated professionals than to the more individualistic utilitarianism of the propertied middle class.

The Welfare State is also more directly advantageous to the professional, educated sector of the middle class which can pursue careers as functionaries, staff experts, and servicers of the State. The Welfare State, then, constitutes itself as an alliance between the state apparatus—which is the largest and fastest growing sector of the "tertiary," nonindustrial work force—and the educated sectors of the middle class, whose operations are financed by taxation costly to the propertied middle class, and thus more likely to be resisted by them. "Within the services area, it is government and non-profit employment that has expanded the most. Between 1929 and 1960, non-profit and government-employment more than tripled, while total employment and services-producing employment each less than doubled. Furthermore, it is at the state and local levels, the places human services are actually delivered, where the greatest increases in employment have occurred. . . . In 1947, government employment amounted to some 35 percent of manufacturing employment; by 1972, it was 70 percent." ° Finally, and it is this that we will develop in a later volume on *Revolutionary Intellectuals*, the split in the middle class between those grounded in property and those grounded in education is central to the radicalization of the intelligentsia and thus to the development and spread of the revolutionary social movements of the twentieth century.

The alienation of the Enlightenment intelligentsia from the old regime had been spurred by a drastic and visible censorship. The alienation of the post-Enlightenment or romantic intelligentsia was fostered by the new *bourgeois* form of censorship. If the support given by the intelligentsia to middle-class politics had been grounded in the alienation wrought by old regime censorship, so, too, was the intelligentsia's support for the new grammar of *rationality* that universalized the special historical requirements of the bourgeoisie.

Let us then say it as plainly as possible: in part, the elaborated sociolinguistic speech variant, with its culture of critical speech, is a grammar of rationality—an historical, not an eternal rationality—that grounds the various, specific ideologies but is, in itself, the shared ideology of different secularized intelligentsia. That grammar of rationality was always an ideology supportive of the special status interests and social position of the intelligentsia themselves.

This grammar of rationality was an "ideology" partly in the sense that it was functional for the vested property interests of the intelligentsia. Based on the prime injunction of *self-groundedness*, the new rationality justified the transformation of culture, science, and literature into a commodity, payment which could now be claimed by individuals.†

° Alan Gartner and Frank Riessman, *The Service Society and the Consumer Vanguard*, Harper & Row, New York, 1974, p. 57 A.

† To the extent that culture products (including the scientific) were publicly defined either as dependent on an established secular tradition, on a sacred tradition, or on religious revelation, then their products were not "their" products; they belonged instead to the "public domain" or to the church, or, as among the Pythagoreans, to the godhead. The individual producer therefore had no right to individual gains based on the production of literary products whose sale was protected by "copyright" law. The writer-scholar could at most claim a living simply as a member of a group, such as a university or churchly order. (His rights were based on his *needs*, not his literary production.) Nor had the writer any basis for demanding to judge whether his work deserved publication; this, rather, would reside in the established authorities in charge of the tradition, whether secular or sacred.

The self-groundedness central to the modern grammar of rationality is expressive of, and consonant with the special social position of the modern intelligentsia. It is conducive to their vested interests, on the one hand, and on the other, it is cognitively harmonious with their everyday life and with their mundane experience. It is for both reasons that the modern grammar of rationality is the modern intelligentsia's special ideology. That same self-grounded grammar of rationality was an instrument used by the intelligentsia in its struggle for power against the bourgeoisie and clergy. The "warfare betwen science and religion" was not based so much on the specific theories or discoveries of particular sciences, but on the common grammar of rationality all of them shared, and most especially, on their tenet of self-groundedness which was dissonant with Christianity's claims for a supreme being over man.

A self-grounded rationality is the ideology of these new "cosmopolitan" citizens of the World, an intelligentsia defining themselves as above nationalist prejudices (until it comes time to vote war budgets); an intelligentsia whose travels, audiences, and markets allow them to elude the controls of family, neighborhood, and province, as well as of country; and who, even before that, had already begun to break from these older structures, leaving home to attend "public" schools in an isolated and protected site—being itself protected by the claim of self-groundedness—and within which, like-minded students could develop ties of intimacy that strengthened their resistance to parental definitions of social reality. Ultimately, the university becomes a larger and more hallowed coffee house, the holding company of many coffee houses, within which varied forms of "organized deviance" could be cultivated and protected.

The morality of self-groundedness is an ideology congenial to cosmopolitans who can move between cities, between countries and, also, between social classes. Men without property themselves, the new intelligentsia that emerged among the liberal aristocracy had a social position largely dependent, at first, on their superior education. They advance their careers by transforming the culture they produce into saleable commodities; the new intelligentsia *capitalized* its culture. It traded repute for income, and it utilized its education as a cultural capital with which to advance itself. The new intelligentsia lived between the established property classes; between countries and cities; and beyond the control of families and neighborhoods. Central to this capacity to loosen the control of these structures is, of course, the development of a market for literary and cultural products, and which also enables cultural producers to escape the limits imposed by individual patrons, whether of the great bourgeoisie or the liberal aristocracy.

With the development of the mass media, the economic possibilities of the new market place for culture become actualized. Writers can increasingly make a living from their writing. If they have thus substituted the controls of the market for the controls of the patron, it needs to be added that market controls have a certain invisibility, as Adam Smith long ago noted. One is now subject to the impersonal "laws" of the market. A manifest personal "enslavement" has thus given way to a universal constraint which, while powerful, is less visible. The new market for culture products generated a less personal, hence less visible, unfreedom. The cultural producer selling his cultural product is, moreover, now faced with those with whom he can argue, bargain, and negotiate—with editors and publishers—whom he may see as (and who are) suffering a similar constraint, and as transmitting the domination of an anonymous "public," the ultimate, faceless philistine.

This new intelligentsia, then, in its own self-understanding, now makes its way in the world freely and "self-grounded": bowing neither to church nor to patron; free of official control by a state censor; able (via the market) to escape one buyer by selling to another; and able to compensate for the system's control over him by an overweening sense of his own cultural superiority, and by contempt for the ultimate consumers of his products, the "philistine" public. Moreover, even the hegemonic classes in society develop a need for the intelligentsia to help maintain their system of Indirect Rule. Having separated the hegemonic elites and the public, the media (could now) allow the intelligentsia to feel that they, too, are principals, self-grounded gatekeepers between elites and publics.

All this is only the briefest sketch of the institutional and structural conditions contributing to the sense of self-groundedness, and thus to the historically modern form of rationality, seen as the special status ideology of the modern intelligentsia.

2.8

One other consideration is important in the social *psychology* of that self-groundedness. This involves the differences between the traditional forms of face-to-face communication characteristic of pre-bourgeois communication, and the media-centralized system that follows. In media-organized communication there is, as noted earlier, not much chance of feedback to the media senders. The "massified" receiver gets the message and, as it were, goes to ground. He cannot become involved in a dense, multimodal, ongoing pattern of social interaction with the media centers, but can, for the most part, talk only with others like himself.

The new communication media (at least for so long as they were primarily printed), thus created a cleavage between information and affect or attitude. "Information," is in *that* sense the *de*contextualization of cognition; it is the relative isolation of cognition from other parts of personality, particularly from structures of feeling. I have argued earlier that this is one source and characteristic of modern rationality itself. Related to this are other important implications of this split. One is that it transforms "commands" powerfully, for they, like "reports," tend to become "spiritualized" and cognitive. The command now simply conveys *information* about what the media center wants *done*. There is a kind of emasculation of commands as they become reduced to their cognitive contents. Commands lose their power, while reports win conviction, as information becomes decontextualized and split from feeling. This is inherent in print-grounded systems of media, but not in all.

This split is one of the historically unique groundings of the split between "theory and practice." Polemical reaffirmations of the "unity of theory and practice"—as in Marxism—seek to transcend this dissociation between the "is" and the "ought," between feelings and information. This dissociation was also contributive to the new, secularized idealism operating in a universe of discourse that premised a print-grounded system of decontextualized, sentiment-"detached" information.

In this respect, it is interesting that Auguste Comte's preview of normal academic sociology expressly characterized it as an effort to speak about the social world without allocating "praise or blame." In other words, in a specifically nonexpressive language. But, at the same time, Marx and Engels were also moving toward a conception of socialism, and toward a doctrine of the unity of theory and practice, that demarcated theirs from other socialisms by polemically rejecting moralizing "sentimentality." Clearly then, their "scientific" socialism, like Comte's "scientific" sociology, is not only an effort to appropriate the new prestige of specific natural sciences; it is, even more specifically, grounded in the tacit premises of a sentiment-excluding, decontextualizing, notion of information and of the relatively context-free elaborated speech variant that grounds even the natural sciences themselves. Now, given this sentiment-excluding, decontextualizations of print-grounded media, ideas become isolated; ideas can then become *the* Idea. Ideas seem so radically self-grounded that they are now understood as not only free of the social but also, of the psychological groundings of individual persons. The "Idea" could then emerge as the heroic protagonist of that secular passion play, objective philosophical idealism, featuring an Idea allegedly having its own history and cosmic unfolding.

It was exactly such an *objective* philosophical idealism that Hegel had developed. And it was by replying to exactly that idealism that Marxism established its own character as a *re*contextualizing social theory.

The grammar on which all classical ideologies rests requires (1) the "unity" of theory and practice, and stresses (2) the power of consciousness, speech, the Idea—"generic ideology," as I have called it. This grammar of ideology premises an experience with printed media that splits information from feeling. In one part, then, ideology may be understood as a transformative mediation of news that reacts against and seeks to overcome affect-bleached, detached cognition; prodding it to feel and to act; to overcome inertia and passivity; to transcend the *spectator role* induced by the reporting of reified news, whose daily presentation inherently induces readers to view the world as a "spectacle," whose succeeding acts they must await in forthcoming issues.

I have also said above that "generic ideology," the "pathetic fallacy" of the autonomy of Ideas, is likewise grounded on experience with the print-induced decontextualizations that exclude affectivity. It, too, is, I hold, a part of the universal grammar of ideologies. The question, of course, arises as to how, in what way or to what degree, Marxism—which polemically and firmly opposes itself to philosophical idealism—also shares *that* part of the grammar of ideology. This is a problem to which I hope to return in a separate volume focused on Marxism.

chapter 6

Toward a Media-Critical Politics

The analysis of the public as a sphere of rational discourse—of reflective and critical discourse—that had been stimulated by the Chicago School well before World War II languished without significant development until 1962, when Jürgen Habermas published his *Strukturwandel der Öffentlichkeit: Untersuchungen zu einer Kategorie der Bürgerlichen Gesellschaft.*° There is both continuity and basic discontinuity with the earlier Chicago view and that developed by the young Habermas—then more largely under the influence of the Horkheimer-Adorno formulation of Critical Theory.

1

The Chicago view of the "public" had been largely taxonomic and positivistic, liberal in its political assumptions and therefore both optimistic and lacking in historical perspective. It manifested an almost total inability to analyze the public in relation to the emergence and transformation of bourgeois society. Habermas, on the other hand, used analysis of the public sphere as a decisive occasion to explore the prospect of a politics based on critical and reflective discourse. His central aim was to begin clarifying the possibility and requisites of rational discourse in modern society. This is one of the main continuities in his theoretical work, amplified in his present "linguistic turn" and leading to his effort to clarify the requisites of "communicative competence," an effort that generalizes on Noam Chomsky's notion of a more limited *linguistic* competence, and Dell Hymes' work on communicative competence. What Habermas did was to transform his formulation of the problem of rationality. In the *Strukturwandel* the problem

° Cf. the very concentrated statement by Habermas in the Fisher Lexicon, *Staat and Politik*, Frankfurt, 1964, pp. 22–26. An English translation of this appears in *New German Critique* Fall, 1974, pp. 49–55.

138

had been cast in terms of an historically specific and *societal* analysis focusing on the emergence of bourgeois society. With his focus now on communicative competence, the problem of rationality was considered in a less historical and less institutionally specific way. The analysis now moved to the more abstract social *systems* (rather than societal) level, focusing on the interaction of *any* two actors; it is thus akin to a Parsonian ego-alter model. This transition in levels was mediated by Habermas' critical assimilation of ordinary language philosophy, sociolinguistics, and a philosophical version of communications theory.

The continuity, then, is largely a continuity of his value problematic: the investigation of the social conditions requisite for rational discourse, i.e., of undistorted, nonideological communication. In taking the fulfillment of this value as pivotal, and in organizing his historical researches around it, Habermas situates himself firmly within the tradition of a critical theory clearly demarcated from the nondialectical sociology of the Chicagoans. It is in this value-grounding of his historical researches, openly making rationality his central problematic, that Habermas makes his most important contribution. In my own view, the more recent linguistic reformulation and change to the social system level is too early to judge in terms of its actual contribution to that problem. The yield for the problem, the illumination it provides of the specific social requisites of rationality seems extremely low, up to this time; certainly its penetration of that problem seems negligible compared to the vast textual discussions and intense philosophical explorations, on which Habermas' work is, in general, commonly grounded.

In his early work, Habermas stressed the historical newness of the emergence of the public sphere and noted that whole new sectors of public life had been opened up to critical discussion—religion, family life, sex. There was developed in the sphere of the bourgeois public a model (part reality and part idealization) of a discourse free of the threat of violence and domination —but which was in fact limited by the actual inequality of persons in bourgeois society. The bourgeois public was thus not only a sphere of liberation but, also, of false consciousness. Habermas realized that the bourgeoisie's opening of the public sphere involved their pursuit of partisan class interests that coincide only temporarily with a larger, more universal interest, but which in time diverge.

In time, the bourgeoisie generates a style of life that blurs the private sphere's distinction from the public, and that places both increasingly under the domination of growing corporate organizations. Bourgeois culture becomes a culture of consumers, rather than of critically questioning and politically concerned persons, of spectators who are now to be entertained. Critical individualism is attenuated as people are assimilated into the growing private and government bureaucracies. Once a sphere for critical discourse among persons, now the "public" is superseded, managed and manipulated by large organizations which arrange things among themselves on the basis of technical information and their relative power positions. The "public," then, no longer connects the state apparatus with the everyday life of society. Politics becomes managed by the corporate associations and by the state. People increasingly reject politics and seek psychological individuation through the exploration of privatized (or depublicized) life styles.

The public sphere, then, tends to disintegrate with the development of bourgeois society. As the entrepreneur is replaced by the "organization man" under bureaucratic control and is subjected to the influence of mass media selling entertainment as culture, and as organizational management operates with internal technical investigations of its problems, the public loses its ability to participate critically and reflectively in the political process.

Habermas thus links both the emergence and deterioration of rational public discourse to the evolution of the bourgeois economy. Bourgeois individuation gives way to the dominance of corporative forms within which discussion is not public but is increasingly limited to technicians and bureaucrats. The excluded "public"—the public that has not yet been privatized and "dropped out"—now becomes a condition of organizational action, to be instrumentally managed—i.e., manipulated.

1.1

Yet in grounding this historically specific rationality in bourgeois society, Habermas is not to be read as arguing that it is the bourgeois *class* structure *per se* that generates the essential limit on rationality. Certainly, the inequality of a bourgeois class and property system contradicts the ideal of the public the bourgeoisie had fostered. If I read Habermas rightly, however, what he is suggesting is that the historically specific class system is only the intervening variable of *domination*. It is domination, then, that is held to be fundamentally inconsistent with the requisites of a rational public, and such domination can be found before and can persist even after the passing of the bourgeoisie.

Thus even the revolutionization of bourgeois society *need* not remove the conditions destructive of public rationality; for *domination* may be grounded in *political* power, no less than in property advantages; people who have the power to shoot or to put their opponents in concentration camps can stop or distort a discussion just as effectively as those who can withdraw advertising from privately owned papers,· or starve striking workers into submission. If such political power persists after the bourgeoisie have been removed, then domination remains, and with it the corruption of public rationality and the depoliticization of the masses. It is domination, whether mediated by economic or by political power, that subverts rationality; a class system, such as that of the bourgeoisie, is only one intervening mechanism conveying domination and thereby limiting rationality.

Habermas' focus on domination is based on his refusal to *identify* capitalism and the capitalist class with the corruption of public rationality. This, in turn, is grounded in his experience of the political catastrophe of Stalinism and in a concern to prevent its recurrence, as well as in his own experience of Nazism.

The occasionally strange, tortured, if not Aesopian, formulations of Habermas may obscure the fact that the foundation of his social theory is fundamentally his concern with *freedom* from domination and terror, and with *freedom* as the ground of rationality. It is this value grounding that *unifies* his response to the historically overlapping phenomena of Stalinism and Nazism. For both entailed a transcendence of familiar bourgeois society but, nonetheless, both obviously remained profoundly irrational. By the end of World War II, however, this assessment was already the common achievement of Horkheimer and Adorno; it was, we might say, their legacy to Habermas.

By the time of writing *Strukturwandel*, however, something different was emerging in German politics, particularly among radicalized university students. The manipulated hostility toward Soviet Communism, as an instrument in the "cold war," was then in the process of being shunted aside by the New Left, as an impediment to any radical effort that went beyond liberalism or social democracy. The emergence of the youth movement of the 1960s launched a renewed politics of anticapitalism and an affirmation of social equality. The German student movement, like its counterparts elsewhere, was often swept by a revulsion against the bourgeois press. The New Left escalated its activity and promoted a politics that often seemed (at least to others) more like the surrealistic dramaturgy of a spectacle than a true revolution.

Although deeply involved in the organization and struggles of the German youth movement, Habermas also sensed its openness to irrationality and its profound ambiguity about freedom. On one occasion, Habermas spoke publicly of the danger of a Left Fascism *(Links Fascismus)*—a term never to be forgiven by the dogmatic segment of the left. While some regard this phrase as an unfortunate inadvertence, I suspect it to be a clear symptom of Habermas' enduring dilemma—which is partly responsible for his failure to bring his theory to some politically manageable focus.[*]

The dilemma is that Habermas' theory is value-grounded in his concern with freedom,[†] but the practical politics of the Left centers less on freedom

---

[*] Cf. the view of Dick Howard, "A Politics in Search of the Political," *Theory and Society*, Fall, 1974; pp. 271–306.

[†] For Habermas, for example, a "public sphere" is one in which a public opinion can be

than equality. In its struggle to extend equality, the Left sometimes manifested an indifference to already institutionalized spheres of freedom in parliamentary societies, and tended to deprecate them as a disguise for class domination, rather than to foster them as necessary and valuable. Many on the Left one-sidedly "unmasked," discredited, and undermined these liberties, and began to reproduce conditions reminiscent of the Weimar Republic preceding the advent of Nazism.

Habermas sought to integrate classical German philosophy's stress on freedom with socialism's stress on equality in a transcending linguistic theory of "communicative competence." He sought to establish the character of "the ideal speech" situation that would permit *all* to participate in a public discourse productive of truth, freedom, and justice, and which discourse would constitute the site of a developing *rationality*. The philosophical foundations for this, and for Habermas' larger "communication theory of society," are extensive and cannot be discussed now in any detail. What interests us *here*, rather, is the sociologically concrete specifications of the "ideal speech situation." Once seeing its implications at the level of praxis, one may better understand why Habermas' theory has been accused of lacking a "politics."

2

Four "simple" elements seem crucial for the practical production of Habermas' ideal speech situation—(1) no violence, (2) permeable boundaries between public and private speech, (3) allowance of traditional symbols and rules of discourse to be made problematic, and (4) insistence on equal opportunities to speak. (Claus Mueller is particularly clear that the society-wide media must be accessible to all, although his formulation of the open, nondistorting ideal speech situation—to which I shall return—is formulated with more specificity at the societal and institutional level.) A few comments about each of these may quickly indicate the scope of the problem and how unresolved it yet remains.

First, there is no doubt that the existence of violence makes it impossible for many to speak clearly or truly, to themselves or others: violence commonly distorts communication. But if this was all there was to the matter, the torture of captured enemy personnel—a common practice by military and paramilitary forces throughout the world today—would make no sense. (In antiquity, it was also commonly assumed that slaves could best be believed only under torture.) Under *some* conditions, then, it seems violence is

---

formed via unrestricted conversation, and with institutionalized freedom of assembly, freedom of association, and freedom of speech. Cf. the Fisher Lexicon article, ibid., p. 220.

expected to (and perhaps *does*) *remove,* rather than impose, communication distortions. Indeed, under some conditions violent actions themselves constitute *ambiguity-reducing communications,* unmistakenly saying where those who engage in them stand, and what they are willing to do to achieve their ends. If some group says, "we are prepared to kill to achieve our ends," can they state that with any greater *clarity* than by killing? Moreover, must we necessarily and invariably regard this as a rationality-*reducing* statement? If this communicative action makes viewers better aware of the speakers' true character and motives, does this not, to that extent, also make *them* capable of more rather than less rationality? Violence plainly indicates that some things are not open to discussion—it marks the limits. At the same time, however, violence may also motivate men to enter, rather than avoid, discussion *within* those limits, and to bring that discussion to some conclusive agreement. Let me say it plainly: I find violence detestable; but I remain unconvinced about the conventional argument that it is always and necessarily inimical to *rationality.*

Physical violence is the deliberate infliction of pain injurious to animal survival or bodily integrity. Beyond physical violence, there is also, as Pierre Bourdieu reminds us, "symbolic" violence; the use of symbolic means to inflict pain and impose costs on others; which is to say, symbolic violence is speech intended to hurt others' "feelings," their self-regard or their sense of security; or which is understood by the speaker to have that *effect* on the listener, even if that is not his intent. Such symbolic violence, no less than physical violence, may also inhibit and distort communication. But to call someone's attention to the fact that he is impairing or violating the requirements of rationality, or the ideal speech situation, may hurt him deeply. Should we then forgo *all* symbolic violence? Does not rationality require that persons be socialized to place so high a value on having a *rational self,* that they will be *pained* to be told they are behaving nonrationally? Indeed, is not the ability to feel pain at one's own nonrationality conducive to increased rationality?

Second, that there should be no compulsive, rigid, and unexaminable barriers between the private and public is eminently desirable for rational discourse. And who decides which of these barriers may be violated or must be respected, should also be open to examination. But to say (or imply) that *all* barriers between the private and public are to be removed, or should be considered suspect, is quite another matter. There is no reason why anyone should be allowed or encouraged to say publicly anything that comes into his head; and there is no reason why everyone should be obliged to hear out *any*thing that someone wishes to speak.

Unless there is *some* limit on what may be said, when, and to whom, there is no possible predictability in human discourse, and no possible way of maintaining a consistent and logical line of discourse. Without such a limit, any reasonable discussion may at any time be disrupted indefinitely by the acted-out fantasies or autisms of one of the parties. Rationality does, of course, require that certain persons should be available to others at certain times and under particular conditions, persons with whom one may ventilate one's fears, anxieties, or express one's fantasies. It is the institutionalization of such a social desideratum that *is* a matter of the common, public interest. But it is not in the common interest that each may say anything, to any one, at any time.

Much the same may be said about making traditional rules and symbols open to critical reexamination. No rule or symbol should be given *compulsive* conformity, nor should anything be done to foster *such* conformity. Nonetheless, it is impossible to examine critically *all* traditions at the *same* time. Habermas knows this, but my impression is that certain other critical theorists do not. For then, nothing would be speakable, and we would have to remain silent, since there can be no language that is totally self-grounded, self-constituted, and self-justified. We are then back to the limits of Gödel's Theorem. But there is no good reason why anything once taken as given and beyond examination cannot, in time, be reconsidered and made problematic. To make all things problematic at the *same* time is conducive not to rationality, but nihilism.

2.1

Finally, there is the question of the role of equality in the "ideal speech" situation. Fundamentally, equality is a value-affirmation which one group makes as a *critique* of the privileges held dear by another group, *but which are irrelevant to its own values.* Bureaucrats and bureaucracies thus "level" the privileges of the traditional aristocracy. Again, as Max Weber indicated, churches tend to democratize the dispensation of grace, making it accessible to all their members, and thus churches "fight principally against all virtuoso-religion and against its autonomous development." Equality is the leveling of differences that are valued by some group other than the "levelers," but it is never the leveling of *all* differences.° For the equalizers themselves always affirm some high value—in the ideal speech situation, truth and justice—and they must thus differentiate those who most exemplify or produce that high value. The ideal speech situation thus generates a *new* system of stratification, rather than abolishing all; its affirmation of equality is

° No one calls for compulsory plastic surgery to make all equally beautiful, for compulsory surgery, to make the smaller as big as the taller; for compulsory drug injections to make all equally great lovers or thinkers. And why should some, simply because they happened to be born earlier than others, be denied an equal prospect of future longevity? In fine: the inequalities condemned, and the equalities demanded, are always highly *selective*. But on what standards?

a way of excluding the interests and pressures that other groups exert on behalf of different values. It is noteworthy that in stressing the centrality of freedom, truth, and justice in the ideal speech situations, a certain ambiguity is injected concerning equality. The focus on "justice" serves as a kind of equality-container, or equality-substitute and, perhaps, as a *sublimation* of equality, much as it was for Plato.

Claus Mueller's effort to develop Habermas' theory of communication requires persons to share a language at the same level of linguistic competence, and also requires them to have a similar semantic, syntactical, and lexical knowledge. The question arises, however, whether such equality is preferable to that inequality in which the less competent can learn from the more competent. A group can consist of linguistic equals, but their equality may be at a commonly *low* level of competence. Is it better for such low competence speakers to be kept together, or to be separated from one another and, as it were, "bussed" into groups with those more competent? From Mueller's standpoint, it might seem that children should talk only to one another, never with adults. (Again, one is reminded of the Platonic fantasy of separating all youth from their parents at an early age to prepare them for the ideal Republic.)

Assuming an initial equality of linguistic competence, what must also be assumed about its subsequent development? Do the parties involved stop developing linguistically and thereby maintain their equality? Will they always change and improve, but at an equal rate of improvement? If they develop *un*equally, what is to be done about the new inequality produced by the initial equality? If one represses the faster learner, then the ideal speech situation has suddenly metamorphosed into a new system of repression. Or does one disregard these emerging inequalities, simply *defining* everyone as equal, no matter how their performances differ? But then the ideal speech situation has been transformed into the breeding ground of a new false consciousness. Or, does one remove the faster learner, relocating him with others of a like high competence? Here the ideal speech situation is generating a whole new system of stratification among groups who, while internally equal, are unequal to other groups.

Clearly, communicative competence implies linguistic competence. Even in the ideal speech situation, persons of different language histories, linguistic competence, and linguistic codes would be brought into interaction with one another. Whose language or code would be used when these differ? If the choice is made to establish communication only among those already equal or similar, does this not immediately set up patterns of speech segregation and stratification? If a situation akin to speech-"bussing" is arranged, with less competent speakers brought together with the more competent speakers, who decides, and how, whose language or code will be used in their intercommunication? Insofar as communicative competence entails linguistic competence, there would seem an inevitable moment of domination embodied in choosing the concrete language (or specific code) to be used for communication, exactly as there is in teaching children their first language.

To labor the obvious: I have not meant to enter upon a systematic exploration of the problems presented by the notion of an ideal speech situation, or of communicative competence in general, but only to open up this matter sufficiently to exhibit plainly the ambiguities involved. For one suspects that it is these ambiguities that generate so much of the distorted communication about communicative distortions.

2.2

The failure of Habermas' theory to effect a polity derives partly from its being grounded in a value commitment divergent from that of "normal" radical politics which, whether of the New or Old Left, was *always* more committed to equality than to freedom. The left—at least the nonsocialist or nonsocial democratic left—has commonly refused to make freedom under socialism problematic, and more recently, has sometimes stolidly acted as if Stalinism was simply a myth invented to slander the left. The New Left of the 1960s tended to focus on issues of personal—e.g., sexual—freedom, and on political freedom defined as diffuse and spontaneous "participation." But the real political work of the movement was its struggle to extend equality. There was, then, a real difference between a sector of the New Left and Habermas.

Habermas' theory of communicative competence may be read in this way: as an effort to extend, to generalize, and to consolidate a new theory of *censorship*. The theory of communicative competence may be seen as a new critique of censorship. It seeks to go beyond Enlightenment rationalism with its focus on churchly superstition and governmental censorship, to the manner in which the structure of communication allows some issues to be seen and spoken, while inhibiting and diverting attention from still others. Language behavior is seen as the intervening variable between social institutions, the class system, and the state, on the one side, and, on the other, persons' capacity to interpret the social world rationally and do something with others to change it. It is in this linguistic emphasis that Habermas moves to generalize a critique of censorship, the linguistic providing a framework within which he can encompass characterological inhibitions and irrationalities implanted by socialization in particular types of family systems, and the limits imposed on language behavior by the class system and class origins of the speaker, along with more familiar forms of censorship by the state apparatus. These diverse institutional strands are now drawn together in their ultimate effects on language use in public discourse.

But it is precisely because of the focus on the role of language, as an intervening variable standing between the inputs of dominant institutions and established arrangements, on the one side and, on the other, persons' behavior in everyday life and politics, that this theoretical gain also generates a sense of the theory's political irrelevance. For while the language level is an essential mediating element (most directly affecting the quality of public discourse and political behavior), language is not *easily* accessible as a lever of political intervention for emancipatory change.

2.3

Another dimension is added if we notice that complaints that Habermas' theory lacks a politics are operating with a concept of politics that is largely unexamined. Thus, it may not be that Habermas' theory lacks a practice; it may be quite consistent with a *new* practice, but one the left does not regard as a *politics*. Seen from the standpoint of the kind of practice it implies, it may be that the "praxis" consistent with Habermas' ideal speech situation is that found in the early "group dynamics" movement launched by Kurt Lewin, by the Bethel Laboratory with its training or "T" groups, by Moreno's psychodrama and sociodrama, and by their more recent derivatives, "encounter," "sensitivity-training," and "co-counselling" groups. All this suggests that there *is* an organizational infrastructure and, indeed, a social movement to which Habermas' linguistic theory of communicative competence corresponds, and for which it may supply a certain philosophical foundation. But this is to find the *practice* of "communicative competence" in the newer counterculture, rather than in the party vanguards familiar to the left. From the standpoint of the left, this will be taken to mean that Habermas has "no" politics or no "serious" politics. In truth, however, such a judgment may simply mean that the Left has a very limited concept of politics and—we will return to this later—it may be that it is the left whose politics is reactionary.

Habermas' theory will be judged *a*political by those operating with an historically limited Leninist conception of politics-as-revolution-via-vanguard party, for whom the paradigm of revolution is the October Revolution of 1917. From *that* standpoint and in *that* interpretation of what is politically relevant, Habermas' theory will seem politically unproductive. But such a critique is limited by its own truncated historical perspective. For in a longer historical horizon one would have also seen that in the historical transformation through which capitalism itself came into power, political revolution was only one moment in a longer process. It was at best a culmination of the slow transformation of the consciousness, of the social relationships of everyday life, and of the new forces of production and communication. Modern capitalism had a complicated development of which the Revolution of 1789 was the political climax, and of which the Reformation was an important stage.

Partly as a reaction to Oblomovist passivity, Leninism fostered a compensating fantasy of the power of planned revolutionary initiatives—a fantasy which underestimated the initiative of ordinary people, as well as the significance of the vast variety of changes that had to occur before vanguard initiatives could begin to succeed. Vanguard initiatives have generally succeeded only in relatively underdeveloped areas where (or because they were underdeveloped) the vanguard did not confront a well-developed state apparatus; and/or where the state's armies had been crushed by another state; and/or where the state had little access to the mass mobilizing power of a modern technologically advanced media. Vanguard initiatives have only succeeded where mass loyalties to the state were undermined by vast military catastrophes, and by the humiliating subservience of its own elite to the imperialism of aliens and foreigners.

These several concrete conditions largely account for the success of vanguards such as the Bolsheviks or the Chinese and Indo-Chinese Communist Parties. With their conquest of state power, however, conditions changed substantially because vanguards elsewhere could use them as a buffer and from whom they could receive military training, hardware, and other resources, in the inaccessible "hinterland" where state power had already changed hands. Communist accession to power in Czechoslovakia, for instance, had little to do with the successful initiative of the local Communist vanguard and much to do with the Soviet military presence. This, of course, is not revolution but military conquest, a kind of Bonapartist exportation of new forms at the point of bayonets, which the Soviet Marshal Tukhachevsky once advocated as "revolution from without." These are tactics to which underdeveloped areas are vulnerable.

Within advanced industrial nations, whether the USA or the USSR, revolutionary vanguards waiting an opportunity to "pick up power in the streets" in a moment of chaos, will wait in vain. But while waiting, they will be manipulated and infiltrated by highly trained antirevolutionary and antiterrorist state agencies, who will subject them to technologically advanced surveillance, to infiltration by medically conditioned and controlled informers and provacateurs, to counterterrorism including assassination—as well as to legal pressure and media influence. The West, therefore, must have its reformation before it can have its revolution. The theory appropriate to such a social strategy is a critical theory focused on the production of change in language, in communication, and in media. Habermas' work may be read as a contribution to *such* a politics and to such a conception of revolution. The theory premises that "Der Weg . . . ist der Umweg." And those seeing this as "resignation" or "accommodation" have simply not begun to understand the difference in mass suffering in the West as compared to the Third World.

2.4

The politics of a linguistically grounded critical theory raises the question of how *change* in a linguistic code or communication practices can be achieved as a matter of *political* effort. For one thing, the theory must take into account the fact that language behavior has long been affected by initiatives of the state apparatus. The modern state has traditionally but profoundly affected language through proliferating schools and by the reform and extension of modern mass education, over which the state soon won nearly complete hegemony. Governments have also affected language behavior by influence on the media, via direct censorship, through pressure exerted by the licensing system, as well as by more diffuse impositions in the form of legal action or taxes.

In organizing a politics against censorship in modern society, critical theory needs an emphasis on the institutions connecting the state and language, the most important of these being the media and the public school systems. In focusing on the special role of the State, as a source of language-consequential initiative and as a focus for a counterpolitics, I have certainly not meant to suggest that a social theory sensitive to the linguistic and communications dimension should limit itself to the search for political leverage. On the contrary, the repressive censorial consequences of class inequalities or of sexist family structures can be countered directly as well as by political pressure on state policy and the media. Finally, although we cannot elaborate on it here, it needs remembering that an inescapable medium of politics—its sociological infrastructure—is face-to-face communication. Such communication can, and commonly does, serve as an instrument by which established "opinion leaders" transmit and reinforce media messages. But it can also foster a critical view of the media and implant a new language, a new set of values, skills, and a body of information, at variance with those supported by the dominant media. The elemental speech process remains a fundamental agency for the distancing of persons from old languages and unexamined lives; word-of-mouth is the ultimate medium of the masses, if not the newest innovation in mass media.

In the end, there is probably no more powerful mechanism of social change than people's talk. In a society where there is a constant tendency for the growth of centralized media, distant and unresponsive to persons who have no real opportunities for feedback, the real impact of the mass media will often be considerably less than it is thought to be by those who point with alarm to—or who profit from—their growth. The relation between personal speech and the media is a complex one that changes with the development of the media themselves. While studies of political persuasion still leave much unanswered about this connection, the classic work by Paul Lazarsfeld and his colleagues in 1944 is still reliable. They found that "the effect of the media to be rather small. . . . People appeared to be much more influenced in their political decisions by face-to-face contact . . . than by the mass media directly." ° (And if this is so, what does it mean to have declared the "public" to be an obsolescent social structure?) To a large extent, the media operate by strengthening dispositions already developed by other social forces. Conventional media and communications research concentrate on clarifying the conditions under which the *media* will be more effective (in political and other kinds of persuasion). It remains a central task of critical theory to focus on face-to-face communication. In the context of a concern for political persuasion, it may be that studies of communicative competence on the social system level can yet have political relevance and theoretical importance for that reason. Here the decisive question would be, how to make interpersonal speech persuasive without turning it into a manipulative rhetoric that treats the other simply as object to be managed instrumentally. This, in turn, may be understood as asking, how can persons *speak to* one another so as to strengthen their capacity for rational judgment and free them from the control of external or built-in censors, *without* the prior institution of an already ideal speech situation?

3

The Left's politics of equality, sought through the disciplined heroism of party struggle, is inevitably a politics in which the state becomes central. The struggle seeks to influence or capture the existing state as an agency for the reallocation of wealth in the existing society; or it seeks to smash the old state and build a new one, as the control and planning mechanism for a new socialist society. Habermas' theory of communicative distortion is a new Fabianism aimed at extending rationality and communicative competence by removing the system of domination grounded in private property by socializing property more widely; but it does *not* assume that the new system will be devoid of a drive toward domination. To achieve a new distortion-free communication, Habermas' theory implies the capture of the state, as well as strengthening the state so that it can overcome the limits established by the old property systems and the resistance of those privileged by it. This, however, generates a new system of domination grounded in the new politics

---

° P. F. Lazarsfeld and Herbert Menzel, in W. Schramm, ed., *The Science of Human Communication*, Basic Books, New York, 1963, p. 96.

and its state apparatus. Facing this dilemma, Habermas can neither clearly renounce the old combat politics requisite for the reform of property domination nor firmly commit himself to it.

This, then, is a dilemma of a Habermasian theory. If it does what it must to foster the equality necessary for communicative competence, it inevitably undermines the freedom it also prizes. The doctrine of communicative competence seeks to mute this contradiction by developing, at the level of *theory,* so abstract a conception of communicative distortion that the place of *state* censorship and the growing domination of the modern state over communication is hidden. But a theory of communicative competence or distortion that glosses over the new power of the state—socialist or otherwise—that says little about its vast domination of communication, such a theory simply cannot have a politics. Certainly, left politics is the pursuit of equality through the struggle for power in the state and by the exercise of domination through that state.

Paradoxically, Habermas' theory is politically aborted precisely because it is politically committed. Like its critics, it too lives within its own political horizon. For Habermas, that political horizon is the familiar social democratic version of socialism, a version of classical Marxism. Habermas knows this. He also knows the profound failures and vast dangers of this socialism. Albrecht Wellmer has already made that plain enough,* from the standpoint of a critical theory. The trouble with the socialist politics to which Habermas remains sentimentally attached is that, in simple *historical* fact, it confronts him with the choice between social democracy's capacity for accommodation to brutality (for voting the war credits), on the one side, or, on the other, the active infliction of mass genocide by Stalinism. These have been the dominant historical pathologies of modern socialism.

Given this political horizon, Habermas is rational in being reluctant to draw clear political implications from his theory. But it must be acknowledged plainly, that, like his critics, Habermas is operating within a limited political horizon; living within the contradictions of historical socialism, Habermas lives within the *socialist* counterpart of the Weberian "iron age." It is clear that Habermas does not manifest Weber's capacity for "heroic" self-torment and grinding stoicism; but it is not yet clear whether this is an improvement.

As for Habermas' critics, most tacitly base themselves on a very limited understanding of what politics and revolution are and might be. Theirs is a fading, unreflective Leninism that views politics as a kind of a career; as the sublimation and routinization of heroism. For them, politics is "made" by

* Wellmer's slim volume on *The Critical Theory of Society,* Herder and Herder, New York, 1971, is surely one of the most lucid products of the Frankfurt School, as clear in its political import as in its philosophical explorations—a marvel of economy, force, and clarity.

"professional revolutionaries," banded together in a self-transcending vanguard, applying the steel forceps to history to extract the reluctant revolution. Essentially and unavoidably they are Europeans dwelling in a museum of revolutionary memories, which enshrines as the paradigm of revolution the obsolescent revolution in Czarist Russia of October 1917.

A linguistically sensitive theory of social change and politics would, however, consider and open us to a larger history: to a history that goes beyond Europe, and also to a history that goes deeper into Europe; into a Europe in which the Soviet Revolution was a lineal descendant of the capitalist revolution; and in which that very capitalist revolution, too, can be a paradigm—a revolution nurtured in a social space liberated within the still functioning routines of feudal society, within the liberated social space of the growing medieval cities, where "city air made a man free," even though still surrounded by the feudal landscape. The paradigm of this capitalist revolution stresses the significance of the mass transformation of a consciousness disciplined and energized by the this-worldly activism of highly organized Protestant sects. The capitalist paradigm suggests that the ecologically organized sects were a counterculture that diligently imprinted the new consciousness on everyday life.

3.1

Implicit in the above is the assumption that the central semiotic effort of modern politics is the capturing and evocation of a symbolism of freedom and/or equality. Its central dilemma has to do with the manner in which energies and other resources are to be allocated among these two powerful symbols. (Habermas' theory became unfortunately entangled in the dilemmas of precisely this bimodal symbolism.)

The theorist who has done most to open inquiry in this direction is the social psychologist Milton Rokeach.° Rokeach's formulation is organized around an affirmation and a denial. Its denial is that politics can be understood as *uni*dimensional, stretching between "left" to "right" as a single line. Rokeach's affirmation is that there are *two* (orthogonal) dimensions that together constitute the semiotic space within which politics moves: freedom *and* equality. One cannot know or predict a group's commitment to one symbol simply from knowing its commitment to the other. The semiotic space of politics then is *bi-* and not *uni*dimensional. "Radicals" then, are *not* simply liberals but only more so and to the "left;" reactionaries are not simply conservatives who are further to the "right."

° M. Rokeach, *The Nature of Human Values*, Free Press, New York, 1973.

The major variations in politics, says Rokeach (*I* would say in the *ideologies* of *modern* politics), "are fundamentally reducible, when stripped to their barest essence, to opposing value orientations concerning the political desirability or undesirability of freedom and equality in all their ramifications." * To Rokeach, then, "politics is mainly about . . . a fundamental concern or lack of concern with equality and freedom." Here I would ask the key Weberian question: What of the *struggle for power* in the state—where does that fit into politics? Having omitted that, one must conclude that Rokeach mistakenly *reduces* politics to the values and ideologies on behalf of which politics is pursued, and under whose banners its protagonists struggle for power. Rokeach's contribution, then, is *not* to a theory of *politics* but to a theory of political *ideologies*, which is exactly its relevance for us. It is precisely because Rokeach is not really dealing with an ahistorical politics in general but, tacitly, with a historical, specifically *modern* politics, that its ideologies center on the symbolism of equality and freedom.

Rokeach suggests that capitalism, socialism, communism, and fascism can all be located in this bimodal semiotic space. Fascism, says Rokeach, places a *low* value on both freedom and equality; socialism places a *high* value on both; capitalism values freedom highly but equality less so; while communism values equality much more than freedom. He also notes that "Americans of all political persuasion, whether liberal, moderate, or conservative, are generally alike in caring a great deal about freedom, varying mainly in the importance they place on equality . . ." But this is so only when one does not separate whites and blacks. Blacks place equality slightly ahead of freedom; whites place freedom substantially ahead of equality. It should be clear that what is referred to, as freedom and equality, must be interpreted as an *ideology* that refers not to the actual *conditions* in which Americans live or which they foster in other countries. Once again: Rokeach's is a theory of political *ideologies*.

Rokeach establishes, convincingly, that there is not one but at least two "left" political ideologies, the socialist and the communist, and that they vary in terms of their differing commitments to freedom and equality. As mentioned, socialist ideology is committed to both equality and freedom as salient values. Communism, however, values equality highly but gives little importance to freedom: ". . . the socialist frequency score for freedom ranks first among 17 terminal values. Equality ranks second . . . for Lenin the order is reversed, equality ranking first and freedom last . . ." † Further: "A content analysis of the values contained in the New Program of the Communist Party USA, published in 1966, yields an equality-freedom pattern

* Ibid., p. 169.
† Ibid., p. 173.

that is similar to that found for Lenin's works which antedate 1917. For nine terminal values extracted from this work, equality is the one most frequently mentioned, whereas freedom is sixth down the list." °

3.2

The fundamental part of Rokeach's work is its insistence on the *bi*modality of (the ideologies of) modern politics. A fundamental difficulty with Rokeach's formulation is its failure to pursue the implications, not simply of the bimodal character of these ideologies but, the full implications of their relative *independence* (or orthogonality) of one another. Because of their independence, it is now possible—not necessary, but *possible*—that freedom and equality *can* conflict with one another; thus the pursuit of freedom can lead to vicious inequalities while the pursuit of equality can and has produced despotism and authoritarianism.

When the French Revolution invoked "Liberty, Equality, and Fraternity," thus implying their *simultaneous* achievement, this was mythological. It is precisely this affirmation of the possibility of achieving *both* freedom *and* equality, together, that *defines* the concrete political symbolism underlying the nineteenth-century concept of *progress*. Progress tacitly implied that one might and was, achieving *both* freedom and equality. Subsequent political experience indicated that this too was a myth, since some classes preferred freedom but glossed over equality, while others were committed only to equality and (at best) gave lip service to freedom—it is this visible *cleavage* that accounts for the death of the nineteenth-century concept of progress.

The grimness sets in when political activists come to believe they have to choose one (and surrender the other) value; when political "realism" comes to be defined as the stern sacrifice of one on behalf of another, high value; and when political "tact" (or statesmanship) is understood to mean systematic silence about the value that is to be sacrificed. The importance of Rokeach's work is not that this dilemma is seen, but that it sets forth a semiotic space for a politics that generates that dilemma.

In the simplest possible terms, modern politics could pursue two possible values, freedom and equality; but it often found, like a hunter who had sighted two rabbits, that it could not pursue both simultaneously. It had to make a decision about which one to pursue and which to let go; but it could not clearly admit that it had made a decision to sacrifice one.

These dilemmas of freedom and equality are mediated by the essential instrumentality of all politics, the struggle for power in the state. The reduction of inequality in an old society, or its fostering in a new one, means that the old state must be taken hold of, or else it must be smashed and a new state erected. In either event, the state, old or new, will be strengthened. The

° Ibid., p. 185.

state then inevitably becomes a growing center of societal domination, whether it is the so-called "welfare" state or the "totalitarianism" of a so-called socialism.

The ultimate contradiction, however, is not between freedom and equality. It is not that the pursuit of equality must inevitably take a dark detour through a freedom-surrendering politics. More ironically, that very surrender of freedom destroys conditions vital for engendering equality and for protecting it. In surrendering or in glossing the problem of freedom, the pursuit of equality undermines its own ambitions. The affirmation of equality and rejection of inequality is crucial to any democratic politics; no modern politics that is decent and potentially effective can boggle at that issue without corrupting itself morally and destroying itself politically. But both things are true: if freedom is not possible without the determined pursuit of equality, equality is precarious and defenseless (if ever achieved) without freedom. Michael Walzer has said it well: "liberty and equality are the two chief virtues of social institutions, and they stand best when they stand together." °

3.3

The tensions between equality and freedom become dilemmas primarily at the level of a *practice*, at the level therefore of political action and struggle, but, not necessarily, at the level of social *theory*. The crux of the matter is that the production of theory does not face the fundamental "economic" problem of scarcity in anything like the same way that it confronts political practice. Since Hegel, it might be thought that theory can, in principle, resolve all contradictions, if only given enough time. But this was always at the level of "pure reason," as distinct from *practical* reason (in Kant's sense). In pure reason, there is always "time enough" to resolve dilemmas, simply because pure reason rejects all limitations of time. Practical reason does not, and operates in a limited time, and therefore has limited energies which constrain choice.

Political action requires sacrificial choices among values in ways not required by merely symbolic action. Indeed, this is exactly one implication of saying that the latter addresses itself to "academic problems" while the former deals with "practical" problems. Academic problems do not necessarily require the sacrifice of values, for one can delay their solution indefinitely, or until such time as a solution, presumably without sacrifice, can be invented. Practical problems, lacking in elastic time, cannot defer decision and they cannot therefore avoid sacrificing *some*, even high, values. Theory should be "system flung" while action and politics must always be problem

° *Dissent*, Fall, 1973.

centered. It is theory's systemic concern that constructs a structure of thinking that *can* enable it to correct for, to avoid, or to transcend the problem-focused limitedness of political action, and to *speak* the silences of problem-focused ideologies of politics. This is not at all to say that a system-flung theory has no foci of its own, and no lacunae or occlusions of its own. It clearly and most emphatically does. It is simply to say, however, that system-theoretical thought generates a structure of rational thinking that transcends the tunnelized narrowing imposed on an ideologized vision limited by the scarce resources of political practice. And all this, after all, is a way of talking simultaneously about the unity *and* disunity of theory and practice, of what theory can *contribute* to practice and of why, in part, it finds itself in *tension* with it.

Within the limits of the scarce resources of all political action—further and powerfully constrained by the anxieties, hate, fear, envy, callousness, studied ingratitude, sheer terror and brutality of political *struggle*—the pursuit of any one precarious value, or of an ideology centered on it, commonly defocalizes other values important even to those seeking the first value. Commonly, ideologies focalize precarious or scarce values. If they neglect certain things, it is not always because they do not esteem them but, often, simply because they already *have* them, and thus mistakenly take them as given securely.

But it is this tendency to take certain values as given securely that places them in jeopardy. This danger is generated precisely by the commitment to precarious or scarce values. But this means that achieved values enable a concentration on others' values, those not yet satisfactorily available. Achieved values thus allow ideologies to focus on precarious and scarce values; these, in turn, paradoxically undermine the very achieved values that they had first premised. Ideological thought, then, is a tunnelizing problem-focused structure of thinking inherently fostering discontinuities and oscillations, first focusing on the scarce, precarious values, then back again to the value which has been neglected during the pursuit of the former; it is self-negating and self-transcending. Ideologies thus always generate thick and dangerous silences even as they publicly dramatize scarce values.

The fundamental silence and false consciousness of modern political ideologies is their tacit but perduring premise of political *uni*dimensionality, the allegedly *single* line that presumably runs from the reactionary to the revolutionary, via the liberal and conservative. Modern political ideology, however, implicates at least *two* values; but it can commonly speak only one. This is the fundamental dilemma of any ideological politics, with which it commonly copes by imposing a silence on and glossing over the other values on which modern politics is based. The false consciousness of ideological politics—that is, of all modern politics—is that politics is one-dimensional. The fundamental silence of every modern politics is that its victory may require the sacrifice or subversion—and certainly the risking—of its other values.

4

The entire development of the "counterculture," during the second half of the 1960s, has made it plain that publishers and other media controllers governed by considerations of profitability will actualize and foster this "counter" culture, even though it runs "counter" to their own assumptions and cultural requisites, doing so simply because counterculture *sells*. Ownership generates a set of limits patterning the media in directions supportive of the property system. At the same time, however, considerations of marketing and short-term profitability, grounded in that same property system, generate internal contradictions leading publishers to tolerate (and promote) a counterculture hostile to their own *long*-term property interests. The need to turn a profit disposes producers to manufacture any and every noxious product that might sell. They will and have sold an adversary culture that openly alienates masses of youth from their parents and government because, and so long as, it is profitable. Indeed, at some point the media develops a vested interest in maintaining the counterculture. The system's long-term interests are sold out for short-term profits.

The hegemonic class's profit imperative therefore ends by undermining the very culture on which its own legitimacy rests. This is not, however, simply saying that the journalism schools of genteel universities breed "class treason" in the sons of the middle class (as Daniel Patrick Moynihan once seemed to suggest). It is primarily a matter of the profit imperatives of their *parents* that corrodes the legitimacy of their own social and cultural position, and thus fosters "the seeds of their own destruction."

It is, however, precisely this internal contradiction, born of the imperatives of profitability, that contributes to the *rational* side of the mass media. The rationality of the dialogue in bourgeois society is in part, but in *part only*, a matter of small competing entrepreneurs' fostering diverse accounts that complement and check one another in the "market place of ideas." It is also importantly a question of having differing official accounts and media accounts. All this is real and substantial enough; especially for a period when small media producing units might still survive. But even in an age of huge, immensely capitalised and increasingly centralised media, there abides the essential bourgeois contradiction between producing anything that sells, on the one side, and allowing only what is supportive of existing institutions, on the other. In the end, the system subverts itself because there exists no protection for its own *future* that might rule out quick turnover profits at the cost of the system as a whole.

Historically concrete rationality, today, means the *maintenance* of this contradiction; for there is no transcending resolution of it in sight. It means a *resistance* to any regressive reinstitution of censorship that seeks to reduce the gap between official accounts of social reality and those distributed by the media system. Historically concrete rationality now means the generation, defense, support, and fostering of any and all *gaps* between accounts of social reality fostered by the managers, owners and leaders, of the society *and* those coming from the media and any other sources defining social reality, including the social sciences. Rationality, today, means an insistence that the media conform to their own supposedly autonomous and supposedly "professional" standards for producing accounts of reality; it means "unmasking" and public criticism of them, when they fail to do so; it means the development of specialized watchdog agencies, associations, action organizations, and social movements constantly to monitor these reality-defining media and institutions; constantly to expose their lapses; and constantly to expose and resist pressures by the managers of institutions to impose controls on the media.

4.1

To strengthen public rationality today means the strengthening of the *contradictions* internal to that system of producing accounts of social reality that is grounded in private ownership. It means seeing both sides of this contradiction, rather than only "unmasking" the media's corrupt support for property-favoring definitions of social reality. It means seeing that the greatest danger is the *fusion* of media accounts with manager accounts of social reality. It means seeing that this threat is now lodged primarily in agencies of government and in a political subsystem embarrassed by residues of media autonomy—which can be substantial. It means that the contradictions of our present private-property system of information cannot in the *slightest* be resolved, improved, let alone transcended, by the *nationalization* of the mass media. It means seeing that such a "solution" is fundamentally a regression to the censorship of archaic "old regime" societies, a regression now immeasurably strengthened by the newest media technologies.

One of the most fundamental ways newspapers contribute to societal rationality is not by competing with one another, but by providing alternatives to and critiques of official (and especially governmental) accounts of social reality. The standard simple-minded and middle-aged critique of current media systems, from a supposedly "socialist" viewpoint unmasking the property-grounded bias of the bourgeois press, willfully ignores the visible, brutal reality of the Soviet alternative, and stonily grounds itself in a capitulation to archaic Stalinism. Such "unmasking" does not prepare the way for transcending bourgeois domination, but for the catastrophic *regression* of public rationality.

Unless all this is said plainly, theoretical discussion about clarifying the requisites of "communicative competence," *re*mystifies rather than *demys-*

tifies the current predicament. The struggle for public rationality is given political substance and leverage only when it restores and deepens the concept of *censorship* as one center for the critique of contemporary society. Politically viable critique means to turn critique increasingly on the system of information publicly available through the concretely organized mass media. It means making the relations between media and *government,* no less than between media and property, a central issue of political struggle, rather than a peripheral question of the "superstructure." It means understanding that what is now regarded as a "socialist" critique is not an alternative to bourgeois corruption but a part of the same imperial system.

The fundamental intentions of all political movements today can be appraised, and can be archeologically unearthed, by revealing the theory and practice of censorship with which they operate, tacitly or overtly, whether these be movements of the *status quo* or those opposed to them. The emancipatory politics of a "one-dimensional society" must begin by seeing that it is *not truly* one-dimensional. It cannot be one-dimensional for reasons essential to its own property form, and to the profound contradictions these generate. The public critique of current industrial society as "unidimensional" is itself contradictory. For if modern industrial society was really unidimensional, there could be no *critique* of that unidimensionality made or heard.

Contradictions within the system are mystified when that system is characterized as unidimensional. The "long march through the institutions" must begin with, center on, and recurrently exhibit the concrete condition of the mass media. What is needed is critique of the mass media, and not *only* an exposition of the theoretical requisites of "communicative competence" formulated at the level of an abstract, ahistorical "social system" composed of an ego-and-alter, in general, for *they* are only the nameless systematization of Robinson Crusoe and his "Man Friday."

The march through the institutions cannot begin by analyzing a sociological island beyond history. It must begin within history, on the societal, not the social system level, and it must deal not only with language and symbolic interaction but, *also,* with the concrete revolution in media technology. It must also see critique, not as deploring the abominable taste of capitalist media, but as the exhibition of its economic contradictions. It must see that the media are not at one with the system of ownership, but are in profound tension with it.

A politics appropriate to a critical theory must have some interface at the public level. One way it can express itself there, on the plane of practical political struggle, is by refocusing the issue of censorship and self-censorship; and by deepening public understanding of what censorship is within the mass media themselves, and in their relations with other spheres and subsystems of the society, exhibiting the meaning of the media's accommodation to, and its tensions with, the managers of these other spheres. A new and deepened critique of censorship on the level of the mass media can contribute to a new politics.

Critical theory must reopen the question of media *freedom*. It must recenter that problem, exposing the manner in which all kinds of *freedom* today hinge on issues of media censorship—of news, news interpretation, and of entertainment. Without such freedom, expressed concretely and histori-cally, all talk of equality is false consciousness; or, at worst, it is the instrumental slogan of mass mobilization and manipulation. Without *that* freedom, we can expect only a circulation of elites, the replacement of an old by a new elite, but not the transcendence of elitism itself.

It is through the mass media and through them alone that there is today any possibility at all of a truly mass public enlightenment that might go beyond what universities may elicit, i.e., beyond small elites and educated elitism. It is through the media that the system may be made to "dance to its own melody," or to expose itself. From *l'affaire Dreyfus* to the Watergate scandal, the powerful role of the media in monitoring the management of public affairs has been notable, even if sporadic. For those who can see, it is profoundly at variance with any simple-minded stereotype of media simply as an agency reproducing the existent system of domination.

The path from critical theory to the long march through the institutions must go over the bridge of the mass media, and undertake the struggle for and critique of these media for what they are: a complex system of property interests, technologies, professionalizing skills, strivings for domination and for autonomy, all swarming with the most profound inner contradictions.

This is not, and is not intended to be, anything like a "complete" politics for a critical theory. Indeed, no convincing reason has ever been given why such a "complete" politics should be required of critical theory. The struggle for the mass media may, however, be one opening wedge in the fuller development of the politics of a critical theory, for it is a strategic hub that moves out in all directions. The struggle for the media is also a vital way that critical theory can contribute some of its distinctive and special insights, and can support critical theory's autonomy from both the irrationality of the status quo and, also, from the by-now obsolescent but dominant modes of struggle against it.

5

There remains an important question concerning the *politics* of critical theory's diagnosis of the breakdown of the modern public, and it had best be put directly: does not the breakdown of the public necessarily imply that the institutions it grounds—parliaments, congresses, and other representative assemblies—must now be a sham? Does not the critique of the public inevitably imply a denial of the very legitimacy of electoral and representative institutions and undermine any loyalty they may claim? For on the Kantian premise that ought implies can, the impossibility of the public in modern society implies it can make no moral claim upon us.

The critique of the public, the doctrine that it has undergone a breakdown, casts into shadow differences between liberal and authoritarian societies, between those societies making some serious claim for their representative institutions and those others where this is all too patently a sham. Jürgen Habermas' critique of the western public is compelling. But this bourgeois public cannot be appraised in the abstract. It cannot be appraised simply by comparing what is with what was or should be. It is also a question of what, given the real conditions in which we now find ourselves, *might* be and what *can* be. We are back to the question that Merleau-Ponty raised: is it possible to align realism and the dialectic, or does the dialectic require the sacrifice of realism? To give due consideration to what Merleau-Ponty called the density and opacity of history, having a momentum of its own, must we not also ask: what are the realistic alternatives to this decayed bourgeois public?

What, for instance, of *socialist* freedom and of a socialist public? To ask the question is to answer it. In the light of *that* comparison, the bourgeois public—far from being dead—remains a paragon of vigor, liveliness, honesty, and freedom. Without insisting on *that* comparison, we are living in Cloud Cuckooland. Neither the advocates of Critical Theory nor any one else will, in the foreseeable future, establish an oasis of *socialist* freedom and a new *socialist* public in Germany. Germany will no more have a free socialism than could Czechoslovakia. And for the same reasons: socialist freedom in Middle Europe means civil war, or at least vastly intensified conflicts and tensions in Soviet territories to the East. It will not be countenanced by the USSR.

The question, then, is not whether there is a "third" way in Europe that is neither Soviet nor corporate capitalist. There are countless third ways that are conceivable, many of which are eminently preferable to these two alternatives. The question here is not morality, but history and geography and power. To limit consideration of the issue to a comparison between what is and what was or should be, to compare the decline of the bourgeois public with the possibility of an ideal speech situation, and to ignore the density of the Soviet Union and its weight on Europe, is to surrender all politics.

The doctrine of the breakdown of the public is the political counterpart of the Marxist doctrine of the economic crash (*Zusammenbruch*) and of the declining rate of profit, which, in some readings, automatically spells the downfall of capitalism. Like the economic crash, the doctrine of the breakdown of the public is a Sorelian myth. For it premises that there had been a "golden age" of the public, but this never existed. Only when measured against this nonexistent standard can the modern "bourgeois" public be declared degenerate. But where and when did the gilded age of the vigorous public exist? In Bismarck Germany? Chartist England? At the turn of the century, when the European working classes were being drilled into passivity and coopted into the preparing war machines? In the small towns of the United States that beat up itinerant I.W.W. organizers and "agitators"?

The bourgeois public was never democracy-in-being. It was and is a small and precarious social space, with significant institutional support, from which to expand freedom and to win rights; but it is not freedom secured. Its vast and continuing importance cannot be overestimated even if it provides "only" an opportunity; and, indeed, Marx himself lauded it. Although perhaps too sanguine, it was even Marx's "prediction that the mere introduction of universal suffrage—bourgeois democracy—would ensure the advent of socialism in England." °

When it fails to speak to the present and attend to the future, a critique of the bourgeois public may be twisted into a theory of "social fascism" that obliterates the substantial distinctions between liberalism and authoritarianism. ("Social Fascism" was a doctrine of the 1920s that paved the way for the advent of Nazism.) The doctrine of the breakdown of the public may be used to sanction any and every form of violence and terror whose provocations aim to reveal the fascist essence presumably hidden by the parliamentary appearance.

The reference to Nazism here will be thought harsh by some. But the problem needs to be raised, especially with Americans, who tend to have a short historical memory and who live a long way from Europe. European countries share a continent with the Soviet territories; America does not. The future of parliamentarianism and representative institutions in Europe will not be determined by Castro's Cuba, by Hanoi, by Gramscians, or by Gauchiste sects. The future of representative institutions in Europe will depend largely on the nature of the Soviet Union's social system, *and* on the political license that the United States grants the Soviet Union in exchange for access to Soviet markets and profit opportunities. In the end, the United States may weigh these markets and these profits against European parliamentary institutions. Those who fail to see this have no calling for politics, least of all for socialist politics. They are the gentle brothers of a new religion.

So to speak of the Soviet Union and of Nazism in the same breath may seem irreverent but it is not irrelevant. The association will be regarded as outrageous by those promoting *détente* between the Soviet Union and the United States. But other and significant parts of mankind do not share that indignation. For example, the Chinese *People's Daily* (8 January 1974) asserts that there are a thousand detention camps, akin to Nazi concentration camps, in the Soviet Union and that these hold more than a million prisoners.

° *New Left Review*, July–August, 1974, p. 14.

"Anyone who expresses discontent and resistance to the fascist rule of Soviet revisionism," maintains the *People's Daily*, "will be declared a 'lunatic' or 'unbalanced' and forced into a mental hospital. . . ." Mao has called the Soviet Union a Hitlerite regime.

Such judgments need careful weighing. Certainly the Chinese judgment of the Soviet social system must be appraised in the light of their adversary relationship. Yet it should also be asked: which is cause and which, effect? That is, is this adversary relation the cause of China's condemnation of the Soviet social system, or is the Chinese diagnosis of that system what led them to take up the adversary relation? Is there, moreover, any reason to believe that the Chinese diagnosis of the Soviet society is any more self-serving than that implied by the *détente* policies of the American administrations of Nixon, Agnew, Ford, and Rockefeller?

For my part, I *do reject* the Chinese diagnosis of Soviet society as a form of Nazism. Nazism was characterized by a systematic and open policy of racism and anti-Semitism; the Soviet Union and the Communist Party of the Soviet Union do not avow such a policy. But both are/were one-party states, with a strong cult of leadership, and both have or had growing elements of state capitalism. The working class of the Soviet Union has no more control of its society than had that of Nazi Germany. The last effective representative institution of the working class in the USSR was the "soviets" or workers' councils, and these were at once reduced to a nullity when the Communist Party of the Soviet Union took power. Despite these important similarities between the USSR and Nazism, nonetheless, there are important *cultural* differences, the Soviet Union retaining, in grotesquely distorted form, a continuity with Enlightenment thought that had largely been renounced by Nazi irrationalism, and which underlay its racism.

Let me state emphatically that I am *certain* that the great theorist of the breakdown of the public does not endorse a politics that sees no difference between liberal democracy, on the one side, and Nazism or Stalinism, on the other. For my part, I am confident that his intent is freedom-strengthening. But his theory has a life of its own, and has its own ideological susceptibilities and functions.

The theory of the degenerate bourgeois public then does have a profound if unwitting political potential, being usable to "unmask" representative institutions as a lie. The only political alternative is to assert that these deteriorated institutions must be revitalized and made genuine. But how? Here we are back again to the dilemma of Habermas' theory, and to its impasse within the framework of a conventional politics. With the framework of conventional socialism—i.e., of a social democracy or a Leninism based on a "Scientific Marxism"—there is simply no way (and, indeed, no reason) to revitalize representative institutions and the freedoms they grounded. That socialism always contained more than a trace of positivism in which politics was an epiphenomenon. It assumed that the transformation of economic institutions, of science and technology, would by themselves suffice, and suffice automatically, to yield a new political freedom. Indeed, that Marxism —as Lucio Colletti has correctly noted—scarcely has any specifically political theory at all. Neither the bureaucratic oligarchies of social democracy nor the Communist Party cadres, with their Sorelian myth of the "dictatorship of the proletariat," have the least intention, or the least capacity, of revitalizing political freedoms. They mean to rule, not to represent. For Habermas' theory of the breakdown of the public, then, there is absolutely no way forward to an authentic socialist freedom, and there is no way back to the freedom of a desiccated liberalism.

For those in want of a politics, Habermas' exploration of the "ideal speech situation" will be condemned as an empty baggage train. For them, the real payload will be carried by Habermas' critique of the public, from which some of them will conclude that representative institutions are a sham. His critique of the public, then, has a profound political spill-over, impugning the legitimacy of electoral institutions and political democracy where they already exist, and forestalling struggle to institute them where they do not. Consider what that theory means to the Portuguese or Spanish. The critique of the public unwittingly provides theoretical materials justifying a mythical dictatorship of the proletariat: Myth built on myth.

This floundering thing we call parliamentary democracy is surely riddled with corruption and hypocrisy and it is a forum for every kind of lie and swindle ever perpetrated. Yet it possesses one incomparable advantage over the peoples' (i.e., puppet) democracies—important, at least, to some. It is advantageous, by far, to those who hold their politicians in suspicion and contempt. For those whose tastes run in opposite directions, and perversely permit their politicians to hold *them* in suspicion and contempt, it must be admitted that the higher forms of democracies, the "democratic dictatorships," are superior.

The modern revolutionary period, with its drive toward a vast social reconstruction through the intervention of a strengthened state apparatus has, in some places, yielded a reorganization of instututions in which the economic and the political spheres, always only incompletely separated in bourgeois society, are once more, as they were in feudalism, reunited and fused. These "new" and advanced forms of society, immodestly calling themselves "socialism," thereby arrange that all incomes and all livings are now bestowed by state bureaucrats. Persons who do not conform to official definitions of social reality are declared insane or, more simply, prevented from working, as may be plainly seen in the Soviet Union, Hungary, and Czechoslovakia. There is, therefore, no "public" in these "socialist" countries—if by that is meant a social place where persons may talk about their common problems and interests without risking their livelihoods, or having their sanity impugned.

Any society that entails the strengthening of the state apparatus by giving it unchecked control over the economy, and re-unites the polity and the economy, is an historical *regression*. In it there is no more future for the public, or for the freedoms it supported, than there was under feudalism. In such a regressive society, the domination of the individual employer—who could be opposed by unions—has been replaced by a dominating state bureaucracy who can now finance its own projects and who possesses unlimited instruments of violence.

If socialism is to mean a new human emancipation, one thing is certain: it can*not* mean the nationalization of the means of production. The historical functions of such societies has not been to produce human emancipation but to force-feed industrialization. A state-dominated socialism is but a continuation and culmination of corporate capitalism. It involves the ultimate concentration: taking the step from oligopoly to state monopoly, it completes capitalism's drive toward the concentration and centralization of the means of production. This has always been one of capitalism's most powerful tendencies. Such a "socialism," then, is a state *capitalism* whose own law of absolute immiseration is: concentration and cumulation of power in the hands of the state bureaucracy, and the concentration of passivity and subservience among the masses of people. The further concentration of the means of production, or the means of the production of *ideas*, in the hands of the state, brings capitalist society to a regressive culmination, rather than constituting its socialist antithesis. An emancipatory socialism requires the spread and diffusion of the people's ownership and effective control over the means of production, not their further concentration. Otherwise, socialism can only mean the re-institution of the "company town," on the level of the nation-state.

Bibliographical Note

Among the studies of communication that I have found most useful for present purposes are the mimeographed lectures (in English) given by Jürgen Habermas as the Gauss lectures at Princeton University and, to the best of my knowledge, not yet published. These have to do with the philosophical foundations of a communication theory of society. Also of basic value in his *Strukturwandel der Offentlichkeit*, Luchterhand, Neuwied und Berlin, 1969. Basic data is to be found in certain UNESCO publications and in I. de Sola Pool, *et al.*, eds., *Handbook of Communication*, Rand McNally, Chicago, 1973, and in W. Schramm, ed., *The Science of Human Communication*, Basic Books, New York, 1963. See also Robert E. Park, *Society, Collective Behavior, News and Opinion, Sociology and Modern Society*, Free Press, Glencoe, Illinois, 1955, for the relevant contribution of one of the founders of the

"Chicago School." Other useful compendia include Denis McQuail, ed., *Sociology of Mass Communications*, Penguin, London, 1972, and the Swedish scholar, Jan Ekecrantz, *Readings in the Politics of Information*, mostly translated into English but presently only in xeroxed form. Articles by Jan Ekecrantz include, "Mediating Factors in the Production of Systematic Ignorance under Late Capitalism," an expanded version of an article originally published in German by the Sektion Journalistik der Karl Marx Universiteit, Leipzig, 1974; "Concepts of Social Control and Communication"; and "Notes Toward the Reconceptualization of the Concepts of Social Control and Communication," mimeographed. Herbert I. Shiller, "The Mind Managers," valuably updates information about the growing concentration of information systems in the private sector and their increasing fusion with government, in Western societies and especially the United States. One would like to know, however, what workable and democratic alternative news systems are conceived by critics of Western news concentration. In other words, what is a model of an "ideal speech situation" on the level of *mass* media? The full meaning of critiques of media "concentration" cannot be appraised seriously unless there is a clear specification of the alternative arrangements sought or condoned. One work that begins to move in that direction is Claus Mueller, *The Politics of Communication*, Oxford University Press, New York and London, 1973. An admirable piece of work is Hans Magnus Enzensberger, *The Consciousness Industry*, Seabury Press, New York, 1974. Other valuable works include: Hugh D. Duncan, *Communication and Social Order*, Oxford University Press, New York and London, 1962. Duncan epitomized some of the best traditions of American Midwest sociology. He is, in some part, the creative synthesizer of Kenneth Burke's great *oeuvre* which was important as a source of intellectual nourishment for the early Chicago School. Many cognate themes of relevance here are explored in Lewis Coser's knowledgeable *Men of Ideas*, Free Press, Glencoe, Ill., 1965, as in Melvin DeFleur, *Theories of Mass Communication*, McKay, New York, 1966. Apart from the classics in communications research by Paul F. Lazarsfeld and Robert K. Merton, other useful contributions in the Columbia University tradition include Herbert Menzel, "Quasi-Mass Communication," *Public Opinion Quarterly*, vol. 5, no. 3, and Richard Maisel, *Information Technology*, Conference Board Inc., New York, 1972. Edward J. Epstein has written much of value for the problems considered here, including *News From Nowhere*, Random House, New York, 1973. Over the years Dallas Smythe and Herbert Gans have continued to make contributions of considerable substance.

chapter 7

Ideology, the Cultural Apparatus, and the New Consciousness Industry

There is a special connection, we have said, between the spread of modern ideologies with their historically special rationality, on the one side, and the unimodality and lineality of printed materials, on the other. Writing, and especially printed communication, then, is a basic grounding of "modern" ideologies, at least as we have come to know them. The future prospect of ideology will thus depend, in part, on the future of writing; on the production of writing and printed objects; on the consumption of writing and written objects; and, also, on the reproduction of audiences and markets for writings—"readers." Writers produce writings for readers. Hence anything that effects the production of writing, and the competition of printed objects for audiences, necessarily impinges on the role of ideology in the modern world. The position and structural character of ideologies is affected by changes in reading behavior, and by the changing interest in (or time available for) reading. We shall thus attempt to explore, with great tentativeness, some of the ways in which the recent, full-scale emergence of modern communication technologies and of the consciousness industry of which it is a part, may impinge on ideology and its prospect.

1

Hitherto, the fundamental symbolic means of ideology has been conceptual and linguistic. The relationship between ideology and society was mediated by the enormous development of printed matter. Ideology did not "reflect" society in a direct way but mediated the news and newspapers while, correspondingly, much of ideology's reciprocal impact on society was through its publication. Modern ideologies were made available, first, to readers, a relatively well-educated but small sector of the society—the "reading public" nucleated by a literate intelligentsia—and then through them to a larger public. Ideology was diffused via a relatively highly educated reading elite and spread to a larger public through written interpretations of "popularizations" of the ideology in newspapers, magazines, pamphlets, or leaflets, and through face-to-face oral communication in conversations, coffee shops, class rooms, lecture halls, or mass meetings.

In this "two step" model of communication, the dense information of complex ideologies is transmitted or "filtered down" to mass audiences by the media and, in particular, through a mediating intelligentsia. The mediating intelligentsia, then, serve partly as interpreters and partly as proprietors of those printed objects in which an ideology is defined as authoritatively exhibited. An intelligentsia may be said to have a proprietary relation to the printed object when (and to the extent that) they can certify readings of it as correct or incorrect, and certify others as possessing competent knowledge of it.

1.1

In contrast to the conventional printed objects central to ideologies, the modern communication media have greatly intensified the nonlinguistic and iconic component, and hence the *multi*modal character of public communication. The communication breakthrough in the twentieth century begins with the spread of the radio and the cinema and is now coming to a culmination in the spread of television.° The worldwide diffusion of television marks the end of one and the beginning of a new stage in the communications revolution— the development of a computerized mass information system. We are presently at the early stages of a radically new communications era in which computerized information storage and retrieval systems will be integrated with "cable" television. The computer console will control the computer's information storage and order it to produce selective bits of information, making them directly available in offices and homes via television scanning through cable television, or through specially ordered print outs.

Television is not just an experience substitute *or* merely another experience; it is both, and hence is an historically new mass experience. Such

° From 1946 to 1967, monochromatic sets in use in the United States increased from 8,000 to more than 81,000,000 while, in 1967 there were also some 12,700,000 color sets in the United States. This and other basic communication data are critically condensed in the solid volume by Melvin L. DeFleur, *Theories of Mass Communication*, McKay, New York, 1966.

ideologies as the television watchers accept must be successful in integrating and resonating the residual iconic imagery—"pictures-in-the-head"—generated by media-transmitted films as well as by their own "personal experience." In effect, this residual iconic imagery is a new, technologically implanted paleosymbolism; a type II paleosymbolism directly affecting, resonating, and reworking the type I paleosymbolism residual of early childhood experience. In brief, things people could not normally speak about are now being affected by other things they cannot speak about, in ways and with results they cannot speak about. To that extent, the *characterological grounding* of ideologies, normally changed only slowly and in the course of life experience, is being impinged upon and changed in new ways and, quite likely, at far more rapid rates. Television has instituted a new modality and tempo of experience.

If we can think of ideology and history as connected by the "black box" of personal experience, that black box has now been technologically amplified and we may therefore expect a decline in the *manifest* connection between ideologies and history, or people's social position in historical processes. In one way, this may be *experienced* as an "end of ideology," as the "irrelevance" of ideology, or as the "meaningless" or "absurdity" of life, of society, and culture. As the paleosymbolic materials of persons' character are now technologically touchable by six hours of television watching per day, which is to say, almost 40% of the person's waking day, the disjunction grows between the "personal" and the sociohistorical.

With such a technologically induced mass transformation of the paleosymbolic elements of character, changes will have to be made in the mass belief systems available, including the ideological. But it is not simply that different ideologies, ideologies having different public projects and appealing to different audiences, become necessary but, rather, that the entire lineal and activistic rationality of *any* kind of ideology—the very grammar of ideology— may be undermined. Television is a "you-are-there" participatory and consummatory activity. One is not commonly left with a sense that one needs to do something actively after a viewing. The viewing is an end in itself.

As a participatory experience, the viewers' sense of critical *distance*, one basis for the rationality premised by normal ideology, has been diminished. If there is residual tension after a viewing, it does not necessarily call for intellectual clarification of the kind provided for by ideology but for a "resolution" in the sense that a drama or piece of music may be "resolved." Ideology always implies a measure of rational social criticism, which is the specification of a social target and the readying of the self to change it. A *viewer's* participatory experience, when intellectualized at all, implies a *dramaturgical* criticism of an object to be consumed and experienced. Dramaturgical criticism does not prod a viewer to do something or change something, but simply to "appreciate" something in its givenness. The viewer presented with a negative dramaturgical criticism of something is not expected to produce a better showing, but to better "understand" it, to recommend others view or avoid viewing it, and to look forward to or avoid the next production by the same dramaturgist. Ideology implies rational criticism as preparation for action; dramaturgy implies the cultivation of the viewer's sensibility as the passive spectator of events as presented.

1.2

With the shift from a conceptual to an iconic symbolism, then, the very fundamentals shared by any ideology may be attenuated. The response prepared by the transition from a newspaper- to a television-centered system of communication may not take the form of ideological performances that vary around a common grammar of ideology, but of altogether differently structured symbol systems: of analogic rather than digital, of synthetic rather than analytic systems, of occult belief systems, new religious myths, the "discovery" of Oriental and other non-Western religions. In this, however, there is no "end" to ideology, for it continues among some groups, in some sites, and at some semiotic level, but it ceases to be as important a mode of consciousness of masses; remaining a dominant form of consciousness among *some* elites, ideology loses ground among the masses and lower strata. In consequence of television, it may be that the traditional undermining of "restricted" speech variants by the public school system is counter-balanced by television's reinforcement of it, and that "elaborated" speech variants become increasingly limited to an elite.

The "end of ideology" thesis of the 1950s was rooted in a kind of optimism and in a tacit myth of progress. The idea was that ideology would be replaced by the victory of technological, scientific, and rational-pragmatic modes of consciousness; in short, by a "higher" mode of consciousness. The view suggested here is that the mode of consciousness likely to compete with ideology among the masses, at any rate, may not be more rationalism but less, not a higher rationalism but a lower. Ideology and the critics of ideology both remained rooted in the Enlightenment. The critics of ideology overlooked the fact that, when ideology faded, it need not be replaced by something more rational but by something that *they*—as Enlighteners—might regard as regressive and irrational. This is not to say that there were no limits to the Enlightenment's rationality that needed transcending, nor even that the Western drift to occultism and Oriental religions does not rest on certain irrationalities of present societies. It is, rather, to doubt that occultism and Oriental religions successfully surmount these irrationalities.

2

People who do not read can have only kind of secondhand relationship to ideologies and ideological movements. If they are to be convinced, they must be convinced by other means or in some other way. Since there has been a profound change in the symbolic environment with the emergence of radio, cinema, and television, there must also be an important change in the role of ideology as a spur to, interpreter and director of, public projects. Correspondingly, certain places—such as schools and universities—or certain social strata—such as the relatively well-educated—remain structurally advantaged with respect to opportunities for ideological production and consumption.

With the growth of the system of mass education, the consciousness of the population of advanced industrialized countries becomes profoundly split: there is an intensification among some "elites" of the consumption and production of ideological objects; but at exactly the same time, there is also a growth of "masses." "Masses" are here defined as those to whom ideology is less central because their consciousness is now shaped more by radio, cinema, and television—being influenced more by the "consciousness industry" than by the ideological products of the "cultural apparatus."

2.1

In industrial countries there is considerable tension between the "cultural apparatus," largely influenced by the intelligentsia and academicians, and the "consciousness industry," largely run by technicians within the framework of profit-maximization and now increasingly integrated with political functionaries and the state apparatus. For that reason, such technicians may seek to avoid overt political acts, lest they offend potential markets as well as offend the political preferences of the industry's owners and managers, or political leaders and state functionaries. This is not at all to say, of course, that the content of the "entertainment" produced by the consciousness industry is apolitical. Far from it.

"The Cultural Apparatus" was a term that C. Wright Mills first used in a BBC broadcast in 1959 to refer to "all the organizations and *milieux* in which artistic, intellectual, and scientific work goes on, and to the means by which such work is made available to circles, publics, and masses. In the cultural apparatus art, science, and learning, entertainment, malarkey, and information are produced and distributed and consumed. It contains an elaborate set of institutions: of schools and theaters, newspapers and census bureaus, studios, laboratories, museums, little magazines, radio networks."

This formulation tends to conflate two different things whose separation repays analysis. One is the *sources*, the creative persons, circles or milieux, in which or by whom critical reason is displayed and exercised, in which science and technologies are developed, and in which sensibility is symbolically evoked and explored. These *sources*, however, are quite distinct from the *media* through which they are conveyed to audiences and publics. If this distinction between sources and media is not made clearly, there is a tendency to blur the social marginality of the cultural apparatus, their ideological isolation and their political powerlessness. Correspondingly, to emphasize such a distinction is to indicate systematically that the producers of "culture" in modern society cannot communicate their work to mass audiences except by passing through a route controlled by media, and those who control the mass media, the consciousness industry.

This is not to say that the cultural apparatus is altogether devoid of its own media or has no control whatsoever over these. It does control certain magazines, theaters, and radio stations which are relatively small and, especially so, in the audience reached and in the influence exerted. The media directly under the influence of the cultural apparatus allows its members to communicate internally *with one another,* and thus to constitute themselves to some extent as a community; but it allows them little routine access to mass audiences. Often, they convey only elaborated codes.

Mills' discussion of the three stages through which, he held, modern culture was publicly supported essentially culminates in the consciousness industry. The first stage was the aristocratic patronage system, especially in Europe. The second was the bourgeois public for whom the cultural workman worked via the mediation of an anonymous market. The third was the one in which "Commercial agencies or political authorities support culture, but unlike older patrons, they do not form its sole public." It is in this last stage that (following Hans Enzensberger) what is called here the consciousness industry becomes the dominant force, as the medium of public communication.

Mills stresses that the earlier system in which cultural workers and buyers were integrated was unified only indirectly and as the unwitting product of the common taste of patrons or bourgeois publics. In contrast, however, in the third period now dominated by the consciousness industry, Mills notes that the definition of reality, values, and taste once diffusely shaped by a cultural apparatus are now, however, "subject to official management and, if need be, backed up by coercion . . . the terms of debate, the terms in which the world may be seen, the standards and lack of standards by which men judge of their accomplishments, of themselves or of other men—these terms are officially or commercially determined, inculcated, enforced." Much the same point had been made (in 1954) by the dean of critical communications studies in the United States, Dallas W. Smythe, who remarked: ". . . as our culture has developed it has built into itself increasing concentrations of authority, and nowhere is this more evident than in our communications activities." °

Written at the end of the so-called "silent decade" of the 1950s, Mills' analysis minimized the conflict between the cultural apparatus and the consciousness industry. Mills then emphasized the subordination of American academicians and intellectuals to business values of usefulness and efficiency, and their gratitude for business philanthropy. "Joseph Schumpeter's notion that under capitalism intellectuals generally tend to erode its foundations," declared Mills, "does not generally hold true of the United States." Mills was more nearly correct, if we take the focus of his remarks to be American intellectuals rather than Europeans. But, for the most part, however, we shall argue that it was Schumpeter who was correct.

There was a tendency on Mills' part to underestimate the alienation long felt by American cultural establishments from the society's dominant values. This alienation was fully visible at least as early as the American transcendentalists; it was an alienation that became more pronounced after World War I, as symbolized by Randolph Bourne's rejection of John Dewey's pragmatism; it was an alienation plainly visible during the Depression and the Marxism of the 1930s; and it was an alienation that would once again be evident only a few years after Mills' own talk on the cultural apparatus, a talk which, in itself, exhibited the very alienation whose absence it decried.

Speaking a decade after Mills, Herbert Gans remarked that "the most interesting phenomenon in America . . . is the political struggle between taste cultures over whose culture is to predominate in the major media, and over whose culture will provide society with its symbols, values and world view." † Gans also called attention to the continuing tensions "between the distributors and creators of culture," ‡ another expression of the conflict between the cultural apparatus and the consciousness industry.

2.2

The tensions between the cultural apparatus and the consciousness industry are, in part, derived from the tensions that arise between any kind of sellers and buyers. Here, however, there is the additional problem that those in the cultural apparatus are essentially small scale, handicraft workers who are ever in danger of domination by a narrowing circle of enormously powerful buyers. The buyers in the consciousness industry can establish prices and

° Dallas W. Smythe, "Some Observations of Communications Theory," in *Sociology of Mass Communications*, Denis McQuail, ed., Penguin, London, 1972, p. 25.

† Herbert J. Gans, "The Politics of Culture in America," in McQuail, ibid., p. 378.

‡ Ibid., p. 380.

create political blacklists, exert continual economic and ideological pressure on the cultural workers, and violate the latter's sense of autonomy—of craftsmanship, of artistic or scientific integrity.

It is in part the very control exerted by the consciousness industry, on behalf of values opposed by cultural workers, that generates the latter's continuing critique of "mass culture." This bitterness is accentuated by the vulgarity of the standards that the consciousness industry is felt to impose. The relations between the two are also strained by the widespread feeling in the cultural apparatus that sheer contact with the consciousness industry is threatening to their deepest values. The consciousness industry is often viewed as a "dirty" business threatening the "purity" or authenticity of the cultural apparatus. Hans Enzensberger has noted sympathetically that, considering the nature of the consciousness industry, it is no wonder that "the temptation to withdraw is great." He adds, however, that "fear of handling this is a luxury a sewer-man cannot necessarily afford." °

2.3

An essential characteristic of the modern communication system is that it is a *mass* media system, which means that it can make an increasing number of low-cost messages available to an increasing proportion of the members of any society, and to an increasing number of societies throughout the world. This, in turn, has largely been a function of the technological innovation, the invention of printing, with which the communication revolution began. Enzensberger recently formulated a list of technological innovations in the last 20 years or so in communication: new satellites, color television, cable relay television, cassettes, videotape, video tape recorder, video phones, stereophony, laser techniques, electrostatic reproduction processes, electronic high-speed printing, composing and learning machines, microfiches with electronic access, printing by radio, time-sharing computers, data banks. "All these new forms of media are constantly forming new connections both with each other and with older media like printing, radio, film, television, telephone, radar and so on. They are clearly coming together to form a universal system." † In the next forty years, the symbolic environment and political systems of the world will, once again, be revolutionized by this newest communications revolution.

Both the cultural apparatus and consciousness industry parallel the schismatic character of the modern consciousness: its highly unstable mixture

---

° Hans Magnus Enzensberger, *The Consciousness Industry: On Literature, Politics and the Media,* Seabury Press, 1974, p. 105. Enzensberger is one of the ornaments of the German intellectual life, whose independent neo-Marxism has a tough Voltairean glint.

† Ibid., p. 99.

of cultural pessimism and technological optimism. The cultural apparatus is more likely to be the bearer of the "bad news" concerning—for example—ecological crisis, political corruption, class bias; while the consciousness industry becomes the purveyors of hope, the professional lookers-on-the-bright-side. The very political impotence and isolation of the cadres of the cultural apparatus grounds their pessimism in their own everyday life, while the technicians of the consciousness industry are surrounded by and have use of the most powerful, advanced, and expensive communications hardware, which is the everyday grounding of their own technological optimism.

Cultural apparatus and consciousness industry thus each define the world quite differently and are, as a result, in a tense if somewhat one-sided relation with one another; one-sided in that the former worries more about the latter than the reverse. Clearly, the largest section of the populace in advanced industrial societies is now under the direct and immediate influence of the consciousness industry, while the cultural apparatus has little if any direct contact with this great public. In short, the cultural apparatus is largely without direct access to or influence on the rural peasantry or farmers, the poor, the blue-collar working classes, blacks, and women.

The differences between the cultural apparatus and the consciousness industry do not exactly parallel differences between the politically involved and the *a*political, or between the "left" and the "right" ideologies in politics. There are some tendencies in that direction, but they could be overstated. For example, there are some involved in the cultural apparatus whose fastidiousness makes politics boring or offensive to their sensibilities. Correspondingly, the consciousness industry, perhaps particularly in its pop-music sectors, often fosters a deviant subculture isolated from mainstream consciousness. As we suggested earlier, it sometimes generates a *counter*culture that unwittingly undermines the very characterological and cultural requisites of the hegemonic class and the institutions that sustain it. It does so, of course, not because its personnel harbor a deliberate intent to sabotage, but from the most "respectable" of motives—to produce and sell whatever turns a profit—regardless of its consequences.

The cultural apparatus largely organizes itself in and around the modern university and its supporting facilities; it is therefore constantly threatened with isolation from the larger society and from any politically consequential following. In effect, the elites of the cultural apparatus surrender the mass of the populace to the consciousness industry, *so long as the elites continue to conceive of influencing others via ideology and ideological discourse.* For now, with the split between consciousness industry and cultural apparatus, ideology continues to ground an *elite* politics but loses effective influence over the masses.

Those who are ideologically mobilized and ready—the people of the cultural apparatus—are thus vulnerable to increasing political frustration, isolation, and impotence. The sense of self-identity and achievement implicit in and reinforced by ideology is here threatened. Even the ideologically mobilized are now, under the conditions of this split, tempted toward the rejection of ideology itself. They, too, are tempted toward a politics increasingly open to the irrational, in order somehow to make contact with the mass public from whom they have been cut off, and who do not respond to the conventional ideological appeals. Something of this was exhibited in what may be called the "Weatherman Syndrome," which is an impotence of the ideological that generates "days of rage," of violence and trashing, as a way of suppressing a sense of ineffectuality and of overcoming inclinations to passivity. In the Weatherman Syndrome—and in terrorism more generally— discourse ceases and ideology collapses into the propaganda of the deed. If the growth of the consciousness industry and its tensions with the cultural apparatus did not produce an "end to ideology" it certainly fostered a crisis for ideological discourse, making the limits on ideology's traditional modes of discourse all too evident.

2.4

There is now a growing mass of the populace in advanced industrial countries who are incapable of being reached by ideological appeals and who are insulated from ideological discourse of any political persuasion. It no longer seems merely mistaken, but is more nearly archaic, to think of the proletariat as an "historical agent" with true political initiatives in societal transformation. With the rise of the consciousness industry the inability of the proletariat to play such a role may now be beyond remedy. As E. P. Thompson has suggested: "So long as any ruling group . . . can reproduce itself or manufacture social consciousness there will be no inherent logic of process within the system which . . . will work powerfully to bring about its overthrow." * The conclusion is sound, however, only if we omit discussions of the contradictions of the consciousness industry itself.

Thus one may not conclude that the working class remains reliably controllable, even if it is continually vulnerable to the consciousness industry. Indeed, the proletariat in various countries, Italy, for example, may yet serve as the clean-up men of history, picking up power in the streets as their society's hegemonic class fumbles and collapses in the face of some abrupt crisis. But that is a far cry from being an historical agent with initiative and with a consciousness of its role.

The great and successful revolutions of the twentieth century, in Russia

* E. P. Thompson, "An Open Letter to Leszek Kolakowski," *Socialist Register*, Merlin Press, London, 1973, p. 75.

and China, occurred in societies that were not only behind in general industrial development but, also, in the development of their communications technology. To this day, the Chinese Cultural Revolutions make important use of wall posters to mobilize their forces. Indeed, one might add that the Cultural Revolutions themselves seem to have been precipitated when Mao lost control over (and routine access to) Peking newspapers, which refused to print his criticisms of Peking's mayor.

3

In countries with an extensive development of the consciousness industry, talk of "revolutionary solutions" is primarily indicative of ideological rage at political impotence and of the fear of personal passivity. In other words, it is a symptom. At the same time, however, neither the continual readiness of the cultural apparatus for ideological arousal and mobilization, on the one side, nor the growth of deviant and countercultures among masses, on the other, can allow one to assume any persisting social stability and equilibrium. A potentially mobilizable mass coexists alongside of an easily arousable ideological elite. Presently, the "stability" of modern society results in some large part from the mutual isolation of these sectors. Indeed, one should think of the present not as any sort of stable equilibrium but simply as a temporary "inertness." But whether that coexistence of mass and elite—an inert adjacency without much interaction and mutual influence—can long persist remains to be seen. Nevertheless, revolutionary solutions remain mythical so long as ideological elites and their cultural apparatus can reach masses only by going through the consciousness industry.

The paradoxical character of the present becomes even more visible if it is noticed that the *managers* of the consciousness industry, as of others, are also likely to be among the relatively well-educated, university-trained persons most extensively exposed to the cultural apparatus. Their ambiguous social role must yield an inevitable measure of ideological ambivalence. They cannot easily be dismissed by the cultural apparatus as philistine, illiberal, enemies of the mind. Indeed, the hegemonic elites have recently taken to accusing some in the consciousness industry of favoring the "left" and of being class traitors. This was, to some extent, the import of the Nixon-Agnew accusations against the press and of Daniel Patrick Moynihan's suggestion that university-trained journalists are one-sidedly critical of the *status quo*.

The tension between the consciousness industry and the cultural apparatus can become *a* center for a politics sensitive to the importance of the media and of the modern communications revolution. In one part, this will entail a struggle for public control and access to the burgeoning new communica-tion's technology. In another part, this politics will concern itself with the cultural apparatus' isolation from the mass media and the public it reaches. The tension between the two exists in some measure because the consciousness industry has socially isolated the cultural apparatus and has successfully imposed an institutionalized form of tacit censorship on it. The political struggle between the two will, in part, concern itself with the maintenance or relaxation of this censorship.

But this is not a conflict in which the consciousness industry will be unambivalently opposed and solidary in its response to the cultural apparatus. The reliability and controllability of the technicians of the consciousness industry and even of some of its managers is, indeed, in question. For, as we have noted, they too have been exposed to the perspectives of the cultural apparatus and share its hostility to censorship. Moreover, to the extent that the cultural apparatus can produce products that capture and hold attention, and can be sold or used as a vehicle to sell other things, then the cultural apparatus *will* be given access to the media and publics controlled by the consciousness industry. A media-centered politics, then, will amplify the common values and hostility toward censorship shared by the consciousness industry and the cultural apparatus, building alliances around these. It will, at the same time, exploit the contradictions of the consciousness industry that dispose it to publicize any cultural outlook that helps maintain its own profitability.

chapter 8

Ideology and the University Revolt

If, as we have said earlier, ideologies have a special relationship to written objects and to writing, this necessarily implies that ideologies will also have a special relation to those places in which writing and writers are to be found in some density. In some part, this points to the special importance of modern universities for ideologies and ideologues; for they are places where writing, writers, and written objects are highly valued and where this value is consciously transmitted.

1

An adequate sketch of the historical origins of modern ideology would clarify the special position of the university-trained intelligentsia most immediately involved in articulating ideology as a set of symbols. Here several points need mentioning. First, we must note as a kind of arbitrary base point that following the Enlightenment there was a profound loss of authority of the traditional, "organic" intelligentsia, of an intelligentsia integrated with other social strata—in short, of clerics. This, for two reasons: one had to do with the clergy's notorious alliance with the aristocracy in the class struggle that overthrew the old regimes. Another reason for the clergy's decline was cultural, not political; it remained too closely tied to the older humanistic, language-centered scholarship to be related effectively to emerging science and its growing public prestige. Both these factors were involved in the clergy's failure to respond persuasively to the critique of the old regimes mounted by the *philosophes*.

The *philosophes* themselves, however, were characterized by their integration—via the *salons*, their publishing audiences, and their mistresses—into the very society they subjected to scathing critique. The *philosophes* were often successful men, both in terms of public prestige and income. Among the social arrangements that the French Revolution destroyed, however, were the very structural requisites of the *philosophes* as a distinctive type of intellectual elite. After the passing of the old regimes, the remaining institutions—the market structure and university system—that might integrate intellectuals into the new society were, at first, only newly and weakly developed. Both, at first, provided only limited outlets for a humanistically trained elite while the newer scientific elites, technicians, engineers, and even doctors, were more readily integrated into the new industrialism. Being less integrated into and less rewarded by the new industrialism, the *humanistic* intelligentsia were considerably less sympathetic to it. They were the structurally alienated, quite free to feel disdain for the blunt venality and rough egoism of the new bourgeois. It was essentially this group of intellectuals that was the core of what Karl Mannheim called the free-floating, "unattached intelligentsia," presumably being unbound by class privileges.

It was only slowly, after 1789, as the public school and university system was reformed and expanded, and as it became a substantial labor market for intellectuals' services, that this system became a mechanism through which part of the unattached intelligentsia was slowly transformed into a new kind of corporate intelligentsia, more deeply integrated with the state and indirectly with the dominant social classes. The classical age of ideologies, of nationalism, socialism, liberalism, and indeed of Saint-Simon's (if not Auguste Comte's) positivism, was the product of initiatives taken by a sociologically distinct group of ideologues: the "unattached" intelligentsia. It was not directly a product of the university itself, although profoundly influenced by its products and training.

It was because of a unique historical situation that, following the French Revolution, the unattached intelligentsia could take important initiatives and had much autonomy. This intelligentsia faced a discredited aristocracy and clergy, on the one side, and, on the other, a publicly inexperienced, only precariously legitimate new bourgeoisie, who were separated from the direct exercise of violence or from the production of the culture and ideas that might legitimate them. The newly unattached intelligentsia could thus live in the interstices and unresolved antinomies between elites, between an old aristocracy that was historically outmoded and a new bourgeoisie that was historically immature. This unattached intelligentsia might then curry the favor and custom of the new bourgeois to his face, while sniggering at him in the coffee shops.

This was the distinctive social situation in which ideology at first developed and which endowed it with certain special characteristics: first, a certain autonomy which was real enough, especially while the class equilibrium mentioned above was fragile. Second, the very use of science for political and social ends, specifically, to serve as a legitimation of the new hegemonic class; this in effect allowed *non*scientists to define and speak for science thus once again enhancing the new ideology's autonomy, this time from science itself—as in the case of Saint-Simon. Third, the historically unique autonomy of this unattached intelligentsia was also reflected in ideology's concept of the unity of theory and practice. The very emphasis on this unity was grounded in the formulation of ideology by a social strata that, being alienated and unintegrated, itself stipulated social goals and ends, no less than proposing means to achieve them.

This unattached intelligentsia had no compunction—as later generations of intellectuals would—about articulating objectives for the larger society and prescribing the reorganization that it deemed necessary to bring them into existence. This very unity of theory and praxis prescribed by the grammar of ideology was grounded in the transient historical specificity of the unattached intelligentsia which allowed them substantial initiatives in the specification of group goals. Like independent contractors, they built their intellectual edifices where and how they wished, investing their energies in them on "speculation," i.e., without commitments in advance from specific patrons, working in the hope that their products would be marketable. The early ideologues were in that sense intellectual entrepreneurs.

But this situation, in which autonomy and alienation were two sides of the same process, was a transitional one. The expansion of the university and public-school systems, the creation of a national reservoir of teachers, meant a growing labor market for a language-manipulating and essentially humanistic elite and brought a corresponding reduction in their structural alienation. Regular livings, decreasing their autonomy, made them respectable and, in some places, even eminent men with a substantial stake in the new *status quo*. Moreover, the aristocracy waned slowly—much more slowly than those who think that Europe's history is reducible to the history of its revolutions—and at the same time adapted their resources and character to the new opportunities—which they had indeed begun to do well before the revolution of 1789. (Actually, the final death blow to the reactionary nucleus of European aristocracy did not come until the Soviet Army occupied Prussia). As the middle classes' old enemies grew weaker, or married their daughters, the new bourgeoisie achieved increasing influence in the state apparatus while facing increasing challenges from a new enemy, the rising urban proletariat. At least until World War I, the bourgeoisie grew stronger economically and politically. And even after, as industrialism provided a growing basis of consumerism, the working class threat diminished in Central and Western Europe, and the Communist Parties became in time essentially parliamentarian social democrats. With this consolidation of bourgeois rule in Central and Western Europe, the bourgeois need for legitimating ideologies was minimized and the new technological society came into its own. With this, the age of ideology and of an ideological politics began to become circumscribed or encysted within a surrounding technocracy.

There was, then, a certain rationality in the "end of ideology" prophecy. A certain structure of ideology *was* drawing to an end, although not ideology itself. From an historical standpoint, this cannot be otherwise and those who reject entirely the end of ideology thesis must be careful to avoid putting themselves in the unfortunate position of conveying a conception of ideology as a deathless entity above and outside the history.

2

One way of taking hold of the current condition of ideology is in terms of the theory-praxis problem. As we have seen, the unity of theory and praxis, enjoined by the grammar of ideology, was originally grounded in the sociological character of the ideologue as "unattached intelligentsia," as an intellectual entrepreneur who confronted problems of his own selection, and who took initiatives in formulating public policies and the social goals to be pursued. The ideologue was characterized by a genuine *personal* commitment concerning social problems that he himself selected for attention.

It is in the emerging era of the technocrat and of technology that there develops a rupture of this unity between theory and practice—a rupture which, at least until the mid-1960s, was expressed in the largely unchallenged definition of the role of the "professional." In saying that the new technological era introduced a split between theory and practice, I do not mean to suggest that technology is devoid of a praxis and concerns itself only with theory. If anything, the opposite is true, in that technology *per se* is primarily a praxis. In its self-understanding, what "technology" does is to present itself as a universal, all-purpose praxis, as a practice fit for the pursuit of any and all goals and as available to all and every group, whatever their goal. In between this universal all-purpose utility, and the universal needs of diverse publics, there is, of course, one important mediation: payment for services rendered. What integrates all-purpose polymorphous societal needs with the presumably all-purpose polymorphous need satisfier, technology, is the all-purpose mediator: money. In other words, the split between theory and praxis now takes the specific form of "sophistry," analytically construed here as the offering of one's talents or skills in exchange for money.

The split between theory and praxis is, then, twofold: first, the new technician himself has no interest in or binding commitment to the use of his skills in a limited way; he is, in principle, willing to consider any offer and regards himself free to accept an offer quite apart from the social purposes to which it will employ his skill, perhaps on the basis of its pecuniary advantage alone, providing only that it is not expressly illegal. This disunity between theory and practice is, in a way, also a split *within* the technician himself, his refusal of responsibility for the ends to which his virtue-skills are to be put.

This split takes a second form; it involves the allocation of the right to specify these ends to those paying for the technician's skills. Now there are two groups: technicians who supply the instrumental means, and contractors who formulate, specify and control the ends on which these instruments will be put to work.

It is precisely this societally supported definition of the technocrat's role that has usually enabled the hegemonic class to control technological skills without having to sequester them politically or deny them legally to others. It is essentially this definition of the technician's role that now enables the dominant classes to control the largest part of technocrats' time and skills. When intellectuals are willing to sell their services for a fee, and to allow others to specify the ends to which their skills are put, the intelligentsia become controllable technicians and technocrats; part of the once alienated, unattached intelligentsia now becomes an integrated appendage contributing to the reproduction and maintenance of the *status quo.*

Since "ideology" grew out of an unattached intelligentsia formulating its own goals, the emergence of technocrats working on behalf of others' goals does indeed draw a boundary line around classical ideology; this was one important phase-change in the history of ideology. (Although this is a project for a separate study, I later suggest this phase too, is drawing to a close.) Let me be clear that this new phase was not necessarily limited to, or brought about only by, specifically economic or market mechanisms. The party ideologue, for example, who surrenders party policy to party functionaries, and who confines himself to legitimating policies formulated by others— showing it to be consistent with what Marx "really" meant—such a party ideologue has become a technician specializing in symbol manipulation under the direction of party superiors. He is not much different from the market researcher who seeks ways of marketing carcinogenic cigarettes by showing them to be compatible with "the good life." Neither the party technicians nor the market researchers are any longer an unattached intelligentsia conscientiously committed to recommending only what they themselves believe. In their own somewhat different ways, both are now species of corporate intellectuals—kind of "company men."

As the unattached intelligentsia wane, ideologues come to be supplanted by technicians, bureaucrats, or technocrats, working to achieve goals specified by others. It is this change that was part of the rational core of the "end-of-ideology" prophecy. But how does this leave the end-of-ideology thesis—vindicated, refuted, or what? There is no serious answer possible without clearly seeing what the nature of the objections to the end-of-ideology thesis was at bottom. Essentially, the objection to that thesis expressed resistance to any implication that technology or science, and especially *social* science, were socially neutral, impartial, or "value free." What those opposing the end-of-ideology thesis rejected was any idea that technologues were "above the social struggle" and truly available to all comers with an impartial zeal.

The idea of the impartiality and autonomy of technology was doubted for good reason. For what does the impartiality of a technology mean if, via the market mechanism, it is more systematically available to the rich and to their distinct purpose? Moreover, the contention was also made, most definitely by Max Scheler and by the Frankfurt School, that science and technology have extra-scientific values built into them.

Those rejecting the end-of-ideology thesis had assumed that "impartiality" was a lofty virtue entrenching those who claimed it in a strong moral position. But if such impartiality comes down to the assumption that all goals must be treated as if they were equal in value, that one course of public action is no more valuable than another, then the new technocrats are grounded in the oldest venality. Why should one think that this venality endows anyone with a strong moral position? It is *independence*, not impartiality, that is the decisive consideration here, for *such* impartiality is only the most ancient of sophistries. As Socrates held, sophistry is essentially the readiness to sell one's "virtue" for money. If such sophistry is impartiality, it is the impartiality of the whore. Seeing the matter in this light, the end-of-ideology thesis was grounded in the waning of the *unattached* ideologues who worked on their own initiative on behalf of what they believed, and their replacement by technicians who sell their skills to those who have the price. Thus the new technologue is in no way morally superior to the old ideologue. His superiority is not moral and not even political; it is only a superiority of effectiveness. He is a man who can get things done. To regard the new technocrat as in any way superior to the older ideologue we must judge him entirely on *technical* grounds alone, and in doing this, we must prefer an anomic to a moral life.

In considering the relationships between the hegemonic classes and the intelligentsia, a special effort is required to avoid oversimplifying formulae and dramatizing dichotomies, and to exert every effort to see their relation in something like its true complexity. The hegemonic class is neither seducer nor, certainly, the pawn of the intelligentsia. And the intelligentsia is scarcely the *dis*interested embodiment of an historical idea that governs society. If we see the individualized venality of the bourgeoisie, we must also have no illusions about the systematic cravenness of apolitical academics and the obsessions of technocrats on the one side, and the susceptibility of the political intelligentsia, on the other, to anti-intellectual self-hatred, hysteria, resentment, and rage. And we must see both social strata as historically evolving—even though evolving with different timetables—and recognize that neither social strata has a patent on immortality. The task then, is not to deplore the limitations of a one-dimensional society but to explore a richer

Lukácsian vein: the opportunities for social development provided by the contradictions of contemporary culture.

Certainly there is little doubt that the hegemonic class remains an alert and effective shopper for ideologies. At the same time it is important to see that the influence it is able to exert on ideological development has its limits. One central site of their influence, which also establishes certain *limits* on that influence, is the modern university.

3

The university today is the key modern institution for the training of ideologues: it is also that single institution from which most modern ideologues derive their livings. Indeed, the university today is the single largest producer both of technocrats and ideologues, of *both* science and ideology. While the political dispositions of the university-based ideologists are quite various, there is little doubt that the modern university is also the largest single site for the production and storage of *anti*establishment ideologists; this means antibourgeois ideologists in the Western countries and anticommunist ideologists in the Eastern. (The recurrent waves of cultural repression, for example, of McCarthyism in the United States or of Mao's "Cultural Revolutions" in China, make it perfectly clear that in each case universities or their counterparts were a prime target.)

3.1

The student rebellions that culminated in the last half of the 1960s in the United States and in other countries of Western Europe were in part efforts to transform the universities; most specifically, they were attempts to change the formal, higher power structures of universities in ways that would "democratize" them. This means: to bring the formal governing apparatus of the university into greater correspondence with the actual distribution of *ideologies* in the universities' infrastructure. At the lower social levels of the university a liberal-to-Left ideology was generally far more prevalent than it was at the higher administrative levels. The university rebellions of the 1960s may, to stretch the point, be conceived as analogous to the bourgeois revolutions against old-regime politics. I mean this in the specific sense that the bourgeoisie had then already captured and controlled the *infrastructure* of old regime society prior to 1789. What "their" revolution sought was a corresponding control over the society's leading *political* institutions. In like manner, the "student" rebellion sought to bring the top polity of universities into closer correspondence with the ideological distribution in the infrastructure. And, we might add, the university revolt of the 1960s was not a "student" rebellion any more than the French Revolution of '89 was a "Jacobin" Revolution. It was essentially a rebel alliance between junior (and other) faculty and students, in which the students (whatever their self-consciousness) were the open fighting force; the students were the Jacobinry of a larger alliance.

This rebellion, however, had another concrete objective that was economic and which was as important as the political goal. This economic objective was to capture *livings* for those ideologically friendly to the rebels. Specifically, it aimed to win *tenured* posts for them. This objective had two related functions. First, it sought to consolidate the liberal/Left presence in the university, reducing its vulnerability to the inevitable *revanchism* of ideological enemies who occupied the administrative high ground. Secondly, the effort to win increased numbers of tenured livings within the university sought, in effect, to provide a basis of *economic* independence for those who were leading the Left's political effort to transform the *larger* society, not simply the university, and who wanted to secure the university as a fulcrum with which to lever the larger society leftward. Ultimately and clearly, the university revolt was a means to a larger societal reconstruction.

Let me draw a political parallel. *Full-time* politicians are the power center of *all* modern politics. There can be no serious political movement of any continuity without a substantial number of full-time leaders. But full-time leaders must have economic support, otherwise they have no free time for politics. The problem, then, is the *economics* of politics and, more especially, the particularly difficult economics of a *left* politics. For it cannot expect to be financed by enemies in the very establishment it wants to overthrow. In effect, then, tenured university posts were sought as a basis of financing the political efforts of those liberal-to-Left ideologues who wanted to devote themselves to the transformation and reconstruction of the larger society.

If, in the 1960s, the doctrinaire Left in the university commonly denounced the university as the instrument of the conventional power structure, it nonetheless did in practice proceed in the genuine hope that it might accomplish both its political and economic goals. While some on the Left held that they undertook the struggle primarily to "educate" others about the true nature of the university, nonetheless, many in the movement seemed to believe that they might genuinely increase their influence on university structure. And, in truth, they did. There was, indeed, some success in "democratizing" the university administrative structure, or at least, in increasing democracy there, even if not forcing power from the hands of those who had long monopolized it. There was also some modest success in winning tenured posts for movement-involved ideologues. This is at variance with the movement's own publicly expressed grievances, which naturally focus on universities where there was (without doubt) a bloodletting of the ideologically deviant. Nonetheless, from coast to coast, the movement succeeded in shifting attitudes and seeding new personnel. If the movement did not achieve its highest hopes, neither did it fail altogether. It moved forward. More than that, it may even be that those academics in the movement who won some tenured place outnumbered those who were purged. As a footnote, it seems curious that the movement preferred to define itself as having been brutally martyred and defeated rather than acknowledge that it had won a modest, small-scale success. The reader is referred back to the discussion of the tragic and the utopian, for a glimpse of such dynamics.

3.2

The fundamental political mistake that the movement made was underestimating its *own* strength and potentialities within the university, as well as the university's relative readiness to comply with its demands. In part, the trouble was that the Left succumbed to its own ideology. Believing that it could not expect support from those it fiercely denounced and humiliated—and it was surely right in this expectation—it generated a self-fulfilling prophecy. Heedless of the maintenance of its alliances, it often unleashed an indiscriminate campaign against and within the university, thus ensuring that many apolitical and uninvolved scholars, *Luftmenschen* normally interested only in their puzzle-engrossed scholarship, would lose their neutrality and could be mobilized against them.

The Left's campaign thus won less than it might simply because it made more enemies than it needed to. It failed, primarily, because it was based on an essentially faulty diagnosis of the university that overstressed its complicity as an ally of the establishment and correspondingly underestimated its relative autonomy. It also failed because it settled for the short-term pleasures of "trashing" rather than keeping its attention rivetted on the essential structural factors: enlargening the economic basis within the university for a radical critique and political transformation of society; a university basis which might strengthen the movement's ability to contribute to the long-term transformation of the national consciousness, as well as serving as a *locus* for mobilizing the community outside.

Still the very campus rebellion of the 1960s, however limited its successes, should make it perfectly plain that the hegemonic classes do not control the university in the way that doctrinaire dogmatists among the rebels had claimed. The hegemonic classes' capacity to communicate and enforce their ideological requirements and to find intellectual suppliers for them, is limited: by the apolitical other-worldliness of many specialized academicians; by the university's prevailing ideology of intellectual autonomy; by the degree of ecological and cultural separation between the university and the larger community; by the very "irrelevance" of the academic of which the Left most complained; and by a modest but palpable tradition of self-governance and autonomy. In some measure, granting "autonomy" to the modern university, as well as opening the university to larger numbers of students, was one way in which the nation-state could counter the influence of the church, exert direct influence over its masses, and ensure the loyalty of the elites and the skill of technical cadres required by the state's bureaucracy. The university and its faculty were thus key agencies in completing the modern separation of church and state. The "autonomy" of the university and its faculties was in effect the price that they had prized from the state by allying itself with the state's *Kulturkampf* against the church. University autonomy, then, was never an autonomy from the state itself.

The university's role as an incubator of ideologies was, in the beginning, condoned if not sponsored by the state itself in its effort to formulate a systematically secular definition of its own powers and prerogatives, enabling it to compete against clerical authority and churchly conceptions. The university became the state's source of "staff" experts and of culture resources, of ideologies no less than technologies, on which the state's growing power was based.

In some part, the period *after* the Enlightenment was an age of ideology precisely because there was then a great development under state auspices of universities, colleges, and other schools that provided livings and careers for the new secular ideologues. But while this autonomy of the university was grounded in these historical conditions and in the support of the state, what was won was nonetheless a real (even if limited) autonomy within which the whole modern system of sciences was cultivated, and by which the consciousness of modern elites was progressively secularized.

The development of the university as a center of secularism coincided with the requirements of the hegemonic economic class to produce persons with the desired vocational and professional skills. At the same time, however, the world outside the university, including the hegemonic classes and the state itself, tended to lose direct influence over the secularized consciousness that was being fostered by the more "isolated" faculties, colleges, and depart- ments—in the humanities and social sciences—whose product was not as successfully marketable in the larger society as those from professional and technical schools were. It is especially these "isolated" and "useless" parts of the university that tend to support and produce deviant and rebel ideologies. These segments may sometimes experience their autonomy as a rejection and as an isolating alienation; unswerved by temptation—indeed, untempted, if not untemptable—they could cling to older, humanistic values from whose perspective they could reject the successful technicians as narrow, servile, venal, and hypocritical careerists. Purified by social neglect, they could become a moral elite.

3.3

The development of the modern university, then, has tended to be contradictory. On the one side, it produces ever increasing numbers of technicians for bureaucratic offices—people with neither aptitude nor taste for ideological discourse, people who believe that society's problems can and will in time be solved by nonideological, technological appraisal, and purely scientific solutions. On the other side, however, the universities have also been producing a substantial, and perhaps even an increasing, *number* of intellectuals greatly interested in the production and consumption of ideologies. As *technical* and scientific education expanded, the *educated* middle class underwent a kind of binary fission, between the technical and the humanistic intelligentsias. The latter achieves a growing, "fissionable" mass of ideologues even as they decline in relative influence within the university's own proliferating technical colleges, thus becoming all the more vulnerable to alienation.

4

What has been happening in universities, then, is not altogether well expressed by speaking of the destruction of the "public space" due to the growth of a technocracy inimical to public political discourse. What is happening to politics is something different and more varied. It is, on the one hand, the continuing growth of a kind of new psychedelic "Hellenism," of the new occultism, of the emergence of "dropout" strata who are "into" the expansion of consciousness, who are also partly in the business of buying and selling, consuming and experimenting with, a changing variety of drugs, music, macrobiotic foods, television, clothing, travel, new religions, community-formation experiments, and the reorganization of sexual roles. All this is a demanding (indeed, exhausting) business. It leaves its adherents little time or energy for conventional combat politics. This seeming apoliticism has little or nothing to do with the burgeoning of modern technology and the technologues' preemption of citizen prerogatives.

What may be discerned is, partly, the narrowing of the public sphere, by reason of the growth of a technocracy inimical to mass political discourse, as well as the *transfer* of that public space, its *movement* from the larger community into the smaller and more limited public space of the university itself. What has been happening increasingly is the closing down of the *community* as the arena of political discourse and as the authentic site of the public sphere. Politics and political participation are thus, indeed, inhibited because of the pressure of the technocracy and because of the public unintelligibility of its proceedings. This closure of the larger community to politics, however, is also happening because intensifying public apathy about conventional politics was given a positive value by psychedelic cultures. As distinct from the more conventional form of political apathy, the psychedelic "dropout" was not reluctantly leaving the place of politics; he was *going gladly* to a better place, to a far, better world. . . . In that sense, then, the dwindling of the public space in the larger community is partly a pilgrimage and is, therefore, only partly a retreat.

The transformation of modern politics is rooted in an ongoing historical migration of the public sphere from the larger community to the university, and the outcome of this transformation will depend on the demographic forces that are mobilized. In other words, if those involved in colleges and universities continue, as they do in the United States, to increase in number more rapidly than do the nonuniversity segments of the population then, with their technical skills and openness to ideological enthusiasm, this university-related group can become a very powerful political force, and indeed, one of a very new kind.

This transformation is also closely linked to the issue of whether or not advanced education in the colleges or universities can continue to involve the masses and whether it will be free, both economically and intellectually. In this respect, the policy of the administration of the State of California during the late 1960s and early 1970s is instructive if not encouraging. There the nub of the matter was that the dominant classes and establishments quite clearly saw that the California University system did, indeed, threaten to become a center of politics that was autonomous and powerful. Its response to this threat was to mount increasing political pressure against ideologically deviant faculty and students and by budget cuts, to starve the university to death.

On a wider plane, the Nixon administration similarly contrived, by budget cutbacks, to create a *managed* recession in the American university system as a whole. The goal was to reassert the establishment's control, to squeeze the rebels out, and to warn university administrators that they faced financial ruin unless they "put their own house in order." The current contest for the control of educational facilities is radically new and consequential. Colleges and universities are no longer, as they once were, merely peripheral spheres of political mobilization or of incidental ideological embellishment. They may well be a holding ground of the public sphere and the main rallying ground of a new political power.

What I am saying, then, is that the growth of technocracy does not mean the "end" of ideology, the end of politics, or the end of rational discourse in the public sphere. The public sphere was always, after all, the sphere in which small elites sought to mobilize and manipulate masses via ideologies, even as it was also a sphere in which some (usually limited elites) fostered and participated in rational discourse. Ideology continues; it is by no means "dead." At the same time, however, it no longer preempts the modern political consciousness. The ideologue is forced increasingly to retreat before the technocrat's pressure. This retreat seems in the longer run likely to concentrate ideologically rational, political discourse in a university-centered political sphere. Yet such a concentration also risks isolation.

For if it has no links with the larger community, with strata associated with modern technical culture, and with the consciousness industry, the political consciousness of universities may become elitist and ritualistic. It presages the evolution of the larger public sphere in plebiscitarian directions. It means that political discourse will increasingly partake of the nature of "consultation" rather than decision-making, and in the ritualized ratification of well-merchandised glosses of the technocrat's proposals.

There can be no effective modern politics without finding ways to bridge the discourse of technicians and ideologists. The university with its auxiliary institutions is probably the best site to connect these different strata and modes of discourse. The problem, of course, is the structure of hegemony of that discourse. The danger in such a discourse is that it may simply become the mechanism by which technocrats either neutralize or coopt the ideologues; this, in turn, largely depends upon the relative power of the technical and professional faculties vis-à-vis the others within the university as a whole. It becomes clear, then, that what were once provincial questions of "mere" university politics, questions that were presumably the concern of only narrow, musty men, might come to assume a radically different aspect as the new fulcrum of a society-wide struggle.

PART TWO

Ideology and the Modern Order

chapter 9

Ideology and the Bourgeois Order

The "dual revolution" with which the modern era surfaced—the Industrial and the French "Revolutions," each a revolution in its own different way—was accompanied by a third revolution of which we have spoken in previous sections. We have spoken of it at length in part because it was, somehow, an invisible revolution, a symbolic explosion whose full impact is only now beginning to be seen and felt, like the light long ago emitted by some distant star and visible only now to the astronomer. It was in part "invisible" because it was enshadowed by the then more dramatically visible dual revolutions, with their forceful uprooting of European institutions and everyday life. The communications revolution was invisible, also, because it was in part the medium through which the other revolutions were followed and seen. Like the eyes with which we watch events around us, it was the events watched, not the eyes watching them, that were centered in attention. Thus the communications revolution was the revolution that was not only the seen-but-unnoticed revolution, it was a revolution *in seeing* that took time to see.

There were some few who saw its import almost at once and interestingly enough, among them, were the young Marx and Engels who, in *The Communist Manifesto*° and elsewhere, spoke of the communications revolution in the same breath with the bourgeois revolution in production—but it was the latter revolution to which they devoted their intellectual lives. They saw the communications revolution; they noticed; but their attention was elsewhere.

Having given attention in previous chapters to the submerged connection

° For example: "Modern industry has established the world-market, for which the discovery of America paved the way. This market has given an immense development to commerce, to navigation, to communications by land. . . . The bourgeoisie, by the rapid improvement of all instruments of production, by the immensely facilitated means of communication, draws all, even the most barbarian, nations into civilization." *Communist Manifesto*, authorized English translation edited by Engels, trans. Samuel Moore, Charles H. Kerr, Chicago, 1888. Pp. 14, 17.

between the communications revolution and the emergence of ideology, I now want to return to the more manifest connection, that of the relation between the bourgeois order itself and ideology. This connection is a familiar, well-worn and, indeed, a shop-worn one, precisely because Marx and Engels spoke of it at length, and, in a way, "discovered" it. Given the power and originality of their discovery, and the subsequent vulgarization of it, it is difficult to speak about the connection between ideology and the bourgeois order without first involving oneself in an exegesis of their views on the matter, and without taking a stand on these views, for or against. In my view such a course of analysis is today relatively profitless.

For me, Marx and Engels' theory of ideology, or my reading of it, assumes importance when and insofar as it is assimilated into our own analytic perspective, and helps us get on with our work. Its importance here is its capacity to do *that* and not as a center of theoretical struggle or sectarian polemics. The discerning reader will note that what follows is often (not always) consistent with the Marxian theory of ideology, and that what is important about the relation of our position to theirs is not the points of convergence or divergence, but rather my effort to clarify, explore, and provide an articulate and new *grounding* for certain aspects of their theory of ideology.

The discerning reader will note also that my reading of Marxism is heavily influenced by Hegelian preferences, by the standpoint of a "critical" rather than a "scientific" Marxism, and, especially by the young Lukács.

1

Eric Hobsbawm tells us that the term "ideology" surfaced in the sixty years from 1789–1848, along with a flotilla of other new terms: journalism, strike, pauperism, capitalism, industry, working class. "Ideology" manifests itself, then, hard on the heels of the French Revolution, as unmistakably born of the transition from the old regimes and of the first stirrings of the new bourgeois order. It is as importantly connected with the new sciences and with their accelerating prestige, as with the new politics of mass mobilization. Indeed, "scientist," "statistics," "engineer," and "sociology" itself, are among the new terms with which the modern consciousness begins to think.

The first great assembling ·of ideologies in Europe was shaped by their presence in transitional societies, societies only recently revolutionized, or on the verge of it. In these societies there were groups that had a deep sense of the need to change and to carry change forward to some new stable plateau; and there were others who had a will to restore society to what it had been, and to create new social forces to prevent impending but undesired changes from going further. Whether "liberalism," "socialism," "nationalism," or "monarchical paternalism," all were relatively new ideologies and none expected to achieve their aims by the politics of the camarilla. All aimed at the mobilization of masses. The Enlightenment became the age of ideology when the mobilization of masses for public projects was undertaken via the rhetoric of rational discourse. But if ideology reaches forward toward political projects it is also grounded in economic transofrmation no less than in the communications revolution that accompanied it.

There is absolutely no way forward to an analysis of ideology; there can be no serious understanding of ideology in the modern world that is not grounded in the historical quandaries of the new bourgeois society, in the bourgeois revolution, and of course in bourgeois property. Any historical discussion of ideology that blinks at this and does not relate ideology to the problems of the new society, any discussion of ideology that thinks this an oversimplifying vulgarity, will discover that it has bought sophistication at the price of impotence. Those who want to talk "ideology" must also talk "property."

1.1

But we had best add at once that those who think property—especially "private" property—is a matter of narrow *egoism* are laboring under a profound misapprehension that is not only theoretically misguided but can, also, father practical political catastrophes. The hunger that a man cannot endure, which his ego cannot survive, is not his own but his child's. The hunger that puts the spur to revolution is not a stomach question alone. Men will beg and they will kill, they will steal and rebel, when the social world in which they live prevents them from protecting and nourishing those persons and things they love, and to whom they are bound by duty and affection.

The power of property interests, as either stimulus toward or as a brake upon revolution, cannot be understood simply as an expression of a narrowly individualistic venality, or as a selfishly pursued egoism. There is, paradoxically, a deeply altruistic component in property. For the property interests of the bourgeoisie—as of the peasantry and other strata—have always been enmeshed in its family system. The middle-class concern to extend or defend its property was always motivated, in important part, by the viability of the middle-class family, by the bourgeois' felt obligations to it, and by his concern to use property to protect and advantage "his" family. The bourgeois, in short, acted as the leading member of a family group to whom he felt responsible, and by whom he might be held accountable. Property's power to mobilize the most profound motivations and anxieties relates to the fact that economic and family roles are fused; the threat to property generates panic not only because it threatens comforts but because it thwarts the proper performance of family obligations, family roles, and of the selves that are grounded in these.

Imagine a middle class consisting solely of men and women who neither had nor wanted family and children of their own. As has been suggested since Plato and recently reiterated by John Rawls, such a class would be better able to do justice to others precisely because it had less interest in accumulating heritable private property. For it, property would be less significant a consideration in making political decisions. This would be a class, on the one side, whose defense of property interests would be more temperate and would, on the other, be less likely to shrink from policies against property. In short, property's influence on political decision is importantly (not exclusively) due to its embedding in the family system.

Correspondingly, those of the urban poor with little or no property and who (partly in consequence) may also lack stable family structures have, in turn, less motive to acquire such transmissible property and certainly less reason to protect the property of others. The political policies of the poor do not aim at the protection (or even the acquisition) of heritable property but are, rather, concerned with consumable goods. This, for example, was the central economic policy of the French Revolution's *sans-culottes;* it sought to provide and distribute relief and to limit prices. It is not amiss to note here that urban pauperism was, at the beginning of bourgeois society, as at the present, connected with the deterioration of the family system of the poor, as was female or child labor, individual migration to the cities, squalid housing, and itinerancy.

1.2

The slow deterioration (or revolutionary destruction) of the old regime's corporative order during the bourgeois emergence never quite entailed the radical atomization of society that some critics have imagined; for at least the middle-class family remained a viable group. The deteriorating social system at first fell back on simpler social structures, the family unit, which became the nucleus around which new, more complex social structures could develop. In other words, family units became the organizing centers of commercial and industrial enterprises. They provided stability in bourgeois society because of the family's intergenerational continuity and its inheritance of property.

These consolidations of effective social structure—fusions of family and enterprise—were then essentially defined as *private* spheres, and were believed to be legitimately such. The central problem of the new society therefore concerned its *public* sphere and especially its political institutions; the viability of its private sphere was taken as given, at least among the rising bourgeoisie. Political issues came to center on the kinds of social structures that might provide continuity and stability in a public sphere where family transmissible privilege was no longer accepted, since the state was no longer defined as the private property of a dynasty.

While the bourgeois economy could be reorganized around an old, established structure, such as the family, the social structures organizing the public polity had to be newly created, invented, and debated. For there existed nothing in the public sphere comparable to the families through which authority could over time be transmitted, legitimated, implemented, and maintained. The one exception was the state bureaucracy, which, *defined* as a purely technical instrument presumably above clashing private interests, became the decisive vehicle of continuity in the *public* sphere.

The crisis of the bourgeois order was then defined as residing in the public, not the private sphere. The focus of political concern at first devolved on the development of new public institutions for which a wave of constitution-building became one kind of response, on working out the relationship between the state and the individual person, and on extricating the economy from the state.

2

The French Revolution's "Declaration of the Rights of Man and the Citizen" epitomizes one such effort at developing new public institutions. The "Declaration of the Rights of Man" was in effect a model charter of bourgeois society, and a closer view of it may enable us to see the ideology-generating quandaries of that society. Such declarations were, in effect, social plans for the organization of the public sphere. These plans embody the images or maps of a proper social order shared by the men formulating the plan and who bound themselves to it by making their commitment (to the plan and to one another) a *public* act. It thus took the form of a "declaration."

Embedded within the Declaration there was also an explanation of the protagonists' behavior toward the old regime and of their expectations of the new regime. The Declaration thus contained an account of the way the planners felt the new world *should* be organized, as well as of the way in which they thought it *had been* organized. It was both a political theory and a civic morality, a set of reports and of commands. This mapping of the projected social world, however, was not only an intellectual projection; it was also a political product. As such, it was not an embodiment of what one "planner" wished but, rather, of what the polity of leaders could commonly agree upon, and further, of what they hoped might appeal to a larger public. The plan, therefore, was also a rhetoric, intended to be publicly persuasive.

2.1

The Declaration began by reporting that public misfortunes derive from a disregard for the rights of man. The bourgeois revolution was thus presented as lacking in a particularistic or merely local coloration; it was presented as one special case of what happens when a more general condition arises; the revolutionists thus identified themselves with humanity at large, and they endowed neither themselves nor their time with any special privilege or unique character.

In attributing the revolution to the violation of human rights, the revolutionaries made no mention of *interests*, or at least of their own specific interests. The rights violated were described as both "natural" and "sacred," which implied that the revolutionists were not initiating anything new, that they were only protecting something old against new violations. Conceived as both natural and sacred, the rights are thus both normative and existential. The Declaration did not simply contend that they were good but also that they were real and existent; thus morality and theory, commands and reports, were fused. It premised a species of natural law conceived as under the governance of some "Supreme Being," whose secular interpreters were the people themselves rather than priests.

So far as these rights are concerned, men are born free and equal and remain so. The differentiations among men "may be based only on common utility." It is utility rather than wealth or lineage that was held to legitimate social differentiation and, especially, social rankings. In other words, it was presumably men's *usefulness* to the commonweal that justifies social distinctions and inequalities, not their traditional character or their imputed origins.

Here, then, the divine right of kings gave way to *utility* as the standard of legitimacy; authority was held to rest on (or emanate from) the nation and it was thus secularized and stripped of its mystique. Moreover, all rights and customs not authorized expressly now became of dubious legitimacy and subject to criticism, however traditional; correspondingly, rights and entitlements might be entirely legitimate even if new or only recently adopted. Traditionalism, which entails the right of the old to bind the young, or the right of previous generations to bind successors, was thereby declared null and void.

The society conceived here was one in which certain spheres of freedom from interference by public authority were established. The constitution of the public and private sphere was simultaneous and complementary. The role of the state was conceived not as actively encouraging the pursuit of various virtues, or of providing means for their realization. The new society protects "liberty" which is conceived negatively, as that which is *not* a duty required by law or is *not* injurious to others. These are the only limits on liberty: "No hindrance should be put in the way of anything not prohibited by law." Moreover the only legitimate limits on rights are to be those *legally* enacted. Thus any legal limit may be enacted if it protects the rights of others, and whatever is not prohibited (by law) is permissible. Restrictions resting on custom or tradition alone are, therefore, dubiously legitimate hindrances on action and vulnerable to challenge and criticism. All custom, then, is intrinsically modifiable by law for the protection of human rights, and is subject to a rational appraisal of its utility.

There is now a clear operational test of the legitimacy of (restrictive) *custom*—its correspondance to and validation by positive law. There is, however, no equally definite test of the legitimacy of the *law* itself. Law lacks legitimacy if it is not needed to defend the collective interest from injury, but this need is difficult to impute. Law is also not legitimate if it is not universal, i.e., "the same for all"; but in so far as it is, it may legitimately enact any penalty or provide any service held to be in the interests of the commonweal. Thus while affirming the sacred rights of *individuals*, the Declaration also reserves for and endows the *state* with enormous discretionary powers. As if concerned about this, the Declaration of Rights also announces very specific protections for property: "Property being an inviolable and sacred right, no one may be deprived of it except for an obvious requirement of public necessity, certified by law, and then on condition of a just compensation in advance." Equal access to public employment, allocated only on the basis of competence, is also affirmed, as is freedom of opinion, including religious opinion and its communication, and so, too, is taxation in accordance with ability to pay.

Implicit within the Declaration of Rights, then, was a distinctive image of man and a distinctive theory of society, which had something of the following character: it postulated individuals deemed essentially alike, at least in their possession of certain sacred rights and in their relationship to constituted public authority. Whatever other socioeconomic differences they have, these are not to be regarded as inequalities relevant to the state or to be remedied by it. The state is to take no notice of man's social differences in the protections it affords or in the justice it distributes; i.e., men of property presumably have no special advantages.

The state is essentially a referee, ensuring that the contestants fight a clean fight and do not infringe upon one another's natural rights. The state, however, has no obligation to prevent mismatched or unequal contests. Still, this is somewhat ambiguous, for the state does have an obligation to see that one party does not infringe on the rights of another. But an existent social differential between contestants does not *prima facie* constitute such an infringement, and therefore the *redress* of such differentiations does not constitute a *prima facie* obligation of the state. It is, rather, the obligation of some private party to initiate the contention that certain traditional social differentials do inherently limit the sacred rights of some persons. The state, however, is obliged to recognize different levels of competence and to allocate public employments to those with the superior competency; but it has no *prima facie* duty to redress the *traditional social differences* that regularly reproduce different levels of competence.

The social world is thus viewed as one large contest, overseen by the state. Men are expected to pursue their private interests by working and by contesting with others, but to do so without infringing on their rights; the social relationships envisaged are, therefore, not actively cooperative ones, nor are citizens expected to have any more regard for the state than a prize fighter has for the referee. That is, men do not enter into an intimate communion with one another or with the state. They are not required to feel a common devotion to a common past. Their common customs are conveniences—"rules of the game," as we now call them—rather than a "sacred heritage" which is deeply internalized. Such rights and duties as men have are to themselves and to the families they represent, or to the state. While they are expected to honor the rights of others, which means that they will forgo injuring them, they are not required to assist others actively and positively in the achievement of their rights. Generally, it was not men's duties but their *rights* that the Declaration declared to be sacred. And such rights as men have, they have primarily in their capacity as *citizens* and thus in their *political* relationship to the state as such.

It is clear, then, that the Declaration was only the most skeletal map of a social order in which "individuals" are engaged in a contest refereed by the state. It was a social map whose stark outlines would seem particularly bleak when contrasted with the still familiar feudal map of a hierarchically arranged society of three orders, in which the differences among men were at least acknowledged and composed, and in which there was a place for the guild and the Church as well as the state.

2.2

The Declaration of Rights and the new bourgeois order never faced up to the question of how an equality of public political rights could be effected among those who had unequal wealth or powers in society. Indeed, it endorsed differentials of wealth by declaring property rights to be sacred. The bourgeois order entailed an affirmation of equality which, like all such, implied a critique of *old* privileges and disguised the emergence of *new* inequalities. It was not inequality in general, and certainly not inequality in wealth or property, that the Declaration sought to abolish; it was primarily inequalitities unrelated to individual talent or achievements. It was *feudal* privilege that the French Revolution sought to abolish and it was bourgeois privilege with which it replaced this. And it was not even all privileges based on *birth* that the revolution struck down, but primarily *public* privileges and distinctions; for it clearly did not intend to abolish the right of succeeding to family property. In short, the middle class sought to remove limitations in the political and public sphere that prevented *it* from achieving political influence and public distinction commensurate with its wealth, and which it could in turn use to augment its class position.

The Declaration of Rights took no notice of other, nonfeudal but still traditional social distinctions, insofar as these entailed social inequities. While it acknowledged and sought to remove impediments to freedom of religion, this was only a recognition of a right to hold and communicate diverse religious beliefs insofar as these did not disturb public order. But it undertook no responsibility to restrain religious prejudices or discriminations, even though these constituted career handicaps and other kinds of market inequities. Hence while the Declaration enlarged religious tolerance, it also countenanced anti-Semitism and, for that matter, other forms of ethnic discrimination. Although speaking for a generalized equality, it left ancient distinctions of race intact as well as many traditional restrictions on women. The new bourgeois society, then, entailed an accomodation to "racism" and "sexism."

The bourgeois could, of course, be content with such a purely *legal* universalism for *it* already possessed the means to prosper and to exploit the new opportunities it had created. Yet equality under the law was of course something quite different for the urban poor and the emerging working classes. For even when enfranchised, they could not eat their votes. Out of this tension between legal universalism and the strengthening of the state, on the one hand, and abiding unequal wealth, on the other, there in due course emerged the "welfare" state. Similarly, the continued maintenance of traditional ethnic, racial, and sexual distinctions, in the context of a strongly affirmed legal universalism, also created tensions and contributed to various social movements aiming at the redress of these inequalities.

Equality as an ideology was generalized and abstract; it was an unspecified affirmation that all "men" should be afforded the same rights and be treated in the same way, particularly with respect to public authority. It did not specify to which men, or to which roles, or in which times or situations this applied. The burden of justification was thus placed on those who wished to *limit* its application and to treat others differently. This theory and the everyday culture out of which it grew, tends toward the implication that, apart from such *ad hoc* exceptions for which argument is offered, the right to equality is universal and unlimited.

The formulation of bourgeois ideology (or of any ideology) tends to generality and has a zone of indeterminate application. In contrast, however, the middle classes also had more concrete and specific *interests* and limited class "paradigms" in mind, when they vaunted equality and denounced privilege. They wanted equality under the *law*, equality in the *public* sphere, and an end to the *legally* sanctioned privilege of the nobility in the public sphere. "Ideologies" are thus public commitments embedded in a more *focal* awareness, while "Interests," being partisan, are commitments maintained in a more *subsidiary°* awareness, all the more so as they are variant from the ideology held and as this variance generated dissonance.

The bourgeoisie thus rarely gave "equality" unambivalent support. It was primarily the educated rather than the propertied members of the middle class, the professional more than the businessmen, and the intellectuals more than the professionals, who developed a politics centered on equality. It was the intellectuals, more than any other group, who could develop a Jacobin fervor and revolutionary intransigence on behalf of equality.

3

Why did bourgeois societies have such a strong impulse to *generalize* claims, to put their particularistic interests into a universalistic framework? In one part, this was because, at least for an historic period, the interests of the bourgeoisie were actually consistent with those of other groups. The bourgeois revolution was made in the name of Reason, in which all men were held to participate. So while it was bourgeois property that, among other social forces, corrupted and qualified public rationality, it was also the bourgeoisie who brought Reason onto the historic scene.

Moreover, it was in bourgeois societies that all members of the nation, the "people," were first admitted to the public arena. It was the bourgeoisie who really first created modern politics as action in a truly public arena. Unlike the ancient Greeks, who excluded well over the majority of their cities' population—the slaves and *metics*—from political participation and from the

° To clarify this distinction between focal and subsidiary awareness, which I use occasionally in this volume, let me quote from Michael Polanyi, from whom it is derived: "When we use a hammer to drive in the nail, we attend to both nail and hammer, *but in a different way*. We *watch* the effect of our strokes on the nail and try to wield the hammer so as to hit the nail most effectively. When we bring down the hammer we do not feel that its handle has struck our palm but that its head has struck the nail. In a sense we are certainly alert to the feeling in our palm and the fingers that hold that hammer. They guide us in handling it effectively, and the degree of attention that we give to the nail is given to the same extent but in a different way to these feelings. The difference may be stated that the latter are not, like the nail, objects of our attention but instruments of it. They are not watched in themselves; we watch something else while keeping intensively aware of them. I have a *subsidiary awareness* of the feeling in the palm of my hand which is merged into my *focal awareness* of my driving in the nail." M. Polanyi, *Personal Knowledge, Towards a Post-Critical Philosophy*, University of Chicago Press, Chicago, 1958, p. 55.

public arena, the bourgeoisie—or a section of it—opened this arena even to urban masses, especially when they needed a fighting force against their political enemies, particularly the nobility. Indeed, in principle, they included all except the nobility and clergy in the "nation" and "people" in whom they claimed that sovereignty now resided.

The people, in short, not only had a new power in the public arena but this new power was also legitimated. The creation of a public sphere with a measure of democracy, along with the definition of the people as the basis of sovereignty, along with the dissolution of traditional social structures, meant that the masses were far more politically mobilizable than ever before. The urban masses, in particular, were then in a much stronger position either to block or to further the politics of elite interests. It is the development of such a new role for the masses that necessarily requires that their views, beliefs, and convictions be taken into serious account.

It is partly for these reasons that private interests come to be generalized into universal claims. The modern "egalitarian" politics of the bourgeoisie meant that they were constrained to *take the role of the other,* and be sensitive to his view of the world; for, without this, there would be no persuading him. Conversely, one can more readily ignore the standpoint of the other when he is powerless than when he has institutionalized access to power. Persons who lack such sources of power can, indeed, be subjected to manipulation and be externally influenced. They may be moved about as if they were goods in a store. Elites need not bother about the views of the powerless except in an instrumental way.

In the context of empowering democratic institutions and, also, in the context of the cultural sanctioning of equality, the masses had to be treated as "human." One now had to make an effort to persuade them, to make them *want* to do and to believe in what they are called upon to do. They could no longer be treated as instrumentally manipulable and deployable resources who could be openly *ordered* to do something against their will. The new culture of "equality and fraternity" was dissonant with manipulation of the masses in that impersonal and visible manner. They now had to be given reasons. And the reasons that they had to be given could not be grounded in discredited traditional authorities and had to have the same universalistic and generalized character as those offered to others; for now all were "equals."

Thus impersonal manipulation and traditional hierarchy no longer sufficed to coordinate modern politics, or to mobilize the masses to action. This became one of the central tasks of ideology.

3.1

In societies prizing egalitarian values, it becomes particularly important to blur the existence of hierarchy and to conceal domination. Above all, it is important in such societies for superiors not to be seen as issuing "orders"; for it then becomes inescapable that those ordering are dominant and those obeying are subordinate. It likewise becomes particularly important not to resort to brute force and violence. Direct orders and open violence are dissonant with a social system premising egalitarianism and disposed toward free rational dialogue as a way of determining who is to do or to get what.

Dominant groups need not issue orders to subordinates, and they need not exercise force and violence over them, under the following conditions: (a) if they can determine the rules by which subordinate's behavior is to be governed, and this would include their processing of information—that is, the rules of data processing; and (b) if the resultant definition of the situation— the "What Is"—is established in conformity with these rules, or is otherwise subjected to influence of the dominants, whose definitions of "What Is" are given greater weight than those of other strata. The influence of dominants in defining social reality is not confined to their influence over the rules but may, in a less systematic way, simply derive from the credibility attributed to them by reason of their social position. Given the ability to influence general information-processing rules, and specific definitions of reality, the dominant group can now get others to do as it wishes without being compelled either to resort to force or to issue direct orders. Once someone complies with the rules of behavior and accepts the conception of reality favored by others, then he will willingly and "spontaneously" behave in ways that the latter wishes, without having to be *forced* or ordered to do so. In effect, ideologies facilitate the production or maintenance of some power hierarchies (even if they undermine their adversaries). Domination is concealed when certain courses of conduct, definitions of the situation, or conceptions of what is real, are internalized by subordinates so that they give willing compliance to the expectations directed at them. For to internalize an ideology is to internalize a set of commands and reports. That being so, the struggle between social groups is now mediated by their struggle to shape the ideologies relevant for various situations and groups. There is, in the result, a struggle to control ideologies with their built-in system of reports and commands that structure the behavior of the politically involved.

3.2

When it was first surfacing to public visibility and mounting its revolutionary effort, the new bourgeoisie had special needs; they had to legitimate themselves and their political aspirations *vis-à-vis* their competitors for power, the old elites and especially the aristocracy, who had largely preempted the political services and allegiances of the clergy and Church. Established religion had cast its fate with the old order and old elites, ratifying this ancient connection even after the French Revolution, as was made clear during the Restoration period and the Metternichian effort to impose a European-wide political stasis. There was thus crystallized a widespread public view of the Church as allied with premodern forces and as manifesting a class partisanship.

Excluded from the political favor of the Church, the new, rising elites sought new sources of legitimacy for their political claims, as did the new states that were then also developing. It is thus that they turned from ancient modes of legitimation to the newer legitimations that could be provided by a secular intelligentsia acting under the growing authority and prestige of science and to the development of universities under the aegis of the new states.

Enlightenment ideologies at first united all social classes under the rubric of the "nation," as a social entity apart from and against the old regime of priesthood and aristocracy. Correspondingly, the development of *anti*-Enlightenment ideologies sought a symbolic rubric for a new solidarity of classes within the nation. They sought ideologies that would include the *aristocracy* and reestablish its hegemony over the other and newer classes. In both cases, what was needed was an ideology that could contribute to the blurring of certain, but in each case different, class differences and to the consolidation of new polities. In the beginnings of the bourgeois era, ideologies were needed to provide secular legitimations of the middle class's political ambitions and to ground the modern state as a nonpartisan, above-class, institution in a secular culture fostered by a newly autonomous secular intelligentsia.

David Apter correctly notes, "ideology helps support an elite and to justify the excercise of power." Still it is apparent that ideologies as such do not at first provide support for *any* and all elites; for old regime traditional elites are supported by *religious* belief systems; *ideological* belief systems appeal to the newly established elites of emerging industrial society, the rising bourgeoisie, who are congenial to the emerging sciences, once more affirming the link between science and ideology.

There is, however, not only accommodation but also growing tension between this emerging hegemonic class and the new intellectuals. The new bourgeois elite welcomes science and scientism as a critique of the belief systems, and hence legitimacy, of older traditional elites. Ideology, then, is at first grounded in a consciousness open to the new prestige of science, emerging when the older elites are beaten or on the verge of defeat, but while the new elites are still precarious and insecure. Ideology's opening toward science functions to provide both a new epistemology as well as a new technology to legitimate and empower the new elites' consolidation of its power.

The old elites had initially sought to respond to this challenge by revitalizing their ties with traditional religion, in part by seeking to coopt the new romanticism as a critique of science and of the life styles and consciousness of the new elites associated with science. Essentially, romanticism's strategy was to formulate a belief system that made it possible to accept modernity without rejecting religion. But in the end it could not do this without the most profound transformation of religion itself. Beginning with Kant and continuing through the other great German idealists, Fichte, Schelling, and Hegel, religion was sublimated into a rational philosophy which, refusing to limit itself as a "specialization," came to produce a secularization that was more profoundly dissonant with traditional religion than science itself.

Ideologies, then, are beliefs systematized by a stratum of intellectuals separated from power and property, from which they initially seek support and sponsorship. Unlegitimated by tradition or church, these new intellectuals authorized *themselves* in the new rhetoric of science and through rational discourse. It is clear, then, that science was pushed toward scient*ism* not only, and not even mainly, by scientists themselves.

3.3

Ideology was at first produced by humanistic, symbol-manipulating elites to coopt science or, at least, its prestige for its own public projects and for those of the new elites with whom it desired to be associated. Being useful to the new elites, the ideologues won some support from them, so long as they clearly accepted their hegemony, at least in the "secular" sphere. The new hegemonic elites did not really want to wage war against the Church so much as they wanted the Church to limit its support of the old elites and to accept the new bourgeoisie and state. Thus some of the new ideologies, such as positivism, commonly did not reject religion. They sought to reform and modernize it, pushing it toward a kind of ethical culture and "rational" religion—Saint-Simon's and Comte's "religion of Humanity." But scientism essentially remained the ideology of the newer technicians and engineers. By contrast, romanticism's own infrastructure was more congenial to the older, humanistic elite of writers, poets, and musicians, who had once been integrated into the older patronage system of the traditional elites, but who, with the new industrialism, had been left adrift.

In compact outline, these are some features of the social situation under which the first age of ideologies prospered. The situation changes, of course, when the bourgeoisie are no longer a new and precarious class and when they come to be more fully integrated with the state and accepted in society. Does the bourgeoise then need ideology to legitimate its influence and power? What happens to ideologies when they no longer need to swim upstream against powerful resistance, and have freinds and clients in the state apparatus, and when their once eccentric ideas become the commonplaces of state-supported textbooks? The ideologies and the need for ideologies change, moving from sectarian matters of personal conscience and faith to become the churchly, official ideologies of well-accredited establishments and state systems. With the bourgeoisie's entrenchment, with its growing self-confidence and experience with power, the old ideology loses much of the appeal that it earlier had.

chapter 10

Interests, Ideologies, and the Paleo-Symbolic

In the course of its struggle against the old regimes, the bourgeoisie deauthorized the aristocracy and legitimated their own claims by affirming a new set of standards for allocating enjoyments. They shifted the standard from ascription to achievement, from what a person "was" to what he *did*. The new standard called for allocating rewards on the utilitarian basis of persons' differential "usefulness," rather than on the basis of their family or birth. The aristocracy and court were condemned for their uselessness to the nation. Imagine them all dead, asked Saint-Simon, what loss would it be to France?

1

This bourgeois critique of the aristocracy was itself grounded in a distinction between (1) the gratifications persons enjoy, on the one hand, and (2) the conditions or situations on which these depended, on the other. There is thus both a distinction and an interlocking of the subjective and objective dimensions of "interest." what is *in* our interest are out-there gratification-producing conditions, and is epistemologically "objective." At the same time, not any condition that exists apart from us is in our interest. It needs to be stressed emphatically that I reject totally any objectivistic view of an "interest" without at all embracing a subjectivistic one. This means that it is decidedly *not* that conditions are in our interest only or whenever we think them so, or that whatever we may want is in our interest. Nor do conditions constitute interests simply by reason of what *they* are. They constitute interests only because of what they *do* and do for someone, and exist as "interests" therefore only in relationship to some persons. An out-there condition is in our interest insofar as, and only insofar as, it produces an in-here gratification for us. An "interest" then is never just an interest in general. It is always *someone's* interest. What an interest is, therefore, always depends on the character of an out-there condition *and* on *our* character. It is thus not what some men *want* that make certain things in their interest but on what these men *are*. Thus interests depend on the nature of the gratifications men require and are capable of experiencing, and, also, on what certain conditions do to produce gratifications for them. Whatever produces gratification for persons is in their interest; property and wealth are certainly among the most common interests men have but so, too, may men have interests in a nation-state, in an ethnic or racial group, in their education and knowledge and linguistic skills, and they may also have an interest in the success of their ideologies. Here, then, we begin to explore some of the links between ideology and interest. But first we require a deepened understanding of an interest.

1.1

It is essential to the concept of interest that it is ambiguous as to whether the gratification it entails for persons is "known" to them. This allows both for (1) the possibility of a rational calculation concerning these conditions and, (2) it sometimes permits these gratifications to occur without persons "knowing" what produces them. It also means that persons may not know whether or not those gratifications affect their response to the conditions producing them. Not knowing what produces a gratification may make it difficult to maintain it; but it may, contrariwise, allow us the continued enjoyment of it under certain other conditions which, did we *know* them, might interfere with our enjoyment or require us to forgo it. Specifically; if the conditions producing our gratifications are known to us, it will also be known to us whether they are *unjustified*, which may, indeed, impair our enjoyment and, perhaps, spoil it altogether.

It is in this context that a word may be said about "false consciousness." As I use it here, this simply refers to a view or "consciousness" concerning the sources of one's gratifications—or of what is "functional" for one—that is *wrong*. To say that it is "wrong" implies a judgment validated by some group other than the persons having the "false consciousness." When anyone asserts that some persons have a false consciousness, it implies his acceptance of some *other* group as a superior source of cognitive validity; it implies a reasoned preference for *their* standards of judgment as against those whose judgment has been found wanting.

As used here, then, the notion of false consciousness has no necessary connection at all with the relationship between dominated and dominating groups, nor with the failure of the former to understand that their own interests are in conflict with the interests of the latter, due to the manipulation of the dominated by the dominating. As far as we can see, this is by no means always the case. Where it does sometimes occur, it is merely a special case of the notion of false consciousness used here. The interests of the dominant are not always in conflict with those of the subordinate. There *are* times when their interests coincide; when, even in the Marxist formulation, the bourgeoisie are a "progressive" class, the interests of the proletariat are *not* in conflict with theirs. Nor is the mistaken judgment of the subordinate class always due to their manipulation by the dominant class. The dominants *themselves* do not always know what is in their interests, and thus cannot always impose this view on others. Moreover, even if they do know what is in their interest, and do attempt to impose it on others, they sometimes fail. Successful manipulation implies the *vulnerability* of the manipulated, as well as the culpability of the manipulator. The German working class did not fall prey to Nazism simply because of manipulation by the bourgeoisie, or the Nazis.

1.2

Interests then imply a distinction, and a *possible* improper conjunction, between gratifications as experienced and the conditions producing them. The latter are our objective interests, know them or not; they may become interests to which we may attend, i.e., subjectively interesting things we "want," to the degree that they produce gratifications. And yet, as noted, there are certain conditions under which it is in our interest *not to know* what is in our interests.

The quest for gratification, therefore, often fosters rationality but, under certain conditions it may also foster ignorance. Essentially this has to do with whether the gratification and the condition imputed to produce it is defined as illicit or justified. The distinction between gratification and the source of gratification thus inherently allows for two possible connections, one legitimate and the other illegitimate. Indeed, the bourgeoisie developed the distinction in part to indicate that, for the *aristocracy*, the connection was improper, thereby undermining their position.

Justification and gratification are potentially independent experiences. We may, but need not, be gratified by justifiable conduct and we may do it only as a chore. The inventory of unjustified gratifications people have enjoyed is as long as the list of justifications people have invented. Nothing inhuman is alien to man. People prefer repeating experiences they have reported to be gratifying. And they are loathe to surrender conditions they believe productive of gratification, or which they somehow associate with it. Gratification and the evaluation of the gratification are distinct experiences. One may be unable to enjoy something defined as wrong, or one may like that which is believed bad; and one may want but may *not* enjoy the good.

Indeed, gratification is *pre*symbolic and prelinguistic and is therefore premoral.

The impulse to repeat gratifications and to maintain conditions associated with their production may therefore exist quite apart from whether the enjoyment and its source is justifiable. To that degree, gratification and attachment to their sources may generate *limits* on rationality. One way this is commonly done is by refusing to discuss certain gratifications, or their sources, and by placing them beyond examination. Most men will not question whether they are to be allowed to live; they will usually not submit *that* to rational discourse. Somewhat fewer, but still most, men will not make problematic nor gladly enter into discourse about whether their comforts, privileges, and property are to be removed.

A limit on rationality is also imposed when there is cognitive dissonance between gratifications and the justification for them. Pressure is then exerted to formulate beliefs that provide justification for gratifications and continuing access to the conditions producing them, or which reformulate beliefs impairing, inhibiting or reducing such gratifications, or access to them.

1.3

Gratifications, and beliefs about the good, each limit one another. Beliefs may repress gratifications or require them to be forgone; gratifications may generate cognitive distortions that serve to induce dissonance. In the latter case, where "unjustified" social conditions are generative of gratification, we may say that these social conditions are *interests* inhibitive of rationality. Interests, then, foster both the rationality *and* the limit on rationality that characterizes ideology.

The "command" dimension of an ideology is thus never simply grounded in its report dimensions, but is also grounded in some interest. "What is to be done" always depends in part on the pursuit or defense of an interest under conditions indicated in the "report." Correspondingly, reports about "what is" in the social world embedded in ideologies always further some interest; thus reports are always caught up in a functional relation with some interest. This has two different implications for the relationship between knowledge and interests: (1) to the extent that knowledge is grounded in interests, its pursuit is *energized* and motivated by them and, at the same time, (2) knowledge is always *limited* by these same interests.

The pursuit of knowledge always entails interests—subjective *and* objective interests—above and beyond the gratifications provided by the knowledge alone. To have a purely "technical" interest is tacitly to have an interest in maintaining the larger social system in which such *technical specialization* is encouraged and supported. The technical "inside" interest always premises an interest in the nontechnical "outside." To have technical interests in knowledge is to have an interest in those various social conditions that protect technicians from "distractions"—that insulate them from other claims that would divert them from their technical interests. Those wishing to pursue technical knowledge have an interest in someone else shopping for and cooking their dinner; in some person or condition that will tend their children and keep them out of the study; in maintaining income sufficient for their "needs"; in magazines that will publish technical findings; in mail systems that will convey these; in protection from people who want to blow up their computers or their persons.

Interests over and above a technical interest in knowledge are, then, an inescapable part of the knowledge-producing process. They both advance, and they limit, the knowledge produced. Gratifications generate commitments to the conditions producing them. There is thus generated (1) an effort to maintain continued access to gratifications and to whatever produces them, as well as (2) to produce justifications for this effort, thereby allowing the unambivalent enjoyment and protection of the gratification. This is not merely a selfish "rationalization," for it pays respect to rationality—at least in the way a thief pays his respects to the law when he uses stealth.

Ideologies are grounded in this tension between gratification and justification in the bourgeois epoch, and in the particular forms this tension takes in that epoch. For the bourgeoisie, gratification was justified primarily when it was earned by work and social usefulness, while "unearned" gratifications were defined as illicit. But by insisting on performance or achievement as the justification of gratification, the bourgeoisie undermined the inheritance of private property; for this clearly entailed *unearned* gratifications, rent, interest, profits, which might accrue to heirs who had never earned them. Indeed, given private inheritance, property might now pass to those who wasted it rather than those who made it useful.

Ideology, then, is a contradictory thing. It is pushed toward rationality by the interest on which it is grounded, but is limited in this rationality by that same interest. Ideologies are grounded in interests of which they may not speak with ease and freedom. But the very grammar of rationality to which ideology submits calls upon it to be *self*-grounded. This self-groundedness is sealed by the interaction between ideology's theory and the practice it advocates, and by the imputed grounding of the ideology's "commands" in its "reports." Ideology is thus characterized by its *inhibition* about addressing the question of its own *grounding*, and thus by self-imposed restrictions on its own reflexivity. It is this impaired reflexivity, concerning its grounding, that is the analytical essence of the limit on the rationality of ideology.

1.3.1

In other words: the limit on rationality—the *non*rational—is that which may not be scrutinized critically because it cannot, or will not, make its own assumptions problematic intellectually. The system thus limited is only willing (or able) to operate with (and within) its own assumptions of the moment; and it can only "apply" them to different circumstances. It must move outward— "externalize." In short, the limit on the rationality of ideology is fundamentally a defect of *reflexivity*. It is unable to transform the "resources" of its own analytic machinery into "topics," and thus it leads an unexamined life.

Ever since Socrates and Plato, such reflexive self-examination has been one of the great virtues of the dialectic—particularly, of the dialectic within the *idealistic* tradition. Theirs was a dialectic that always "soared upward," searching out the unstated premises of an argument and then, in turn, the premises of those premises, etc. But the idealist dialectic has the vice of its great virtues: the narcissism of world avoidance; the refusal of world encounter without which its own *criterion* of truth must always remain ungrounded.

It is essentially this nonreflexive working within limits of the given that also characterizes modern science and social science and is, indeed, a central basis of such success as it has had. Divorced from critical philosophy, the modern sciences have simply had to assert rather than ground critically, their own criteria of truth. If science could not step backward, in the "regressive" manner of the idealistic dialectic, it could and did inch forward into that limited kind of world encounter involved in experiment and technology. "Normal science," as Thomas Kuhn conceives it, is exactly that fusion of intellectual vices and virtues: it is immersed in a paradigm and in involved puzzle solving *within* it; it is the intensive working out of the minute implications of the paradigm taken as a given. It is this "nit-picking," as it sometimes seems to outsiders, that entails a cautious venturing forth into things, while all the while building up self-isolation. Science is world encountering, but encounters the world as broken down and sliced up into minute scrapings. Science is context-destructive because it proceeds by taking small, limited regions and amplifying their inner structures and functioning. At the same time, normal science lives *within* its intellectual paradigm, taking this as a given rather than critically exploring its boundaries, precisely because its energies are captured by the puzzle of the paradigm and the working out of its implications. The intensive exploration of a minute world sector ("adding another brick"), this activistic externalization so characteristic of "normal science" is the other, complementary side of a normal science whose energies reject the critical contemplation of its own basic intellectual premises, defining this as a pathological "navel gazing." Such normal science, then, also has that inability to make its own grounding problematic, which Jürgen Habermas correctly sees as the essence of "positivism."

Clearly, a lack of reflexivity concerning one's own grounding is a limit not only of ideology but, also, of science and especially of normal social science. Both ideology and sociology are vulnerable to the pathology of externalization—the headlong push into the world. Sociology wishes to "know" the world; ideology wishes to change it. Each wishes to "get on with the work" of domination. If the idealistic dialectic is vulnerable to narcissism, the materialistic dialectic of science is vulnerable to compulsive externalizing.

1.4

I have suggested that ideology is grounded in the tension between gratification and justification. The question arises as to how beliefs are cognitively warped by gratifications, and why—or under what conditions—the failure to justify gratifications is generative of a dissonance reduced by ideology. Why isn't enjoyment without justification possible?

One answer, of course, is that it is indeed possible and happens frequently. But it is more costly to those having internalized self-images as rational persons. Justification is necessary for gratification to the extent that being a "normal" person in a culture requires people to give reasons for their actions. "Reasonable" men require that they give, that they be given, and that they heed reasons; although what will be taken to be a convincing reason varies widely in different times and places. The giving of reasons is a way of securing consent to a given allocation of gratifications that is functionally alternative to the exertion of domination, where others are compelled to accept things for fear of violence. To give reasons is to communicate something about the self: that one is the kind of person who is loathe to use force and violence. To give reasons is subliminally to assure the other that violence against him is not imminent. To give reasons presents oneself as a responsible agent acting on his own account and accepting the other as such, rather than, say, simply as an agent susceptible to control by magic or by gods to whom one can appeal. To give reasons implies also that the other could withhold his cooperation (or forebearance) and that he cannot be coerced into this.

1.5

As an historically emergent concept, the idea of an "interest" that surfaces with bourgeois society implies a kind of *rational* desire. That is, it is not just a passion, appetite, or lust. An interest is the concern of a *reasonable* man and implies a measure of deliberation and reflection. An interest thereby implies a certain *justification* in and of itself.

An interest implies a kind of cerebralized hedonism, in which persons' pursuit of pleasure (or avoidance of pain) is not seen as a demeaning animalization but as a symptom of vigor and honesty, as expressing health and authenticity, as a proper acknowledgment of the "natural" in man, rather than as pretense and insincerity. *Such* an interest is experienced as demystification, in contrast to self-serving accounts of behavior bound by conventional piety and sentiment. Contempt for "sentimentality" is a critique of sentiment from the standpoint that claims itself too honest to wish, and too strong to have, to conceal its own character. Interest is the standpoint of the historically specific "honest" bourgeois, Jacques Bonhomme.

What makes the open acknowledgment of such hedonism permissible is a specific premise: that private vices produce public benefits, that others do not lose, but rather gain, by reason of our concern for our own interests. The historically specific ideas of an interest implied self-seeking behavior conjoined with a sanctioning usefulness to others. The justification, then, was in the *consequence* and it is here that justification via interests is vulnerable. For who knows how to reckon consequences? Are the consequences to be considered the "immediate" ones or those "in the long run?" And how does one add up gains and subtract losses, establishing the "net balance" of consequences? How does one establish that a given set of outcomes are, indeed, the outcomes of a specific set of inputs? In the end, consequences are often only loosely imputable. The self-interested intent of an action is often plainer than the social value of its ultimate consequences.

An "interest"—as an historical emergent *accounting* for behavior—implies reasonableness, reflection, and social utility conjoined with egoism, selfishness, and narcissism. It is an unstable and precarious mix, easily suspect and highly vulnerable to challenge. One may therefore agree with Virginia Held that interests stand *between desires and rights*. Interest is not a "right" which, being already socially recognized, does not need be justified. In that sense, those having "rights"—say, freedom of speech or association—need not justify them; but those wishing to abrogate rights are required to give good reasons. That is why rights are sometimes called "natural." Correspondingly, sheer desire is that which one wants but which may have no social sanction at all. Desire simply presents itself, having a "givenness" apart from justification, sometimes unexpectedly and on inappropriate occasions, and may thus be totally lacking in acceptance by others. If rights are fully accepted they need not be argued; if desires are lacking in acceptance by others they may be beyond communication. Interests, however, make a disputable claim to acceptance. They want the consensual validation that desires may never even seek; they foster argument and require communication.

But it is inherent in interests that their public communication will dramatically accentuate only one side of their ambivalent structure, their imputedly useful character, while repressing their other, private and egoistic side. It is on this structure of ambivalence, inherent to interests, that ideologies arise.

To refer to an interest, to one's own interests, is to argue that one's behavior is *rational*. It is to offer an accounting for one's behavior that recommends it as *not* arbitrary, capricious, changeable, inconsistent, and unpredictable. To refer to an interest is to refer to that which must be *reckoned* with. To tell another of one's interests, then, is to threaten him with determined resistance should he encroach upon them. To speak of one's "vital" interests is to speak of what one will fight for, thus of things that are in a sense *beyond discussion*. Interest refers to such resistance as a kind of fact of nature, whose sheer potency, not its morality, makes it relevant. There is thus a certain positivism already present within interest itself; for interest claims recognition on the sheer ground that it *is*, that it is a reality that has a force and, as such, cannot be neglected.

Interests are a warning of potential violence that claims the sanction of reason. Interests persuade, then, partly by intimating the costs of refusal; but they are less persuasive to those whose interests conflict. Given a conflict of interests, discussion becomes a negotiation in which diverse claims are compromised in terms corrsponding to each parties' willingness and capacity to fight. Interest fosters shifting alliances but does not mobilize abiding solidarities or enduring communities.

This is not to say that interests do not have or constitute a rhetoric. To the contrary—they are indeed a rhetoric, but of a very special sort. They ground their claims in their *being, not* in their propriety; like death itself, interests demand to be taken into account not because they are ultimately good but because they are inescapably real. The rhetoric of interests, then, is the rhetoric of *Realpolitik*, edged with a certain cynicism and brutality. Thus violating public moralities and religions, the rhetoric of interests does not lend itself to persuasion in the public sphere; interests become the language of *closed* politics, the understanding of which marks one as an "insider." This limit on the rhetoric of interests also sets the grounding for the development of ideologies whose grammar, calling for the unity of theory and practice, and for the grounding of commands in reports, transcends the gap between is and ought, between facts and values, and thus seeks what neither ancient religions nor new interests are able to do in the modern world.

2

The development of ideologies makes available general and universal bases of action to which men may appeal to justify their own actions, and by which they may either mobilize others on their behalf, or win their forbearance. There are two foci here: legitimation and political mobilization. The former is a necessary condition for successful mass political mobilization. As a result, ideologies (and the intellectual strata that formulate them) become partly autonomous conditions for effective action in the public sphere. The most fundamental political significance, then, of ideologies and intellectuals is their role in political mobilization.

Ideology entails the impersonalizing of one's own interests, or the publicizing of private interests. Political action in a public realm requires that proposed courses of conduct be legitimated in terms of the good of the whole. Correspondingly, a course of action that comes to be publicly associated with a private interest loses its public authority. Such a loss of authority is politically lethal, for in order to realize their interests, people invariably need the support, consent, or active cooperation of others, especially in a society where politics is conducted in a public arena. Others can obviously hinder or help us, or at least remain usefully neutral. Our own private interests, then, cannot be pursued successfully as *our* interests, but must be redefined as impersonal interests of general concern. Interests must be redefined as matters of principle. It is this that is accomplished by ideology.

Ideologies help transmute self-interested egoism into public goods. Since the visibility of the underlying interest, or its passage from egoism to public morality via ideology, would ruin the transmutation, it must be done cryptically. Ideologies thus always induce a measure of false consciousness because (1) they present private interests as public goods and (2) because this reconstruction would not persuade were it visible. This is essentially a problem in the "reduction of dissonance." Ideologies reduce the dissonance between (1) the recognition that one is seeking a private advantage and (2) one's wish to be seen as pursuing courses of conduct that are justifiable. The public recognition that a course of conduct is grounded in private ambitions threaten and impede mobilization of public support on their behalf. It is the function of ideology, by justifying claims, to solve the problem of how the pursuit of private interests may, nonetheless, generate public support.

2.1

Interests constitute the unnoticed grounding of two kinds of standards for evaluating public action in everyday life. One of these is ideology itself, the other is what may be called a "paradigm." ° The relation between ideologies

° Cf. my discussion on this in A. W. Gouldner, *Wildcat Strike*, Kent State University Press, Kent, Ohio, 1954, and A. W. Gouldner and H. P. Gouldner, *Human Interaction*, Harcourt, Brace & Co., New York, 1963. As used *here*, the notion of a paradigm derives from Karl Mannheim rather than from Thomas Kuhn.

and paradigms is akin to the relation between the abstract and the concrete. Both ideologies and paradigms serve, among other things, as standards to help persons make decisions and to formulate policies. The paradigm, however, is a relatively *concrete* image of what is sought and desired, while the ideology is relatively *general* and abstract. If, for example, an ideology calls on men to "succeed," certain men's paradigms of success may denotatively define success as owning an Aston Martin, or as being deferentially addressed as "Sir." The class paradigm, no less than the general ideology, then serves to channel and direct the behavior and decisons of the persons and groups who hold them. But if the ideology says, "work hard," the paradigm may add, "when working for *yourself*"; if the ideology says, "respect reason," the paradigm, however, may indicate that respect is shown by friendly behavior at the salon, but not by giving intellectuals a vote; if the ideology says all "men" are equal, the paradigm may still feel that a "woman's place" is at home.

In other words: an ideology entails legitimated projects that lay a claim to the support of others; a paradigm, however, does not necessarily entail a good for which a public claim is made; one might enjoy being called "Sir" but need not acknowledge this to others or invite them to that same enjoyment. The paradigm is rooted in a specific and concrete set of experiences and those who have shared them can share the paradigm but it is difficult to communicate it to those who have not. All men place some value on security but those who have lived through an economic depression may share an image of what they want to avoid, and of what had best be done to do so, that will often seem inexplicable to those who have known only affluence. The paradigm is a less context-independent symbol and may be spoken about only with those sharing the concrete experiences enabling it to be decoded. The justification and grounding for a paradigm is thus in a relatively *tacit* knowing which is, correspondingly, relatively lacking in a reflexive articulateness. With paradigms, then, we are back in the realm of a restricted sociolinguistic variant, with some intimation of why that speech variant becomes "restricted."

Being relatively concrete, paradigms vary among individuals and across groups. They will be formed by the patterned but different experiences of different groups. A paradigm expresses and embodies the experience-generated *conceptions* of the special, hence less communicable, interests of particular persons or groups. It expresses their conception of what they believe *desirable*. But this is a concrete *image* of what is desired, and it is thus a standard of gratification, of what is wanted, but not necessarily of what will be recommended for others.

Ideologies also are criteria for decisions, channeling and selecting behavior; but they are more conceptually abstract, lacking a similar specificity, concreteness, and detailed iconic imagery. The ideology is a generalization of the interest-rooted paradigm formulated in the syntax of a rational discourse that authorizes itself by speaking for the public interest. As such, ideology has a broader range of possible applications; it is not as limited and not as private in its applications as the paradigm which, logically, may be only a special case of the ideology.

An ideology, therefore, may entail applications that go well beyond the paradigm; and the paradigm will entail tacit but firm limitations on these applications. Conforming to his paradigm, a man will be satisfied with less than the more ambitious requirements of his ideology. Ideologies, therefore, always entail a more *radical* program of action; paradigms always entail a more *conservative* program. There is, then, a continual dialectic between ideologies and paradigms, a tendency for each to exert a strain upon the other, to create difficulties and embarrassments for the other.

A key issue is: *how it is that paradigms come to be generalized into ideologies, when they do.* Part of the answer appears to be that, while both perform similar functions, they do not perform identical functions. In particular, ideologies and paradigms are not equally helpful as political mechanisms for mobilizing group solidarities. Being more generalized, an ideology may appeal to larger and more diversified groups than does its underlying paradigm and it may, thereby, mobilize more powerful and larger polities. Being generalized, ideologies serve to generate alliances and understandings among those who do *not* share the same paradigm; or whose paradigms differ in significant particulars; which is to say, among those whose concrete experiences and interests are somewhat different and incommunicable, even if not in conflict. (Here, then, we glimpse some of the limits of restricted speech variants and, correspondingly, how elaborated speech variants transcend these limits.)

2.2

At the same time, however, underneath any common ideology there are always centrifugal tendencies among its supporting groups; for each interprets the ideology in terms of its own, somewhat different, interest-grounded paradigm. Moreover, each group will be ready to stop cooperating with the others when it has attained its own paradigm, with the result that the common alliance forged by the ideology will always tend to break down well *before its unifying general value is achieved.*

In consequences, ideologies are always "myths." They always urge something that the group subscribing to them does not exactly want. They allow a pursuit of interests somewhat oblique to the projects publicly proclaimed, even if not contradictory to them. The generalization of an interest-grounded paradigm into an ideology is the price a group pays to mobilize the wider support required to achieve its own more limited paradigm. Ideology is thus the price of politics when masses must be mobilized for public projects in a society with class-divided interests. Paradigms, however, entail an apolitical, public-be-damned, isolation.

Unlike more group-restricted or privatized paradigms, ideologies are a rhetoric of public discourse and produce, what we may call with Erving Goffman, a form of "dramaturgic accentuation." They become foci of public concern that divert attention from the more concrete, interest-embedded paradigm. Yet ideologies are not simply a mask for self-interest: they are also a tacit and a genuine offer of support for different groups. In sharing a common ideology, different interest groups give tacit consensual validation to or condone one another's paradigms. In time, the paradigm is therefore no longer recognized as the basis of the ideology, nor is the ideology viewed as a mere rationalization of the interest-grounded paradigm. An inversion takes place. The paradigm is now viewed as a derivative of the ideology, as a permissible *example* or logical inference of the ideology and, *as such*, is no longer a matter of a partisan but of a general public interest.

For that very connection between the limited interest paradigm and the generalized ideology does indeed motivate each group to support the common ideology. This, in turn, furthers their social cooperation and may contribute, in some measure, to moving all of them somewhat closer to their own more different paradigms, even if not equally so. Ideologies do not necessarily conceal a zero-sum gain but may foster a Pareto optimality. The generalized formulation characteristic of an ideology does, however, serve to conceal the divergencies or the conflicts among allied groups. It is in that way a lie: a "noble" lie, perhaps, because it often enables each group to do more on behalf of its own special interests than they might otherwise achieve by themselves.

Still, the generalization of different paradigms into an ideology does not eliminate these differences or their potential conflicts. Rather, it reduces their salience and visibility, and it provides opportunities for partial gratification of the varying paradigms of different groups.

Underneath the common ideology the group differences in paradigms abide. These differences in paradigms are like geological faults that lay beneath the unbroken surface; they demarcate the boundaries along which subsequent breakdowns of group solidarity will recur, the lines along which conflict will arise. Ideologies, then, are temporary bridgings of group differences. They are inherently precarious because they premise the existence of different group paradigms. That is, ideologies express a point of dynamic equilibrium among different groups' paradigms. They would not be needed were there no such differences. But they do not so much resolve such differences as defer conflict concerning them.

Since men subscribing to the same ideologies do not have the same paradigms, they therefore do not want quite the same things; nor have they the same means of achieving them. In consequence, the larger common ideological alliance will always be a shifting one. Some groups will be continually falling away from the consensus, while newer ones are attracted. The polity's consensus is thus ever crumbling and in need of restoration. It is to be emphasized, however, that the commitment to an ideology and to the solidarity built upon it does not falter simply through *failure*. It falters, also, when one group *succeeds* in achieving the paradigm-limited understanding of the ideology that it, all along, sought. Once a group achieves its paradigm there is less gratification in prospect for it, and now it faces the costs of supporting others in the pursuit of their own rather different paradigms.

Ideologies are thus consistent with paradigms and the interests in which they are grounded, but they go beyond them. Paradigms resolve the ambiguities inherent in ideologies with their generalized values. Paradigms constitute auxiliary criteria in terms of which ideologies will be decoded and concretely interpreted, limiting the imputation of their various possible meanings and their application to concrete situations. In effect, one knows what an ideology *means* only when one also knows the paradigms that are keyed to it.

An ideology always requires that persons do something *more* than their paradigms want; paradigms always dispose persons to do something *less* than (and different from) their ideologies. Ideologies always require that persons transcend their paradigms and hence their interests. Paradigms always dispose persons to compromise (if not to subvert) their ideologies. The two, then, are in a constant tensionful dialectic with one another. Ideologies, then, are not to be viewed as inherently order-maintaining, solidarity-inducing, or *status-quo* reinforcing elements of culture. For ideologies generate tensions as well as reduce them. The more men commit themselves to and believe in their ideologies, the more these exert costly strains upon the paradigms and interests to which they are also committed.

2.3

Ideologies are focalizations of the grounds on which a group has been able to achieve some consensus. They embody the tacitly negotiated compromises of the different paradigms held by different members or subgroups of the larger polity. They express a compromise already achieved by a smaller band of articulate notables, and they propose, in effect, a compromise that might be attractive to a larger polity with new, potential allies or constituencies. An ideology is, therefore, a "program" or project for public action whose rhetoric functions to further power-mobilizing alliances by defusing differences, and by formulating the goals of the alliance in a manner that harmonizes the different paradigms of various subgroups.

For example, the French middle class's generalization of its own paradigm into the Enlightenment ideologies mobilized support for it among other social classes—the peasantry, the urban masses, and even the liberal aristocracy. To do this an ideology must remain silent about differences or disguise conflicts, thus providing a basis of unity among diverse, potentially conflicting groups. The function of ideology, then, is two-sided; it is not merely to report and to reveal, but also to *blur* and to *conceal*. It performs its social functions not only by its reports but also by the silences it imposes. Ideology then is a "noble" myth whose subsequent troubles derive from the high promises it is unable or unwilling to keep, from the confusion generated by its distortions and omissions, and from the existence of problems about which it cannot speak.

Both ideologies and paradigms are symbol systems, more or less shared modes of communication, particularly concerning things not necessarily visible in the everyday world of their believers. Paradigms are grounded in group-limited interests that may be unintelligible or unattractive to others, while ideologies transcend and bridge these. Ideologies facilitate communication in the public realm, by allowing, opening, and focusing communications on certain concerns and, simultaneously, by inhibiting, suppressing, and even repressing other kinds of public discourse. Ideologies thus distort public communication and inhibit a personal awareness of beliefs dissonant with those ideologically endorsed. Ideologies, in short, structure communication, admitting certain subjects for discussion and rejecting others. Paradigms, however, are the elements of a prepublic communication, the shared iconics of those already joined in mutual acquaintance, the flag of those already friends, not the rallying standard of strangers.

3

Paradigms, correspondingly, entail subjects that are screened out, rejected by, or not allowed into open, free, and direct discussion because of the censorial functioning of the publicly dominant system of communication or simply because they are grounded in group limited contexts not shared by others. They are therefore a less publicly accessible symbolic system, a "paleosymbolic" system.

The paleosymbolic, then, constitutes a set of beliefs and symbols of restricted communicability. The purely ideological, of course, assuming it not to be illegal (and requiring cryptic formulation), is however a fully public language. This means it will and can be spoken by (and before) mutually anonymous persons of quite diverse experiences. Correspondingly, the paleosymbolic is at the opposite end of the polarity. The paleosymbolic tends to be spoken in private settings, among those previously known to one another, and who, for this reason alone, as well as others, share interests. At the extreme range, the paleosymbolic is that which is not actually spoken to *known* others, but is only a fantasy-speech to imagined intimates which is not even spoken out to them. Or it may be that which is written only in one's diary and is not intended to be read.

There is thus a certain scale-like dimensionality moving from the publicly communicable ideology to the paleosymbolic of the paradigmatic level. The most ideological, and the least paleosymbolic, is that which may be spoken publicly among strangers. The least ideological and the most paleosymbolical is that which may be spoken to intimates in private settings, only if strangers are not present. The latter is a *paleo*symbolism precisely because it refers to symbol systems older and earlier than a speaker's ideologies, having been acquired before his ideologies were.

On the sociological level, the paleosymbolic is part of the shared, ordinary (and hence "restricted") languages of everyday life learned during primary socialization as children. The paleosymbolic, therefore, is powerfully associated with "significant others." These are persons involved in the teaching of this ordinary language, by linking its learning to their provision of gratification and security for the self of the learner, and hence with the most elemental system of affects. The language learned thus also becomes linked with images of such significant others, and with their relationship to the learner. The paleosymbolic level thus implicates central persons, nuclear social relations, and the affectively laden gratifications and securities associated with them.

The career of an ideology, then, will be effected by its relationship to the paleosymbolic level. Through this connection, it can tap extrarational support, to the extent that it resonates pleasantly the paleosymbolic. Contrariwise, the maintenance of an ideology will entail extra costs if dissonant with or resonating the paleosymbolic level unpleasantly. The interfacing of these two levels means that all ideological communication is always consequential for, or always makes tacit reference to, and always rests on *something other than that intended by the ideologue.*

3.1

Ideological speech, then, must unfailingly be about an-Other, about that which is alien to its own rational discourse, about something more, or something simply different, than that intended by the speaker. The extraordinary speech of the ideologue cannot help but be charged with surplus meanings and affects; for it is grounded inescapably in the ordinary speech of everyday life from most of which it can neither be separated nor reflexively detached. The ideologue simply cannot use the ordinary language without inhibiting or summoning more meaning and motivation than he intends or of which he is aware (thus a speaker urging his followers to "behead the king" may trigger a diffuse fear of authorities, elders, or parents that he never intended, thereby producing an unseemly butchery or a panicky flight that he would have preferred to avoid politically).

The point is most certainly *not* that ideology is a rationalization of the paleosymbolic level. The point is rather there is an unavoidable interface between these two levels with countless, and often unintended, consequences. It is inherent in this that neither level gets exactly what it wanted or bargained for. Each may be inhibitive of the other and, often enough, each may produce blockages and distortions in the communication of the other. Correspondingly, it is inevitable that ideologies are not accepted solely for the good reasons that the ideologue urges but, also, for others of which he is commonly unaware and cannot control.

3.2

One concrete implication of this is that the dynamic of the French Revolution, and indeed of much subsequent European culture, were in important part shaped by a tension between the generalized public ideology and interest-grounded paradigms (of the emerging middle classes) at the paleosymbolic level. This tension arose precisely because the Enlightenment was not some disembodied *Geist*. It was borne by very specific social strata, the bourgeoisie, and it was developed within a limited national milieu. Enlightenment was a universal philosophy that happened to speak French. The Germans *Aufklärung* was quite another thing, in part because it spoke another language. On the paleosymbolic underside of Enlightenment, then, there were vested class interests, national loyalties, and cultural ethnocentricities, all of which limited the Enlightenment's larger promise.

The incipient dissonance between universalistic ideology and paradigms, rooted in class or national interests, became overt with the eruption of the French Revolution and in the unfolding context of its revolutionary politics and wars. In the eighteenth century, Enlightenment was something brought by a cultural, economic, and political elite to its *own* people. With Bonaparte, however, Enlightenment was imposed by one nation on *others*. There was thus a certain evolution in Enlightenment: from elitism to imperialism. Even at its flood, the publicly prescribed universalism, egalitarianism, and cosmopolitanism of the Enlightenment was in tension with its tacit cultural elitism, and its accommodation to sexism and anti-Semitism; but Enlightenment's universalistic ideologies clashed even more flagrantly with the subsequent nationalism of the Revolution and the imperialism of Bonaparte.

While affirming the claims of men of talent, energy, and achievement—the "useful"—the middle class also affirmed the "sacred" right of private property, thereby reasserting the contrary right of those who might be "useless" to "something for nothing,"—i.e., their *right* to profits, interests, and rents. The middle class's egalitarian ideology was compromised by its inclination to establish property qualifications for political participation. Even the middle-class ideology of "free enterprise" and *laissez-faire* was at variance with those middle-class paradigms that conceived the state as a vehicle for tariff protection, as an agency for controlling labor unrest, and, more generally, for maintaining domestic social order.

3.3

The symbolics of Enlightenment thus had two layers: on one level, it had an ideology layer that served as a rhetoric for public discourse mobilizing interclass solidarities. On the deeper paleosymbolic level, Enlightenment ideology was sedimented with a layer of class and elite interests, of restricted communicability. The rationality of even the *philosophes* themselves was always a class-limited rationality. They proposed to advance education, erase superstition, foster science and liberate reason, while still supporting Deism and without surrendering sexism or anti-Semitism. Throughout, then, the interpretation of Enlightenment ideology was continually limited by the interests and paradigms of the very elite that had formulated and fostered it. But this contradiction exists as a two-sided process: If the class interests of the middle class subverted its ideology, making them less than they claimed, these very ideologies also pressed the middle class toward reforms they did not altogether desire and which were costly to their interests. Thus, Jacobinism.

The Enlightenment crystallized in France in the eighteenth century, but the contradictions it contained were *not* limited to *France*. These went beyond France and beyond the eighteenth century. Other Western European and bourgeois societies possess a similar tension between Enlightenment ideologies and middle-class paradigms. The contradictions visible in the Enlightenment, then, are nothing less than the contradictions of all those Western European societies that have participated in its tradition. They are with us still.

Many post-Revolutionary ideologies and theories, such as romanticism and Marxism, are not merely reactions against the Enlightenment but are efforts to transcend certain of its contradictions. The main problems of post-Revolutionary Europe, then, are not intelligible simply as the product of the breakdown of the old feudal order. They derive also from the very nature of the new order, from the new tensions and new conflicts, that it itself created. Most fundamentally, the new society was one that could not be kept together except by affirming ideologies that excited ambitions that its leading elites were often reluctant (and commonly loathe) to satisfy, and who often moved toward the fulfillment of these ideologies only when threatened by the costs of conflict.

But the new society was also a society that generated ideologies with a Jacobin thrust; ideologies dissonant with its own limited class interests; and its venality fostered, at least among the rebels, recurrent waves of moral revulsion at establishment hypocrisy. In general, it was a society with a capacity for moral fervor that it passed on to its adversaries, and it is often hard to choose between the self-righteousness of the rebels and the smug piety of the establishment. It was a society whose ideologies often condemned "vested interests" (the right, as Veblen said, to "something for nothing") and retained a permeating disgust for the "useless." It was a class society whose ruling class's interests often subverted the very ideologies on which this class first developed; as, for instance, the consumerism of modern advertising contradicts the bourgeois ideologies of hard work and deferred gratification. It is a society that required conflict to revitalize its commitment to its own ideologies.

It was not, then, simply the social vacuum of an incompleted transitional period, after the collapse of the old regimes, that brought recurrent demoralization, self-hatred, and social conflict to modern industrial societies; rather it was the very self-contradictory nature of the new bourgeois order that had emerged and which could not and cannot make itself coherent except by promising what it only half-believed and only begrudgingly provided.

chapter II

Ideology and Indirect Rule: Technocratic Consciousness and the Failure of Ideology

It is not possible to understand ideology without understanding the historically unique system of social classes that characterize modern capitalism. In contrast to the ruling class of earlier Western societies, unlike the slaveowners of antiquity or the ruling nobility of feudalism, the dominant class under capitalism is actively and routinely engaged in the conduct of economic affairs. Rich Athenians, for example, who wished to become richer might invest in various commercial activities; but they commonly did not view the mundane administration of these investments as the preferred way to spend their days; the spear-won prize was always honored in ancient Greece. Similarly, the feudal nobility did not *prize* the routine administration of economic affairs but the honorific display of bellicosity.

Certainly, this relative disinterest in everyday moneymaking, in the routines necessary to make money, was not an ascetic disdain for money or an inability to enjoy what it can buy. But the routine management of economic affairs in capitalist economies is a different matter: partly because it *is* indeed commonly seen as a fit way for a grown man to spend his life; partly because the formal rationality and competitiveness of capitalism require vigilant attention and mobilized energies; and partly because the structural differentiation of capitalism means that an involvement in the economy necessarily *dis*involves one from other social structures.

This means, as George Lukács long emphasized, first, that members of the ruling class under capitalism do not normally have the time and energy to make their own contributions to the development of culture and, secondly, that the ruling class must give others the actual, at-hand, control over the means of violence and coercion, thereby placing this *ultimate* protection of their own class position in the hands of others.

1

As a structurally differentiated economy develops, there correspondingly develops a differentiation of other social structures within bourgeois society— the military, the judiciary, the police and penal institutions, in short, the organization of the *state*. With this there is the development of a specialized stratum, the *administrative* class we may call it, engaged in the full-time and routine administration of the affairs of the state. A basis is laid for the fullest development of a bureaucracy. Correspondingly, just as the demands of a differentiated and developing economy withdraw the ruling economic class from the creation of culture and from the day-to-day administration of coercion, so, too, does it also withdraw them from day-to-day involvement in politics, from the *routine* mobilization of power and mundane decision making. This, too, becomes the specialized activity of a distinct stratum, the *political* class.

In consequence of these developments, the system of stratification under capitalism differs profoundly from that of previous societies. The position of its ruling class and its total class system are historically unique. We will adumbrate a few of the ways in which this is so. With the growing differentiation between the economic, political, and bureaucratic *orders*, and with the growing specialization among different *personnel*, each of the newly differentiated spheres develops a measure of *autonomy* and, we might add, of "slippage," from the other. The operating personnel of the administrative, the political, and the ruling classes, each develop specialized standards and skills for dealing with their own spheres, thereby making the latter less intelligible and less manageable by those in the other spheres. But this means that the political and administrative classes are now also less intelligible and less accessible to the direct supervision of the dominant economic class. The ruling economic class under capitalism must thus rule quite differently than ruling classes before it. Its rule is a *mediated* rule.

1.1

This at once creates a special problem for the ruling economic class. Indeed, it is *the* political problem for it. The problem is: how may it exercise influence over the other sectors and ensure their loyalty? This is a problem that did not exist in the same way for the ruling classes of the slave societies of antiquity or of feudal societies, where such differentiation did not exist and where the ruling econmic class also had both political power and the administration of coercion in its own hands. Those ruling classes were brutal; the capitalist class is only callous.

Ideology assumes special importance as a symbolic mechanism through which the interests of these diverse social strata may be integrated; through the sharing of it the several dominant strata are enabled to make compatible responses to changing social conditions. The ideology held by the political and administrative classes is a mechanism by which their loyalty to the ruling class is strengthened, or by which it might be weakened. The solidarity of the dominant classes, and the ruling classes' influence with the political and administrative classes, is now contingent on and mediated by the *ideologies* to which they subscribe. Ideology thus assumes a new historical role in the maintenance of social solidarities and class control.

Never before in a class society did the security of a ruling class depend so much on the presence of belief-systems appropriate to its rule. The new dependence on ideology by the ruling economic class under capitalism makes it a special ruling class, a class which must win influence over the minds of men, and especially over those of the other dominant classes; it is a class exceptionally dependent on ideologies in whose terms its dominance is defined as *legitimate*. The importance of an ideologically sustained legitimacy makes the ruling economic class under capitalism a new kind of ruling class—a *hegemonic* class (to use Gramsci's term).

There is good reason to question whether the slaves of Athens or Sparta obeyed their owners because they believed them to be *rightful* masters to whom they accorded legitimacy, and correspondingly, whether the slaves believed themselves rightfully to be slaves. It is more probable by far that the slaves obeyed not because they believed their masters to be legitimate authorities, but because they were afraid. And lest they forget, they would be given reminders of their vulnerability, such as the Spartans' occasional butchery of their slaves. Plato speaks of even Athenian slaves (the slaves of "violent-wreathed," cultured Athens) as ready to massacre their owners, if only they could hope to do so with impunity.

We might similarly question just how much peasant obedience on the feudal manor was based on the peasant's conviction of the Lord's moral right to rule, and how much was based on simple convenience, prudence, apathy, or on an expedience rooted in the essential fact that peasants' everyday life was a ghetto-like existence which had little to do with their masters. It was not unimportant, but it was decidedly *less* important, what slaves and serfs *thought* than whether or not they obeyed. Under capitalism, however, the situation of the lower and working classes differs. Beginning with their poor houses and mad houses, and going on to publicly controlled compulsory education, and later to the outpourings of the mass media, it is clear that vast energies and resources are expended in shaping what the nonruling class thinks.

1.2

In saying this, however, I do not mean to suggest that ideology is the only, or even the most important, mechanism by which the dominant classes are coordinated and by which the influence of the hegemonic class is strengthened in capitalist societies. This hegemonic class is also protected by the development and stability of the economy, with whose successes or failures it is associated. Given a condition of prosperity, of increasing consumer goods, of controlled inflation, then the social *credit* of the hegemonic class will be high and the readiness of other classes to accept its definitions of the social world (with only loose demonstration) will be correspondingly high. There is thus an interaction between ideology and economy.

The following discussion of other methods by which the hegemonic class fosters its dominance and coordinates social action with other classes may at first seem a digression, taking us away from an understanding of the function of ideology in the political economy of capitalism. In point of fact, it is not. For the career of ideology under capitalism will depend on the other mechanisms of dominance and integration available to the elites. Obviously, if there are few or no alternatives to ideology, then one would expect it to receive more support and cultivation and that it will remain more central.

Suppose, however, that there are many functional substitutes for ideology, providing alternative ways of integrating social action and winning the collaboration of others. Under these conditions one would expect that the career of ideology under capitalism would be more precarious and threatened. This is essentially what I will contend. More than that, it is precisely because the hegemonic elite is *separated from* the means of culture, including the production of ideologies, that ideologies developed in capitalist society may often be discomforting to the hegemonic elite, so that they prefer other mechanisms of dominance and integration more fully and routinely accessible to them. In short, although the hegemonic elite in capitalist society, more than those in other societies, needs ideological legitimation, it resists, and as I shall argue later, quite reasonably so, a reliance on ideology and on those who produce it.

Let us consider the nature of the problem that the hegemonic class faces: it, itself, is *not* seeking to make day-to-day decisions. The hegemonic class is more nearly like the chairman of the board than like the company president who actively manages daily affairs. What the hegemonic class wants is a sympathetic and knowledgeable responsiveness to its problems available among the other classes. It wants to create a *readiness* to respond protectively to its changing needs. The central political problem of the hegemonic class is to have the other classes define the social world in ways congenial to its own concerns and interests, and supportive of the interlocking institutions within which they exist, and whose normal functioning reproduces the hegemonic class.

The primary *political* problem of the ruling, hegemonic class, then, is not to rule directly but to ensure the compatibility, the responsiveness, and loyalty of the administrative and political classes, their loyalty to itself as a class and to the institutionalized social *system*, within which it is reproduced. The hegemonic class's main problem, then, is not to have these other classes *obey* "orders" it gives, but to have them perform in ways that support the social system, the institutions and policies, whose normal functioning permits the ruling class to maintain and reproduce itself. Ideally, the most effective arrangement for this ruling class is one that protects its interests without having directly to issue orders that would do this.

What the hegemonic class finally requires of the others is neither right thinking nor even obedience but, rather, the effective and reliable performance of certain functions. Short, however, of the performance of these functions by machines, an alternative never ignored, right behavior commonly turns on the prevalence of appropriate ideologies, as on the viability and growth of the economy, and on the development of effective organizations.

It is central to the effectiveness of a society using a system of "indirect rule," that its organizational instruments be reliably controllable from the *outside*. These several organizational characteristics—reliability of performance, control by outside interests, without a continual flow of monitored concrete "orders," and high effectiveness—are typical of the dominant organizational form, the "bureaucracy" using general standing rules, run by full-time experts, administered from the top by *non*bureaucrats.

The society thus depends greatly on appropriate socialization and education of the administrative and political classes. These develop expert skills, and create a readiness to *credit* the hegemonic class, to define it as a "responsible" and effective stratum dedicated to the commonweal; they define its role as legitimate and, also, generate loyalty to the social system. What is required is a *system* loyalty, not merely a class loyalty; nonetheless, this is a loyalty to a social system within which there is a certain hierarchy of institutions—a structure of dominance—that systematically benefits the hegemonic class and protects its vital interests. In addition to these basic institutions, by which the influence of the hegemonic class is exerted and protected, there are also certain special mechanisms (*ad hoc*, but recurrent) that help maintain the ruling class.

1.3

Among these there are direct *bribes*. To some, the mere mention of these *morally* "vulgar" things makes it seem as if one is being vulgar intellectually. Not so.° Direct bribes are a significant mechanism by which the ruling class, or its agent lobbyists, influence the administrative and political classes. Indeed, they do not even have to be particularly large to exert influence. It is astonishing how much political influence a modest bribe can buy.

Bribes may be profitably compared with the very modest sums, often 20 to 30 pounds or a few hundred dollars or marks, with which secret services pay spies for treachery to their native country, and for their really quite hazardous, "dirty" work. If a man may betray his country or risk his life for a few hundred dollars, it should not be surprising if members of the administrative or political classes will betray their oath of office, or their country's *institutions* for similarly (or, at least, relatively) paltry sums. In both cases—national treachery or political corruption—the paltry sums involved obviously suggest the existence of *other*, nonpecuniary, motives that lead men to betrayal. There is resentment of, and alienation from, those whom they betray. Correspondingly, there is often affection or respect for those *to* whom they "sell out," sometimes simply because they share a common foe. Yet, the pecuniary is important in its own right, even if only as a precipitating factor that sometimes tips a precarious balance of loyalties and alienation. In addition to direct bribes, then, there are also "favors" and other opportunities to make money, that are also among the *ad hoc* mechanisms by which the hegemonic class is enabled to influence the political and administrative classes.

In this way, the administrative and political classes *capitalize* their strategic social positions. They thus acquire advantages which, unlike their political and administrative status, *are* bequeathable to their children, and constitute economic advantages that can be transmitted across generation lines. Moreover, "favors" need not even entail monetary costs: they simply may involve the transmission of strategic "insider" *information* enabling the recipient to acquire a capitalizable economic advantage. In this manner, the hegemonic class may, even without a pecuniary outlay, provide economic advantages to its allies.

Both bribes and favors have a special advantage from the recipient's standpoint in that they constitute "unearned income"; no additional or special work is required of the political manager or administrative person receiving them. They are thereby enabled to remain active members of the

° Obviously, this was written *before* the Watergate scandal reminded us of the prevalence of direct bribery.

political or administrative classes, without having to attend to moneymaking activities. This is precisely why campaign donations or contributions are more important than may be measured by their sheer monetary value. They not only pay a leader's bills, but do so without his having to withdraw his time and attention from politics in the way that "working" would.

Intermarriage opportunities are another mechanism for integrating the hegemonic and other social classes, and are of similar import. Here again, one of the less noticed functions of such marriages is to enable persons to support their political habit, permitting them to become or remain a *full-time* member of the political or administrative classes, without having to work. Among other mechanisms by which the hegemonic class may influence the others, there are the creation of *communities* or pseudocommunities in which "promising" members of the political and administrative classes are admitted into the personal presence of members of the ruling class, or of those known to be close to them, and may thus have symbolic intercourse with them—the "pleasure of their company." Such diffuse, unfocused participation induces some sense of a common destiny among the classes (as does intermarriage); it fosters a feeling of solidarity not limited to specific problems and issues; it promotes a readiness to credit the hegemonic class, to see them in their full "humanness" as decent persons, rather than as the "exploiters" their enemies claim them to be. Now, each of the dominant classes learns to take the role of the other. It thus makes the "other" an *internalized* audience, so that the political and administrative classes' policies may be influenced by the hegemonic class even without *communicating* with it.

2

The hegemonic class under capitalism rules at a distance; it rules through others who actually exercise the coercion and the force on which its system (like others) ultimately rests; it rules through the political managers and administrative classes, who routinely man the system of governance and coercion.

This has profoundly important consequences. It means, for one thing, that the most vital interests of the hegemonic class now depend directly upon the action of other classes. The ruling class under capitalism has a degree of dependence upon others that is historically unique. But this interdependence does not mean, as Emile Durkheim supposed, that now all social strata are equally important in managing the society. It does mean that now the hegemonic class must pursue its aims in new ways and with new mechanisms. It means, in some part, a *bargaining* relationship between itself and the administrative and political classes: it means that the latter's responsiveness is dependent in *part* on the terms that the hegemonic class is willing to offer, the favors and advantages it is willing to convey. It means that the hegemonic class must (in effect) *negotiate* with the other classes to establish the terms of their mutual exchange; it means that it is exposed to some degree of nonresponsiveness, to resistance to, or even threats against, its interests. But this resistance is not an expression of independence from the hegemonic class by these other sectors; resistance is the way negotiation proceeds and terms are established; it is the process by which the political managers and administrative classes surrender a measure of their autonomy in exchange for other advantages.

Inevitably, however, this entails a weakening of the centralized and unified direction of the society as a social system. It fosters a social system in which outcomes are not fully and directly controllable by the hegemonic class, or, for that matter, by the others. The structural differentiation and *relative* autonomy of the various sectors of society means a *decline* in the *power* of the hegemonic class, along with an increased sense that the society is no longer a pyramidal "hierarchy" ruled from the top. The image of "hierarchy" gives way to that of a "system." Society is now more nearly a *system* which has its own system imperatives.

Since the actual outcomes produced by the system correspond less and less with the policies of any one class, the system is, in that sense, "out of control." Fewer and fewer people get precisely what they want. Everyone experiences an alienation, a sense of the "unanticipated consequences" of their own politics and action; there will be a growing sense that the system as a whole has become unmanageable. The hegemonic class no longer governs *outcomes*, howevermuch it strives to do so, to anything like the degree it would wish. Increasingly subject to the proliferating constraints and strains of the social system of which it is a part, the hegemonic class is increasingly less of a *ruling* class and increasingly more of an "upper" class. But while the political *powers* of that class have declined, its income perquisites remain unaffected and may even expand. Its privileged incomes continue even if shaved by taxes, while its ability to procure desired outcomes has been constricted by the increasing systemness of the society, and by the increasing powers of the political and administrative classes.

2.1

While the hegemonic class's structural situation has in this sense deteriorated, there are still certain changes that it cannot permit; there are limits on what it can allow if it is to survive. Essentially, these limits are those that define its own social reproduction as an upper class.

These revolve around several things: first, control over property and above all, over investment policies, so that it can determine allocations of capital in terms of the returns. This, of course, implies the continued existence of an opportunity structure for private investment; markets must be available on which things and labor power can be bought and sold profitably. In other words, the hegemonic class' *capital* position must be protected against unprofitable operations, unsalable inventories, confiscatory taxes, direct expropriation, and against destruction by foreign soldiers or domestic insurrectionaries. It must also be protected from foreign competitors or suppliers who might undersell it, deprive it of its markets, its raw materials, energy supplies, or of opportunities for reinvestment of its surplus capital. Indeed, it must also be protected against any tendency for the rate of profit to decline. Under any of these conditions the capacity of the hegemonic class to reproduce itself socially is seriously threatened, and it will undergo a convulsive crisis.

The upper class will oppose anything that threatens its ability to reproduce itself by threatening the profitability of its holdings, and thereby its capacity to *reinvest* and make more profit. In effect, then, it is the protection of *capital* and hence of profitability that constitutes the interest that the hegemonic class under capitalism cannot allow to be undermined, and limits the rationality it supports. But this, of course, is only the hegemonic class' *defensive* strategy or, in other words, its minimal "program." It can live with and tolerate this program, but it does not regard it as desirable or optimal.

But if the central *political* problem of the hegemonic class under capitalism is the development of its influence over the administrative and political classes, on the state apparatus and governing regime, this influence is not a mere option that the hegemonic class can *elect* to exercise. For this class' interests are critically involved. These interests require protection of their currencies in international money markets, controlled taxation, access to distant markets for finished commodities, energy supplies, and raw materials. All these need the national coordination of banking services and of labor supplies. Under the modern conditions of bureaucratized corporations, whose profits are primarily a function of the sophistication of its technology, great sums are also necessary for "R & D" and for the development of a system of mass education for technologists and scientists. Much of this is supplied by "socializing" these costs through taxation. For a class whose needs encompass all this, a mere "alliance" with the state does not suffice. What it imperatively requires is a degree of integration with the state that is far more than an alliance, and which in fact is continually increasing. This is one of the fundamental structural characteristics of modern neocapitalism.

Michael Miles characterizes the emerging situation with succinct clarity: ". . . the government, the profit-making corporations, and the non-profit institutions of the knowledge industry are so interlocked at the directorial level, so interwoven at the middle levels, so meshed in functions, that they are hardly distinguishable." °

A key mechanism for this structural integration, commonly stressed by Miles, by Seymour Melman, and by Severyn de Bruyn, is of course, the military, and its civilian interface, the Defense and War Departments. It is this ministry that provides the strategic bridge between the state today and the hegemonic class, providing as it does for massive contracts for private industry, subsidies for research and development, which more or less guarantee the profitability of these supplying firms. To stress, as we have, the structural differentiation of the various social class and institutional orders under capitalism is clearly, then, not to imply they are mutually isolated or unconnected.

The structural differentiation of the several institutional orders and social strata under capitalism creates certain potential *advantages,* as well as dangerous vulnerabilities, to the hegemonic class and to the societal system of which it is a part. One of the most important advantages is that differentiation between the economic and the political-administrative spheres enables the latter, the state apparatus, to *appear* autonomous and impartial toward the other sectors of society. The *relative* autonomy of the state apparatus is publicly defined, for reasons to be discussed later, as an *un*qualified autonomy. In other words, the state apparatus is defined as that institutional sphere which *controls* society. What this occludes, however, is that the administrative-political classes are *not* autonomous; they are, in fact, in tacit alliance with the hegemonic class; are greatly subject to the latter's influence through various pressures and temptations; have entered into a mutually gratifying system for the exchange of reciprocities with the hegemonic class; and that some have become members of the same *subcommunity.*

The differentiation of the several social spheres in modern society also enables the hegemonic class to remain hegemonic by keeping at some remove from the political sphere, which serves as a "lightning rod" for the successes or failures of the society, thus protecting the hegemonic class' public repute. The corruption and scandals of the politics-administrative spheres need not taint the reputation of the seemingly distant hegemonic class.

2.2

The autonomy of the state apparatus *vis-à-vis* the hegemonic and other classes is a real if only relative autonomy, but is not simply a monotonic function of any one variable. More than that, a proper analysis of the relative autonomy of the state in modern industrial societies, especially capitalist

° Michael W. Miles, *The Radical Probe,* Atheneum, New York, 1971, p. 151.

nations, must recognize that it is an internally contradictory phenomenon. In dealing with it we must, on the one hand, avoid vulgarizations that simply see this autonomy as a useful illusion, presumably hiding the essential truth of its bondage to the interests of the hegemonic elite. On the other hand, we must also avoid a vulgarization that simply affirms the growing power of the "political sphere" in modern society without also seeing that it is not some monolithic force acting in integrated unison to impose itself on the rest of society. The industrial state's power is greater than ever; but it is also a power riven by internal contradictions and these, too, grow stronger. The modern state is neither monolithic nor isolated from other sectors.

The autonomy of the state is a complex function of several factors, among them: (1) its direct access to and control over the means of violence; (2) its licensing, taxation of, or direct military or legal control over the communication media; (3) the organization of a highly developed expert bureaucracy under the imperative control of a centralized authority; (4) the development, projection, and amplification of ideological appeals, as a direct mode of mobilizing the populace, which is available to the highest executive sector of the political class. Having already discussed the first two factors at some length, the following remarks will focus on the last two factors.

2.2.1

The organization activities of the state apparatus, as, indeed, of the industrial sector, are increasingly bureaucratic in character—in Max Weber's classically delineated sense. That is, the organizational form values expertise, and roles and authority in bureaucracy are allocated on the basis of certified expertise. The bureaucratic form is thus not that of the popular stereotype of foolish inefficiency, but an historically superior form of efficiency and relative instrumental effectiveness. For it entails an administration by full-time experts that links the bureaucratic form, on the one side, to training and credentialing institutions such as colleges and universities, and, on the other, to institutionalized science situated in universities and elsewhere. Interestingly enough, the views of Saint-Simon and Max Weber, although differing profoundly in many ways, nonetheless agreed that modern organizations would be and were characterized by their reliance upon rationality, at least the *formal* rationality of science and technical experts.

Modern bureaucratic organizations in the state sector or in the production sector systematically evaluate the degree to which their policies are effective and make cost-benefit analyses of them; they appraise rationally the relative effectiveness of the various departments within the organization; they conduct public opinion and market researches that keep open contacts with their suppliers and outlets; they select new recruits and continually reevaluate all members with various kinds of psychological and performance tests; they defend policies with the use of research; they struggle and wage war against others with rationally documented argumentation and information— "facts and figures"—they prepare for unforeseeable contingencies by briefing their administrators with scientifically accumulated "background information" and with systems analyses allowing for different "scenarios" involving alternative assumptions about events.

The formal rationality of modern bureaucratic forms has evolved rapidly since Weber's analysis, but essentially on the basis he described. The organizations' technological hardware has developed enormously since Weber with the advent of computerization, mechanized retrieval and control of information, and electronic communications systems. But this development was grounded in the prior development of the bureaucratic organizational form that stressed instrumental behavior, formal rationality, and scientific, expert administration. The power of the state apparatus has increased greatly as some function of that technological development. But the goals for which that power is used are, in important part, set from outside the bureaucratic system of formal rationality.

2.2.2

As Weber saw long ago, all bureaucracies are under the control of top executive officers who establish the goals for which the bureaucratic organization is mobilized. The heads of even the most technologically advanced bureaucracies are not appointed simply on the basis of *their* technical credentials or imputed scientific competence. Their appointment is fundamentally based on their *extra*scientific characteristics: their membership in the right political party, family, in appropriate class sectors, their possession of evidenced ideological reliability, friends and contacts, wealth, ownership.

Increasingly, however, if these persons are effectively to assume control over scientized organizations they need technological training and skills of their own, enabling them to negotiate with scientific and engineering administrators and appraise the performances and potentialities of their organizational instruments. Thus the interaction between the technical staff and the controlling administrators appointed over them entails a measure of reciprocal influence, rather than simply the one-way giving of instructions by the political appointees to the technicians and bureaucrats.

Nonetheless, the top administrators have commitments, involvements, and dependencies outside of the bureaucracy itself, which they communicate and represent, and which constitute a nucleus of nonnegotiable interests. Their influence is exerted in part by defining the organization's foci of activity—the issues and tasks made problematic to the bureaucracy—and, also, by defining the *givens* of its problem-solving effort. All problem solving, even within the most scientifically systematized arrangement, always premises that some features of the situation are to be treated as unchangeable and that others are to be changed or to be revised around these. They constitute the "conditions" of action and the "goals" toward which the organization is aimed. Either "conditions" or "goals" may be defined as *givens*, as fixed, unexaminable, and unchangeable; the conditions or goals that are defined as givens will variously limit and constrain the resultant foci of activity in the organization. The administrators in control of the scientized bureaucracies are political appointees who transmit *interests* that define certain conditions or goals as nonnegotiable and beyond examination, thus focusing the bureaucracy on the residual, *non*given, elements from which it selects its problematics.

2.2.3

The rational-scientific elements of the bureaucratic organization remain encased within and limited by nonrational, nonscientific political and economic interests. Scientific and technological expertise thus rationalize and legitimate only the instrumental *means* used to achieve the organizational goals given, but *not the goals* themselves. These can only be legitimated by value systems and ideologies to which the controlling administrators may link their organizational directives. Thus despite the accelerated scientization of bureaucratic organizations, the effectiveness with which they achieve these goals will not only be a function of their technological prowess and scientific development, but also of their ideological vitality and persuasiveness. Even within the most modern bureaucratized state apparatus, science and technology thus operate within limits set by *ideology and interest.*

The rationality of the scientized bureaucracy is only a formal rationality precisely because the Weberian limit abides: it is not men of science, not experts, and not even sheer bureaucrats that set organizations' goals but political appointees; men who, for instance, are understood to understand which demands are to be viewed as nonnegotiable; what issues are beyond discussion; what constitutes ideological reliability; what constitutes fiscal soundness; whose viewpoint cannot be ignored; and who thereby manifest reliability concerning the protection of fundamental interests, material, and ideal. These political appointees in charge of the bureaucracy can thus never have their organizational power legitimated by (but only hidden behind) the organization's science, technology, and expertise. It is at *their* level that there remains an abiding interest in ideology not yet enshadowed by the technological fascinations of bureaucracy's everyday life. It is at the executive level that the ideological direction of the organization will be set, or at which ideological options and needs may be mismanaged or abandoned. The executive level continues to need ideology to legitimate its own authority and projects.

2.2.4

No sociologist doubts that the dominant type of organization today, whether in the private or public sector, is the *bureaucratic* group. Whether armies, hospitals, fund-raising groups, factories, or revolutionary vanguards, they are run by full-time experts deploying technical skill in instrumentally rational ways for the achievement of specific purposes. Even sheer terrorism, by governments or against them, is now organized in essentially bureaucratic ways. The Scarlet Pimpernel is dead.

It is precisely the bureaucratic organization that has, in the modern era, provided for the reliable performance of required functions—the organizational "machine,"—quite apart from ideological conviction, and from any belief in the rightness of the end to which the organization has been committed. It is precisely this *de*moralization and impersonalization that strives to release performance from dependence on belief and ideology and which acclimates persons within the organization to rigorous obedience. I say, "strives to," not necessarily successfully so. It is the implantation of this "discipline" which, as Weber said, is "exact execution of the received order, in which all personal criticism is unconditionally suspended and the actor is unswervingly and exclusively set for carrying out the command"; it is exacty this discipline that enables ideological dissonance to be overcome, declares it to be irrelevant, and makes bureaucracy the perfect tool of a small external oligarchy. It is this conquering organizational form, the bureaucracy, that along with habituation to the use of consumeristic gratifications, provides a functional alternative to and substitute for ideological motivations, and thus competes with and deteriorates ideology.

But the ultimate paradox and contradiction is that this organizational machine, when successful in implanting discipline and technical efficiency, seeks to divert attention from the goals being sought to the means used in seeking them, thereby leaving the legitimacy of the goals unclarified and thus vulnerable to ideological critique. The system works only when the goals pursued by the bureaucracy are not ideologically challenged, and may thus remain *de*focalized. Given an ideological critique of the bureaucratic goals, however, they surface into visibility and must then be defended ideologically. But the skills that the organization has habitually rewarded and cultivated have been technical, not ideological.

Fundamentally, every bureaucratic organization is constructed on the tacit assumption that its goals will *not* be accepted either by many of its own subalterns or by those outside. All bureaucratic organization is grounded in the expectation of resistance, by those whose goals differ from those to which the organization has been committed. This resistance is dealt with by defocalizing the goals, concentrating attention on the means, and instilling discipline so that, it is hoped, there will be obedience even when the goal pursued is rejected. But when the goals pursued by the organization are too much at variance with those sought by its own personnel or others, when the price of obedience is too high, or when ideological challenge makes the dubious goals visible and hence problematic, there is a kind of "return of the repressed"; the fundamental repression on which the whole organization is based surfaces, compulsive concern with technique dissolves, and a disabling *anomie* anarchizes the group.

The goals of even the most computerized bureaucracy still require the justification of ideology to the degree that they require the willing cooperation of persons in and out of the organization. The most significant evidence of this in recent times was the failure of American intervention in Viet Nam, an effort that broke down domestically as well as within the army itself. All the technological prowess of the civilian and military bureaucracies failed to achieve the goals assigned them primarily because they had no ideological justification for the war. If the "end of ideology" thesis was taken seriously by political managers—and there is no doubt it was—the American failure in Viet Nam should have disabused them. Fundamentally, the American catastrophe in Viet Nam was not at the level of bureaucratic expertise, for there the technological instruments were more advanced than anywhere, but, rather, the failure was at the executive level. The war in Viet Nam made plain a fundamental error of the "end of ideology" thesis, as of any view implying that science and technology in industrial societies now have a *self*-sufficient and *self*-justifying hegemony; it revealed the fundamental weakness of the technocratic consciousness.

There is no doubt that some did *believe* the end of ideology thesis; it *was* an articulate view at the presidential level and, also, a permeating consciousness that premised *tacitly* that the existent levels of motivation and loyalty to organizations will, with the available technologies, suffice to achieve organizational goals. In a society in which loyalty and willing obedience have not been problematic for long periods, then the focus (even at the executive level) is given over to the development of new technologies, rather than to awakening ideological sensitivities and resolving ideological quandaries.

2.2.5

Capitalist nation-states have for long now successfully maintained their internal, domestic motivation and stability largely through "material" rewards in particular, with rewards deriving from their expanding gross national product from which many received more than they had previously gotten—even if not receiving as much as others did. It has been Pareto Optimality that was the fundamental basis of social solidarity in the expanding capitalist economies and, quite *rationally*, the major safety valve draining off class conflict.

But where the expansion of the GNP stops as, for example, in the event of a sharp depression, or when there are material or energy shortages and movement toward a "zero growth" economy, then Pareto Optimality ceases. People then no longer receive more than they had known; issues of differential allocation become sharper; class conflict intensifies; the loyalty and obedience to authoritative institutions and symbols attenuates. Now, increasingly, societal 'integration comes to depend on the effectiveness of ideological projection emanating from the top executive levels. And material motivations alone have *never* sufficed to maintain morale, or to mobilize it successfully, in the event of war. For war entails costs, at least for some, for which material rewards simply do not compensate. War generates gratificational deficits that have to be financed by religion, nationalistic fervor, perceived threats to security, and by the compensatory right to express aggression and to kill with authoritative license, or by ideological innovation.

In general, the revolutionizing of productivity following the industrial revolution enabled capitalist society further to break out of the limits of a zero-sum game in its relations with other states. Its own gratifications did not now necessarily imply a corresponding diminution of the gratifications available to other states. Capitalism meant that looting and booty were not *necessary* to increase a nation's gratifications, for the technological revolution allowed the society to play an increasingly powerful "game against nature." Seen from the standpoint of the past, capitalism meant a decrease in looting, in booty, and in wars from which these derived; in general, it meant that "primary accumulation" was only a transient phase. But capitalism also meant that the new societies were increasingly dependent on distant markets, to sell their finished products or invest their capital, as well as increasingly dependent on distant sources for raw materials and energy. This, in turn, makes the advanced capitalist nations seek imperialist control over the backward nations, and puts them in a position of competition with others like themselves who need markets and supplies, from which conflicts and wars might result.

2.2.6

On the one hand, then, capitalist society's ability to integrate itself depends on the maintenance of a certain level of popular ideological conviction, either for the routine orchestration of increasingly differentiated sectors of a society held together by a system of "indirect rule," or for the mobilization of the populace under the critical conditions of international conflict and war. As the colonialized nations of the world are disrupted by imperialist penetration and mobilized by their own ideologies of nationalism and socialism, the supplies and markets of the Euro-American nations and of Japan shrink or are imperiled; scarcities and uncertainties about supplies and prices grow. The ability continually to increase GNP, the fundamental requisite hitherto of the stability of capitalist industrialism, is thus increasingly precarious. These countries increasingly experience an accumulative sociocultural-psychological strain which is soluable only with, as *one* requisite, some basic ideological shift. The grounding for the old ideological equilibrium is rapidly eroded, and the cultural market for new ideologies swiftly accumulates. As humane as it doubtless is, and as correct as it doubtless is in many of its diagnoses of impending shortages, the new "ecological" movement can also be regarded as a new ideology that is being "Shopped" as a possible source of institutional legitimation for a society in which the established basis of equilibrium—the increasing GNP—is threatened. The new ecology movement may thus function, whatever its intentions, as the ideology appropriate for a time of austerity, of material shortages, of declining or static standards of living, of the conservation of energy supplies and raw materials. But the symptoms of the symbolic shift impending scarcely stop with the growing ecological movement. There are also indications of the emergence of a multitude of new preideological symbol systems—new religious, quasireligious, and occultist movements which, in their own different ways, also sanction the "dematerialization" of everyday life.

All this concerns the forces generating a new market for ideological innovations. At the same time, however, there are other fundamental characteristics of a capitalist economy that make it difficult for that need to be satisfied within the limits of its previous institutions. For the practice of these societies, in the recent past, had been to integrate themselves through improved standards of living, by increased "consumerism," and, in general, by any mechanism that was manageable instrumentally, and was subject to the controls of purposive rationality. This pattern of social control has largely generated a tendency toward the *devaluation* of ideological integration— toward the "secularization" of politics, we might say—that discourages ideological skills, sensitivities, and openness. Ideologies then lose their tautness and effectiveness. The ideological dimension is thus repressed. Conformity tends to be maintained more by gratificational conditioning and less by ideological conviction.

As there is a growing connection between consumerism, productivity, science, and technology, many in the society tend to associate their increased enjoyment of life—the improved living standard—with technology. But under these circumstances, it is not correct to say that technology *becomes* the new ideology and replaces ideology; rather, it *represses* the ideological problem and inhibits ideological creativity and adaptation. The new technology has not become a new *mass* ideology, but, rather, for most of the population obedience is conditioned by the *gratifications* it associates with technology.

What then governs mass conduct is not a new *belief* in the moral rightness of technology but, rather, *the sheer experience of gratifications* with it. Let the technology remain unchanged, but let the gratification level decline, and the matter is put to the test. This is exactly the test inadvertently provided when wars and depressions occur. We then see that it is not science and technology, nor even their continued development, that suffices to maintain the morale and loyalty of modern citizens. There remains an abiding need for a justificatory ideology. Growing rationalization, technological hardware, the scientization of bureaucracy, do not circumvent this need. They never did. The authorities in charge of them, and the goals they established, always required ideological sanctioning. This ideological sanctioning is required increasingly with international crises, domestic depressions, and with declines in or threats to the pattern of consumer gratifications which had once maintained equilibrium in these societies.

2.3

The market for ideologies, even in rationalized, scientifically advanced and technologically developed capitalist societies, remains and, indeed, grows. But the *ability* of these societies to make these ideological shifts, and to meet their new ideological requirements is limited. The hegemonic economic class has long been habituated to justify itself in terms of a growing GNP which undermines the entire mystique of authority.

The capitalist class has not only been a revolutionary class in its continual revolutionization of production but, also, in its demystification of social authority. Habituated and habituating others to rule in a demystified manner, in terms of gratifications produced, the capitalist hegemonic elite, always separated from the production of culture, has never had a strong impulse to maintain ideological creativity in society. It has, in that sense, been a force for political "secularization." It has not only habituated the mass of the populace to expect improved standards of living, but the political and administrative classes as well. More specifically, it has provided economic rewards in exchange for the political cooperation of the political classes. Watergate and other scandals were not a pathological aberration but (the sudden revelation of) a normal mode of securing the collaboration of the political class, used by an elite alienated from the means of ideological production and habituated to *paying* for what it gets.

This elite prefers modes of social control that are available to it, which it has at hand and in adequate supply, and which it can produce routinely. Its own tacit ideology of hegemony is that relatively peaceful one of paying for what it wants, in the expectation that it may rely upon the reciprocity of a grateful political class. As a result, while the market for ideologies abides and, indeed grows, especially when the GNP is threatened or when war occurs, neither the hegemonic economic elite nor the dominant political class is capable of satisfying the ideological needs that then surface. They have been too thoroughly secularized and have internalized the ideologically incapacitating consciousness for which the "end of ideology" was a label and a rationalization.

The end of ideology thesis correctly defined the ideological incapacitation of the hegemonic classes in industrial society, but made the gross error of supposing it to be the sign of a new strength, rather than the symptom of an impending crisis of legitimacy. Lacking any critical impulse, the end of ideology theorists accommodated to the ideological incapacitation of the hegemonic elites. It applauded their ideological malaise as a new enlightenment. The end of ideology thesis was itself an ideology that unwittingly signalled the very crisis of the hegemonic class and further contributed to that crisis by fostering the latter's complacency concerning their own devastating ideological weaknesses.

The end of ideology thesis was in part the ideology of a technological elite which, because it sought to equate their own special social requirements with those of the hegemonic elites to whom they appealed, missed the latter's different needs. The career of the end of ideology thesis, then, is an interesting exhibit of the *contradictions* that may exist between certain interests of an intelligentsia, and those of the hegemonic elite with whom they may in fact identify and support.

It is precisely because an intelligentsia always has *special* interests, independent of other social strata, that the ideologies it develops tend to exert a special strain on the interests of even the social classes it supports. The intelligentsia is the ideology-producing social stratum. The social and political interests and tensions its ideologies serve are mediated by its own special interests and social position, which is why no ideology is ever simply and solely the ideology of some economic or political class; the latter's interests are always mediated by and seen through the interests of the ideology-producing intelligentsia. Thus there is, on the one side, no ideology that is *only* the ideology of some economic or political class; on the other side, there is no ideology that is not, in part, an ideology of the *intelligentsia*, reflecting its special conditions.

If, as we said earlier, all ideologies serve to build social solidarities and polities across different groups in modern society, *one* of the special groups always invisibly involved in the solidarity thus fostered is the intelligentsia itself. Every ideology, then, contains a conception, cryptic or elaborate, of the place of the intelligentsia; every ideology deals the intelligentsia a future in the social change it projects. All ideologies, then, are cryptic projects concerning the future role of the intelligentsia. (I shall be at pains to elaborate this conception at length in my analysis of Marxism in later studies.)

2.4

To return to the main thread: I have focused here on the contradictory position generated by the hegemonic elites' need for, but inability to make, ideological adjustments to its routine and special needs. In a society with an expanding GNP, the executive political class, at the societal level and in charge of various scientized bureaucracies, is habituated to expect obedience without ideological conviction. Those whose careers have been involved in normal politics and in top level administration acquire a certain ideological deafness. Those controlling the bureaucracies come to expect obedience without making ideologically resonant "appeals." Those in charge of the political organizations, the parties mediating between the political and hegemonic classes, proceed by the code of normal politics which centers on certain exchanges: the rendering of practical political services to the hegemonic classes, including the provision of votes and other forms of mass mobilization, in exchange for funds or fund-generating opportunities.

Normal politics, then, is not likely to generate ideological sensitivities on either side of the exchange. Indeed, *neither* party to such a political exchange would normally foster ideological projection and mobilization. Ideological innovation and adaptation becomes the power-mobilizing mechanism of those *outside* of normal politics, of those who have not pursued careers in normal politics, or of those lacking the skills and connections of normal politics, or of those who do not have the resources of the state available to them. An ideological disposition is suspect, to those accustomed to normal politics, precisely because it brings "outsiders" into the political arena, or because it gives those using ideological mobilization a base of power in the masses, independent of the support of either the hegemonic class itself, or the bureaucracies, or the managers of the organizations of normal political mobilization. Successful ideological projection may circumvent existing political institutions and place successful ideologists at the pinnacles of power where they can exert pressure to reshape the conventional patterns of allocation previously reached by normal politics.

All the experiences of the hegemonic class, of the political managers, and of the bureaucratic officials, then, are inhibitive of ideological maintenance. The former normally suspect or oppose those seeking to advance their political position through ideological projection. A fundamental contradiction of a capitalist political economy, then, is that it is based on a system of "indirect rule" that requires operating mechanisms of ideological integration, yet at the same time, its own leading elites and classes inhibit the effective maintenance of the very ideological mechanisms required for their own social reproduction. The hegemonic and dominant classes suspect and oppose those pursuing an ideological politics, seeing it as the politics of unsocialized outsiders who do not play according to "the rules of the game," and who, above all, are less responsive to normal interests. Ideological projection may give an outsider his own base of power; a base which may enable him to cut out older political interests, to renegotiate the terms of exchange between the political class and the hegemonic elite, and, indeed, to impose new costs on or even to threaten the interests of the hegemonic elite.

Being relatively unsocialized outsiders, a new political class grounding itself in an ideological revitalization disrupts established political institutions and arrangements and can, in that sense, be or seem to be a revolutionary force. (Precisely that ambiguity was involved in National Socialism or Fascism.) The analysis formulated here suggests that all capitalist economies possess an inherent vulnerability to ideological crisis that may be met, and indeed, at some point met only, by an ideological revitalization borne by groups *outside* of its normal political arrangements. The fundamental danger of fascism, then, abides within even the most stabilized parliamentary democracies. While the structural decline of the "public" in such societies, as a sphere of rational discourse, is an endemic vulnerability of contemporary democracies, their most critical vulnerability remains the danger of fascism.

chapter 12

From Ideologues
to Technologues

Ideologies are project-centered moralities tacitly seeking to reconstruct a frayed, fragmented whole, or, in any event, a totality taken to be defective. Ideologies are defocalized efforts to integrate formerly separated parts, to reknit the unravelled, to extend the boundaries and to reconstruct the moral grounding of human solidarity. Underneath their often limited manifest project, all ideologies are pursuing a *latent* project: the reconstruction of a social whole weakened by the emergence of privatizing interests. It is precisely for this reason that the attenuation of ideologies in the modern world, of which we spoke in the previous chapter, constitutes not simply the deauthorization of political authority *per se* but undermines the legitimacy of the total social order of everyday life in the modern world.

1

It is because of the attenuation of certain older ideologies in modern bourgeois society that there emerged a renewed interest in a "technocratic consciousness" with which the corporate order and its symbols of authority might be newly legitimated.° The thesis of "the end of ideology" was the newly refurbished ideology of positivism, that served as an effort to crystallize the technocratic consciousness.

The new technocracy, like the old bureaucracy, claims that its work is based on the best knowledge and expertise. Like the classical bureaucracy, the new technocracy understands and proclaims itself to be proceeding

° The presence of this new technocratic consciousness was clearly exhibited at the highest political level by President John F. Kennedy in his address at Yale University on June 12, 1962: "What is at stake in our economic decisions today is not some grand warfare of rival ideologies which will sweep the country with passion, but the practical management of a modern economy. What we need are not labels and clichés, but more basic discussions of the sophisticated and technical questions involved in keeping a great economic machinery moving ahead."

without passion or favoritism; and, above all, with that neutrality toward partisan interests that leaves it free to select and implement the best technical solution. What has changed is that the new technocracies are a *maturation* in the direction already foreseen by the Weberian model of bureaucracy.

1.1

Since Max Weber, the connection between technology and science has been intensified, routinized, and institutionalized. As Peter Drucker puts it: ". . . it is certain that the scientist, until the end of the nineteenth century, with rare exceptions, concerned himself little with the technological work needed to make knowledge applicable . . . the technologist, until recently, seldom had direct or frequent contact with the scientist and did not consider his findings of primary importance to technological work." Today, however, Drucker adds, "technology has become science based. Its method is now 'systematic research.' And what was formerly 'invention' is 'innovation' today." °

Drucker further holds that the modern union between technology and science was not so much shaped by the initiatives of science as by those of technology: ". . . science was transformed by the emergence of systematic technology . . . it is technology that gives the union of the two its character; it is the coupling of science to technology rather than a coupling of science and technology," that characterizes the newly institutionalized connection.

In other words, technology has had considerable success in coopting science. It is precisely this fusion that serves to endow technocracy with the mystique of science, to define itself as something more than the honest craftsman's ingenuity, cleverness, diligence and discipline; as something more than a wily practicality animated by a hope for gain and recognition. Now, technocracy could bask in the more lofty, indeed, sacred, aura of science's Promethean struggle for truth, against superstition, for enlightenment; technocracy could now define itself as the modern embodiment of human rationality. Science took technology out of the artisan's dingy shed into the cloistered halls of the university and its laboratories, and thus doubly defined it as a neutral social agency concerned with the benefit of society as a *whole*.†

° Peter F. Drucker, *Technology, Management and Society*, Harper and Row, New York, 1970, pp. 62–63.

† In that sense, Theodore Roszak is correct in characterizing "technocracy" as a science-grounded mode of legitimation: as that "society in which those who govern justify themselves by appeal to technical experts who, in turn, justify themselves by appeal to scientific forms of knowledge. And beyond the authority of science, there is no appeal . . . technocracy is not generally perceived as a political phenomenon in advanced industrial societies. It holds the place, rather, of a grand cultural imperative which is beyond question . . ." T. Roszak, *The Making of a Counter Culture*, Doubleday, New York, 1969, pp. 8–9.

The technocratic consciousness and ideology, then, corresponds (1) to this hierarchical fusion of technology and science, and (2) to the insertion of this new complex into the structure of the *bureaucratic* organization.

1.2

The classical bureaucracy was, most fundamentally, an organization form aimed at the social control of persons resistant (or indifferent) to the goals to which the organization was formally committed. It sought to control the processes in which recalcitrant persons were engaged, or the products they produced. Bureaucratic officials were understood to be acting in compliance, and seeking conformity with, generalized and ongoing rules, rather than directing in extemporized, *ad hoc* and personal ways. It was a system of control through "rules" rather than through "orders." The obedience sought and given was thus formally defined as impersonal. Persons were dominated by the system, rather than by other persons; and they were to be loyal and obedient not to other persons but to the impersonal rules and the system they constituted. In part, then, in the old bureaucracy, legitimacy was grounded in the *rules* and in their rigorous enactment. At the same time, the old bureaucracy also conceived the *bureaucrat* as legitimate because he was selected on the basis of (authoritative confirmation of) his technical training and skills, through testing or credentialling.

The old bureaucracy was thus grounded in a contradictory system of legitimacy. Its legitimacy derived from its rules, from their proper legal mode of enactment, and from strict conformity to them—on the *one* hand. On the other, its legitimacy also derived from the bureaucrats' imputed expertise. A very large part of the old bureaucracy's personnel, however, was simply at a clerical level of skill, meaning that they were linguistically skilled; they could write, read letters and memoranda, they could maintain files, consult rule books, and perhaps type. As literacy spread, the supply of such skills became diffused in the population and thus limited bureaucrats' economic rewards or social status.

It is thus the old bureaucracy's rigorous conformity with the rules that becomes the measure of its virtue and worth. The old bureaucracy then is primarily legitimized by the uniformity and devotion with which it applies these rules. It also focuses on sheer rule conformity in some part because it expects that persons will be disposed to resist or to avoid such conformity when it suits them.

The classical Weberian bureaucrat, then, was vulnerable to procedural compulsiveness—to "red tape"—giving ritualistic conformity to rule-specified procedures, quite apart from the quality or quantity of services or products such conformity yields. The popular stereotypes were correct. Concern with the development of technical skills, and with the instrumental effectiveness of performances, was further diminished in the classical bureaucracy by linking the official's career and his income to his seniority. His motive for improving his output is thus further undermined. In the classical bureaucracy, then, it was not efficiency but uniformity, impersonality, and accountability—nonpartisanship—that mattered.

1.3

This is profoundly changed with the acceleration of technocracy, with the increasing numbers of "staff" experts, engineers, scientists, technicians, researchers, and the higher-level "technocrats" who mediate between them and the older "line" officials. With the development of science and technology and their growing fusion, their implantation in bureaucracy's social system heightens internal differentiation. Bureaucracy begins a fundamentally new phase in its organizational evolution. The growing technocratic differentiation coexists alongside of the older apparatus. It becomes a differentiated subsystem within it, as partly indicated by the developing distinction between "staff" and "line" personnel. The "line" are essentially the older types of officials, whose legitimacy is grounded by the legality of their mode of appointment and their conformity with rules, and whose security is based on seniority. They become the old "snake brain" of the organization, rooted in the elemental impulse of domination. The new technicians, engineers, and researchers are separated from the more purely political-administrative line system and, within the limits of the goals assigned them, they have considerable autonomy.

Unable to make specialized technical appraisals, the line officials cannot *themselves* evaluate technicians or their work. The technical ignorance of the bureaucratic line officials is an important source of the autonomy of the newly differentiated technical staff. The line system is, therefore, compelled to relinquish supervision of the technical *process*, confining its judgments of the technical staff to appraisal of its *product*. That is, bureaucrats must now judge by "results," in some contradiction with their previous stress on rule conformity, and at variance with their effort at central control from the top.

The newly scientized bureaucracy's system of legitimacy is now radically ambivalent, and tensions grow between line officials and technical staff. To reduce this tension, the two systems are at first insulated from one another and then reintegrated through the mediating brokerage of a new high-level specialty, the technocrat—an engineer, scientist, or technician—who functions to administer the new technical subsystem and who maintains communication with the line officials.

The growth of the technical subsystem means the growing influence of a new logic or culture within the bureaucracy. The logic of the technical subsystem is subordinated to the overriding concern with efficiency. Unlike the ritualism of old-line bureaucrats, the new technicians continually reappraise processes and performances from the standpoint of their costs or benefits, continually devising innovations that improve output.

Unlike the bureaucrat with simple symbolic skills, the new technician has a genuine body of knowledge he is able to apply with skill. Unlike the old bureaucrat, then, the new technicians are therefore less concerned about vaunting their social superiority or extracting personal deference from those below them. The sphere of personalized and political domination has been retracted; personal domination is increasingly replaced by impersonal control.

1.4

The old Saint-Simonian vision, in which the control over persons would give way to the *administration* of "things," appears on the horizon. The trouble, however, is that among the "things" now to be "administered" are *persons*. In short: persons are increasingly treated as "thingified" objects, no different from any other object. In Hans Freyer's words: ". . . the ideological formula is only too correct: men are not controlled, but objects are administered. Only the formula forgets to add: objects including mankind, and man necessarily along with objects."

Scientization of the bureaucratic organization thus produces a profoundly ambiguous development. Correspondingly, the refurbishing of the new technocratic ideology, as a mode of legitimating modern society, has both a rational and an irrational component, resting as it does upon this ambiguous structural development.

Since the new technocracy is committed to technical development, efficiency, and growth, it may also enhance productivity and the supply of available gratifications; to that extent, it provides more of the material satisfactions of life. At the same time, however, the availability of consumer satisfactions provides new sources of social control and social solidarity. Yet, however, fetishistic and vulgar "consumerism" is, and conformity based on material gratifications is, it is more earthy and reasonable than that based on ideological projections and promises such as nationalistic glory, racial superiority, the "white man's burden," or the end of human loneliness. Given an increase in gratifications, men will more readily support their social system without being subjected to force and direct domination; and it is reasonable that, within limits, they should.

The growth of the technical subsystem within the bureaucracy has placed *limits* on the sway of purely political forces, even as it provides improved technological instruments for achieving the bureaucracy's own goals. The bureaucratic line officials, and the political appointees governing them from the top, are now more alienated than ever from the new technologies placed at their disposal.

The ambiguity is thus profound: the technical staff is governed by and subordinated to an officialdom which sets the goals, but which knows little about the technical processes used to realize them. The technical staff is alienated from the ends; the officials, from the means. While now developed more than ever before, technology remains subject to the ultimate control of nontechnicians, bureaucratic officials, and political appointees.

2

Where, then, does this leave the "new" technological ideology as a legitimation of modern industrial society? To have conceived it as "the end of ideology" was itself unreflexive ideology. The rationality of the new technology develops within the limits of the old officialdom. It is censured and channelled by direct orders, and by the fiscal support it receives for its "results." It is under pressure to achieve goals established by the political appointees, nonbureaucrats, and nonexperts at the head of the bureaucracies.

This profound limitation on their technical rationality and reflexivity is largely missed in the vision of the new "post" industrial society of Daniel Bell and of the new industrial society of John K. Galbraith. Both see the new organizations as actually governed by considerations of efficiency. In short, the actual structural subordination of technical rationality to managerial power and economic interests is occluded by the ideology of the new technology. The technologists' wish-fulfilling fantasy of being free from the control of purely political, economic, military, or banking interests is a technological ideology, a project mistakenly defined as an already achieved condition.

S. M. Miller has observed that not having to pay, not being "billed," for its external diseconomies or distantly inflicted costs, the firm seems to be more efficient than a proper cost accounting would reveal. Moreover, observes Miller, citing Robert McNamara's record while head of the Ford Motor Company, there is considerable indication that top management does not at all view the recommendations of the engineers and technologists as if they were the voice of an objective necessity, but, rather, often manifests an "impatience with opposing ideas." ° In this view of the matter, the managerial controllers are not forced to bow to technological imperatives, and they do not.

One characteristic situation, long noticed by Harold Wilensky, is that

° S. Michael Miller, "Notes on Neo-Capitalism," *Theory and Society*, Spring, 1975, p. 14.

experts and expertise may simply serve to *legitimate* positions previously taken by management officials. (Cf. H. Wilensky, *Intellectuals in Labor Unions*, Free Press, 1956). In his recent and probing analysis of *Organizational Intelligence* (1971), which focuses on the use of expertise by the military establishment, Wilensky is far from impressed with its top management's use of expert information. His conclusion tends, rather, to converge with Miller's: "To read the history of modern intelligence failures is to get the nagging feeling that men at the top are often out of touch, that good intelligence is difficult to come by and enormously difficult to listen to; that big decisions are very delicate but not necessarily deliberative; that sustained good judgment is rare." °

Studies of the actual interaction between political officials or management, on the one side, and technical experts, on the other, fail to support any thesis of the "end of ideology." Certainly technical recommendations are not "mere" ideology, but it becomes ever clearer with each study of their operation that the technicians adapt in advance, taking anticipatory account of the ideological and interest-grounded views of organizational management. Moreover, as Magali Sarfatti Larson suggests, technicians usually have more than one way of accomplishing some objective: the one they select is chosen partly in terms of efficiency or cost considerations and, also, partly in terms of political and other considerations.†

° Earlier, Wilensky also remarks that "when experts describe their function as 'window dressing' . . . they point to activities common to experts everywhere—the defense of established policy . . . administrative leaders who hire experts tend to derogate technical intelligence and accent the importance of political and executive skills they themselves possess. They throw in their 'research' staff ritualistically, much as a tribal leader embarking on war calls on the shaman for supporting incantation."

In her study of the location of a power plant and the expansion of an airport, Dorothy Nelkin similarly concludes that "developers seek expertise to legitimize their plans and they use their command of technical knowledge to justify their autonomy." Professor Nelkin also observes that even "purely" technical decisions entail technical uncertainties, so that different sides in a political conflict can call up their own experts in support of their conflicting views. Whether technical advice is accepted (and I might add *which* technical diagnosis is accepted), often "depends less on its validity and the competence of the expert, than on the extent to which it reinforces existing positions," and the power of those holding them.

Professor Nelkin also observes that, as differences between experts surface to public visibility, the idea that technical considerations express an objective, immanent necessity, to which one must submit, loses its public force. Controversy "demystifies their special expertise and calls attention to non-technical and political assumptions that influence technical advice." (Dorothy Nelkin, "The Political Impact of Technical Expertise," Social Studies of Science, Vol. 5, No. 1, pp. 51, 53, 54.)

† M. Sarfatti Larson, "Notes on Technocracy," *Berkeley Journal of Sociology*, XVII, 1972–73. Technical ambiguities themselves allow other criteria of choice to enter. Indeed, the more technical maturity, the larger the variety of more or less technically equal solutions to a problem, the more room there is for intervention by *extra*technical considerations to resolve that technical uncertainty. It is thus not simply that the organizational structure places the technological sphere

A technocratic model, then, which sees technicians dominating officials and management, and which sees the modern technologically developed bureaucracy as governed by an exclusive reliance on a standard of efficiency is a fantasy, a utopia, an ideal type. That fantasy, however, was the grounding of the "end of ideology" thesis, as well as of Galbraith's and Bell's vision of the new knowledge-dominated society.

3

What, then, may be said of the differences between older ideologies, e.g., nationalism, *laissez faire*, socialism, and the supposedly modern ideology which seeks to ground the legitimacy of modern neocapitalism and bureaucratic socialism in the idea of a technologically guided society. How much of a change has actually occurred, if any, and in what directions, in the transition to the technocratic ideology?

Jürgen Habermas has raised this question forcibly. Habermas is lucid in stressing certain differences between the two ideologies, their *dis*continuities. He has not, however, been equally incisive in clarifying the nature of their differences; and, in the end, one suspects he has overstressed the differences themselves. Indeed, there are points where Habermas' formulation—written in 1968—so emphasized the *differences* between the new technocratic legitimation of modern society and the old ideologies that it almost slides into a sophisticated statement of the "end of ideology" thesis: ". . . this new form of legitimation," affirms Habermas unequivocally, "has cast off the old shape of ideology." °

Again, Habermas emphasizes that "technological consciousness is . . . 'less ideological' than all previous ideologies." When we ask, in what sense is this so, how or why, then ambiguity ensues and difficulties arise. The new technocratic ideology, says Habermas, is "not a rationalized, wish-fulfilling fantasy, not an 'illusion' in Freud's sense . . ." This, apparently because it is not based on the power of dissociated symbols and unconscious motives. The new technocratic ideology probably means considerably less than the *end* of "illusions" (in the Freudian or any other sense). Here one might well remember that Marx and Engels saw even the earliest, *pre*technocratic bourgeois economy as having exactly the same "illusion"-destroying character that Habermas claims for the "new" technocratic ideology:

> The bourgeoisie . . . has left remaining no other nexus between man and man
> other than naked self interest . . . it has drowned the most heavenly ecstasies of

---

under the control of *goals* formulated by management officials at the top, but the selection of technical *means* or instruments too, may also be affected by interests or norms that are taken as nonrational givens. The maturation of a powerful technology, then, does not eliminate norms and interests that restrict and limit the influence of technology.

° J. Habermas, *Toward a Rational Society*, Beacon Press, English translation, 1970, p. 111.

religious fervour, of chivalrous enthusiasm, of political sentimentalism, in the icy waters of egoistical calculation . . . for exploitation, veiled by religious and political illusions, it has substituted naked, shameless, direct, brutal exploitation. (*Communist Manifesto*, authorized English translation of 1888, p. 15)

The above pamphleteering extravagance, which imposes new illusions as it exorcises ancient ones, does have a point, however, especially if we remember that, in their more Apollonian moods, Marx and Engels were the first to analyze how the age of new ideologies did impose new illusions. And that they did so is, I assume, part of what Habermas had in mind.

3.1

What is involved is a continual process of disenchantment in which at "first," men imagine themselves motivated by religious piety, and account for their actions by their love of God, religion, and the sacred. This was succeeded, in the bourgeois age, by ideologies which, with a *coupure*, did away with the heavenly iconography of the human reality; men now presented themselves as doing what they did for the earthy happiness of all. Ideological smugness thus replaced religious piety.

Marx and Engels, then, were right: the old illusion that could not, being sacred, be forthrightly challenged gave way to a new *secular* illusion, that could be. The new technocratic ideology, however, does not simply claim to produce something better for all, but also claims this happy administration of things is supervised by a kind of secular ministry, the scientists, who are interested in no gain for themselves, and whose work can be judged by its fruits, superior consumerism, comfort, health. There is here perhaps a certain businesslike realism, secularism, loss of illusion. Disenchantment has taken another step, except so far as scientists are concerned.

"The new ideology," suggests Habermas, "is distinguished from its predecessor in that it severs the criteria for justifying the organization of social life from any normative regulation of interaction. . . . Technocratic consciousness reflects not the sundering of an ethical situation but the repression of 'ethics' as such as a category of life."[*] This last conclusion is less convincing, however, if one recollects that the Marxist version of socialism, itself part of the age of classical "old" ideologies, sought to distinguish itself from earlier forms of socialism, particularly from "utopian" or "true" socialism, by insisting that it, unlike them, was not based on moralizing sentimentalities; that it was grounded in what *is*, and in what was coming with historical inevitability, rather than in what *should be*. Marxism clearly

---

[*] Habermas, Ibid., pp. 112–113.

affirms itself, in some formulations, to be a "scientific socialism," which, like other sciences, sought inevitable laws of social development that did not depend on men's thoughts or morality but, rather, *determined them.*

Indeed, one of the central foci for the subsequent development of Marxism, one of the cultural modalities around which Marxism begins to structurally differentiate into a "scientific" and a "critical" Marxism, is precisely this *element* of technocratic consciousness with which it was sedimented and which was intensified by the work of Engels, Kautsky, and Plekhanov. If one recalls Marxism, it seems that Habermas is overstressing the historical *novelty* of the new technocratic legitimation of society.

More generally, however, and as our earlier discussion of the general grammar of classical ideology stressed, ideology is a more rational semiotic system than its critics commonly suppose, even if not as rational as its adherents like to pretend. "Old" ideology developed in this way precisely because it arose in a world in which traditional semiotic systems, religious and myths, were fast dissolving and being replaced by the newly prestigious sciences. Indeed, Marx condemned "ideologies" because they were *pseudo-sciences*, shallow pretensions to true science placed in the service of the social domination of society by the capitalist class.

Habermas' stress on the newness of modern technocratic legitimations, on their escape from Freudian irrationalities, derives from his having taken his starting point in the Marxist critique of ideology. For this critique one-sidedly emphasized the *cognitive* failures, or upside-downness, of ideology; the critique does not see the then new ideologies as partly rational, and as having a relatively heightened rationality. The generic grammar of the old ideologies entailed a rule of the unity of theory and practice, and the grounding of commands in reports, and this always implies a concern with the factual and technical grounding of any ideology's public project. Thus the technocratic consciousness of Marxism, with its plain-spoken resistance to using morality as the grounding of its own public project, is not an ideological aberration; it is an outcome clearly continuous with the general grammar of the "old" ideologies.

3.2

This becomes all the more obvious if we remember that "positivism" began in France precisely during the classical age of ideology. Positivism was a project for the social reconstruction of postrevolutionary France. In its view, the new society that had surfaced with the immature bourgeoisie was a "positivist" one that would transcend the "negativism" of the Enlightenment and the "anarchic" individualism of Protestantism. In their new positivism, the divided society was to be reunited on a scientific grounding. Science would be used to establish which beliefs were "positive"—precisely in the sense of scientifically *certain*, as well as not "negative." It was supposed that, because of science's *authority*, its claims would commonly be accepted by men, thereby reestablishing social consensus.

From its very postrevolutionary beginnings, then, a scientific technocratic legitimation was proclaimed for the emerging society. The French positivists sought to bring into existence a new morality and religion that would be appropriate to the new science and technology; and they generally thought this "lag" could be overcome with*in* the institutional framework of the emerging bourgeois society. Clearly, then, the *element* of technocratic consciousness in Marxism had its academic and religious counterpart in positivism, where it was far stronger. It is plain that the legitimation of the postrevolutionary society, and of its reform in positivism, or its revolutionary transcendence in Marxism, both contain profoundly important aspects of technocratic consciousness; and both are clearly a part of the classical age of ideology, rather than any radically new thing.

Perhaps Habermas has not concerned himself with this because his critique of positivism has characteristically dealt with it as a *philosophy* and epistemology, rather than seeing it as a new social *movement* for cultural revitalization complete with a new *social* theory, and with a project for social reconstruction, including a new "religion of humanity" whose "priests" would assume a new scientific and technical character. Anyone who sees the early technocratic ideology in its flagrant association with a new religion of humanity (complete with catechisms, retreats, colorful and chic clerical costumes), the intoxication of its sectarian controversy, its search for *la femme libre* in the Near East to serve as copriest of the new religion—anyone remembering this will have little confidence that technocratic ideology is not a "rationalized wish-fulfilling fantasy," not an "illusion" in Freud's sense. This colorful and "spiritual" side of the technocratic consciousness was, in fact, thoroughly compatible with the then emerging romanticism.

3.3

But this is not to say that the recent form of technocratic consciousness has now actually stripped itself of "illusions" and "fantasies." The technologic consciousness no longer structures these in religious forms. Illusion now takes the form of a kind of "naive" consciousness, infantile and adolescent in its repressed yearnings for association with an unlimited power. Scientific and technological power serve, in part, as the secularized symbol of the unlimited potency and cosmic unification once provided by religion. Science and technology assume a panacea-like character; given only time, the fantasy is that all problems will capitulate to it. Man is really Promethean and there is presumably nothing he cannot accomplish.

The technocratic consciousness, then, fantasizes science and technology as the utopian absolute, being the perfect fusion of both unlimited power and goodness, and to which as such all willingly submit, hence reconciling all social conflict. The technocratic, then, becomes the secularization of deity.

Magali Sarfatti Larson suggests (or implies) that the technocratic fantasy thus takes on a classical character as "ideology," being the very *inversion* of social reality characteristic of ideology—in the Marxist formulation. That is, the actual situation in the social structure is inverted. In the real social structure of the modern bureaucracy, technocracy actually remains limited and restricted by real interests and the structures of domination of power elites; but in the technocratic ideology this is inverted; science and technology are fantasized as the power to which all, including the hegemonic elites and their managers, must bow. Thus seen from the standpoint of a Marxist conception of ideology—as well as my own different conception— there remains a fundamental *continuity* in the character of ideology, even with the emergence of the technocratic consciousness. The technocratic consciousness and legitimation of modern society is fundamentally an emendation and a fulfillment of the grammar of ideology, rather than the end of ideology.

There is, however, one aspect of the character of the technocratic consciousness that differs from other ideologies and that is its *time* orientation. The technocratic consciousness premises that its project is already at hand and already exists. It is in this respect *not* future oriented, but is oriented to that which already is; it is thus classically "positive" in character. The technocratic project turns men away from a fascination with the future, discouraging a view that the fulfillment of hopes will be found there. It tells us the future is already here, in essentials if not in its full maturity. The future comes, then, as incremental addition rather than as structural transformation.

From another perspective, this says: things are not going to get better; there are no culminations to come; it is the present that counts. The technocratic consciousness, then, is the end of transcendental hope. It says we have much and will get more, but not all we have dreamed of and really wanted. It is thus comfort, and the end of comfort. The problem is whether people can stand so much comfort. The technocratic consciousness invites us to "grow up," and it tells us that growing up means the end of heroism and youthful "enthusiasm." Can this be borne?

The fundamental "weakness" of the technocratic consciousness is really that it does *not* promise "pie in the sky." It says, rather, look around you at the things already at hand, and it says that these suffice, and will become more sufficient. The rationality of the technocratic consciousness is that it invites men to judge on the basis of their experience, on the basis of what they can see and is already at hand. This invitation to judge by one's experience is reasonable. But it is also vulnerable and the society legitimated in these terms has a corresponding vulnerability. The technocratic consciousness promises both too much and too little.

It tells us that things are essentially sufficient, yet people look around and see the devastation of war, real or threatened depression, the collapse of affluence, the strains of inflation, the impending end of important sources of energy and raw materials, and the unending faithlessness of men. And even when they do not see such concrete things, they know they are not happy: "Men die and are not happy." Why aren't they happy, if things are sufficient? And how can this unhappiness be borne if this is all there is? The technocratic consciousness is the ideology of busy managers, engineers, technicians, persons already content with their work, social position and their comfortable standard of living. It is, in short, a consciousness of elites.

But is there any evidence at all that it is a consciousness of masses? It is not the technocratic *consciousness* that cements *their* loyalty to the system but concrete, technologically improved *gratifications*—"consumerism." The technocratic consciousness says that this is a reasonable way to live. But it really cannot do much with the unyielding remnant of unhappiness. In fact, it makes this unhappiness harder to bear since it envisages no end of it in sight. At this point, the technocratic consciousness is no longer the joyous harbinger of the possibility of happiness in the world, but a subterranean stimulus to depression. And when wars, economic crises, or material shortages occur, the technocratic consciousness has nothing to fall back on; for it has asked people to judge in terms of their experience; it has invited them to look around.

3.4

A fundamental vulnerability of the technocratic consciousness is that it is characterized by a prosaic matter-of-factness: it has painted God grey. It presents itself as devoid of any irrational sense of heroism, as having no impulse toward heroic self-assertion and contest. It is, in some part, this lack of open combativeness that distances the technocratic consciousness from "politics" as it has been conventionally conceived in Western European societies. This lack of public bellicosity makes the technocratic consciousness seem apolitical, possessed of a disinterestedness placing it "above the struggle"; or, from another perspective, over to the *side* of the struggle, by-passed by it. This lack of assertiveness is an aspect of the technocratic consciousness that suits its own structural subordination well, facilitates its domination by political managers and other forces. In part, then, this aspect of the technocratic consciousness provides a kind of adaptiveness and survival value.

In other respects, however, this lack of assertiveness and combative vigor collides with some of the most enduring characteristics of Western culture, particularly its continual need for struggle, the *agon*, its continual drive for mastery and domination over the environment and, in the case of Christianity, over the resistant parts of the inner self. The technocratic consciousness has no well focalized projects which one can "achieve," and movement toward which can provide a measure of success. Its project is already achieved and secured, so there is no more reason to struggle; its project is also never achievable, the goal receding as advances are made toward it, so struggle has no reward.

It is in this respect that the technocratic consciousness makes its sharpest break with certain abiding elements in Western culture, demobilizing and thus often demoralizing people. It is precisely its taste for agonic struggle that has been identity defining and has energized the West. It is the enormous energies activated by agonic struggle that have commonly induced the West to experience struggle itself as the very quintessence of the "life" force. As Euripides said: struggles make up our life. As a result, the rise of the technocratic consciousness has been widely experienced as a kind of "Deadening." Many who oppose technocratic society, literally see *death* in it. This tells us that the resistance in the West to technocratic society and consciousness is not a recent, shallow, or transient mood, and should not be dismissed lightly as a mere romantic reaction.

The critique of the technocratic society and its "mathematical project" began close upon the French Revolution with the emergence of a self-conscious romanticism which, from its very beginnings, was antimechanistic, antimaterialistic, and disposed to a pantheistic (if not animistic) conception of all things as infused with their own life spirit. Opposing the mechanistic deadening of things moved "merely" by external forces, the romantics affirmed that, far from God being dead, he, the supreme life spirit, was everywhere and in all things, however lowly or trivial. Romanticism *thus* "romanticized" the world. It is on this ground that romanticism begins the earliest critique of technocratic society. This critique, of course, was actually preceded in the most direct way by Rousseau's work, and, most especially, by his prize-winning Dijon essay which affirmed, against the common contention of the *philosophes*, that advances in knowledge and science were *not* making men's everyday life better.

That this critique of technocratic society is often denigrated as "mere" romanticism partly reflects the fact that the judgment made on romanticism is largely made from the very standpoint romanticism criticizes, and is to an extent defensively self-serving. The critique of the technocratic society *is* grounded in "romanticism;" but the critique of romanticism *is* grounded in the technocratic project. Having said this, however, one may miss the fact that romanticism is not some separate tumor of the imagination, Goethe's *krankheit*, which provided the foundation for a subsequent critique of the technocratic society, a foundation which, being "sick," already disqualifies the critique. Rather, the very foundations of romanticism already embody a critique—originally, but no longer, based on Christian standards—of the utilitarian assumptions of the new society.

In short, it is not that romanticism produced a critique of the new society because it was sick; to the contrary, romanticism became and was made "sick"—in some part—because it went against the stream, resisting the forces becoming dominant in the new society. And in any event, the romantic critique, in its turn, conceives the technocratic society to be the really "sick" society. It condemns the technocratic society as one in which the goals of life go unexamined; in which men compulsively fasten on the instruments of action; as a society run by grey men without spirit, where freedom, spontaneity, imagination, will, and creativity are crippled; where individuality and personality are buried under the growth of formalization and routinization: "sick."

4

As scientific and technical development proceed, the sheer complexity of technical analysis and work accelerates and, with this, there is increased difficulty in accommodating technological development to the requisites of a democratic political existence. Jürgen Habermas and others have stressed that there is no longer an arena of effective public discourse because of such technically difficult and specialized developments. As suggested in a previous chapter, this is scarcely all that is undermining politics today but, surely it is an important part. At the same time, it also needs to be said at once that the development of a technocracy has not simply crippled the possibilities of *democratic* control. The technocracy has, also, greatly limited the effective exercise of power even by those in *control* of the bureaucratic organization. It is not simply the "man in the street" but the hegemonic classes and elites themselves whose power is now limited, even though it enhances their legitimacy, to the extent that they proclaim their decisions to be governed by scientific considerations.

The pattern of "indirect rule" that was from the beginning a distinguishing political characteristic of the bourgeois hegemonic class, making it dependent on others for the actual at-hand exercise of violence and for the development of culture, has been intensified by the great development of a technocracy which now becomes the main source of a general utility, all-purpose, instrumental-purposive action. Now, in the old (Alfred) Weberian sense, neither "culture" nor "civilization" are directly produced by the hegemonic class. Now, the means of violence and, with the communications revolution, the means of manipulation, are both mediated by others. Now, the most fundamental *organizational* instrument, the bureaucratic organization itself, has developed within it a great growing "black box," a social space that requires ever greater investment and from which profound consequences emerge, but the hegemonic class knows not how.

This new technology mobilizes immense power for the hegemonic class; at the same time, however, this very development creates a new center that limits the options open to the hegemonic class. The growth of the technocracy increases the power, but reduces the *functional autonomy*, of the hegemonic elite. The security and survival of the hegemonic elites, then, becomes ever more dependent on others, and particularly the technocracy.

Let us here raise the question, not of the technocrats' own interest in power, but in the *uses* to which any power aggrandizement it secures might be put. In other words, the question here is the kind of ideology to which technocrats are susceptible. But, be it noted, I raise this question in a different way than those for whom the ideology of technocracy is a foregone conclusion. I do *not* premise that technocratic ideology is concerned solely with efficiency and instrumental efficiency. *That* appraisal of technocratic ideology is fundamentally mistaken precisely because it assumes that it can be solely technocratic; it thereby tacitly accepts the "end of ideology" thesis. Here, however, the question of the ideology of the technocrats is raised from a standpoint that *rejects* the end of ideology thesis, thereby rejecting any premise that "technocrats" are technocrats *alone* and are interested *only* in increasing efficiency and "instrumental rationality." A conception of technocratic ideology that reduces it to instrumental rationality is an illusion of philosophical idealism. It begins by recognizing the technocrats' technical and "ideal" interests and then proceeds to imagine that these are their *only* interests. Which, of course, ignores technocrats "material" interests, including their *political* interests.

Seen from another perspective, the question here, then, is: to what extent, and under what conditions, is the technocracy a conservative or progressive force in society? By which I mean two things: (1) to what extent does it contribute to the development of society's *productive* forces and to the rational use of these productive forces, and (2) to what extent can these forces contribute to a correct *understanding* of the nature and problems of a society?

The technocracy is turned in two different directions, toward the bureaucratic officialdom above them, with a quite *focal* awareness; and toward the working class below them, with considerably less clarity and unity. Serge Mallet suggests that the technocracy is willing to increase worker self-management in certain areas—in managing the "social surplus"—say, the amount allotted for plant crèches or health programs—and may even accept worker participation in incentive setting, in raising and equalizing salaries. Generally, the technocracy prefers to motivate workers by increasing consumerism, strengthening job security, and providing other incentives, rather than by extending workers' control; for the technocrats wish to retain control for themselves over investment policies, price setting, and production strategy.

There are, however, two other ways in which the technocracy are clearly progressive. One is in their resistance to the bureaucratic officialdom; the other is in their technological innovations. The two are profoundly connected. The larger import of the technological intelligentsia for social rationality and emancipation is that today it is they, more than any other single force, that now revolutionize productivity. As Marx formulated it in the *Grundrisse*:

> To the degree that large-scale industry develops, the creation of real wealth comes to depend less on labor time and on the quantity of labor expended, and more on the power of the instruments set in motion during labor-time, and whose powerful effectiveness . . . depends . . . on the general state of science and the progress of technology . . .

A fundamental difference between the older bureaucratic officialdom and the newer technocratic elite is that the former are fundamentally disposed toward systems of social control that simply "order and forbid." ° Bureaucrats expect to produce their objectives by inflicting costs and punishments upon those who do not conform. Technocrats, however, are generally much more disposed to use systems of material incentives and educational indoctrination as their mechanism of social control. This is partly because they are confident in their own ability to increase the available supply of material rewards through their technical innovations. Technocrats are also less punishment prone partly because—unlike the older bureaucratic officials whose ego-damaging low levels of skill lead them to become status centered and deference demanding—they really *know* and can do certain things with their knowledge. The technocracy is thus a more *task- and work-*centered elite, and has considerably less status anxiety; or more precisely, their status concerns are directed toward their own *professional communities.*

° A striking example of this kind of bureaucratic consciousness is related by Egil Krogh, Jr., the former special assistant to former President Richard Nixon, with responsibility in the federal government's "war" against crime: "I had been given the District of Columbia liaison responsibility in February 1969, and I remember a meeting with the President, he said, 'All right, Bud, I'd like you to stop crime in the District of Columbia; [Washington, D.C.] and I said, 'Yes,' I would do that. So I called the Mayor, Walter Washington, and asked him to stop crime, and he paused for a moment and said, 'Okay,' and that was about it." (cited in an article by E. P. Epstein, "The Krogh File—The Politics of Law and Order," *Public Interest*, Spring, 1975, p. 102).

It is in these professional associations and communities that they wish to be well-regarded, and whose good opinion can, to some extent, provide compensatory rewards. What happens within their own employing bureaucratic organization is therefore (relatively) less important to these more cosmopolitan technocrats. The bureaucratic officialdom who have no extra-bureaucratic base of support and security, however, must rely entirely for their protection on their position within their own bureaucracy. They are therefore a more conservative force, whose loyalties are focused on the particularistic characteristics, with which their privileges and status are intertwined.

At the same time, however, although the technocrats are more cosmopolitan and have a greater "task orientation" and less status narcissism, they may also be less sensitive to the *persons* around them, who may be affected adversely by their work. Nonetheless, to the extent that the technocrats' work successfully enhances productivity, the system then has more rewards to allocate; it can then generate a more *willing* consent, and needs punishment less as a mechanism of control. Without doubt, technicians are not committed to a radical equalitarian allocation of rewards; and without doubt, they favor using the material incentives—"consumerism"—they generate, as the central mechanism of motivation.

4.1

But the fundamental choice that technologically developing countries face is between two different modes of organizing *bureaucracy*. Their choice is between: (1) a mode of *punishment-centered bureaucracy*, in which the older bureaucratic structures predominate, and whose system of social controls necessarily focus on the infliction of punishments because its rewards are limited, and, (2) an organizational structure, a *representative bureaucracy*, in which the technocracy plays a much larger if not the leading role, generating a willing consent and integrating the system through the allocation—unequal, to be sure—of the increased productivity they generate. Far from being the single-minded advocates of a stripped down ideology of "instrumental rationality," the technocrats are able, precisely because of the increased productivity they can generate, and because of their greater commitment to work rather than to status-deference, and because of their elaborated linguistic codes and higher education, to organize a more rational *and more collaborative* organizational system.

Seen in this perspective, Maoism is essentially an egalitarian effort to *avoid* choosing either the authoritarian, punishment-centered bureaucracy *or* the (more collaborative, but still hierarchical) representative bureaucracy, grounded in science and expertise. In the end, China cannot avoid that choice. Whatever its own self-understanding, *this* is what Maoism is: it is an effort to establish a strengthened bargaining position for the working class in its inevitable forthcoming negotiations with the technocracy. Insofar as Maoism accomplishes that, rather than fostering contempt for the technocracy and the technical intelligentsia, then, Maoism is a profoundly progressive social force. In effect, the Cultural Revolutions will have cut off the option of developing a punishment-centered bureaucracy in China; it will ensure that the new organizational equilibrium point will be the representative bureaucracy. For its part, Stalinism was a profoundly retrograde force precisely because it subordinated the proletariat, along with the technical intelligentsia, to the most archaic organizational elite, the old bureaucratic officialdom.

The options facing technologically advanced society today are not between bureaucracy and the commune, not between bureaucracy and *non*bureaucracy. The real choices are between two types of bureaucracy; between a bureaucracy in which the old bureaucratic officialdom hold unrestricted domination, and whose rule is authoritarian and punitive, and a representative bureaucracy whose technocrats increase available material gratifications, and whose control systems can therefore focus on rewards rather than punishments, and who, in consequence, can enter into closer collaboration with the working class and elicit its willing cooperation rather than having to dominate it.

The older bureaucratic system centered on an officialdom with a more restricted linguistic code and who, when asked to *justify* their orders and forbiddings, grounded them in their *formal position of authority*. The older officialdom thus had no *reasons* they could speak. They legitimated their directives by their positions and only rarely justified them on the grounds that they would achieve some desirable ends. In the Weberian sense, their bureaucratic rules became a "basis of action for its own sake"—in short, a form of ritualism.

In such punishment-centered bureaucracies, rules are treated as ends in themselves; in the *expert-centered* bureaucracy, however, rules are treated as means to something further desirable, beyond themselves. Shall we then say that the punishment-prone, archaic officialdom manifests a "higher" rationality than the technocrats, because they manifest a *value* rationality, while the technocrats manifest a more mundane and merely "instrumental rationality?" In truth, the authoritarian bureaucrats manifest the most powerful *limits* on rationality. If, indeed, the technocrats foster "the end of ideology," the bureaucrats foster an end to *rationality*. This, in fact, is inherent precisely in *value* rationality. For its essential contention is that, at some point, persons must stop asking for *reasons;*° indeed, they say this rather quickly when the

---

° Clearly, at *some* point persons must; but it is one thing to do so out of the need to come to some decision in the face of a pressing problem and to allow the matter to be reopened after the

examination of reasons focuses attention on their own authority and on its powers and privileges.

Technocrats, however, being less status defensive and more work centered, are trained to give and to ask for reasons. They do not justify their work by making references to their authority. In contrast to bureaucrats' relatively restricted linguistic code, technocrats speak an elaborated linguistic code that demands reasons. It is just this pattern, in which things are *not* done for themselves alone, that has been condemned as their "instrumental rationality" and which Jürgen Habermas fears is destructive of morality.

Technocratic consciousness and instrumental rationality, suggests Habermas, "severs the criteria for justifying the organization of social life from any normative regulation of interaction, thus depoliticizing them. . . . Technocratic consciousness reflects not the sundering of an ethical situation but the repression of 'ethics' as such as a category of life . . ." ° From this standpoint, the technocratic elite is isolated from its practical alternative, the archaic and reactionary officialdom, and the judgment pronounced on the technocracy is the Durkheimian one, namely, that it spreads an *anomie*, a normlessness. There is, I believe, an important truth in this. The technician's instrumental rationality is a form of utilitarianism that does induce a strain toward *anomie*, taken by *itself*. The problem is, is instrumental rationality ever taken by itself?

4.2

If we divest ourselves of any notion of instrumental rationality as a *Geist*-like, disembodied wraith, and see it instead as part of the occupational culture of experts and technicians who constitute a *specific status group* with *status interests* they wish to protect and advance, and for which they require political allies, and which, in turn, require an ideology acceptable to these allies, it then becomes clear: technicians and experts are forced to go beyond instrumental rationality, and to *generate* a larger morality.

The question, then, is not what are the consequences of the technocrats' "consciousness" or of instrumental rationality, but what are the moral consequences produced in a social group facing certain political tasks. These inevitably lead to alliances and collaborations with other social groups. These alliances, in turn, require an encompassing ideology, which is surely *generative* of a new morality and not simply destructive of old ones.

Given the technocrats' political and status interests, they also have an

---

crisis has passed, and another, to do this quickly, punitively, and permanently. It is one thing to do this in connection with a limited, small number of questions and, quite another, with many.

  ° Habermas, Ibid., pp. 112–113.

interest in their own social *legitimacy*. The crucial question is whether their own expert competence *suffices* to generate that legitimacy. Looked at with any care, it is quickly visible that it does *not*. Technical expertise is not sufficient to generate legitimacy, when this expertise is *not* exercised on behalf of the values, goals, or interests of those others who are expected to bestow or withhold that legitimacy. The inmates of Nazi concentration camps did not view the doctors who experimented on them as legitimate medical authorities, despite the latter's technical training.

Two conditions, then, are necessary and sufficient for the legitimacy of experts and technicians: technical competence *and* the application of that competence on behalf of the interests of those from whom legitimacy is sought. If experts and technicians are to maintain or acquire legitimate authority in a group, they must support some of its interests and share the goals, ends, and *morality* of that group, or, at least, some part of it. The politics and social alliances of the technocracy, then, become *generative* of a morality. Expert authority is validated and legitimated only when it contributes to certain ends. Expert authority is legitimate only when there is the fusion of rationality with goals acceptable to some group.

The legitimacy of the technocrats, and hence their capacity to mobilize power useful to themselves, constrains them to choose sides, to opt for the interests, values, and goals of some other segment of society. Then, far from being the end of ideology, technology launches ideology upon a new stage in its career. Technicians and experts have, of course, traditionally dealt with this problem by repressing it; which means that they have tacitly supported the morality of those for whom they worked, but never made this focal, stressing instead their supposedly exclusive devotion to the development of means and instruments. Repressing the ends and the morality they supported, they occluded the group alliance they had made.

4.3

This repression and this group alliance have become more difficult to maintain. The decisive, most visible, change occurred after Hiroshima. The sheer horror and public visibility of the goals the scientists had urged or condoned—and it was not only the military but certain leading scientists who also wanted the bomb used—generated an historical *rupture* in the unexamined givenness of technocrats' instrumental rationality, and in the group alliances it had traditionally supported. Hiroshima was an historical crisis for the technocrats because it no longer allowed them to take as *givens* the goals and groups their technology supported. It began to make problematic and visible, to physical scientists themselves, their need for other group connections, for some role in goal setting, and for a *value* rationality; in other words, for a morality and moral commitment of their own. Since that time there has been a continual development of various "socially" committed and concerned causes in the sciences, of "radical caucuses" in professional associations, as well as the spread of a variety of journals and magazines devoted to expressing scientists' own political judgments.

A second, long-term development seems likely to be conducive to the same ideology-fostering and autonomy-strengthening result. This is the sheer growth in the numbers of technicians, scientists, and engineers, partly indicated by the growth of the "knowledge industry," the service and tertiary sectors of the economy, the vast development of universities since World War II, and the great increase in advanced technical schooling. James O'Connor has commented:

> The most expensive economic needs of corporate capital as a whole are the costs of research, development of new production processes, and so on, and, above all, the costs of training and retraining the labor force, in particular, technical, administrative, and non-manual workers. Despite the rapid advance of technology during the first half of the twentieth century, until World War II the industrial corporations trained the largest part of their labor force, excluding basic skills such as literacy.°

During World War II, however, O'Connor, Maurice Dobb and Richard Deaton argue that these costs began to be socialized, paid for, that is, by the society at large through taxes levied by the state. After World War II, liberalized government grants and fellowships for advanced schooling, as well as government funds for the development of academic plant and equipment were increased. The result, further intensified by post-Sputnik competition between the USA and the USSR, meant a great increase in the numbers of technicians and experts on the labor market, and which, at some point, acts to depress their economic conditions. "The professional and technical occupations contain most of the scientific workers, and," according to S. M. Miller, "is the fastest-growing category of the main (US) census occupational categories." While this may be far from "proletarianizing," it seems likely to give the technical intelligentsia a greater sense of their own corporate interests, making more problematic to them the goals which they should pursue, as well as increasing the power at their disposal.

5

With the world-wide emergence of the "ecology" movement, in itself an international and multiscience grouping, some scientists have now authorized

° J. O'Connor, *Corporations and the State*, Harper & Row, New York, 1974, pp. 126–128.

themselves to evaluate the consequences of their work quite apart from its success or failure in achieving the goals of some bureaucracy, once more making problematic technology's traditional alliance with organizational management. In ecology, technology itself starts a critique of its own traditional instrumental rationality, commits itself to new moral evaluations, and takes initiative in searching for new political alliances.

One notable consequence of this is the emergence of a new group of ideologists from ecology. Their function is to bridge the technical work of the many scientific specialities relevant to ecology with a larger public. Going beyond the closed discussion of bureaucracies, and the mutual isolation of normal sciences from one another, they increasingly address themselves to one another, providing a medium whereby experts in one speciality can understand developments in others, and, secondly, they may also write to a larger public of the relatively well educated, in magazines such as the *Scientific American* or *Science*. Not yet aware of the thesis that the old public is "dead," the new ideologists of ecology—"technologues"—proceed as if it were not. They have largely discovered from widespread responses to their dismal predictions, particularly in North America, and in Western and Northern Europe, that the rumors of the death of the public may have been somewhat exaggerated.

The ecological movement promises to strengthen the autonomy of scientists and other experts because it has brought them into increasing and direct contact with a larger *public*, by-passing bureaucratic definitions of the situation. All this, of course, is distressing to some scientists who quite correctly recognize that, except for *biological* ecology, a *general* ecology does not yet exist as a true science, and that it is an assemblage of diverse specialists who as yet lack a coherent *scientific* basis. There is, however, no doubt that the ecological movement incorporates many disconnected empirical generalizations of scientific validity and of considerable practical import for the future. But this means that the ecological movement has provided a general impetus to the development of an *ideology*, and is producing new types of ideologues, the technologues. This ideology is likely to enhance the scientific community's sense of itself as a corporate entity, and to allow it interaction outside of the bureaucracies that once monopolized scientists' time and enclosed their horizon.

In effect, then, scientists' growing connections with the ecological movement suggests that "instrumental rationality" no longer monopolizes their professional consciousness, if it ever did. It means that instrumental rationality is being augmented by, or fused with, a new *goal*-concerned ideology. Certainly, there are segments of the ecological movement, or sectors seeking to make use of it, that do indeed manifest an older, more conventional technocratic consciousness, hoping and intimating, that all can be remedied with "technological quickies," if only enough money is spent on certain new hardware. There is money to be made in the ecological movement; that is, there is public money to be privately appropriated, and the *technocratic* response panders to such interests. But this is very far, indeed, from the dominant character of the ideology exhibited by the ecological movement.

Although often unrealistic and naive about the differential class costs of their proposals, it seems plain that the ecological movement leads science increasingly toward politicalization and political programs, and toward a more unified, autonomous ideology of its own. Ecology may be the historical stimulus for the development of science's interdisciplinary and international corporate self-consciousness. When the American Barry Commoner asserts that the essential source of the emerging ecological crisis is industrial technology, as it has been used, and when a leading Swedish biochemist and ecologist, Gösta Ehrensvärd, calls for the mobilization of science to develop measures leading rapidly to a new *agricultural* (rather technological) society, it would seem that important sectors of the international scientific community have surrendered the old technocratic consciousness, have rejected a stripped down instrumental rationality, and have now authorized themselves to act as critics of the technological present and as technologues affirming new human ends.

Bibliographical Note

For an extended analysis of the distinction between what I have called punishment-centered and representative bureaucracies, as well as for an analysis of the conditions under which the technical intelligentsia will be defined as legitimate, see Alvin W. Gouldner, *Patterns of Industrial Bureaucracy*, Free Press, Glencoe, Ill., 1954, especially chapters nine through thirteen. For my fuller position on and analysis of the contradictions internal to bureaucratic organization, see A. W. Gouldner, "Organizational Analysis," in R. K. Merton, L. Broom, L. S. Cottrell, Jr., *Sociology Today*, Basic Books, New York, 1959, pp. 400–429. There is a theoretically and politically significant set of researches on bureaucracy, stemming from the critique and extension of Max Weber's work following World War II, that has yet to be harnessed and used by independent neo-Marxists who have recently rediscovered the problem of "bureaucracy." It is thus peculiar to note Americans "rediscovering" the work of Claude Lefort and of the Paris "Arguments" group on bureaucracy, when so much of that work was precisely an effort to fill in the Marxian lacunae concerning bureaucracy by using the studies of Max Weber and other sociologists informed by his perspective. The discussion on the Left today concerning bureaucracy and technocracy will wastefully recreate the world unless it assimilates—and critically—the probing theoretical and rich empirical work of "normal" sociologists such as: Peter Blau, Robert K. Merton, Philip Selznick, Melville Dalton, Orvis Collins, Raymond Mack, Reinhard Bendix,

Morris Schwartz, Burton Clark, Renate Mayntz and Michel Crozier. The Left is presently in danger of capitulating to a merely newspaper sociology of bureaucracy, devoid of any first-hand field study or even of closely analyzed readings of first-hand studies of bureaucracies.

There is no better critical appreciation of the ecology movement than the splendid piece by Hans Magnus Enzensberger, "Critique of Political Ecology," *New Left Review*, March/April, 1974. Barry Commoner's *The Closing Circle*, Knopf, New York, 1971 is of course one of the ecology movement's own classics and justifiably so. On a theme that he has developed in a parallel way independent of O'Connor, see Rick Deaton, "The Fiscal Crisis of the State in Canada," pp. 18–58, in D. I. Roussopoulos, *The Political Economy of the State*, Black Rose Books, Montreal, 1973. One may profit also from Henry Jacoby, *The Bureaucratization of the World*, University of California Press, 1973, and Ralph Miliband, *The State in Capitalist Society*, Basic Books, New York, 1969.

On the technocratic emergence in modern society see also: Daniel Bell, *The Coming of Post-Industrial Society*, Basic Books, New York, 1973; John K. Galbraith, *Economics and the Public Interest*, Houghton Mifflin Co., Boston, 1973; Alain Touraine, *The Post-Industrial Society*, Random House, New York, 1971. These, of course, are the contemporary emendation of a venerable intellectual project whose antecedents include James Burnham, who was taken far more seriously in Europe and on the Left—for example, by the *Arguments* group in Paris—than by the Left in the United States—for instance, Paul Sweezy's early polemic against him in *Science and Society*, Winter, 1942. The work of András Hegedüs is also noteworthy here, as is Claude Lefort, and, of course, some of Bruno Rizzi's early work. Much of this stems from an effort to develop or formulate a critique of Trotsky's analysis of the distinct character of the Soviet state as a transitional "bureaucratic deformation." It thus often involves a creative hybridization of a Leninistic Marxism, on the one hand, and, on the other, the great seminal work of Max Weber on bureaucracy. The project reaches back, on the American side, to Thorstein Veblen's *The Engineers and the Price System*, (1921), where the technical intelligentsia's potential for political autonomy is prophetically analyzed. This may be understood, correctly I believe, as working through the *radical* potential of positivism (in Veblen's distinction between "business" and "industry," and their contradictions) already found in the work of the Saint-Simonians, Enfantin and Bazard. Thus the root of the project comes to its origins in the work of that most prolific genius, Henri Saint-Simon. On the surprising continuities between the Saint-Simonian formulations and the Weberian, see also my article on "Organizational Analysis," cited above.

chapter 13

Ideology Critique and the Tension of Parts and Whole

The fundamental power situation under capitalism, I have held, is that of a tacit alliance and community of certain classes: the capitalist hegemonic class allied with the political and the administrative classes. What is the position of this alliance in the larger society? How is it viewed and understood?

In large measure, there is great public uneasiness about this alliance and, indeed, downright denial of its existence. There is a widespread feeling that such an alliance is (or would be) morally dubious and, at a minimum, of uncertain legitimacy. The class alliance, when glimpsed, is commonly defined as an only *incidental* immorality, as an aberrant illegality, or as "deviant" behavior. In short, it is treated as the exception rather than the rule; as a breakdown of the system, rather than its conventional structure. What is in fact the usual relationship between the classes in capitalist society is redefined as an unusual occurrence; the normal structure is redefined as an abnormal event. Things are indeed thus ideologically inverted. Why is this the case?

1

Essentially, this has to do with the fact that public perception of the community alliance of the dominant classes would undermine the legitimacy of all the classes involved. For this reason: the administrative-political classes in capitalist society are defined as *independent* of other classes, as a group devoted to the commonwealth, and not as furthering its own private interests by attending to the interests of the rich. It is defined as trustworthy, as capable of helping all groups in the society, as capable of adjudicating differences among them, precisely because it is supposedly *not* allied with any one of them more than others, and because it does not pursue private interests that might compromise its impartiality. Such a view of the political and the administrative classes as selfless and impartial is essentially possible only under capitalism.

1.1

The manner in which the capitalist system actually maintains itself is deeply at variance with conventional conceptions of how the system is maintained. In fact, it is a system in which the hegemonic class may not appear in public, may not appear as "ruler" and may not even appear as "upper." Thus public scandals that rock the political order may not even touch the repute of the hegemonic economic class, which is one way it maintains its hegemony. For it is a society in which the very *existence* of their class is widely denied, or concerning which there is an uneasy silence.

The system defines itself as one in which persons are respected as ends in themselves; in which all have an equal voice and equal franchise; in which the society is seen as directed by competent persons who, whether elected or not, are viewed as devoid of selfish and especially venal interests; in which rewards are seen as proportionate to accomplishments. All these conceptions of how the system works do in fact help the system to work. If *dis*believed, the system's legitimacy would be greatly undermined.

The society is maintained then, in some considerable part, by the beliefs shared by its members, and in particular by those bearing on the legitimacy of the political and administrative classes. These beliefs enable these classes to win public credit and foster a willing obedience. Ideologies such as these, then, help perpetuate the specific system within which the privileges and powers of the hegemonic class and its allied classes exist. They do this, above all, by concealing and defocalizing attention from the manner in which the class system actually operates. To that degree, ideology is a system- and privilege-maintaining falsification of reality.

2

In all modern societies, one major source of ideology is: partisanship; egoism; the press for self-advantage; for personal or for group advantage. Ideology is rooted in a kind of one-sidedness, in "part-iality." In other words, ideology is rooted in a conflict between the part and the whole, the individual and society, private and public interests. It is precisely because—and to the *extent* that—each social group has interests separating it from others, and from the whole, precisely because—and to the extent—each has interests that others do *not* have and, indeed, *may* have interests *opposed* to the others, that such interests are precarious, that satisfaction of them is difficult because, being only of limited interest and of uncertain legitimacy, they are resisted. It is because of this that partial interests become opaque, occluded, and unarticulated, and are made inaccessible to the larger society and to other groups.

One-sidedness, then, is the fundamental grounding of ideology. It is because and when our grounding is one-sided that we are cut off, and cut ourselves off from our own grounding, and become as incapable of knowing our own grounding as we are of speaking it. Partisan character *alienates* us from our own interests. These *interests*, the very grounding of our social character, are thus made alien to the very persons who devote their lives to them and who base their lives on them.

In still other terms, ideology implies a lack of "objectivity," if by that is meant the ability to "take the role of the other" validly—that is, in ways the *other* willingly confirms. Ideology is that lack of objectivity which is produced by (and within) a structure of rational discourse, within an elaborated speech variant, when there is an inability to reach forward to the other because the reaching self has something to hide and is unable to reach downward into its own existence and to speak its own grounding.

The ideological situation, the ideology-generating situation, then, is this: it is above all a situation of work-and-communication, where some men must collaborate with one another to achieve anything at all, and where their discourse serves to arrange and motivate this necessary collaboration. Such discourse then is work and project intertwined, constituting a pattern of social interaction driven forward by the imperative of a collaboration whose linguistic medium is in *part* an elaborated language variant. This requires that reasons be given and the parties to the collaboration are called upon, and call upon themselves, to speak what they may not speak without impairing the grounds of the very collaboration they seek *and* the grounds of their own socially situated being. In effect, they are driven to talk and to be silent at the same time; to reveal and to hide at the same time; to speak rationally and to limit that rationality at the same time; to express their interest in social collaboration and to suppress their private interests in that collaboration, at the same time.

Ideology is born of a situation in which socially organized work and public projects will produce privately appropriated gratifications, gratifications that will in fact be allocated differentially. Ideology is that speech that seeks to reduce the dissonance between mutual dependence and differential allocation; it seeks to reduce the dissonance between the fact that *nothing* can be accomplished without others, while at the same time allowing differential rewards despite this radical, mutual dependency.

Let me repeat one qualification, previously mentioned; although I will only mention it once, it is nonetheless meant emphatically. I have said that ideology and its defective objectivity are grounded in a kind of egoism. Now let me add that I do not, repeat, *not*, mean to suggest that ideology is the only form and source of communicative distortion or "untruth" in the world, and I do *not* mean to suggest that egoism is the only grounding for the failure of rationality.

Altruism and love also may impair our ability to see and say truth, for then "smoke gets in your eyes." The comments above deal with only *one* major impairment of the ability to speak truly; they refer only to *ideology* and its grounding in partisanship.°

2.1

For all of Marx's emphasis on the partisan class interests that underlay ideology, Marx's very objection to this *as* "part-isanship" itself indicates that ideologists themselves do not, repeat *not*, accept the *validity* of such "part-isan" interests as a grounding for their public projects. Rather, such projects quite clearly proceed from a different authorization: from the imputed interests of the *totality* and the good of the whole. It is on this claim that the moral authority and suasion of ideology grounds itself. Ideological discourse is aimed continually at denying the legitimacy of partisan interests; sometimes it even denies the *reality* of partisanship. In the latter case, ideology may seek to demonstrate that partisan interests are only *seemingly* such.

In classical liberal ideology, this is quite evident: "private vices, public benefits." Here the claim was that aims and consequences had to be kept distinct. There was the tacit implication that consequences (as distinct from intentions) were the ultimate reality, and that partisan aims might and did—without the individual's intending it—have a public usefulness. The problem inherent in this liberal standard is that one never traces out and cannot know all the brachiating consequences of an intention acted upon. Consequences are thus never more than partially and selectively attended to. In the end, it may be said that "private vices yield public benefits" simply because the consequences being attended to are the publicly *beneficial* ones.

The task of liberal ideology was *recovery* and revelation: to make manifest or to "recover" what had before been occluded—i.e., the public good imputedly produced by the pursuit of private interests. Liberal ideology then was tacitly grounded in a doctrine of "recovery." That is, it was committed to making *visible* certain hitherto structurally neglected aspects of the pursuit of partisan interests. It need not be read as having asserted that *all* public

° A systematic treatment of these *various* limits on rationality or, at least, the statement of *my* position on them, will have to wait for the fourth volume in this set, *On The Sociology of Cognition.*

consequences of the pursuit of private interests were necessarily beneficial. This is part of the rational side of liberal ideology. It correctly saw that, just as it might be true that the "road to hell" was paved with good intentions, the opposite might also be true, that the road to salvation might be paved with evil intentions. Liberalism *generalized* a disjunction between intent and consequences, and it began a cultural development that eventuated in undermining the importance, the value and the reality, assigned to "subjective" factors. The liberal thus never justified the validity of private interests as being an end-in-itself, but, rather in terms of its consequences for the *whole*. The *ultimate* standard, for the liberal, then, was the totality.

What may be said of Marxism in respect to this issue? At first sight, it may seem as if Marxism differs from liberalism in that the former is a species of unembarrassed partisanship, of proletarian partisanship; in some readings Marxism does indeed eventuate in *ouvrierism*. But such partisanship is no more the intent of Marxism than of liberalism. Marxism's central thrust, its most elemental impulse, was always toward the restoration of (a true) *community*. Like the Hegelianism from which it sprang in part, Marxism aimed at the ultimate surmounting and reconciliation of all contradictions.

From the beginning, then, Marxism was grounded in the standard of the totality. The proletariat's interests were supported because it was expected to be an irreconcilable foe of fragmenting capitalist egoism; the proletariat was therefore to lead the struggle for socialism, the free association of united producers. Engels certainly later acknowledged that the bitterness and brutality of the class struggle could (and should) not permit the proletariat to indulge a humanistic sentimentality that dwelled on the future human solidarity; rather, it was the struggle, the social conflicts, and divisions that had now to be focused on. Yet Marxism certainly never denied the *ultimacy* of the standard of the whole. Marxism, then, was an advocate of the need to restore the human community and social solidarity uprooted by the capitalist revolution. (Nationalism, as the third · great ideology of the nineteenth century, began, of course, with its focus on the political unification of a society. In the end, however, it gave way to national egoism and to the entrenchment of national rivalries and international disunity. As *Realpolitik* and *Machtpolitik*, nationalism also prized "hard" objective consequences and devalued "mere" talk.)

Marxism also continued and intensified the drift begun by liberalism toward the disjunction of intentions and consequences and toward the depreciation of the subjective factor. This is intrinsic to the meaning of Marxism's "materialism"—particularly, when read as a "scientific" Marxism —and to its conceptual polarization of economic infrastructure and ideological superstructure. Certainly, we should not overstress the communality of liberalism and Marxism, but they do seem to be convergent in *this* important respect. Like liberalism, Marxism was not necessarily what it seemed to be at first glance. At first, Marxism appears as an ideology that sees material factors as having an absolute importance and asserting their primacy in "the last instance." And the corresponding logical problem for Marxism is that there is no way to determine when the last instance has arrived; one therefore simply stops analytic regression when one has come to a seemingly substantial economic factor, and uses this concrete example to vindicate the analytic generalization.

Actually, however, Marxism like liberalism may also be seen to rest upon a tacit "doctrine of recovery," although the concrete content of what it seeks to "recover" differs from liberalism. Marxism's task, like liberalism's, was to recover what had been, within certain modes of discourse, structurally neglected: the *private advantage* derived from the pursuit of the public interest. Marxism, then, may also be read as a "doctrine of recovery," seeking to make people aware of the class interests in which the pursuit of public good was tacitly grounded. It focused on "material" factors not because of their intrinsic ultimacy, but because this was the *repressed* factor. In that sense, Marxism is a doctrine of discourse, not a "Materialistic" ontology. It is this that is an important part of the rationality of Marxism. Yet it remains true that its *ultimate* aim was to transcend partisan class interest, even if this required an historical detour in the pursuit of the interests of the proletariat. Marx, of course, had long since assimilated the Hegelian understanding that: "Der Weg . . . ist der Umweg."

2.2

Ideologies are thus partly legitimated by the fact that, focally or tacitly, they ground their discourse in the interests of the whole. Ideology, moreover, is always in some part a *counter*discourse, discourse against some other ideology. Thus whether or not its focus on the totality is focal or tacit depends in part on the status occupied by the "totality" in the ideology it *opposes;* it depends on whether this ideology focally affirms the validity of the interests of the whole or, like Max Stirner's, firmly denies the reality of that whole. In some part, Stirner's ideology was publicly aborted because it openly denied the validity of the whole. In some part it was because of this very view, namely, that the very affirmation of a whole was a species of rationalization disguising egoistic interests, that Marx opposed Stirner.

Marx's ideology, indeed, any ideology that is successful, can deny neither the value nor the reality of the whole. Faced with an ideology such as Stirner's, Marxism tends to be pushed toward *affirming* the autonomy of the social whole. Faced with the then more powerful problem of developing a critique of liberalism, an ideology which affirmed the reality and value of the whole, Marx stresses the manner in which the social whole *disguises* the partisan interests of the dominant classes, and allows the value of the whole to sink into the subordinate clauses of discourse.

Each ideology, however, takes itself as engaged in the analysis of an out-there objective reality. In point of fact, however, it is always interpreting, not simply mirroring reality, social reality always being an object constituted in *part* by its own interpretation. Each ideology thus represses an understanding of itself as a world-*constituting* (not merely world-*reflecting*) discourse. But in their relationship to *other* ideologies they are never only concerned about the "world" but also about men in their *relation* to this world. It is in that externalizing way that ideology becomes engaged not only in discovery, but also in *recovery*. This entails a sensitization to how men look at the world, and not only to what the world "is." It is a "recovery," in some part, because it seeks to enable men to recover, to become aware of, their own active role in constructing social reality. It seeks to help them to become aware of what they had once known, guessed, glimpsed about their self and its implication in the world. It seeks to shift what had hitherto been only a part of their auxiliary awareness into focal consciousness.

But nineteenth-century ideologies were, as we said earlier, as "objectivistic" as nineteenth-century science. Indeed, each ideology did not see *itself* as having hidden, and as needing to recover, some part of the social world. It only saw *others* as needing to do this and saw itself as correcting or helping them. It was exactly this limited reflexivity (or self-awareness) that, as Karl Mannheim claimed, made ideology only a primitive precursor of the sociology of knowledge. Correspondingly, says Mannheim, when we move from this partial view to one that regards the views of *all* groups as grounded socially, then we have moved from ideology to the consciousness of the "sociology of knowledge."

One qualification: to acknowledge all groups' views as being influenced by their social position is to acknowledge, but to acknowledge only *tacitly* and hence with diminished force, that *one's own* views were similarly influenced by social forces. To acknowledge that all groups are thus influenced is to acknowledge *en principe*—and then, only if someone should happen to *ask*—that the speaker also has the common human limits. The historical step from ideology to the sociology of knowledge, then, was *not* a true step toward acceptance of *one's own concrete cognitive* limits. It is simply a vague and general admission that, "we are all human," but not a specification of our own concrete "guilt." (This remains visible in "normal" sociology's common unwillingness to apply the "sociology knowledge" to *itself* and in its knee-jerk hostility to a "sociology of *sociology*.")

The essential topic of the "doctrine of recovery," analytically conceived, is the dialectic of the part and the whole. It is about the manner in which people's discourse embodies structurally patterned silences, whether motivated or not. The doctrine of recovery seeks to show how discourse is distorted by reason of the diverse and often contradictory commitments of men, expressed symptomatically in their speech. It does not view silences as passive lacunae, as an "emptiness," but as an energy-full opposition of forces. Ideologies understand themselves as finding out what is important in the world. They tend to speak about what had been hidden by men, primarily insofar as the latter is in contradiction with their *own* assertions about the world. Ideologies speak objectivistically, with limited reflexivity about the world, without clearly indicating that theirs is a *speaking* about the world rather than the world's self-presentation.

To revert and reiterate: ideologies are partly legitimated by their claim to represent the whole. It is precisely in this way that ideology also constitutes itself as a *moral* discourse. As public discourse aimed at mobilizing support for public projects of societal reconstruction, it is normal that the question of "who benefits" from these projects is of central importance. Thus the dialectic of the whole and the parts is an inevitable topic for ideology. It is imperative that, at some point, all ideologies be grounded in a claimed contribution to the totality. For visibility of the private interests in which public projects are grounded always deauthorizes the public project among those not sharing that private interest.

The success of all public projects requires the active support, the consent, or at least the neutralization, of different public sectors. They cannot, therefore, be pursued successfully except insofar as they are defined as *non*partisan, at least "ultimately" and "essentially." To repeat, it is an important part, this requisite of all public action that is provided by ideology.

Ideology is, to this extent, a latent *apologia* for certain partial interests and is thus the opposite of a "critique." "Critique" seeks to expose the private interest latent in the manifest public function. "Apologia" does the opposite —it seeks to reveal the hidden public *worth* of vested private interests. Apologia seeks to exhibit how the good of the whole really rests on and is concealed in the interests of certain parts.

2.3

Both apologia and critique are aspects of ideologies. Hans Magnus Enzensberger is correct in saying that ideology-critique is also ideology: "It's characteristic gesture of 'unmasking' can turn into a smug ritual, if attention remains fixed on the mask instead of what is revealed beneath." It is evident that apologia is compulsively one-sided and partial. What shall we say of ideology-critique, of real historically concrete ideology-critique, as distinct from critique's *self*-ambitions and ultimate project? Is critique, as we actually encounter it today, "impartial?" Is it rational? The rationality of ideology-critique is that it reveals what apologia has hidden. The rationality of apologia, however, is that it reveals what *critique* has hidden. The irrationality of each is that it remains silent about what the other contributes, and each treats the hidden *part* that it reveals as if it were the *whole*, thereby tacitly denying its *own* partiality.

The kind of ideology-critique developed in Frankfurt by Albrecht Wellmer and Jürgen Habermas, correctly stresses the relative autonomy of ideology and rejects any tendency to reduce it to an epiphenomena of the infrastructure. It thus properly recovers what "Scientific" Marxism had *de*focalized— the superstructural and subjective element. (To that extent, Frankfurt's view is a special case of a more general "critical Marxism," which does the same.) Correspondingly, critical theory sometimes tends to *de*focalize what Marx had focalized—the infrastructure, property, technology, power—by its increasing tendency to reduce the societal and the social to the *symbolic*, and to transform social analysis into communication theory. Frankfurt's ideology-critique thus sees the one-sidedness of Marx, but does not always see its own partiality. Nonetheless, I understand this partiality of the "Frankfurt School" as a creative regression toward idealism (in the sense that Marx, in his critique of mechanical materialism, clearly saw how *it* had left men's creative and active side to idealism). It is a regression, albeit creative, to that linguistic sensitivity of an Hellenized Christianity which held that, "In the beginning was the Word (*Logos*)." In short, Frankfurt adopts the standpoint of the older Goethe, but rejects the younger one, who, reinterpreting *Logos*, had at first held: In the beginning was the *Deed*.

Ideology, we have said, redefined the private interest in terms of the public, the part in terms of the whole. It thereby transforms political action into moral conduct. Focally in liberalism, and tacitly in Marxism, ideology transforms "I *want*" into "*you should*" or into, "it is right and proper that . . ." This sublimation of interest and of partisanship into moral discourse must, however, be done *elliptically* and *cryptically*, lest the moral itself come to be "unmasked" and deauthorized. Interests thus come to be secreted in and sublimated by moralities; hence all moralities have a false consciousness concerning interests.

It sometimes happens, however, that we, the "insightful," having some glimpse of our own interests and egoistic partisanship, develop a bad conscience concerning these and may come to underestimate or to ignore their own worth and virtues. It is thus that virtues, no less than vices, may be concealed: e.g., "underneath that gruff exterior . . ." Ideology-critique often fails to see that false consciousness may be based on the fear that one is being too *tough*-minded and hard, as well as on the fear that one is too tender-minded and sentimental.

Ideologies are sedimented with a built-in disjuncture between private and public interests that they (more or less manifestly) work to repair. Ideology *facilitates* the movement of discourse from private interest to public good, on the one side, while on the other, it *blocks* the movement of discourse from the public to the partisan interest. To creep upon and unmask the services performed by ideologies, then, is to strip off a mask, and to lay bare an unresolved problem. This, however, has the possible danger of deauthorizing *all* morality and ideology, by making it seem as if this interest-protecting silence was *all* that ideologies and moralities did, and that they had no autonomy of their own. It was precisely this that Max Stirner saw and pursued.°

To the degree that an ideology-critique does this, then there is a genuine possibility that it will foster cynicism and nihilism—i.e., that it may lead (as Socrates saw that even the dialectic might) to the development of lawlessness or *anomie;* or to a naked egoism and a cynically unashamed pursuit of private interest, whatever their consequences for the commonweal. An unmasking ideology-critique fosters the possibility of an *anomic* egoism that frees itself of all shackling "sentimentalities," brutally concerning itself only with the sheer efficiency of its instruments.

Other forms of ideology-critique have other possible pathologies. Certain forms of ideology-critique do not foster an unabashed egoism, but precipitate unwittingly a "fanatic idealism." Cynical egoism and a fanatic idealism are kindred pathologies, for both premise a sharp disjuncture between private interests and public welfare. Fanatic idealism solves this by denying all legitimacy and reality to *private* interests, and by assigning this legitimacy exclusively to the public weal. Rather than denying any autonomy to public morality, as egoism may, fanatic idealism totally denies the need of morality to accommodate at all to private interests and regards this accommodation as hypocrisy and opportunism. Fanatic idealism solves the problem by premising the total expungeability of the private and the partial. The self silences its fear of its own immorality—of a *self*-betrayal—by mobilizing its moral fervor and by scourging itself and others with it. It mends the disjunction of the private and public by outlawing the private. Fanatic idealism, then, is a tacit claim to *moral* superiority. It is the ideology of a punishing, would-be, moral elite.†

Ideology allows a measure of legitimacy to private interests because (and insofar as) it links them to the public interest; ideology thus paradoxically provides some *protection* against both egoistic *anomie* and idealistic fanaticism. Correspondingly, it may be the *failure,* although not the "end of ideology" that opens the door to both. Ideology-critique sometimes fails to see

---

° The most sensitive and lucid account of this is in John Carroll, *Break-Out From the Crystal Palace,* Routledge and Kegan Paul, London and Boston, 1974, esp. Ch. I.

† Let me add with all the clarity I can muster that this is not a critique simply of *other* ideology-critics—and *least* of all, of Jürgen Habermas—but most emphatically includes *myself.* Certain passages of my *Coming Crisis of Western Sociology* have been criticized, and criticized correctly, for a lack of moral generosity. I do therefore most certainly include myself in this criticism.

the way in which ideology *immunizes* people against egoistic cynicism. Ideologies may also limit and discipline fanatical idealism. Moralities that have been severed from and reject the validity of all private interests do not constitute solutions but are themselves part of the modern social problem, and are a basic source of false consciousness among Jacobin-leaning intellectuals. It is not simply the repression of *instinctual* nature that outrages inner "nature" and leads it to revenge but so, too, do outrages against men's need to substantialize their own individual existence and private concerns.

3

The most elemental source of ideology, we have suggested earlier, is the contradiction between the part and the whole. It resides in the one-sideness and our-sideness of the part—in the fact that, whoever else it favors, it also favors itself, and is on its own side. There is a conflict between the egoistic self-regard of the part and its desire to project an image of itself as being altruistically concerned for the welfare of the group as a whole. This conflict between a part's regard for itself, and its projected image of responsibility to the group, is resolved in some measure by accentuating the visibility of its commitment to the collectivity and, correspondingly, by secreting its commitment to its own more private concerns and interests. This, I have suggested, is at the root of ideology.

3.1

The *Communist Manifesto*'s remarks about the special mission of Communists premise precisely this tension (between part and whole) and they indicate that ideology-generating is to be found not only among establishments but, also, in *counter*establishments. The *Manifesto* acknowledges that working-class parties commonly become entangled in particularistic interests and lose sight of the interests of the working class as a whole, while the Communists presumably do not: "The Communists are distinguished from other working-class parties by this only: they point out and bring to the fore the common interests of the entire proletariat, independently of all nationality . . . they always and everywhere represent the interest of the Movement as a whole . . ." The ideology-generating dialectic between part and whole is thus found also on the rebel underside of society.

The Communist critique of the partiality of other working-class parties was no less true of itself and its own party. There have been very few, if any, "communists" in the sense intended above by Marx and Engels, precisely because most are deeply implicated in special political groups that demand loyalty to themselves rather than to the working class. Conveniently and marvelously, these parties' definitions of the interest of the working class are never at odds with the policies and interests of their own political faction, indicating quite plainly that they *identify* the two interests. We may be sure that this is accomplished, at least in part, by subordinating the class interest to their own distinctive party interests. This mode of resolving these differences in interest must of course be hidden. In effect, Louis Althusser admits as much when he acknowledges that ideology has not ended in the Soviet Union and that it is not likely to do so in the foreseeable future. Since the issue is a significant one, I shall expand upon it in some detail.

Norman Geras puts this matter incisively: "To come to the final consequence of Althusser's idealism: the knowledge which Marxism provides and which intellectuals import into the working class movement has, for him, a very specific kind of directive role. It tries to produce 'a *new* form of ideology in the masses' by supporting and using, or transforming and combatting the ideologies in which the masses live. But Althusser also tells us, in at least a hundred passages, that ideology is a realm of mystification and deformation, of illusion and falsehood and myth, of confusion, prejudice and arbitrariness, of the imaginary and non-knowledge. He thus cuts off the masses, by a necessity he never explains, from the knowledge of their situation which the intellectuals have produced. How then can the intellectuals brandish what they know to be an ideology without violating the first principle of revolutionary politics—to tell it as it is?" °

There is a profound paradox lurking in the above statement, because Althusser, the "Stalinist," is *actually* telling it "as it is" in affirming the continuing presence of ideology in socialism; Geras, his critic, however, is doing the opposite of what he says is needed, "to tell it as it is," and is instead occluding reality. Althusser's affirmation of the abiding presence of ideology is, in one way, an *anti*-ideology; Geras' denial of the *necessity* of ideology ideologizes and inverts reality. Here the Stalinist seems paradoxically less ideological than the anti-Stalinist.

Nonetheless, Althusser's ultimate interest here is in defending "what is" in the Soviet Union, and in protecting it from critique. When Althusser says that ideology abides and will abide, he means to protect the Soviet State from criticism by those viewing it as a deformed Marxism, and by those who hold that the Soviet State has transformed Marxism, into an ideology. Here it is Althusser's very *partiality* that seems to lead him to speak nonideologically, in defense of ideology. But Althusser's motives are at bottom defensive and they serve to conceal certain realities: specifically how and why the Soviet Union transformed Marxism into an instrument of the Soviet State, into a

° N. Geras, "Louis Althusser—An Assessment," *New Left Review*, January/February, 1972, p. 86.

solidarity-enhancing catechism subservient to Soviet society: they thus conceal how and why the Soviet State ideologized Marxism.

Althusser's acknowledgment of the continuing presence of ideology is an accommodation to the requisites of the Soviet State and is an *acceptance* of "what is" in Soviet society. His is the *rhetoric* of "realism," essentially positivistic in its submission to the "facts." Its readiness to tell it "as it is" in the Soviet State has the appeal of candor and frankness. But Althusser's formulation is one-sided.

It is the use of facts as rhetoric; it is the *acceptance* of what is and not simply a *communication* about what is. So here, then, Althusser's partiality has not simply led him to tell the truth about "ideology," but, by acknowledging the sheer fact of its continued existence, he conceals a larger truth. Althusser diverts inquiry from the real conditions that sustain and generate ideology in the Soviet Union by intimating that there is now a certain *inevitability*, almost a "naturalness," in the existence of Soviet ideology. He places Soviet ideology beyond criticism and examination.

In condemning Althusser, Geras is certainly not denying the *existence* of ideology in the Soviet Union or in Communist Parties. What he is denying is its necessity or desirability. He is not clear which, and this is a crucial conflation. For if Geras acknowledges a certain *necessity* in Communist ideology, then the question arises about the grounds on which he can criticize it. If it is necessary, what makes it "wrong?" If it is necessary, how can it be undesirable?

In other words, Geras' critique of Althusser's accommodation to ideology needs to be grounded in a theory about the origins of ideology that would show the social conditions under which it occurs. Unless Geras has some knowledge or, say, some glimpse, of what would be needed to avoid ideology he is arbitrary in condemning Althusser's "realistic" accommodation to ideology. Correspondingly, he is *utopian* in implying that socialists can, here-and-now, expect the elimination of ideology. In short, Geras' critique of ideology is just as ideological as Althusser's apologetics for it. For, the notion that ideology can be removed, and specifically, be removed now from the *socialist* movement, is an illusory goal that obscures the conditions that generate ideology in the *socialist* movement, no less than in capitalist society at large.

3.2

"Ideology," then, is scarcely peculiar to the belief systems of dominant or respectable groups, nor to those that are conservative or reactionary in character. It is no less in evidence in revolutionary outlooks such as socialism and, of course, in liberalism. Wherever there is a conflict between a partial interest and the claims of the whole, made problematic in the special culture of critical speech, discourse, whether it be among conservatives or radicals, the result is ideology. It is, therefore, one thing to be committed to a socialist party organization, a "vanguard" party, and another to be committed to the working *class* itself. For, as the *Communist Manifesto* indicates, the former is always one among a number of parties that *claims* to represent this class; and, as we would add, that party always has a partisan group interest of its *own*, seeking to vanquish other, competing representatives of the working class; it has political interests of its own quite distinct from those of the working class. That this is so is clearly evidenced in the Leninist tradition where the working class itself is *not* thought capable of generating a socialist consciousness, so that this consciousness must be brought to it from the outside, by the vanguard party. Or, at least, so holds the theory.

As there is a difference between the party and the class, so, too, there is a difference between the class and the nation. In the socialist context, there can even be a tension between the interests of the working class and those of a larger society it might govern. One form of this is known as *ouvrierism*, in which the working class' special interests are given precedence and protection over the interests of other social sectors. Insofar as socialism is conceived as control of the means of production by the proletariat, as *workers'* control,° there is a very real question as to whether it will foster zealously the interests of other sectors of the population, for example, the peasantry, farmers—the rural sector.

It is unmistakably clear that the rural sector of the Soviet Union is a subordinated and colonized area and that its peasantry is a subordinated social strata. Until 1975, peasants could not leave areas of the countryside without a special visa. These colonized, rural areas are dominated from remote metropolitan centers where decision-makers (nominally) give priority to the interests of the working class. This colonized character of rural areas by the metropolitan center, and the "land question," † are the two fundamental reasons why the Soviet Union has never solved its "agricultural" question, only recently being forced to buy millions of dollars of grain from the capitalist United States. This condition is no secret but is, rather, something that Soviet urban leaders themselves know and occasionally even acknowlededge.

° And if socialism is not that, not *workers'* control of the means of production and the society and the state, then *what* is it?

† Much of the peasantry still wants land to be assimilated as private property into its family system, so that collective farms still have low productivity in comparison to private plots.

3.3

Quite apart from these specific tensions one question would be how to *justify* such an exclusive, *ouvrierist* control over the forces of production by-the-*pro-letariat*-for-the-proletariat in a socialist society. For the forces of production are a social heritage created by many sectors of society over a long period of historical development. There is, therefore, no reason for the proletariat to control the historical heritage of the entire culture. All the more so, as Marxism suggests that the law of economic "value" does not apply under *socialism*, as it might under capitalism, so that one cannot then justify workers' control by saying that it is they alone who create such "value." The working class, as do other sectors of the population, certainly contributes to the *wealth* of the society; but since this aggregate *wealth* is now increasingly a function of science and technology, a societal product, why should the forces of production be subjected to the control of the workers alone? Here, of course, is one tension generative of ideology within the *socialist* tradition.

But this is not the central, ideology-generating problem confronting socialism. It would be a source of ideology were there a socialism in which the working class actually controlled the means of production. But there is none, anywhere. In all societies that define themselves as socialist, the forces of production are in point of fact under the control of organized political parties and of the state apparatus. The working class may be "consulted," but it does not control.

3.4

All socialist societies, then, have this basic contradiction: their culture is egalitarian but their social structure is hierarchical; their ideology calls for workers' control of the forces of production, but these are actually controlled by the party and the state. This contradiction is the fundamental, ideology-generating condition of socialist societies. It is because this contradiction has never been resolved that Althusser is perfectly right in expecting the continuation of ideology under socialism. And here, once more, we can see how ideologies are rooted in the failure of expectations that are partly grounded in the ideology itself; in this case, the ideological claim that the workers will control production.

The tensions between part and whole in socialism ramify upward still further, encompassing at a still higher level tensions between one socialist nation and another, or between one socialist nation and international socialism as a whole. Stalinism was, in one part, a manifestation of the contradictions between the interests of the Soviet Union and those of other socialist movements which were often subjected to Soviet pressure to forgo revolutionary opportunities in their own society, for fear that these might precipitate wars dangerous to the Soviet Union. These contradictions between the interests of the Soviet Union and of world socialism manifested themselves almost immediately after the Soviet Revolution. When the newborn Soviet Union bought security for itself by signing the peace of Brest Litovsk, it helped give the German high command the freedom of maneuver to smash the emerging *German* Revolution; and ironically this, in turn, helped to *undermine* the very requisites of Russian socialism, upon which Bolshevik leaders had traditionally relied. The subsequent "deformation" of the Russian Revolution was thus paradoxically grounded in the Bolsheviks' own effort to protect their revolution, for this had contributed to the abortion of the German Revolution upon which they had so much counted.

The Chinese Revolution, also, had long suffered from the contradiction between its interests and those of the Soviet Union. The development of Maoism and the radical rupture between it and "Russian revisionism" is only the most obvious evidence of the ongoing contradictions between the Soviet Union and world socialism. In this hierarchical matrix of the contradictions of socialism, a matrix that can only be barely sketched here, are the most elemental tensions between part and whole which it is the function of socialist ideology to repress. Socialist ideology, then, cannot be eliminated, and will only find new forms, so long as this tension between part and whole persists within socialist movements, parties, and nations.

But these are certainly neither new nor peculiar to modern socialism and to its revolutionary thrust. As we have said frequently, in the modern age ideology appears with the decline of old regime societies, when all traditional legitimations of authority and polity have been overturned or deeply undermined. It is now the "people" in whose name all authorities must rule, whether the people are defined as the *source* from which authority derives, or, quite differently, whether the people are said to be the source in which authority continues to *reside*. No longer vouchsafed by Divine Right or inheritance, political authority must now claim the sanction of a popular sovereignty. Socialism, too, grounded its claim in the historic position of the working class who, it argued, does not act only for itself in any selfish way; the proletariat, it was held, moves toward a total human emancipation, even if it must move toward this by opposing an historically transient class, the bourgeoisie, whose partisan interests constrain it to oppose this forward movement. To this very day, "socialist" societies in power legitimate themselves in the name of the working class or, more broadly, the "people," and often define themselves as "people's democracies."

4

All modern and revolutionary polities, then, ground their legitimacy in some version of the ideology of popular sovereignty, claiming to present the needs, the interests, or the will of the masses or the people. At the same time, however, all of them were initially guided and *remain* controlled by small oligarchical leadership groups: elites. While profoundly different from a Leninist "vanguard party," the American colonies' "Committees of Correspondence" were largely self-apppointed, small-scale leadership groups. A revolution, then, is actually *made* by masses and is legitimated in their name; but it is controlled and managed by elites. The societies they bring into existence continue to be sedimented with this contradiction between the way political authorities legitimate themselves, as the representatives of a popular interest, and the fact that they are actually an elite which is, in some measure, a self-perpetuating minority that must come to terms with other classes. Even a conservative such as Talcott Parsons acknowledges that the American political class could not rule against the wishes of the business elite: ". . . political leadership without prominent business participation is doomed to ineffectiveness and to the perpetuation of dangerous internal conflict. It is not possible to lead the American people against the leaders of the business world . . ." ° In short, the business elites in the United States have, at least, a veto over political policy.

The conflict between the practice of oligarchy and the principles of popular sovereignty is a universal contradiction of all modern societies, and of the revolutionary movements in which many originated. It is this contradiction between their claim to represent the whole, and the reality of their partisanship, that is the grounding of ideology today in both capitalist and socialist societies. There is no way forward to the true "end of ideology" so long as this contradiction remains concealed and so long as both types of society are incapable of overcoming it.

This contradiction would not, of course, be a real social force in socialist societies except for the fact that socialist ideology fosters expectations—for example, workers' control of the forces of production, international workers' and socialist solidarity—that are violated by the practice of everyday life in these same societies. Socialist ideology, like others, is a response to the tensions between its own parts and whole. At the same time, however, this ideology also contributes to certain tensions, as well as being a cultural

---

° T. Parsons, *Structure and Process in Modern Societies*, Free Press, 1960, pp. 246–247. For a developed statement of my position on this, see A. W. Gouldner, *The Coming Crisis of Western Sociology*, Basic Books, New York, 1970, especially Ch. 8 on power, wealth, and property.

mechanism for the control of other tensions. Socialist ideology, like others, is thus both tension reductive and tension generative.

To say that it is tension generative, however, means that its ideology constitutes a source of change and development in societies, no less than of continuity and stability. With its promise of a kind of democracy in everyday life, by workers' control of the forces of production, socialist ideology fosters tensions subversive of those structures of domination characteristic of "socialist" nations today. In the end, then, the very distortions of socialist ideology—where, for example, they speak of socialism as already entailing workers' control of the forces of production—may help to overcome the very social reality that falsifies the ideology. In that event, the ideology has the myth-like character of a self-fulfilling prophecy, or at least it has a tendency to function in that way. Socialist ideology, in short, is not only a critique of *capitalist* society; it also serves to ground a critique of *socialist* societies as well, helping to transcend "socialism" no less than capitalism. But this, of course, only guarantees that there will be tension between the promise of socialist ideology and the performance of socialist society. But it is not, of course, a guarantee as to which force will triumph.

Soviet society, then, is a contradictory society and therefore subject to change and crisis. It is that "Integral State"—to use Max Horkheimer's term—whose own ideological egalitarianism undermines its own authoritarian social structure. Governed by a groping bureaucracy which has not yet reached full awareness of its own historical situation, it hides its unemployment with an imposed administrative requirement of full employment, concealing unemployment behind a vast inefficiency, and by paying state subsidies for products rather than for unemployment benefits. Lacking the invisible controls of the market and the threat of hunger, by which an oligopical "private" capitalism disciplines persons, the Soviet Union is an integral state capitalism that is controlled through the mediation of a vast, repressive bureaucracy.

This bureaucracy establishes the basic rate of exchange and monitors it. The exchange is: an improved, but immensely depressed standard of living—"the average monthly wage in the USSR was 135 rubles in 1973" °—with guaranteed employment, in exchange for the workers' right to work poorly and with little motivation, and for his acceptance of continual and rigid state censorship of all media, news, and culture. Quite visibly unwilling to let the Soviet working class govern itself, and quite visibly organized in a steep pyramid of power culminating at a remote but obvious pinnacle, the site of power and responsibility is clearly vested in the

---

° M. Holubenko, "The Soviet Working Class: Discontent and Opposition," *Critique, A Journal of Soviet Studies and Socialist Theory*, Spring, 1975, p. 19.

bureaucracy. The power, the responsibility, and the privileged condition of this bureaucracy are thus not masked by an impersonal market system.

At the same time, however, this ruling bureaucracy lacks a "mystifying ideology. The official ideology in the Soviet Union does not serve to legitimize the ruling group's privileges and power over society. . . . The ruling group is saddled with an ideology which teaches the non-legitimacy of its existence." Lacking a supportive ideology, the ruling Soviet elite "is in a very unstable position, and the Soviet Union is an inherently unstable society." °

But this conflict between Soviet ideology and social arrangements is scarcely peculiar to it. It is as true for oligopical "private" capitalism as for Soviet monopoly state capitalism and its Integral State. As stressed in Chapter Ten, this conflict is intrinsic to all ideology. Ideologies are always myths, urging projects that the groups subscribing to them do not fully want. Ideologies, therefore, are not simply order-maintaining, *status-quo* enforcing symbol systems, whatever the society in which they exist. They not only reduce certain tensions and provide an *apologia* for certain interests, but, also, and everywhere, undermine "what is" because they provide a ground for its *critique.*

Critical theory, the systematic self-reflection of critique, is akin to normal sociology in that it, too, grounds its intellectual work in ideology and does not simply take ideology as a "topic." Yet critical theory and normal sociology are scarcely identical, for critical theory has no illusion about its alleged "value freeness," regarding such a claim as false consciousness. Critical theory knows itself to be, and *wants* its work to be, grounded in justifiable interests and values; it willingly takes responsibility for these, making a continuous effort to deepen its reflexive understanding of its own commitments. Yet at the same time, a critical theory must also be critically aware of itself and understand that what it takes to be its "justifiable interests and values" *may* express the limited reflexivity of any ideology so that its grounding, too, is a grounding in *ideology.* It differs from other sociologies, then, in the emancipatory values it seeks and in the reflexive relation it has toward its own value commitments.

This means that, when it is at its best, critical theory eschews all temptations to claims of moral elitism and superiority, as well as all posturings of innocence. It never imagines—when it is at its best—that its own self-understanding can be taken at face value, or that its commitments are lacking in ambiguities or even contradictions. Critical theory makes a distinction between what it is and what it hopes to be. Affirming human emancipation as a goal, it never allows itself to intimate—when it is at its best—that it itself has already achieved that emancipation and never allows itself to forget that it, too, possesses a repressive potential. It knows that its own rationality, too, is limited by the world in which it exists and by the social

° M. Holubenko, ibid., p. 7.

positioning of those speaking for it. Knowing it will win no easy victories, relying upon its continual work and struggle, as well as upon a sometime quiet capacity for "surrender," ° critical theory seeks to understand itself as well as the world, and it suspects—as self-serving and sycophantic—all offered conceptions of itself that bring it no painful surprises. When it is at its best.

° Here "surrender" refers to the hermeneutic surrender that Kurt H. Wolff speaks of in his "Surrender and Catch" and which Hans-Georg Gadamer speaks of in his *Wahrheit und Methode* (1960) [*Truth and Method*, translation published by The Seabury Press, 1975] as "conquest from underneath."

Index